Sporting Heroes of Essex and East London 1960-2000

Bobby Moore and Graham Gooch

Sporting Heroes of Essex and East London 1960-2000

Bobby Moore and Graham Gooch

Dr. Phil Stevens

Foreword by Tony Cottee

APEX PUBLISHING LTD

Hardback first published in 2010 by

Apex Publishing Ltd

PO Box 7086, Clacton on Sea, Essex, CO15 5WN, England

www.apexpublishing.co.uk

British Library Cataloguing-in-Publication Data
A catalogue record for this book
is available from the British Library

ISBN HARDBACK: 1-906358-65-6 978-1-906358-65-5

Typeset in 10.5pt Baskerville Win95BT

Production Manager: Chris Cowlin

Cover Design: Siobhan Smith

Printed in Great Britain by the MPG Books Group,
Bodmin and King's Lynn

For Linda

ACKNOWLEDGEMENTS

In writing this book I have been encouraged by how generous people have been with their time and ideas. In particular I am indebted to Graham Gooch for his co-operation and support for the project, and Tony Cottee for writing the Foreword.

Writing a book of this kind is inevitably a collective enterprise, and I acknowledge the help of so many colleagues and sport lovers, among them Sinem Cakir at the City of London Corporation, Brentwood's Ken Hobbs, archivist Dave Pracy, sculptor Philip Jackson, David Playfair, Mick Geoghegan, Nigel Hilliard, Geoff Sherman, the Villiers Trust, the Bishopsgate Institute, Dorothy Lumley, Ken and Kath Emberson, Chris Evans at the Essex FA, Michael Grier at Tate & Lyle Ltd, and John Nevill at the Ford Motor Company. I wish to offer them all my sincere gratitude.

Very special thanks to Jonathan Vallerius for his detailed and thorough research, and I am sorry if the time he spent in the library at Lord's intruded into his cricket season. Thanks also to Chris Cowlin at Apex Publishing Ltd for his support and enabling the book to see the light of day. Mark Cripps, a cherished friend, read the manuscript and gave the right mixture of friendly criticism and critical friendship. Finally, thanks to my wife Linda for her support, love and patience.

Graham Gooch was kind enough to give his time in a busy mid-season to reflect on some of the main themes in the book and to express his ideas on coaching and developing young cricketers. As part of the research I have talked at length with local sports enthusiasts, some of whom have memories stretching back over 40 years. Many of their strong opinions and sporting recollections have found their way into the book and it was a delight to meet them all.

It was a pleasure to write this book. I hope you enjoy looking a little deeper into the careers of Moore and Gooch, and the sporting culture that inspired and nourished them.

CONTENTS

FOREWORD

This is a fantastic book which all football and cricket fans will enjoy reading. Bobby Moore and Graham Gooch are two of the genuinely great sporting figures of the post-war period and two of my own personal heroes. Moore's exquisitely-timed tackles and precision passing - Gooch's crunching on-drives and attacking style are clear images in the minds of all sports lovers and were a real inspiration to me and hundreds of other East End kids. Moore was the great iconic figure of the Sixties and Seventies and probably the last of the genuine local heroes, while Gooch's long career spanned the twenty years between 1970 and 2000.

I was born in Forest Gate Hospital, just around the corner from the new Olympic Village and a couple of miles from West Ham's Upton Park ground. When I was four years old, like many local families, we moved out to Romford, always the first stop out into Essex for aspiring East Enders. But despite our new suburban surroundings, like both Bobby Moore and Graham Gooch, we were always stayed close to our roots. The heroes of this engaging book both went to school in Leytonstone, a tough working class borough close to the East End. Like many of us from the East End, Moore and Gooch had the benefit of strong and supportive families, and were extremely proud of their working-class background. Both stayed close to their roots. Dr Stevens's book is the first to compare and contrast the careers of these two sporting greats within the context of a fast-changing post-war world.

If the book is a study of the sporting lives of Bobby Moore and Graham Gooch, it is also the story of thousands of football and cricket enthusiasts who helped to make the sporting culture of East London/Essex so rich and distinctive. The book includes hilarious anecdotes and stories from individuals and clubs, and explains how playing fields like Hackney Marshes, Wanstead Flats and West Ham Park, where many of us played as youngsters, had such a key role in shaping the sporting culture of the area. The book is a celebration of all that is good in local sport.

West Ham United, my old club, and Essex County Cricket Club share a common sporting heritage. Bobby Moore played cricket for Essex as a teenager, while Graham Gooch is a passionate West Ham fan and regularly trained with us at West Ham at the peak of his career. The area that stretches out between Upton Park in the East End and Essex's headquarters at Chelmsford is a hotbed of local sport, and a place which has produced an extra-ordinary number of international sports figures of the very highest calibre. In addition to Moore and Gooch, sporting giants from the area include David Beckham, Dean Macey, Teddy Sheringham, Lennox Lewis, Sol Campbell, Paul Ince, Ravi Bopara, Sir Alf Ramsey, Nasser Hussein, Christine Ohuruogu and Sir Trevor Brooking – the list is endless. Dr Stevens's book identifies what is special about the sporting culture of Essex and East London.

The playing days of Moore and Gooch were golden years when both reached the very heights of sporting glory – Moore captaining England to World Cup victory at Wembley in 1966, and Gooch scoring century after century against the West Indies, one of the most fearsome fast-bowling attacks in the history of cricket. But as we professionals know only too well, sporting lives are short-lived and like all other international greats, our two heroes had to face the challenge of retirement. The book offers a fascinating account of the different ways Moore and Gooch faced their non-playing careers.

This book is a warm tribute to Bobby Moore and Graham Gooch, and to a truly remarkable sporting culture. Through interviews, archives and personal stories, Dr Stevens has managed to capture the sporting essence of the place, and gives the reader a real insight into what drove our two heroes to such dazzling heights of achievement. Sports fans are in for a treat.

Best wishes

Tony Cottee

INTRODUCTION

Bobby Moore and Graham Gooch are two of the genuinely great sporting figures of the post-war period. Moore's exquisitely timed tackles and precision passing and Gooch's crunching on-drives and attacking style are clear images in the minds of all sports lovers. Moore was the iconic figure of the 1960s and 1970s, while Gooch's long career spanned two decades from the 1970s to the 1990s. This book is the first to compare and contrast the careers of these two sporting greats within the context of a rapidly changing social context, and it includes amusing anecdotes and stories from individuals and clubs, tracing the history of football and cricket in East London and Essex during their heyday.

If this book is a study of the sporting lives of Bobby Moore and Graham Gooch, it is also the story of thousands of passionate football and cricket enthusiasts in the area who have helped to make the sporting culture of East London/Essex so rich and distinctive over two generations. For every Moore and Gooch there are hundreds of East Enders and Essex men and women for whom playing sport means as much to them as it does to their heroes. The area that stretches out between Upton Park in the East End and Essex's headquarters at Chelmsford is a hotbed of local sport and a place that has produced an extraordinary number of international sports figures of the very highest calibre. The book examines what is distinctive about the sporting culture of Essex/East London that enabled it to produce not only Moore and Gooch but also a host of world-class sports stars.

I have set the book very broadly between the years 1960 and 2000, a 40-year period during which sport, and society generally, changed beyond recognition. Our two heroes were born just a few miles and 12 years apart, Moore in Barking in 1941 and Gooch in Leytonstone in 1953, a tough working-class area where the East End of London meets metropolitan Essex. Both went to school in Leytonstone, and as emerging young players they had the benefit of strong and supportive East End families, who had made the short trop out to the Essex border. Moore and Gooch were extremely proud of their working-class background and stayed close to their roots.

West Ham United and Essex CCC share a common sporting heritage. Bobby Moore played cricket for Essex Youth as a boy, while Graham Gooch is a passionate West Ham fan and regularly trained with The Hammers at the peak of his career. In the opinion of former Hammers manager, John Lyall, he was good enough to have become a professional footballer.

The playing days of Moore and Gooch were golden years in which both reached the very heights of sporting glory – Moore captaining England to World Cup victory at Wembley in 1966, and Gooch scoring century after century against the West Indies, one of the most fearsome fast-bowling attacks in the history of cricket. But sporting lives are short-lived and, like all other international greats, both had to face the challenge of retirement.

The book provides a fascinating account of the different ways that Moore and Gooch faced their non-playing careers. Graham Gooch was generous enough to agree to be interviewed for the book. The interview took place at Fenner's in Cambridge in June 2009 during the match between Essex and Cambridge University. His reflections provide the book with some fascinating insights into the state of the modern game. Tony Cottee's perceptive foreword offers a genuinely local contribution to a book that is a tribute to Moore and Gooch and to a truly remarkable sporting culture.

Moore and Gooch, East London and Essex through and through, were both anti-establishment figures. The book will focus on the effect of a stubborn streak of independence, not just on their playing careers but also, particularly in the case of Moore, on retirement. Moore and Gooch, both great champions, were socially and psychologically very different characters. Both were intelligent and determined, and they also shared a good sense of humour. Moore was outgoing and confident, although somehow vulnerable, while Gooch was more introspective but very clear in what he wanted to achieve. They were family men who enjoyed a pint with their mates, and despite both being divorced they appeared to enjoy the hurly burly of family life.

These two great sporting stars both possessed a spirit of

optimism, believing that everything was possible. Gooch, for example, never became embittered after his South African experience, but emerged a stronger and better cricketer. Both showed immense courage and fortitude and were very serious professional sportsmen, but they essentially had cheerful natures, despite Gooch's rather dour image. My impression is that Moore was the more vulnerable of the two and seemed to need the emotional support of those closest to him, while Gooch is, perhaps, a more independent character. A feature of the book will be to compare and contrast the two different personalities of these local heroes.

Moore's very sad early death led to an unexpected emotional outpouring, both locally and nationally. There are now statues in memory of the former England captain at the new Wembley Stadium and the Bobby Moore Stand now sits proudly at the southern end of the Boleyn ground. Moore's place in English cultural history is secure, despite, as we shall see, the anticlimax of his non-playing days.

The retirement of Graham Gooch stands in marked contrast to his footballing idol. Since he retired from playing in 1997 Gooch has carefully mapped out his future: some BBC work, coaching at Essex, cricket administration and the establishment of his Academy at Chelmsford. The Academy and his Scholarship scheme have deservedly gained Gooch a reputation as an outstanding and successful coach. His retirement is proving almost as successful as his playing days, as Alistair Cook and Ravi Bopara both testified following their tremendous partnership for England in the Second Test against the West Indies at the Riverside in 2009. The contrast between how these two great sportsmen dealt with life after playing provides a major theme of the book.

West Ham and Essex – sporting soulmates

Both Moore and Gooch are inextricably linked to West Ham United FC and Essex County Cricket Club, the area's premier clubs. These two local sporting institutions have provided the leadership and emotional focus (if we forgive one or two lapses of grace) for tens of thousands of sports lovers in this corner of the UK for over a century. Both clubs have won reputations for playing their respective sports with style and panache, generously laced with a highly developed sense of humour, and both have been hugely influential in the development of football and cricket in the county of Essex and in the East End of London. It is impossible to separate these two great clubs in terms of the affection they hold for sports lovers in the area – like the two places, each club is an extension of the other.

Two occasions in the space of less than one year provide an illustration of just how closely the histories of these two great sporting institutions are interwoven.

At Lord's Cricket Ground in July 1979 Essex CCC won the first trophy in their 85-year history – the Benson & Hedges Cup, with Graham Gooch scoring the first century in a one-day final. On that memorable Saturday in July Lord's resounded to the West Ham anthem, 'I'm Forever Blowing Bubbles', and a definite tinge of claret and blue coloured the parts of the ground occupied by the Essex supporters. Graham Gooch said at the time that he had never heard a welcome as loud as the Essex players received on that sunny July morning in 1979.

Across London on another sunny Saturday the following May, West Ham United beat Arsenal 1-0 in the FA Cup final, with the winning goal scored by Trevor Brooking from an unlikely diving header. This time it was Wembley that was awash with the claret and blue of The Hammers as 'Bubbles' echoed across North London; it was as if the Arsenal supporters had stayed at home.

These two glorious Saturdays were sporting triumphs for East London and Essex. On both occasions observers witnessed the passion and desire of local people for their two clubs, West Ham United FC and Essex CCC.

Londoners over the border

In the nineteenth century, Charles Dickens described people from East and West Ham as "Londoners over the border". East Ham and West Ham were Essex County boroughs until local government reorganisation in 1965, when they became the London Borough of Newham. Both were essential parts of the East End, even though they had been important boroughs of Essex since 1888, unlike their East London neighbours Poplar, Bow and Stepney, which have always been London boroughs and very much part of the capital city.

In football, West Ham United was essentially the club for what is now Newham, although, of course, The Hammers have always enjoyed strong support from Poplar, Bow and Stepney, and, further east, Whitechapel, Shoreditch, Shadwell and Aldgate, all now incorporated into Tower Hamlets. The Hammers have always been dear to the hearts of Essex people from Southend down on the estuary to Colchester, out on the east coast. In the same way, Hammers supporters have turned out in their thousands to support their county cricket team.

The book will explore this close sporting link between Essex and East London, and show how two young sports-mad boys from the same 'manor' went on to conquer the world.

Essex sporting boys and girls

Trevor Bailey, as Essex as it is possible to be, came closest to catching the essence of the area and its people when he wrote:

> *Essex is a large flat, sprawling county, heavily populated, energetic and diverse in its political, economic and social life. In addition to the metropolitan area, comprising London's East End, it has a number of thriving towns, some of them new, as well as many delightful old commuter villages and, of course, popular seaside resorts.*
>
> *- W.A. Powell (2002), Essex County Cricket Club, The History Press.p.5*

One of the aims of the book is to counter the often spiteful image of East London/Essex people as boorish and obsessed with money, 4x4s and tasteless material possessions. Contrary to the stereotype of popular imagination, the true spirit of this special place, as Bailey notes, is derived from its energy and diversity. It is true that this spirit was bent out of shape a little in the 1980s, when Essex, perhaps with more relish than the rest of England, fell for the Thatcher dream.

Energy and diversity are a powerful combination when applied to sport, and we can see this in the strength of the area's sporting culture. East London/Essex is distinctive for the high level of sporting participation woven into its social and cultural fabric. Sport is everywhere. For at least half a century football pitches, cricket grounds, athletic tracks, waterways, golf clubs and sports halls have provided facilities for local people of all ages and, importantly, of all cultural backgrounds to participate at every level in their sport of choice. However, it is notable that this impressive sporting tradition is today, in some areas, in decline. In the research for the book I spent time in schools and clubs, visited local football and cricket grounds, and met volunteer enthusiasts and people responsible for sport and leisure provision across East London and Essex. The research reveals an interesting picture of the state of football and cricket in the area, the place that produced two world champions in Moore and Gooch.

To paraphrase the philosopher Isaiah Berlin, East London and Essex people are like everybody else, only more so; there is an intensity about them. They have always possessed virtues such as hard work and determination, which are important in sport. However, these attributes are not sufficient in themselves, otherwise most sports addicts would be playing at a much higher level than their talent allows. Moore and Gooch inherited the work ethic of their parents and were determined to succeed. Both were also interested in understanding their respective games. Moore was one of the youngest players to take FA coaching badges and was a student of the West Ham Academy under Malcolm Allison, Noel Cantwell and Ron Greenwood. Gooch's cricketing intelligence and thoughtful approach to the game are well known to BBC listeners and to the young players at Essex CCC. Sections of the book include a look at the technical skill and tactical awareness of these two great sporting talents.

Although the careers of Moore and Gooch provide the centrepiece of the book, I am keen to set their magnificent achievements within the local sporting culture. Based around the lives of our two heroes, each chapter of the book is an attempt to construct a social history of sport in East London and Essex over the past 40 years. Sunday morning football on Hackney Marshes and club cricket at Brentwood are all part of the colourful and rich tapestry of sport in the area. Travel around Essex and you will encounter sport at every turn. The book provides a record of the wealth of memories and stories that are the heart and soul of football and cricket and should appeal to sports lovers everywhere.

Can there be another public sports facility anywhere in the world like Hackney Marshes? Football, and to a lesser extent hockey and rugby, has been played at Hackney Marshes since around 1881, and at the height of its popularity there were 120 pitches on the Marsh available for schools and local clubs. An extraordinary number of internationals and sporting household names emerged from the area in the 40 years between 1960 and 2000. They all enjoyed their first experience of sport on the fertile sporting turf of grounds such as Wanstead Flats, Low Hall Farm, Fairlop and the jewel in the sporting crown, Hackney Marshes. Both Moore and Gooch played on these grounds as young boys, and a further aim of the book is to trace the history of these rich sporting grounds and reveal the stories of some of their most intriguing characters.

A sporting hall of fame

In the post-war period the Essex/East London connection produced a host of famous sporting names, in addition to Moore and Gooch. Cricketers included Doug Insole, Trevor Bailey, Keith Fletcher, John Lever, Derek Pringle, Nasser Hussain, Alistair Cook, Brian 'Tonker' Taylor, Barry Knight, Neil Foster, Alan Lilley, Robin Hobbs, Keith Pont and the exciting young prospect, Ravi Bopara. The book will look at the question: how did Essex CCC manage to produce an unprecedented four England captains in 20 years in Fletcher, Gooch, Hussain and Cook.

Footballers from the area include David Beckham, Teddy Sheringham, Sir Alf Ramsey, Jimmy Greaves, Harry Redknapp, Paul Ince, Jamie Redknapp, Sol Campbell, Terry Venables, Martin Peters, Jermain Defoe, Laurie Cunningham, Frank Lampard Snr, Frank Lampard Jnr, Mick Leach, Ian and Roger Morgan, Denis Bond, Ken Brown, Brendon Batson, Derek Bellotti, Alan Curbishley, John Terry and the late Jimmy Neighbour. Dear old Sir Trevor Brooking was born in 1948 in the part of Essex that is now the London Borough of Barking and Dagenham.

Dean Macey, the great decathlete, is from humble Canvey Island, while rugby legend Lawrence Dallaglio and Olympic gold medallist Christine Ohuruogu are genuine East Enders. World champions Ted 'Kid' Lewis, Lennox Lewis, Charlie Magri and Daniel Mendoza came out of East London boxing clubs. If we were really generous we might also include those Essex world champions from snooker, Steve Davis and Ronnie O'Sullivan.

The book will attempt to identify what it is about the area that has produced such an unusually large number of world-class sporting stars.

By any standards this is an impressive record, but it is Bobby Moore and Graham Gooch who have done most to help shape the aspirations of local people, challenging the class-based prejudices of the conventional image of East London and Essex. Bobby Moore, the area's greatest sporting figure, was able to draw on his own considerable personal resources and those of his family to meet the ferocious hopes of a nation in 1966. Like Moore, Gooch drew on his own exceptional ability, pride and resolve to fulfil every ounce of his considerable potential to become a genuine sporting hero to cricket lovers in his native Essex, both as a player and in retirement.

For many, sport is simply fun. It can be a diversion from a stressful or difficult life. Both Moore and Gooch demonstrated a delight in playing and had great fun along the way. Sport is played at all levels for the sheer joy of it and humorous stories abound. Humour will be a constant theme in what follows as sporting tales are told and retold, revealing the true meaning of playing sport. But, of course, there is a familiar, often ugly and violent motive for playing sport. This can be as much a feature of its attraction as playing for the sheer fun of it. Humour and aggression are a part of the rich texture of amateur and professional sport and provide a central narrative thread of the book.

Building for the future

East London has always been a difficult place to grow up. Moore and Gooch had close family support as youngsters, as well as encouragement from teachers and club coaches. From this solid base they were able to realise their undoubted potential and become the best they could be. Young people need role models, and Moore was inspired by his boyhood hero, footballer Duncan Edwards. Typically, Gooch gained inspiration from more local figures such as Keith Fletcher and Trevor Bailey, although his own boyhood idol was, of course, Bobby Moore. Today's promising young sports stars draw on the example of Moore and Gooch, and others such as Lennox Lewis, Macey and Ohuruogu.

Many youngsters from the area show real sporting promise at school, but either through lack of support or negative peer pressure they lose their way. However, despite the often hostile environment of East London and the eastern parts of Essex, many prosper to become successful footballers, cricketers, athletes and musicians or simply go on to secure decent jobs. Singer Leona Lewis, Ravi Bopara, sprinter Jeanette Kwakye and The Hammers' young hopeful, Mark Noble, are all inspirational role models for young people in their communities. In the 2008 Summer Olympics young Kwakye was the first British woman to reach a 100-metres final for 24 years, and her success in Beijing has inspired her to become a mentor for budding young London athletes. In the same way, Lennox Lewis has shown his commitment to helping disadvantaged young people from East London with his college in Hackney. West Ham United, too, are committed to helping their community and there are signs that this is paying real dividends in increasing participation in sport among local kids.

Like Lewis and Kwakye, community leaders and youth workers in the area work tirelessly to counter poverty and deprivation. Schools, colleges and local clubs are committed to maintaining and improving community life in East London's most disadvantaged areas, and there are signs that their hard work is beginning to reap some rewards. In 2009, Repton Boxing Club in Bethnal Green had the most successful year in its long and distinguished history, with an unprecedented five Golden Gloves in the National Championships. Repton's achievement is the result of years of work by scores of dedicated staff and volunteers. The long-term commitment of coaches is vital for the success of such projects. Encouraged by the schools, basketball, athletics and girls' football are all sports in which young people from the area have flourished in recent years as a result of the consistent presence of key people. Moore and Gooch prospered because they had adults around them who gave them the consistency and commitment they needed. These are valuable commodities in building a culture of trust and respect that encourages participation and success among young people.

Graham Gooch has not forgotten the help and encouragement he received as a young man. The Graham Gooch Cricket Academy at Chelmsford was set up in order to develop the next generation of young Essex cricketers. His scholarship scheme is providing promising young players with expert coaching and the opportunity to spend their winters in India, South Africa or Australia. Gooch's efforts are now producing players of the international calibre of Bopara and Cook, and his example shows just what can be achieved with the right combination of encouragement, sensitive coaching and good facilities.

Can East London/Essex produce another Bobby Moore or Graham Gooch? Despite the efforts of schools and clubs like Repton BC, there are signs that a once thriving and proud sporting culture is struggling. The success of the 2012 London Olympics will be judged locally by the contribution it makes to leading a resurgence of sport in the area and to enriching the lives of thousands of young people from East London.

A glorious tradition

Where the right conditions are in place, sport in Essex and East London is thriving. But, as we shall see, there are real concerns for the future of sport in some of the most disadvantaged areas, where schools, clubs and local authorities are struggling to cope with the often conflicting demands of local and central government, parents and legal restrictions. Perhaps the London Olympics, down the road in Stratford, will provide the impetus and inspiration that teachers, coaches and, most important of all, young people now need. The legacy strategy simply has to succeed.

In the post-war years Bobby Moore and Graham Gooch have epitomised the will, dedication and depth of feeling for their sport shared by thousands of local people. Running out to play in front of 35,000 passionate fans at West Ham's Boleyn Ground, strolling out to bat at Essex County Cricket Ground in a one-day semi-final or wandering over to play on Pitch 93 at Hackney Marshes on a wet and cold Sunday morning are part of the same honourable and, at the best of times, glorious tradition. This book is a celebration of sport in this special place. But it carries a health warning. The tradition needs to be renewed and nurtured constantly or it will be squandered and lost forever.

The first section of the book will focus on football, mainly in East London but also out in the non-League stronghold of Essex. In the second part of the book we will travel out on the M11 to Chelmsford and beyond, where the heart of cricket lies.

The book aims to provide a record of the sporting activities of the two generations of people from East London and Essex in the 40-year period that covers the careers of Moore and Gooch. Through first-hand accounts, we will begin to understand their motivations, recognise their achievements and discover just what sport means to the lives of people from this complex and often troubled area.

CHAPTER ONE
BOVRIL TO BABY BENTLEYS

In its long history the East End of London has experienced the effects of every single element of social, political and industrial change in Britain, but with far greater intensity. Unemployment, immigration, poverty, world wars and industrial change have been experienced in places such as Bethnal Green, Stratford and West Ham with so much more force than elsewhere in Britain. Two examples will suffice. Because of the strategic importance of the East End, its docks, shipbuilding works, transport networks, etc., the area, particularly in the Second World War, became the target for the enemies' fiercest and most prolonged attacks. The impact of war on the collective memory and consciousness of generations of East Enders in the twentieth century can only be imagined.

Walk through parts of Whitechapel and Shoreditch on a Friday afternoon when thousands of local people are leaving their mosques after prayer and you could be forgiven for thinking: is this really inner-city London? Local synagogues and chapels are now mosques whose minarets can be seen clear across East London. This is really nothing new, as synagogues and dissenting chapels have always sat comfortably alongside the lovely Nicholas Hawskmoor churches erected in the early eighteenth century in what is now Tower Hamlets. Immigrants have always brought their religion to the area, whether they be Huguenots, Jews escaping from Nazi programmes to the safety of Spitalfields, Africans fleeing from the crimes of Idi Amin or Jamaicans in search of work. Local people from every background have had to adjust and cope with the changes and challenges that shifting immigration patterns have brought to the area. Chinatown in Limehouse is long established and now so-called 'Banglatown' in the area around Brick Lane has added to the rich diversity of this part of the capital. In 1974, the Clifton Curry House was the first Indian restaurant to open in Brick Lane, and today the 'Costa Curry' commercial culture has reduced the authenticity of the experience.

For a time it looked as if the colossal impact of two world wars, the challenges of immigration and the trauma of industrial decline would bring the East End to its knees. But as is their habit, local people managed to roll with the punches and survived once again, to such an extent that parts of the East End have become fashionable, and with the 2012 Olympics based in Stratford the future looks bright. The one element that stubbornly refuses to change is the fortunes of West Ham United, who continue to bring joy and frustration in equal measure.

Much of the credit for the recovery of East London since 1945 must go to the post-war generation of East Enders. The parents of Bobby Moore and Graham Gooch were part of the wartime generation, and Moore himself was a war baby. Both families experienced the harsh post-war East End world of austerity and rebuilding in which as one observer put it,

This community, gone forever, was once bound by a common element – poverty.
- John Rennie (2009), 'Bound Together by Poverty', East End Life (free weekly Tower Hamlets newspaper).

Growing up in these difficult times influenced the way our heroes came to see the world. They were both self-motivated achievers who learnt the hard-won values of discipline and commitment in a tough and unforgiving environment. East London took two generations to recover from the shock and devastation of the Blitz. It was in this period of renewal that Moore and Gooch embarked on the early parts of their careers.

Bobby Moore was an East Londoner through and through, and Graham Gooch continues to show his gratitude and loyalty to the area through his work with young Essex cricketers. But before we examine the local influences on Moore and Gooch in their own time, it is worth reflecting on some of the history of this very special part of London where our two heroes were born and raised. Sport can never be isolated from society in general, and it is interesting to reflect on the wider events that shape the lives of great sports figures.

Courage in adversity

Most British professional football clubs emerged from working-class communities at the end of the nineteenth century, usually in inner-city areas. West Ham United are no different, and we can understand the club and its supporters a little more if we take a brief look at these communities and their history. In the nineteenth century a handful of great industrial pioneers established major enterprises around the Royal Docks, from which emerged a whole culture of sports and leisure clubs. Henry Tate built a sugar refinery in Silvertown in 1878, while Abram Lyle opened a similar works at Plaistow Wharf a few years later. The two firms combined in 1921, forming what became the world-famous sugar company, Tate & Lyle, a major employer in the area for generations. One of the company's first projects was to establish a sports club, complete with a private ground and clubhouse in the heart of the East End, a major contribution at the time to the growth of local sport in the area.

Heavy industry has been a feature of life in East London since the mid-eighteenth century. The River Lea's network of canals, employed today to carry materials up to Stratford for the new Olympic Stadium, have been used for industrial purposes for 200 years. House Mill, built on Three Mills Island, was once the largest and most powerful tidal mill in the UK. Clock Mill was built in 1817 and the third mill, a windmill, stood on the island until 1838. The mills were used originally to grind grain for flour but were later used in the distilling process. There were also tanneries and smoked salmon sheds on the urban sections of the Lea, along which barges carried gunpowder to Waltham Abbey in Essex.

As far back as 1852, the year of the last outbreak of cholera in East London, the industrial pioneer S.W. Silver established a rubber company down by the river, and Silvertown was born. Local people quickly acquired industrial skills of every type and there was no shortage of work, although conditions were usually unpleasant and often dangerous. In 1880, as the industrial revolution took a firm hold, the Royal Primrose Soap Works was opened by John Knight, again in Silvertown, a further source of employment to hard-working locals. This accelerated development of new industry had both positive and negative consequences. The jobs were welcome, but the accompanying rapid population growth caused severe housing problems as jerry-built estates were thrown up on swampland in Canning Town and West Ham. Population growth and inadequate housing caused a crisis in public health, as noted by Albert Dickens, brother of the even then famous Charles, in his Board of Health report, published in 1855:

It was impossible to describe the miserable state Canning Town was in: there was neither drainage nor paving; in winter the streets were impassable; cholera raged very much in this district.
- J. Bird (2002), The Newham Story: A Short History of Newham, ed. S.E. Kirby, London Borough of Newham.

Despite these often appalling social problems, the rapid rate of industrial growth in the East End continued with the largest gas plant in the world opening in the Plaistow area in 1869. Named after Simon Adam Beck, the company's President, the area around the works soon became known as Beckton, as it is today. Industrial expansion brought with it a huge demographic shift, with the Royal Docks in particular responsible for a significant increase in population in the East End. The first official census in the UK states that in 1851 the population of West Ham was a surprisingly low 18,000 and that East Ham had as few as 3,000 residents. The 1901 census shows staggering increases in both boroughs, with the population of West Ham rising to 267,000 and East Ham to 96,000. Immigration was a contributory factor to these increases, as people from all over the world were attracted to the area by the work to be found in the docks and surrounding industry.

Teenage rebels

East Enders are known to possess an independent spirit acquired in hard and difficult times. As the area became the industrial heartland of London in the late nineteenth century, locals began to earn a radical reputation as they sought to improve their wages and standard of living. The famous Match Girls' strike in 1888 at the Bryant & May factory, another major employer in the locality, is a powerful example of the area's militant industrial history. The strike began when three female employees were fired for stirring up unrest among the girls employed in the factory. Angry at the sackings, over 100 girls left the firm at Bow for the Fleet Street offices of radical journalist, Annie Besant. She quickly became the spokesperson for the girls and began to organise them into strike action. All the girls were teenagers and became inspired by Besant's militant example. The Match Girls' Strike lasted for three weeks and ended with the firm acceding to all the girls' demands and recognising the Women Match Workers' Union. Annie Besant was important to the success of the action, but the strike would not have occurred without the natural sense of justice of a group of strong teenage girls who were angered by Bryant & May's refusal to increase their pay of 4 shillings a week, despite the firm being hugely profitable.

The true spirit of East London

Despite the evidence of an extremely hard-working industrial past, there is an image of East Enders as naturally feckless and indolent, preferring crime to hard work and self-improvement. West Ham United have some of the most aggressive fans in Europe, and in some respects are 'brand leaders' for the type of football violence that almost ruined the professional game in Britain in the 1970s and 1980s.The Kray twins from Bethnal Green have their own hard-won reputation for violence and intimidation. I prefer to look to the courage of the Match Girls, the growth of trade unions in the late nineteenth century and the anti-fascist protests of the 1930s as a reflection of the true spirit of East London and its people. This spirit is evident in the determination and courage displayed by Bobby Moore and Graham Gooch as they set out to conquer the sporting world in the latter part of the twentieth century.

The kind of lazy thinking that misrepresents East End people ignores the fact that they have shown real independence and ingenuity in solving some of the social problems caused by industrial decline, war and immigration. The Workers' Educational Association (WEA) thrived in East London in the early twentieth century, while library membership increased significantly at that time and continues to increase to this day. Town halls and libraries opened in Canning Town and Manor Park around the end of the nineteenth century, and the much-respected Toynbee Hall opened for local people in 1884. A Technical Institute for trade and science courses was opened in East Ham by the Prince and Princess of Wales in 1905. But, as one of Charles Dickens' characters said, "We can't always be a-learning."

East Enders enjoy a night out, and by 1917, prior to the

outbreak of the First World War, there were an astonishing 17 cinemas in West Ham alone. These community initiatives introduced at the end of the old century are evidence of a healthy civic energy and are a tribute to the resourcefulness and ambition of local people, despite their undeserved reputation to the contrary. East Enders fought hard to win for themselves the kinds of opportunities in education, community life and culture that were mostly denied them in the nineteenth century. They also began to make their voice heard, largely through the election of Keir Hardie in 1892, the first Labour MP in England, as the nineteenth century democratic revolution reached East London.

Metropolitan Essex

London's East End has never been a recognisably single social entity. Bethnal Green, Shoreditich and Whitechapel, close to the City of London, have always been London boroughs, whereas the area further east around what is now known as Newham, which includes Plaistow, Newbury Park, Stratford, East Ham and West Ham, were metropolitan boroughs of Essex County Council up until 1965. This is the traditional home of West Ham United.

The local professional football club emerged in the mid-nineteenth century in metropolitan Essex. In 1846 C.J. Mare & Co. opened a shipyard at Bow Creek, although the company's name was later changed to the Thames Ironworks and Shipbuilding Company. The firm's football team eventually became West Ham United Football Club. Newspapers began to refer to the team as 'Hammers', but the fans, with a good sense of history, still use the original 'Irons'. "Come on you Irons" is still the chant you are most likely to hear ringing round Upton Park today.

A feature of the area's history is that, as the population increased, local sporting facilities began to spring up across the East End to complement the libraries, cinemas and music halls. West Ham United Football Club was established in 1900, while in 1905 local footballers were accommodated in the newly opened Plashet Park and Central Park in leafy East Ham. Memorial Park was opened in industrial West Ham in 1909, complete with splendid cycle and motorcycle tracks. Further east, the Forest Gate Public Hall introduced a roller-skating rink in 1909, and out on the fringe of Epping Forest Wanstead Flats offered football and cricket pitches, the Whit Monday Fair and open spaces designed to ease the stresses of living in overcrowded accommodation and working long hours in the factory or down at the docks.

A slow decline

If the industrial revolution of the mid-eighteenth century established the employment patterns for the area for 100 years, after 1900 we begin to see a gradual decline of the old East London staple industries such as the docks, sugar refineries and shipbuilding. High levels of unemployment led West Ham to become the first borough to set up a Distress Committee under the Unemployed Workers Act of 1905, to provide assistance to those without work. In an attempt to lower the unemployment figures, the government set up the controversial emigration scheme to Australia or Canada. In 1906/07 1,204 men, women and children left the area, preferring to take their chances in a new land. As in the industrial north of England, new technology and the increased use of sophisticated machinery meant fewer jobs, and the work that remained was usually dull and repetitive, further alienating workers from their means of livelihood.

The event that most clearly signalled the end of a rare period of economic growth and relative prosperity in East London was the construction of *HMS Thunderer*, the very last ship to be built at the Thames Ironworks before its closure in 1912. Dockers were the heart and soul of the East End and formed the core of West Ham fans. However, business has no sentiment and, operating on the precept that unemployment drives down wages, local employers were quick to act and wages across all industries were drastically cut, making it even more difficult for families to make ends meet. The 'call on' system in the docks, which involved men turning up in the hope of being picked out by the foreman for a day's work, illustrates the hardships that local people faced. Gus Webb, a former docker, recalls the 'call on' in the 1920s:

> *I can remember as a kid, five or six years of age, they used to take dockers on at the top of my turning and on the way to school of a morning the place would be full of people, and half an hour later*

there wasn't a soul there. It was a hard life, If your face didn't fit you didn't get picked.
- Bird (2002).

Even up to the early years of the twentieth century it was still thought that if you were unemployed and poor it was your own lazy fault, and this view became more entrenched as unemployment began to bite. But a group of local men named the Plaistow Landgrabbers helped to change attitudes to the unemployed when in July 1906 they occupied some waste ground in St Mary's Road, cleared the site and planted vegetables. The Triangle Camp, as it became known because of the shape of the plots, was eventually taken back by the council, but not before the men achieved their aim of showing that they were willing to work and that waste ground could be made productive. The men made their point, displaying the courage and sense of purpose common to people of the area. As the twentieth century developed they needed to draw on these qualities with increasing frequency.

As things began to get worse, two very different sets of people had no trouble finding work. Prostitution was endemic down in the streets of Whitechapel and Shoreditch, and East End girls would travel to Soho and the 'other end' to work for organised vice racketeers. But another set of people reacted in a different way to the growing problem of poverty and hunger in the area. The churches in East London have always had a charitable rather than merely a preaching function and they were keen to help as well as convert. Local churches opened a series of soup kitchens in the hardest hit areas, delivered hundreds of meals to the poorest families and provided shoes and clothing to those in need. One particular church in West Ham, in a neighbourhood of high unemployment, opened their kitchen four days each week and fed over 300 people a day.

The churches were keen to keep people out of the workhouses at all costs. There were workhouses all over the East End who were ready to give a home to the most destitute families. The official line of the Parish Unions was that admission was restricted to the criminally insane, imbeciles or idiots, but unofficially they admitted many families below the breadline. But these were harsh and unwelcoming places that operated a very strict regime. They really were the last resort. The workhouse authorities split families; husbands from wives and children from their parents. The food was appalling and the accommodation was damp and rat-infested. Many were sizeable institutions. At the end of the nineteenth century the Bethnal Green workhouse housed 109 people, 46 men and 63 women. It is worth remembering that there were no benefits available in those days, just a little parish poor relief for the worse off. Some of the sturdier local women were so desperate to keep their families out of the workhouses that they earned 'nubbins', or pin money, by taking part in organised street fighting in front of large crowds on Sunday afternoons. The Whitechapel Workhouse in Vallance Road, home of the infamous Kray family, later became an infirmary, before emerging in the twentieth century as St Peter's Hospital. This was quite a common change of use, but most of the workhouses were demolished in the middle of the twentieth century and all were closed down in the 1930s. Most have been turned into pubs, almshouses, local museums or trendy apartments for the new inhabitants of the area.

East Enders are endlessly resourceful and, in addition to the free food offered by the churches, private kitchens and cafés were quickly set up by enterprising locals. One such was Rumfords in Hackney, whose delights included the following: boiled beef and vegetables; 3d; half a pound of rice plum pudding, 1d; and a pint of pease soup, 1d. Not your gastro-pub food of today's trendier establishments around Hoxton Market, but nourishing nosh for the poverty-stricken unemployed of the late nineteenth century.

Churches also offered schooling to local children. This was of dubious quality and the Ragged Schools and Scattered Schools probably offered a more rounded education, as we can see today at the Ragged School Museum in Mile End. In 1899 the Grays Scattered School was established out in Essex, an indication that metropolitan Essex was not without its own problems.

It would be a mistake to think that East Londoners were cowed by unemployment, poverty and poor housing. Apart from the emergence of leisure and cultural facilities in the nineteenth century, there was music and dancing in clubs and dancehalls across the area. Most pubs had live music at the weekends, with banjo bands being a particular favourite. Music halls were extremely popular and, like bathhouses, provided places where people could meet, socialise and lift each others' spirits. However, in the early part of the twentieth century their spirit was to be tested by forces that were completely outside their control.

The Great War

The Great War brought shortages and deprivation to East London, as it did across the whole country, although unemployment decreased, largely because a shocking 100,000 men from West Ham alone joined up to serve in the armed forces. Among these was Jack Cornwall VC, who joined the Royal Navy in 1915 at the age of 16. He was killed at the battle of Jutland onboard his ship *HMS Chester* on 31 May 1916. His Commanding Officer paid this tribute:

> *... John Travers Cornwall was mortally wounded early in the action, but nevertheless remained at a most exposed post, ... awaiting orders..., with the gun's crew dead and wounded around him. He was under sixteen years of age.*

Jack was awarded the Victoria Cross posthumously, one of only 634 recipients of the honour in the First World War, and was buried in Manor Park Cemetery. There are few that are given to act as heroically as John Cornwall, but thousands of local men had lost their lives by the time the Great War ended on 11th November 1918. You will see memorials to the fallen all over East London; at West Ham bus garage, St Mark's Church, Silvertown and East Ham Memorial Park to name just a few.

After the war had ended, unemployment once again became the most pressing social problem in East London. Many families from the 'deserving poor' received 'outdoor relief' from the Board of Guardians, and by 1925 over 70,000 people in West Ham were receiving relief, which put an enormous strain on cash-strapped local authorities. Councils argued that unemployment should be a national rather than local issue, and West Ham council were forced to borrow money from central government to meet the rising costs of the depression. The council then defaulted on its loan from Westminster and was removed by the Guardians in 1926, the year of the National Strike. But the boards were themselves abolished in 1929, with the result that, finally, unemployment became a national problem requiring national solutions.

White horses and black shirts

The 1920s and 1930s were a troubled time for East London, but despite the hardships experienced by most locals life did take on a more settled normality. Markets continued to be held in Green Street and at Stratford, while on Sundays East Enders flocked to Petticoat Lane. Sport, as always, continued to provide an antidote to difficult times. West Ham United were always guaranteed to raise the spirits in East London, so when they reached the FA Cup final in 1923 hopes were high. Sadly, victory was denied their long-suffering supporters and The Hammers were beaten 2-0 by Bolton Wanderers in the famous White Horse final, named after a police horse whose calm dignity prevented a potential disaster when the huge crowd at Wembley spilled out across the pitch.

Just like my dreams they fade and die …

But East Enders are ever resilient and continued to build a civic and sporting culture even in the difficult years between the wars. West Ham speedway stadium opened in Prince Regent Lane in 1928, and the local team quickly became one of the most successful in the country. The stadium remained open and active until it was finally closed in 1972, and in addition to speedway it also hosted greyhound racing, stock car racing and football matches. It is a sign of a changing sporting culture that speedway and greyhound racing, once so popular in most areas of London up until the 1960s, have almost dropped off the local sporting radar. For a short time Thames Association FC used the old speedway stadium as their home ground, but the club folded in the 1930s. West Ham United never played there and stayed local to the Boleyn, their home from 1904.

Away from sport, the economic depression of the 1930s continued unabated. Times like these can exploit potential divisions in society and lay them bare, so to speak. Oswald Mosley's Blackshirts dared to exploit poverty and hardship in the early 1930s by revealing their prejudices and taking the easy and banal route of blaming immigrants for high unemployment. The target for Mosley and his henchmen was the local Jewish community, who had opened a synagogue in the Barking Road in 1923 and owned many successful businesses in East Ham. As today, there was some local hostility towards Jews and other immigrant communities, but there was greater opposition to the Fascist movement. In 1935 Mosley ran the gauntlet of over 700 protestors at a fascist rally at Stratford Town Hall, where his inflammatory rhetoric couldn't be heard over the noise of the protestors, and later, in 1937, the British Fascist Party was routed at the historic battle of Cable Street in Stepney. There has always been a degree of racial tension in the East End, and a minority of local activists like nothing more than to stir up trouble. Largely, however, they have been marginalised and the various ethnic groups living in the area exist side by side with a degree of co-operation and mutual tolerance, if not always real harmony.

West Ham United set a good example by becoming one of the first professional clubs to have black players in their first team. The legendary Bermudian, Clyde Best, Clive Charles and Ade Coker followed John Charles into the West Ham sides of the 1960s and 1970s. Apart from Best, all were born locally, and even the great Bermudian liked to think of himself as a local. Today, of course, it would be impossible to imagine a Premier League side without a strong ethnic mix of players - one of the most welcome sights in British sport.

East London under siege

On 3rd September 1939 war was declared for the second time in a generation. The paraphernalia of war at home was quickly brought into everyday life. Air-raid shelters and sirens, gas masks and blackouts became routine. In East Ham 9,000 people volunteered for civil defence duties, as the area moved tentatively through the period of the 'phoney war'. In September 1939, West Ham ARP (Air Raid Precautions) issued 1,700 respirators for children under two years of age, and the local registry offices wondered how they were going to keep track of newborn babies. Eighty underground stations were converted to protect local people from the Nazi night raiders, but many preferred to take their chances with their own crude back-garden shelter or simply, as my parents did, bundled the children under the stairs when the siren sounded.

With the fear of bombing uppermost in their minds, local

authorities moved quickly to evacuate children and expectant mothers away from the area. By 15th September 1939 the *Stratford Express* reported that 16,000 people had been evacuated from East Ham and 32,000 from West Ham. Newham Archives reveal that approximately 40,000 local people were evacuated to the country during the first few weeks of the war. By any standards this was a phenomenal achievement. Most were sent to counties in the south-east or up to East Anglia, but they gradually returned as the anticipated bombing raids failed to materialise. But, of course, the bombing came and when it did nobody could have predicted the devastation it would cause. The first bomb fell in Beckton Road, West Ham, on 28th August 1940, and the Blitz itself began on the night of Black Saturday, 7th September, with 300 German bombers dropping 300 tons of high explosives on the East End. The docks and heavy industry were the obvious targets, and it was said that on that night you could read a newspaper in Shaftsbury Avenue from the light of the fires in the Royal Docks. Fires burnt for a week as volunteer firemen fought to contain the blaze and keep the docks open. Local Iris Warren remembers the first night of the Blitz:

> *On that Saturday night, that we were first bombed, I walked from Walthamstow to Maryland Point and got on a train home. I got off at Manor Park because I lived at East Ham. All along the High Street was on fire, Woolworth's had been bombed on Station Hill and a furniture shop was on fire.*
> *- Newham Archives, Stratford Library.*

One of the most tragic incidents in the East End during the war was the disaster at Bethnal Green Underground Station, which was used as an air-raid shelter, on 3rd May 1943, the worst civilian disaster in Britain in which 173 people were killed. A young woman carrying a baby tripped and fell, causing hundreds of people heading down to the Central Line platforms to collapse on top of one another, the casualties being crushed to death by the weight of the bodies. This incident was particularly tragic since its cause remains a mystery. By this time people were well used to air raids and usually headed calmly for the shelters, as they had done many times before. But on this occasion something was different; there was no air raid, and they did not recognise the explosions they heard. Frightened people abandoned their usual stoic calm and rushed into the station and down the escalators, with tragic consequences. Ironically, the explosion turned out to be artillery fire from home troops drilling in nearby Victoria Park. Tragically, Bethnal Green Station was under construction at the time and there were no handrails on any of the staircases, which added to the chaos as men, women and children tumbled down the escalator. The horror of the disaster was unimaginable – 62 of the dead were local children (Descendants of the victims of the Bethnal Green Underground disaster have organised a campaign to have a Stairway to Heaven memorial erected at the station (March 2009).

Gas masks and goalposts

We know from Anton Rippon's wonderful book *Gas Masks for Goal Posts* that football continued to be played in the area for most of the war. It will hurt Millwall supporters to admit it, but their club was forced to use Upton Park as their home ground after The Den was badly damaged by the Luftwaffe in 1940. Rippon informs us that in 1939,

> *West Ham United's landlords, the Archdiocese of Westminster, offered the club the Upton Park ground for a yearly rent of only a £1 …*
>
> *- A. Rippon (2005), Gas Masks for Goal Posts: Football in Britain During the Second World War, The History Press, p.97*

Upton Park was used by the military for drill and as a practice range. It was hit during the early days of the Blitz and the West Stand, housing the club's admin staff, suffered extensive damage. Temporary office accommodation was found outside the ground in the Green Street House pub, known by all Hammers fans as Boleyn Castle. All the club's records were lost in the war along with, as Rippon reveals, those of the London FA, which had recently moved into temporary offices in Upton Park. Not content with inflicting damage on the hallowed ground once, the Nazi bombers struck again in 1944. A dreaded flying bomb fell on the pitch, causing extensive damage to the South Bank stand, and it was not until 1947 that the club were given permission to repair it. The club therefore had to play all their home-game wartime League fixtures away from Upton Park, until they could safely return to Boleyn Castle when hostilities ceased.

In 1938, the West Ham chairman of the time, W.J. Cearn, suggested that his first team players help the war effort. He encouraged them to join the local Territorials and the reserve police, thus ensuring that the club would be able to put out a decent first team for the duration of the conflict. But many Hammers players saw this as being unpatriotic and later joined the Essex Regiment where they were more likely to be called into active service. In spite of the obvious difficulties, the club did manage to field a decent side during the war and reached the final of the War Cup in 1941. This time they were successful, beating Blackburn Rovers 1-0 in front of 42,000 spectators at Wembley Stadium, at the time temporary home to,

> *Hundreds of bewildered French and Belgian refugees who had fled Hitler's blitzkrieg into their countries.*
> *- Rippon (2005). P.171*

It was generally felt that football, both amateur and professional, would help morale during the war, despite many of the grounds being given over to the military. A police chief in the area remarked at the time that local football should be encouraged; after all, he continued, no one had suggested that people should stop going to church. "Police cells would be full of young men with no outlet for their energies, if things like football were outlawed," he commented rather ruefully.

Professional football raised significant sums for the war effort and continued to be played and watched in East London, despite the lack of transport and the continual threat of German bombs. Local park football in the East End continued where possible, but many grounds were dug up for planting vegetables and Wanstead Flats was used as the site of a prisoner of war camp. Of course, most young men from the area were either away in the war or fully occupied at home in the war effort.

South Hallsville School

Blitz stories are legion and often desperately hard to take. Ordinary tales emerge of people diving for cover when low-flying Nazi planes began spraying the streets with machine-gun fire. But one tragedy stands out and provides an insight into the depth of suffering that the bombing inflicted on local people. On 10th September 1940, South Hallsville School, full of bombed-out families waiting to be evacuated, suffered a direct hit. The official estimate of dead was 73, but locals claimed that as many as 400 people lost their lives in the worst civilian disaster of the war. It is estimated that a total of around 1,700 civilians in the area lost their lives to the German bombs, a number that would have been much higher but for the provision of air-raid shelters. (The Stratford Express reported that West Ham had space in air-raid shelters for 200,000 people). Unfortunately, these private means of shelter were subject to flooding and more public spaces had to be found. One of these was the crypt of St John's Church on Stratford Broadway, converted in the war to a public shelter. Local Len Shingler remembers sheltering there:

> *There was a woman down there and she sold pies and cheese and cakes you see. All the cakes were laid out and all the bodies were buried in the walls! There was signs on the wall saying here lays ... these old-fashioned names, you know. And people had bunks down there and they'd go to sleep on them all night.*
> *- Newham Archives.*

The Blitz was largely over by May 1941, after seven months of the most appalling privation. The war had taken a heavy toll on the area, with thousands dead, 16,000 houses destroyed and a quarter of all families losing their homes. The effect of the war on local communities, schools, hospitals and employment was incalculable. In 1939, the year the war broke out, the population of West Ham had been 294,278 and in 1951 it was only 170,993. Many had died, either at home or in action, and others had moved away to somewhere safer and had chosen not to return. The process of recovery was long and hard, but slowly day-to-day life began to settle down and improve. New homes were built to house the homeless and to prevent overcrowding. The Kier Hardie estate was one of the most ambitious schemes, but progress was slow and building materials were scarce. By the Coronation year of 1953, only one-third of the houses destroyed during the war had been replaced. The East Enders had been hit hard by the war, harder than anywhere else in

Britain. They entered the post-war period of reconstruction punch drunk, but ready to face the next challenge.

We never had it so good?

Bobby Moore was an icon of the sixties, and for many of us 1960 represented a turning point. Socially and culturally the world quite suddenly seemed to become a very different place, new and exhilarating and, best of all, alive. The 1950s were fog-bound, dark and dreary by comparison. Park railings had been ripped out during the war, shops were shabby and unattractive, and crime rates were soaring. In 1938 there had been 58,000 violent crimes in England and Wales; in 1948 there were 130,000. The pre-war world of the 1930s must have appeared altogether more appealing. What was called at the time 'a modern matrimonial landslide' saw divorce rates rise in the UK from 4,100 in 1935 to 60,300 in 1947, as wives struggled to cope with returning soldier husbands, who often had post-war trauma to deal with, as well as children who viewed their father as a stranger in the house.

There is a great deal of nostalgia around for the 1950s: the decade of family values, Ladybird t-shirts, Kia-Ora Suncrush, Saturday morning pictures, Bing Crosby and Dickie Valentine, and London smogs. In the great smog of 1952 12,000 people were killed within just four days in the capital, but little fuss was made of the disaster. Holidays were spent on a windswept beach getting soaked to the skin, with little to do but the occasional donkey ride. Not much to get nostalgic about there. Two things helped to alleviate the boredom. Firstly, the first independent TV channel was set up in 1955 as a rival to the stuffy BBC; and secondly, there was football. Huge crowds were attracted to Football League matches in the 1950s, entranced by the sublime skills of Wilf Mannion, Tom Finney and Stanley Matthews. Just to indicate how popular professional football was at this time, in the 1953/54 season an average of 7,000 people attended Accrington Stanley's home matches. Of course, there was no footie on TV and games always kicked off at 3.00 p.m. on Saturday afternoons. There was little else to do aside from watching wrestling or horse racing on tiny black and white TVs. But things were about to change.

Somewhere around 1960 British people decided to leave behind a post-war world created by the BBC's Light

Programme and Home Service radio stations and chose a more embracing, liberating and popular culture. In 1962 I can clearly remember hearing The Beatles' first single, 'Love Me Do', for the first time in a state of jaw-dropping shock – life would never be the same again. Rapid change occurred in sport as in other areas of life. The minimum wage in football was abolished in 1962, along with the professional/amateur distinction in cricket. Other sports followed cricket's example, although a little more reluctantly where class prejudice was more deeply ingrained.

In 1960, when Bobby Moore was setting out on what was to become one of the greatest careers in sport, the patrician Harold Macmillan was Prime Minister. In March of that remarkable year Elvis Presley returned from US Army duty in West Germany and promptly hit the top of the charts with 'It's Now or Never'. While Elvis was enjoying his return to civilian life, the newly formed Beatles began a 48-night residency in a Hamburg night club, as a prelude to changing popular music forever. In November 1960 the young Senator John Kennedy was elected President of the USA. The *Lady Chatterley* censorship trial in 1960 helped to change the cultural consciousness of a generation and allowed writers and artists the creative freedom they had been denied by British law. The struggle against apartheid in South Africa, in which Graham Gooch became entangled in the 1980s, took a decisive, if tragic, turn with the Sharpeville Massacre in 1960. These events transformed the cultural and political landscape and were to have a dramatic impact on our sporting culture.

Sport is easily dwarfed by such world-changing events, but in the post-war period it felt the force of the revolutionary changes crashing around its often insular world. In 1960 St Paddy won the Derby, Neale Fraser and Maria Bueno were Wimbledon champions, and Arnold Palmer, of course, won the US Masters and the US Open. In the same year Francis Chichester enthralled the British public with his solo adventures in *Gypsy Moth 111*. Despite these notable performances, the most important sporting event of 1960 was the Olympic Games held that year in Rome. American Wilma Rudolph, the greatest female sprinter of her era, won three gold medals, but perhaps the greatest athletic achievement in Rome was the victory of Ethiopian Abebe Bikila, who memorably won the men's marathon while running in bare feet.

The gold medal for heavyweight boxing in Rome was won by the greatest boxer the world has ever seen, Cassius Marcellus Clay, who later the same year fought his first professional fight. Clay, who later changed his name to Muhammad Ali, is reputed to have thrown his gold medal away in disgust after being refused service in a Louisiana restaurant. Such discrimination led to the escalation of the civil rights movement in the USA throughout the 1960s. The Alabama marches, the death of Martin Luther King, and the increasing influence of the Black Panthers, to whom Ali was associated, were all events of the sixties, culminating in the Panther protest by medal-winning African American athletes Tommie Smith (gold) and John Carlos (bronze) at the Mexico City Olympics in 1968. Who said that sport should be kept out of politics?

Two years on, back in East London, Bobby Moore was in his fourth season as a professional for West Ham and his progress had been spectacular. In the summer of 1962, at the age of 21, Moore played in all four of England's World Cup matches in Chile, the last of which was the quarter-final defeat by Brazil and his first encounter with the unparalleled Pelé. In 1962 Sir Geoff Hurst was offered a professional contract by Doug Insole at Essex CCC at £6 a week, but Hurst played just one first-class match for the county. Little did he know what fame would engulf him four years later. On a less elevated level, in East London Leyton Orient FC, in many ways West Ham's younger East End footballing brother, enjoyed their first ever season in the old First Division.

In the decade that followed the sporting year of 1960 the pace of change at home and abroad was rapid and relentless, in politics, the visual arts, film, broadcasting media and particularly music. In Britain in the sixties the world seemed to be full of promise and endless possibilities from the moment that 'Love Me Do' hit the charts. The incomparable Beatles, who quickly became the spiritual leaders of a spirited generation, followed their first British hit with a string of chart-topping singles and albums in Britain, America and half the countries of the world. The world had seen nothing like it.

In sport the decade reached a dizzy climax in 1966 when, on 30th July, the England football team gloriously won the World Cup against West Germany, with all four goals in the final scored by West Ham players, Geoff Hurst (3) and Martin Peters

(1). The other West Ham player in the winning team was, of course, the England captain, Bobby Moore. The East End club had recovered from the war better than most and was producing players of real international class. In 1966 footballers suddenly became celebrities in their own right – indeed, in the last years of that famous decade football was to have its own 'fifth Beatle' in the great George Best. Things couldn't get much better than this. In 1966 was also notable for the following:

• The average house price was £3,840.
• Harold Wilson increased his majority from 4 to 96, joking that England only won the World Cup under a Labour government.
• Ian Brady and Myra Hindley were found guilty of the Moors Murders.
• A slag heap at Aberfan in South Wales engulfed a primary school, killing 116 children and 28 adults.
• John Lennon claimed that The Beatles were "bigger than Jesus".

But some things were slow to change: right up to the early seventies you could still buy a steaming hot cup of Bovril in the shed behind the West Stand at Upton Park and stir it with a dirty old spoon attached to the counter by an old piece of string.

Park life

Strolling through Ridgeway Park in Chingford in the late sixties, where David Beckham played as a young boy for Ridgeway Rovers, enjoying a summer's evening on Wanstead Flats, or passing Hackney Marshes on a 38 bus, you would have witnessed dozens of youngsters enjoying energetic games of football and cricket. Some would have been impromptu kick-abouts; others were more serious and competitive matches with players changed and wearing proper gear. They would often involve fantasy league and cup competitions, complete with detailed statistics of every match played. Every morning break time in my Chingford school playground, using sections of the chain-link fencing as goalposts, we played out a complex set of fixtures which, over the winter, amounted to a full First Division programme. Stout shoes bought with hard-earned wages were ruined in weeks, to the anger and frustration of hard-up parents. At the end of the 'season' one of the boys produced a detailed league table for our very own Division One championship.

On summer evenings in Marsh Lane in Leyton, Low Hall Farm in Walthamstow, St Mary's Church Playing Fields in Barking and the intriguingly named Nutter Lane at Wanstead were all given over to young people, often highly skilled, playing sophisticated games of football, with coats as goalposts. In some games the standard would not have been out of place in London's senior amateur leagues. Indeed, the casual observer might be forgiven for failing to recognise the young centre forward who on Saturdays knocked in goals for Walthamstow Avenue in the Isthmian League, or the talented inside forward who had recently joined Leyton Orient on semi-pro terms and regularly turned out for Leytonstone FC in front of 5,000 regulars at their High Road ground.

But in the early 1970s something changed. These once tranquil escapes from the clamour of urban streets became dangerous and menacing no-go areas. You could still make the same bus trip, if you were brave enough to make the effort, but you would see a very different picture. The hundreds of games of casual football and cricket where the young Bobby Moore and Graham Gooch displayed their emerging skills had all but disappeared. You would find little activity of any kind apart from that directed by drug dealers, gang crews, and groups of depressed-looking young people stuck in the squalid surroundings of urban living. The decline of London parks between 1970 and 1990 was a symptom of a change in the character of British society, which became polarised and divided as greed and envy were installed as the dominant values of the day. A culture of fear gripped the streets and public spaces in East London as gang culture spilled over into gun and knife crime.

Elvis Presley once said that values were like fingerprints - you leave them everywhere. The old East End values of hard work, achievement and looking out for your neighbour, which nourished Moore and Gooch, were being distorted. But all is not lost. Certainly, Newham Council have recognised the importance of public open spaces to community life and have begun to restore their council parks to something like their former glory. Park-keepers are being reinstated, and floodlit all-weather pitches are being installed, as a different, more organised kind of open space emerges.

Stirring up trouble

As local people began to recreate their lives, the post-war period saw further increases in settlers from abroad to the area. There were acute labour shortages in the transport and health sectors, and Britain ran recruitment campaigns in the 1950s, particularly in Jamaica, designed to attract people to come to live and work in England. Later, in the mid-1970s, hundreds of East African Asians settled in East and West Ham after being thrown out of their Ugandan homeland by the military dictator, Idi Amin. Fascist groups such as the National Front (NF) or the British National Party (BNP) are quick to exploit potential divisions in society wherever they exist. The NF targeted the East End at this time, attempting to drive a wedge between the newly arrived immigrants and local young men. They gained a small but dangerous following among local skinheads and the hardcore of Upton Park's North Bank. But East Enders rejected the fascist rhetoric and fought back through organisations such as Red Wedge, Rock Against Racism and the Anti-Nazi League. Metropolitan Essex boy Billy Bragg, a passionate Hammers supporter, was behind much of the local opposition.

Later, in the 1980s, racial tension did threaten to spill over, with several racially motivated murders in the area, which today might be called 'gangland killings'. However, the neighbourhood ethnic groups fought back, forming political and community organisations to represent their views and interests. Many of these groups have become established and today are integrated into mainstream local politics. There is little doubt that the white working-class, indigenous population had genuine grievances against the housing policies of both Newham and Tower Hamlets, which right-wing group quickly exploited. In fairness, both councils had the difficult task of allocating scarce housing resources between the urgent needs of recently arrived families and locals who had been born and brought up in the area.

Unemployment was also a local political issue in both boroughs and reached a staggering 20 per cent in the 1980s, figures similar to those of the 1930s, as the effects of the latest recession hit East London. Between 1951 and 1975, 40,000 jobs were lost in Newham alone (Bird (2002). Many long-established

East End firms closed down, including Tate & Lyle, Trebor Sharpe, Standard Telephones and Cables, and Scruton Maltby. But it was the closure of the docks that had the most devastating impact. The slow death of the Royal Docks from 1966 to 1975 accounted for the loss of 20,000 jobs in the area. The Docklands Development Corporation were set up in 1981 to regenerate the district around the old Royal Docks, and the legacy of the 2012 Olympics is designed to have a positive impact on employment and housing. We shall see.

Dockers, Printers and Times International

Harold Wilson's white heat of technology revolution did little to improve urban squalor and poverty in the poorer parts of London. Deprivation and unemployment were only ever a recession away for thousands of people in this part of the capital. The unreal sixties world of the young Beatles, Twiggy, George Best and Bobby Moore was becoming a fast-fading and dreamy illusion, as a harsher economic climate began to bite in the late seventies.

The final closure of the Victoria, Albert and George V1 docks in 1981, 100 years after their opening by Queen Victoria in 1850, signalled the end of old and settled working habits and practices of generations of East Londoners. The stranglehold of the dock workers' unions on the industry was broken by the employers and by government legislation. The docks themselves were closed because the new juggernaut container ships were too large to navigate the old river's shallow waters around the Pool of London. Now they end their journey in the relatively deeper waters of the estuary at Tilbury. The closure of the docks robbed thousands of West Ham supporters of a major source of employment. The second development had a similar effect.

The printing chapels of Fleet Street controlled the printing industry in much the same way as the dockers dominated working practices on the Thames. When the newspapers, led by Rupert Murdoch and Times International and supported by the government, shut down their Fleet Street operations in 1986, moved lock, stock and barrel to Wapping and introduced new digital methods of producing newspapers, they effectively destroyed a major source of employment in the area, putting hundreds printers out of work. At least 6,000 local workers were summarily sacked in Murdoch's relentless drive to 'modernise' working practices. One by one other newspapers followed the example of *The Times* and, inspired by Eddie Shah, fled Fleet Street and moved their high-tech operations to out-of-town safety. The unions and their friends fought the closure of the Fleet Street plants and there were pitched battles in the streets around Wapping reminiscent of the 1984 miners conflict. Their protests were in vain and the closure of the old printing industry was a further blow to the Hammers' faithful and their families. Sadly, there was little compensation to be found at Upton Park at the time, as the team went through the usual routine of either being relegated or just avoiding that fate.

The closure of the docks and Fleet Street paved the way for the gentrification of parts of the East End and its colonisation by artists, city-rich wide boys and media types. The new Docklands and the area around Spitalfields became a honeypot for the credit-worthy, young middle-class. Shoreditch and Whitechapel followed as lower property prices east of the City became too low to resist. Many of these young tyros adopted football as their sport of choice. Some became the 'new prawn sandwich' brigade of Manchester United supporters, or took their 4x4s over to Stamford Bridge or Highbury, but with a few notable exceptions they stayed away from their local club just a short journey away at Upton Park.

Football became a political issue as violence and hooliganism spread across the country and into Europe. The Hillsborough disaster, although not a result of football violence, led the authorities to take action to improve the appalling state of British football grounds. The Taylor Commission was set up in 1989 to discover the causes of the Hillsborough tragedy that disfigured our national game, almost beyond redemption. Published in 1990, the *Taylor Report*'s main recommendation was for modern all-seater stadiums. The English Premier League fully accepted Taylor's conclusions and football stadiums at all levels of the game were transformed over the next ten years. Backed by Rupert Murdoch's Sky TV, the Premier League quickly became a worldwide success and brought a degree of wealth into the game that would have been inconceivable even up to the late 1980s.

Following Taylor's recommendations West Ham's Boleyn ground became unrecognisable. Out went the beloved old 'chicken run', the hot Bovril stall under the West Stand, and the pre-match entertainment provided by the Salvation Army band. And, almost unbelievably, the infamous North Bank became all-seater. Today the Bobby Moore Stand sits proudly at the southern end of the ground, and you can even get married in the West Ham Hotel on match days and celebrate by watching the game in luxury with friends and family, although it's probably best for the newly-weds not to expect their special day to end with a Hammers win. Club membership is necessary to gain entry to most parts of the ground – no more paying cash through the old turnstiles. But some things never change and 'Bubbles' still rings out as the teams prepare for the kick-off, the anticipation somewhat diminished by watching the sides warm up on the pitch for a full 30 minutes before the game. A nicely refurbished Boleyn Tavern still guards the entrance to the west side of the ground in Green Street and its new Sir Trevor Brooking stand.

The improvements to Premier League stadiums, although timely and welcome, stand in stark contrast to the condition of the surrounding neighbourhoods. For example, despite the glitter and sheen of the new Boleyn ground, the streets around the stadium and the communities across Newham continue to have to cope with the difficulties and complexities of living in East London. Newham Council's website claims that Green Street is now

> *... the Bond Street of the East End with over 400 independent shops representing cultures from around the world, selling food, jewellery, designer saris and a myriad of cafés and restaurants serving authentic international cuisine.*
> *- Newham Council website, www.newham.gov.uk, March 2009.*

This is a slightly disingenuous picture and totally ignores some of the worst housing and living conditions in the whole of London. It is true that the East End is undergoing a transformation. For example, Newham is at the centre of plans for the 2012 Olympics, and the home for the 80,000 capacity Olympic Stadium in Stratford. The Olympic Park, also in Stratford, will contain schools, offices, hotels, a shopping centre and 4,500 new homes. Canning Town and West Ham itself will be subject to numerous regeneration schemes, so the Olympic dream can benefit local people. The opportunity is there to make the East End an area rich in culture, sustainable jobs, better housing and good transport links. This is the very least that local people deserve as the area begins to embark on a new period in its history, finally emerging from the hard and difficult times of the previous 50 years.

Ups and downs

Crime and the fear of crime are at the top of everyone's worry list. East London/Essex has gained a reputation as a dangerous place – the Chingford funerals of the Kray family were as 'East End' as it was possible to be. Some of Bobby Moore's more dodgy mates were rather too close for comfort at times to the brothers' criminal fraternity. Today the nature of criminal behaviour in East London has changed – neighbourhood gangs of alienated young people and spectacular and audacious feats of criminal activity have replaced the more organised, ordinary, but no less vicious 'gangsterism' of the Krays. It is little wonder, against this background, that casual games of football in the local park, which could be seen all over East London on most summer evenings, have all but disappeared, along with young people's opportunity to let off steam playing outdoors with their friends.

In the 1970s Ian Dury wrote a song about the ups and downs of a year in the life of his Essex family. Dury used the song, Profoundly in love with Pandora, to make the point that ordinary life goes on in much the same way, whatever the latest shifts in economic, political or cultural thinking. The divisive policies of one government after another failed to drive out the instincts of our communities to make things better for themselves and their families. But when these families do break down, as the young Drury's did, young people are often left to fend for themselves.

A home from home

Unforgiving urban landscapes are often punctuated by buildings that offer relief and escape from the clamour of city life. One such building is the Stratford Public Library, located just a mile or two from Upton Park and a short walk away from Bobby Moore's old pub, Two Puddings. The library is in many respects a microcosm of the East End itself. It has been said that the single most important thing in encouraging children to read and take an interest in education is books in the home. As a boy I was taken to the public library by my parents every Friday after school. My old library in Chingford looks tiny today, but at the time it seemed cavernous, and for a young boy from a bleak housing estate it opened up a whole new and exciting world. By the age of 16 I had read Hemingway and Dickens, while being introduced to the fascinating worlds of Denis Compton, Peter May and Stanley Matthews. Modern libraries are very different. At Stratford there are rooms for borrowing computer games, DVDs, CDs, magazines and, of course, books of every kind. All these treasures are available in many languages, and there are reading groups, book clubs, and an archive and research centre where local people can trace their family history or find out more about their area. Library staff are kind, sympathetic and knowledgeable. But what struck me most on a recent visit was a spacious reception area with newspapers, magazines and, amazingly, a huge TV screen showing the latest local news and sport. Schoolchildren and adults, numbering 30 or 40, sat quietly in rows watching the screen, warm and comfortable on a bitterly cold late February afternoon. Across the room was a row of desks where kids in school uniforms were chatting in whispers to their friends while pretending to do their homework. The place was calm and relaxed. Modern libraries like Stratford, right next door to a city-centre supermarket, provide a secure space for local people to spend a couple of hours of their day. Young people who for one reason or another cannot go home find the library welcome and reassuring.

It is interesting how our memories are attached to places. The stability of place is important for all communities, particularly those in inner-city areas, and libraries are places where individual and social memories are formed and reinforced, as are football and cricket clubs. It is important to retain such places, as they are integral to our social identity; too often they have either been destroyed or dismantled.

East and West Ham libraries between them issued 80,000 tickets in 1963/64, the year before they were absorbed into Newham. In 2007 the population of Newham was 246,000 and in that year there were more than two million visits to Newham libraries. From these figures it is safe to assume that libraries in the area are in good shape and immensely popular. It is encouraging to know that someone, somewhere, has got it right. Libraries are important public institutions that provide safe and neutral places for local people and are an indicator of the cultural health of a community. Modern urban libraries act as a hub for social cohesion and engagement, although they were never set up for this purpose, and it is to their credit that they have been able to evolve along with their communities.

Diversity and deprivation

The majority of West Ham supporters live in Newham. The population of the borough has increased by 13 per cent since 1991. It is a very young place – the proportion of the population under 19 is a high 23 per cent, while there has been an 11 per cent decrease in the number of people aged over 55. The borough has the lowest proportion of children under the age of one in the country and the lowest population figure for those over the age of 65. Such a young population offers real local challenges in terms of employment, education, social services, housing, sport and leisure, and, sadly, the police. As we shall see, West Ham United are making their own attempt to meet this challenge.

Newham is a fluid, fast-changing place. It now has the highest proportion of non-white ethnic groups in the UK, with 61 per cent of the population drawn from mixed, Asian, black or black British people. The borough has the second highest proportion of Asian people in England and Wales and the second highest proportion of black Africans in the UK. Neighbouring Tower Hamlets tops both these lists. These figures begin to give some idea of the complexity of the place and the extent of change in the streets around the Boleyn ground and also the emerging Olympic Park.

Unemployment remains a troubling local issue. In 2007 the borough had an unemployment rate of 7 per cent, the second highest in the UK behind Hackney. In times of economic recession this figure will rise rapidly. Of the total population who are unemployed and seeking work, Newham has the highest proportion, a staggering 21 per cent, who have never worked. Youth unemployment in 2007 was 25.2 per cent, 34 per cent of local people of working age have no formal qualifications and the borough has a very low level of economic activity among its male population. It is a depressing picture and no better when we look at the standard of local housing. One quarter of households are overcrowded, and the proportion of households in Newham with lone parents and dependant children is the highest in the UK. Two-thirds of all female lone parents in the borough are unemployed. This is the place where Hammers supporters spend their lives, not in trendy Chelsea or the more affluent areas of North London favoured by Arsenal fans.

Crime in the borough in Newham is significantly higher than the average for other London boroughs. The fact that 49 per cent of people in the borough do not own a car probably contributes to this worrying statistic. With a high crime rate, a young and multi-faith population, high youth unemployment and overcrowded housing, the officers and elected members face immense problems and some extremely daunting challenges. High-quality and accessible public services must be at the heart of Newham's future. Despite what cynics say, the Olympics does brings hope. The library service is proving to be up to the challenge, and health and leisure services are making a real contribution to the well-being of local people.

The promised land

In search of better schools and a safer, more ordered way of life, East Enders began to look to Essex as a way out of the deprivation, crime and poor housing. Many achieved their desire to migrate to the calmer environment of Southend, Billericay and Leigh-on-Sea or, for the more ambitious, further north to Chelmsford, Ongar, Brentwood and Braintree. Professional footballers, like Moore himself, preferred the villas and swimming pools of Chigwell, along with wealthy cab drivers and bookmakers from Stepney and Bow.

Historically, East End folk have always wanted to get away - and not only the indigenous white working class of Canning Town. East End Jewish families, as they prospered, slowly migrated to the North London boroughs of Muswell Hill and Finchley, while many local Asian people preferred to stay closer to home in Ilford. In their place came middle-class professionals who began to occupy neighbourhoods in Whitechapel, Shoreditch and Spitalfields, transforming the whole character of the area close to the City. But these newcomers were careful to keep away from the bleak estates that housed the most deprived East Londoners who had failed to make it out to Essex and beyond. In the years between 1960 and 2000 Essex became the new home for thousands of East End families, a phenomenon that for many local people completed the recovery of the post-war period. This demographic phenomenon was to have a positive effect on local sport in Essex, while it signalled the end of traditional types of football and cricket in East London, as we shall see in a later chapter.

Resources for a journey of hope

There are encouraging signs that sporting young people in East London are being offered the kinds of opportunities that were commonplace 40 years ago. Projects such as cricket's Chance to Shine and the growth of new facilities mean that youngsters in the area, given the right support and encouragement, have the chance to play out their sporting hopes and aspirations.

The *Wolfenden Report* (1960) on sport in the UK made a number of far-reaching recommendations, which are discussed in more detail in Chapter 2. As a result of the report, Newham has gained four indoor sport and leisure centres, one of which, Newham Leisure Centre, has its very own athletics stadium. The borough also has a water sports facility and has introduced various initiatives to encourage people of all ages and ethnic groups to participate in sport and leisure. The 'gold card' system means that access to the borough's leisure centres is free to all young people. In addition, Newham Sports Academy, led by former javelin thrower and Olympic gold medallist Tessa Sanderson, seeks to identify and develop exceptionally talented local youngsters. A sports development and coaching scheme has been introduced, designed to create the next generation of sports coaches. In 2004/05 there were 1,600,000 visits to the four local leisure centres in Newham. By any standards this is impressive. In terms of social integration and cohesion, Newham's public culture and sport and leisure services are more than punching their weight. The high-class facilities being built for 2012 should improve opportunities massively for playing sport in Newham and Tower Hamlets for future generations. This will not fully ease Ian Dury's 'ups and downs' of East London life, but sport and culture are resources of hope and should be cherished as such.

I'm forever blowing euros

It has been a long journey for successive generations of Hammers supporters from the Thames Ironworks FC in the late nineteenth century to the glittering Boleyn and millionaire footballers of today. Thousands of East Londoners got some kind of release from the post-war rebuilding efforts by turning up every other Saturday at Boleyn Castle to watch their beloved West Ham United. Against the background of what can be an alienated and pretty desperate city life, football can prove a necessary and pleasing diversion, even with the highs and lows associated with following a club like West Ham. The club had to do their own rebuilding after the war and it wasn't until the 1960s that Hammers teams began to produce the kind of football most associated with the club.

In many ways Moore was the last great local football hero and representative of the post-war generation. The young professional footballers who arrive for training each day at Chadwell Heath and at Upton Park on match days are very wealthy young men. The contrast of their glamorous lives set against those of many of their fans living on the tough housing estates around the training ground may be lost on the current generation of West Ham professionals. The gulf between the fans and the players began with the creation of the Premier League in 1992 and, of course, this is not unique to West Ham. All Premier League clubs and their supporters have experienced this rupture, brought about by television money, sponsorship and astronomical season ticket prices – and the consequent celebrity culture that has engulfed our top footballers.

In 2007 Alan Curbishley, West Ham manager at the time, remarked sardonically that his players were more interested in acquiring 'baby' Bentley limos than earning Premier League points. Curbishley, a good Hammers professional in his time, was making a point about the poverty of ambition of the professionals at his club. An honourable and honest man, he was clearly comparing the attitude of current players to those of his own playing days – among whom were the much-lauded trio, Bobby Moore, Geoff Hurst and Martin Peters. Unwittingly, Curbishley, who resigned the following season after the young defender Anton Ferdinand was sold without the manager's knowledge, was alluding to a wider malaise in British society, the seeds of which were sown in the early 1980s and created the conditions for the 'credit crunch' financial crisis of 2009.

Is it any wonder that expensive cars and showbiz lifestyles would distract Premier League footballers to the extent that a fair football man like Curbishley, brought up on older values, became frustrated with players and club executives who had a very different agenda. It was not always like this. As little as 30 years ago the players lived much closer to their supporters and to the local youngsters who played their sport in the parks and on the pitches of Essex and East London. In the late 1960s and early 1970s West Ham supporters could enjoy a drink on a Saturday night in the Retreat pub in Chigwell, alongside Bobby Moore, Geoff Hurst, Martin Peters and the others. This was an ordinary occurrence and strengthened the bond between the players, the club and the community, which was the essence of West Ham United. This bond contributed to building community morale and a sense of identity vital to inner-city life. In the absence of this close association, young people find other, more sinister, ways to gain an identity and commitment to their area. But all is not lost when we learn that the Hammers' England U21 star, Mark Noble, an East Ender through and through, walks home after every match at Upton Park with his bag slung over his shoulder.

Bobby Moore's first manager at West Ham was Ted Fenton, but when Fenton retired in 1961 the club appointed the man who was to set out the footballing philosophy of the club for two generations, Ron Greenwood. The playing style introduced by Greenwood remains the touchstone for West Ham fans today - they will accept mid-table mediocrity and the occasional FA Cup win if they can enjoy their beloved fast-moving passing game. The playing style of what became known as 'the academy' is the whole point of being a West Ham supporter; without it the club loses its soul, as has happened on several occasions in the years following Greenwood's departure from the club in 1977. Bobby Moore, of course, embraced West Ham's purist approach and, consequently, became one of the greatest players ever to play the game. The playing style dear to supporters' hearts, nurtured by Greenwood and continued by John Lyall, was lost for many years, along with the close bond that had always existed between the club, the players and the fans. The Premier League bought the club a wonderful modern stadium, with players receiving £60,000 in wages each and every week, but for the supporters the result was a joyless sense of loss as the club began to lose their heart and soul. The fans still come each week, high in expectation, yet not sure what to make of it all. They do not forget that the club squandered the best group of home-grown talent that English football has seen since the Beckham generation at Old Trafford. Joe Cole, Frank Lampard, Rio Ferdinand, Glen Johnson, Jermain Defoe, Michael Carrick and Anton Ferdinand all came through the ranks at West Ham and won the club the FA Youth Cup. This fire sale happened as a result of financial mismanagement by senior staff and the board of directors. What else could explain the selling off of the family silver in this way? No wonder the fans are cynical and disillusioned about the club that were once the pride of East London. Given the difficult history of the area over the previous 50 years, they deserve more.

The Premier League ushered in a new era in English professional football. Attendances soared and the spectator experience was greatly improved. But something was lost. The class composition and demographic of people attending Premier League football changed. This unexpected development in the type of people now going to the footie was particularly felt at Chelsea, Manchester United and Arsenal – but no Premier League club remained unaffected. When Roy Keane criticised the new corporate-minded 'supporters' he was expressing a sentiment felt strongly by the more traditional working-class followers of England's premier sport. Keane was responding to the lack of passion and noise that the players felt at Old Trafford during home matches. And there is the rub – wonderful new football stadiums at most Premier League grounds, but a consequent disintegration of attachment. So we have great shiny palaces with facilities to match any in the world, but the passionate, ear-splitting, Bovril-fuelled roar heard in the old run-down terraces, like the Chicken Run at Upton Park, has become a little muted.

If the period 1970 to 2000 saw a slow dislocation of supporters from their club and the players, the introduction of the Premier League and Sky TV hastened the process. Once the Premier League clubs were sold off to debt-crazy, billionaire, leverage merchants from Russia, the USA and Iceland, the process was complete. In 2009 West Ham's Icelandic owners will sell the club to the highest bidder. Hammers supporters patiently await the outcome. Who knows where all this will lead, as managers and players come and go season by season, tossed about by financial wheeler-dealing.

Past and present

The history of metropolitan Essex and East London over the course of the twentieth century was characterised by two things: firstly, the effects of war, industrial change and shifting patterns of immigration; and secondly, enormous and sustained acts of courage by local people. The impact of these seismic political and social developments on both amateur and professional sport in the area has been profound. In the 40 years between 1960 and 2000 professional sport prospered but ultimately became detached from its grassroots support. Local football, once thriving, played out on local parks on Saturday afternoons and Sunday mornings throughout East London and Essex, went into decline. Today It is difficult to see how iconic local heroes such as Moore and Gooch, with their commitment to their area and deep love for their sport and its future, could possibly emerge from today's sporting world of celebrity, bling and 'baby' Bentleys.

The turbulent history of this troubled area of London, at least in part, explains the intense and passionate local attachment to sport, and in particular the emotional pull of West Ham United and Essex CCC. The success of Bobby Moore and Graham Gooch was forged in this emotional cauldron.

CHAPTER 2
GREEN GRASS AND GLORIOUS AIR

On the border of East London and Essex, London's poorest boroughs, Tower Hamlets and Newham stretch out to meet the grim housing estates of Leyton and Leytonstone, before easing into the more comfortable and settled suburbs of Ilford and Chingford. The area abounds with high-quality sporting facilities, both indoor and outdoor. Sports centres, playing fields, parks, all-weather pitches of every type, swimming pools and sailing facilities compete for local people's interest. The long history of these much-loved local amenities helps to explain the sporting success of the area, and why East London and Essex have produced so many world-class sportsmen and - women, not least Bobby Moore and Graham Gooch. But, equally important, this accessible and rich heritage has provided countless local sports lovers with the opportunities to live out their dreams, vent their frustrations and, not least, improve their health and fitness. The heightened experience and sheer intense playfulness of local sport on Saturday afternoons and Sunday mornings can provide a sharp contrast to the boredom and frustrations of weekday working lives.

The story of local sports grounds in East London and Essex such as Low Hall Farm in Walthamstow, Wanstead Flats, Fairlop in Ilford and, of course, the fabled Hackney Marshes, is central to understanding the kind of existence people have in the area. These sports grounds have acquired an important function in providing a focus for social integration and community cohesion – where else can local people from different class and cultural backgrounds play and socialise together within a structured environment and shared purpose? The history of these local sporting arenas also helps us to understand why both Moore and Gooch took such a pride in their origins, and why they were able to develop such a strong sense of place and belonging. I am convinced that this sense of place was instrumental in helping our two sporting heroes to become such great players, confidently able to fulfil their considerable potential.

What strikes you most when visiting parks and grounds in the area is the rich diversity of local football. My own playing experiences in Walthamstow included a few seasons in the Forest & District League for a Sunday team called Britannia FC. Our team included Londoners with Italian, Greek, Jamaican and Irish backgrounds – a typical make-up of most sides in the 1970s. We were all great friends and teammates and got to know each other's families. The sister of one of our players was a sprinter in the Great Britain athletics team and she came to all our matches. Frankie, our tricky Italian striker, brought his mum to most games and she rewarded him with extra spaghetti for Sunday lunch whenever he scored a goal. Frankie, despite carrying a few kilos, was one of the league's leading scorers, and he loved the fact that his football was at the heart of his family. The multi-ethnicity of the teams of the day demonstrates the huge potential of local sport for encouraging and achieving social integration.

Sport being sport, relations with opposing teams occasionally worked against the prevailing sense of social cohesion. While playing for Britannia I had the pleasure of facing as fearsome a centre half as you would ever meet in local league football. Chippy McQueen was a legendary figure on Hackney Marshes and grounds around the East End. With his long dark hair and piratical beard, Chippy was from a travelling family of Romany people and he terrified opposing centre forwards. He could also play a bit. During one memorable match at Wanstead Flats, I once foolishly turned him in the penalty area, but then slipped and fell as I lined up to shoot. As I lay on the ground I watched helplessly as Chippy swung his right boot hard in the direction of my head. He stopped his foot inches from my face – even dear old Chippy could show some mercy. Needless to say, I never attempted to turn him again. But we were good friends for years and always enjoyed a pint together after a game. Such violence, potential or real, was a rarity and hundreds of matches are played out every season in an atmosphere of benign enthusiasm and racial tolerance.

In the 1970s, the Forest & District League on the East London and Essex border country had nine divisions with twelve clubs in each. If you include reserves teams this meant that as many as 2,000 people were playing in just one local league, week in and week out. The sheer scale of this one league shows how important sport can be to the social fabric of local communities. The Forest & District is only one of several such leagues in the East London and Essex area at park level; others include the Essex Olympic League, South West Essex League, South East Essex League and the Southern Amateur League. In the 1960s and 1970s thousands of men and women were involved on Saturdays and Sunday mornings in hundreds of clubs around the area at local park level, an indication of the richness of the sporting culture in this special place. But things are changing, as they must.

Saturday is dead

The 1990s saw the beginning of a period of decline of local league football in East London. Social imperatives and tastes change, and local authority recreation staff in East London and Essex have proved resourceful in the way they have adapted sports facilities to meet the changing needs of local people. For example, Sunday football has been a fairly recent development historically, while the introduction of all-weather floodlit pitches, private and public, has met the demand for more flexible playing arrangements. The classic formula of Saturday afternoon and Sunday morning football no longer appeals to today's young people. These days footballers of all ages, sexes and ethnic groups want to play their favourite sport at an hour to suit their personal work pressures or domestic lives. Today young fathers are more inclined to spend their Saturday afternoons with their families rather than running around on Hackney Marshes with their mates, as might have happened 20 years ago. Midweek floodlit or indoor football is much more likely to fit the life of a modern young family. Similarly, our sporting teenagers prefer to earn pocket money working in supermarkets on Saturdays rather than playing sport – again, midweek provision fits the bill.

The introduction of artificial pitches in the East London boroughs has resulted in an explosion of organised 5-a-side soccer and has encouraged the development of the girls' and women's game. While floodlit, all-weather pitches have enabled the introduction of midweek 11-a-side leagues, the small game version has proved the most enduring and popular. Arguably, the most significant development in local sports provision of the last 20 years has been the introduction of high-quality, specialist indoor sports facilities. Brentwood Centre in Essex, Kelmscott Centre in Walthamstow and Newham Leisure Centre are just three examples of well-run, accessible facilities in the area, built by the local authority and designed for local use. They are a tribute to local ingenuity and a commitment to public health and well-being. They cater for a range of sports, with 5-a-side football benefiting the most, although basketball, hockey and cricket have all made good use of the new indoor facilities. It is interesting that the use of expensive, high-tech health and fitness suites has tailed off after an initial surge of interest. Privately owned indoor sports centres are another matter and cater for a more luxury-inclined, vanity market.

Of course, these developments in local sports provision have occurred in every major town in the UK, but the extent and pace of change in East London and Essex have been dramatic and have had a decisive impact on weekend league football, as we shall see. But somehow, despite the introduction of shiny new indoor leisure centres, the richness of a local sporting culture surely depends on the availability and quality of outdoor parks and grounds. By examining the history of just a few of these, we can begin to gain a sense of how the local sporting culture has changed over the past 40 years. Locals might argue, with some justification, that Dagenham, Barking or Southend offer the best in terms of high-quality playing fields. However, while accepting these claims, I have chosen three sites around the East London and Essex border, where Bobby Moore and Graham Gooch were brought up and played their boyhood football: Hackney Marshes, Low Hall Farm and Wanstead Flats. The history of these three venerable old London sports grounds provides us with an illustration of the way that sporting habits in the area have been transformed. All three have football at their core, while providing additional facilities for cricket, hockey, tennis and rugby.

IS THIS PITCH 96? THE GLORY OF HACKNEY MARSHES

Oh it really is a wery pretty garden
And Chingford to the eastward could be seen;
'Wiv a ladder and some glasses,
You could see to 'Ackney Marshes,

If it wasn't for the 'ouses in between.
- Chorus from a music hall song, 'If It Wasn't for the 'Ouses In Between' (also known as 'The Cockney's Garden'), made famous by Gus Elen (1862-1940).

Late one murky Saturday afternoon in the late 1960s I remember wandering slowly across Hackney Marshes towards the café a few minutes after all the games had finished. I was struck by the atmosphere that hung over the hundred or so pitches, where for the previous 90 minutes opposing teams had played out hard-fought matches. It was almost as though the games continued, played out by ghostly figures in the fading light – but all that really remained, hanging in the air, was the smell of disturbed earth and pungent ointment. But I sensed it was the sheer weight of all those matches, all those people, all that passionate intensity for the previous hour and a half that, having ended abruptly, had left an eerie feeling over the Marsh. Potentially 2,000 players (not to mention up to 100 referees – where do they all come from?) featured in the afternoon's action. After the game, and in a rather undignified fashion, they were washing their boots and bodies in the water troughs outside the dressing rooms before grabbing a warming mug of tea. That special feeling, after the drama of nearly 100 football matches, has sadly diminished since the 1960s with the loss over 40 of the football pitches on Marsh in 30 years. By extension this means that some clubs, having lost their pitch, would have folded without any alternative pitch available to them. Fewer pitches will inevitably mean fewer clubs and fewer playing opportunities. This is a worrying trend and will threaten, or at least diminish, the sporting culture of the area and consequently adversely affect the social fabric of the place.

There is a rich culture attached to local football in East London. On any Saturday or Sunday at Hackney Marshes in the 1960s, once cleaned and changed, most players would have headed straight for the ground's Lammas Café. Generations of players enjoyed a mug of hot tea and a piece of cake the size of a small house brick, served up by friendly tea ladies. The café would serve up to 2,000 people before and after matches at the weekend. It was the social centrepiece of this wonderful sporting landscape. There is a café or some kind of social gathering place on most local park football grounds in East

London and Essex, although it has to be said that these are of varying quality and cannot be compared with the splendours available in many cricket club pavilions. However, they do provide a place where players, friends and families of all teams can come together after a game. Players from teams in the Sunday Hackney & Leyton League would have known each other for many years, and it's interesting how the physical encounters of the games are quickly forgotten. The after-match feeling is good natured, with a great deal of banter and also, in this part of the world, fairly cruel mickey-taking. There are not that many places where Londoners from a range of diverse backgrounds could mix as freely and easily as they did, and still do, in London's premier park football venue.

Apart from their OBEs, our heroes Moore and Gooch have at least one thing in common with David Beckham – they all played football in their early years on Hackney Marshes. Moore, Gooch and Beckham were born in Leytonstone, now part of Waltham Forest, just a couple of miles from the Marshes. As youngsters they shared the experience with thousands of other local young people in the area who were passionate about playing sport. If you lived in East London and played sport it is more than likely that at some stage of your sporting life would be spent on Hackney Marshes – it is difficult to imagine East London without it.

The Marsh is the best known and loved of East London's public sports grounds and its 337 acres were opened to the public in 1890. It comprises a huge area of grassland on the western bank of the River Lea and was created by the flooding of the Lea to form pastureland, which probably explains the absence of development. The River Lea, of course, divides the counties of Essex and Middlesex, and historically it provided an important navigable waterway out to rural Hertfordshire. It is almost a miracle that Hackney Marshes has survived almost in its entirety despite the increased demand for building land in this otherwise densely populated part of London.

Over the years the Marsh has gained a few acres here and there and at other times it has had bits removed. Notable developments on the site include the National Projectile Factory, built after the First World War, while 22 acres were taken in 1937 to build what was to become the notorious Kingsmead housing estate, later demolished. The Lesney die-cast works was built on the Homerton side of the Marsh in the 1940s and became a major local employer. But the factory closed in 1990 when Lesney's iconic Matchbox brand began to lose its popularity. At one time the Marsh had space for 120 soccer pitches, but in 2008 the number was down to 88. It accommodates around 100 local league matches every Sunday, with some pitches being played on twice, highlighting the quality of the playing surfaces. Saturday afternoon adult football, once the jewel in the crown of local league soccer, is now in decline in East London due the popularity of cheap, midweek, all-weather, floodlit provision in the area, for the reasons outlined above.

There are also some Hackney Marshes facts to entertain us:

- All the goalposts are painted white on the front and green on the back, the reason being that if your match is on Pitch 96 - and it can take ten minutes to walk from the changing areas out to some of the more remote pitches - you want to be sure that you are defending and attacking white goalposts and not green ones.
- Goal nets are not available. You have to bring your own and drag the nets, bags of balls, metal pegs and corner flags around the 60 or 70 pitches and then back to the car park at the end of the game. In midwinter it is dark by the time you return to the changing rooms, and taking down the nets after a match on a cold and wet January Sunday morning exposes players to the danger of hypothermia. It always used to be the same players who selflessly volunteered, while their teammates fled for the 'warmth' of the changing rooms. Some more organised clubs, with resourceful secretaries, acquired tiny pairs of stepladders to help the players reach the crossbars and release the net ties.
- Until recently, before the introduction of shower blocks, you did wash your face and boots, and much else, in the muddy stone trough in the changing area courtyard. This was not quite as unhealthy as it sounds. Being outside was generally preferable to the smoke-filled atmosphere of changing rooms in the 1960s and 1970s, when you couldn't see across the room either before or after a match.
- There are sometimes just two metres between the Marsh pitches' touchlines and goal lines. This regularly leads to two balls on one pitch at the same time, while 22 players from a ball-

less game on an adjacent pitch wait for an opportunity to retrieve the ball and resume their game. The close proximity of the matches also means that you will often see two goalkeepers from adjoining pitches deep in conversation, much to the concern of their outfield colleagues.
• Dogs are always a problem on the Marsh. Very often both the ball and players are subject to dog abuse of various kinds, some of which are too indelicate to repeat here.

Arguably, the worst thing that can happen on the Marsh is to begin a game against the wrong team, despite a careful reading of the map on the changing room noticeboard by everyone involved. Although there are no reports of any team playing out a whole game against the wrong opposition, there have been a number of incidents of games when, well into the first half, a casual chat between opposing centre half and centre forward reveals the error. When this does happen it means, of course, that there are two other teams somewhere on the Marsh also playing the wrong opposition. Such confusion has to be resolved by both matches beginning again, against the correct opponents, often with the second half played in near darkness.

I can remember a match on the Marsh a few years ago, on the Saturday before Xmas, when the home team had carefully decorated both sets of goals in true festive fashion – they were still there at Easter. But not all stories are so good-natured. One Sunday morning on the Marsh in the early 1970s a fight broke out between two sets of players after a disputed penalty was awarded towards the end of an important Forest & District Sunday premier league match – there was a great deal at stake. During a violent confrontation, opposing sets of supporters on opposite touchlines began to encroach onto the pitch, thus drastically reducing the size of an already tight playing area. The match was abandoned by default when a roofing lorry, driven by an irate supporter of the offended team, chased the referee across the Marsh as he fled towards the safety of the changing rooms. Not much in the way of social cohesion here – but such is the richness of the local sporting culture.

Matches were regularly cancelled on the Marsh on Sunday mornings because one of the teams would fail to raise the minimum eight players necessary for the game to go ahead. The reasons for absence usually involved the activities of the previous evening. Missing players who arrived late to the ground, lacking sleep and with giant hangovers, could be found squatting down in the bushes at the entrance to the ground, so as not to be identified by either their captain or the match referee. On finding the game cancelled they could return to their beds or continue whatever it was they were doing the previous evening.

Others were keener to play on Sunday mornings. I personally witnessed a taxi being driven out to a pitch on a far-flung corner of the Marsh ten minutes into a game. The passenger leapt out of the cab, grabbed a shirt from the bench and played 80 minutes wearing stack-heel shoes, his club shirt and a pair of stylish corduroy flares. His team went on to win, as I remember, encouraged by the appearance of their eleventh man – a tricky outside left.

Such tales are legion, but if you wander across the Marsh today, when all the games are finished and players are safely ensconced in a warm pub nearby, you will find scattered across the 80+ pitches a collection of abandoned goal nets, corner flags, trendy sports bottles and a variety of substitutes' clothing. All a far cry from the life of the pampered Premier League player up the road at Upton Park, but, I suppose, equally part of this rich sporting culture.

There are hundreds of myths about sporting life on the Marshes, and they hold a special affection in the memory of local people. The playwright, Harold Pinter, who lived in Hackney, wrote this poem as a tribute to his old Hackney schoolteacher, Joseph Brearley:

Dear Joe, I'd like to walk with you,
From Clapton Road to Stamford Hill,
And on,
Through Manor House to Finsbury Park
And back,
On the dear 652 trolley bus
To Clapton Pond
And walk across the shadows to Hackney Marshes.

Pinter's evocative lines express his fondness for the place that local people will recognise.

Football on the Marsh dates back to 1881 when the old boys of

Homerton College founded what was later to become Leyton FC. One of the most enduring projects was the effort by the Eton Manor Mission to set up recreational activities for local young people. In 1901 a local branch of the Eton Mission was formed at premises in Hackney. The Mission was set up by Eton College to bring 'enlightenment' to poverty-stricken and deprived youngsters in the East End of London. The Mission was part of a number of similar charitable projects across the East End set up by Oxford and Cambridge universities to provide recreational and social services for local people. The Dockland Settlement, as these initiatives were usually called, could be found across East London and as far out as Hainault in Essex, a branch that remained active until it was closed down in the 1990s.

While the Eton boys gained some understanding of the lives of the London poor, local people could take advantage of the range of sports that the college initiated, including football, rugby, cricket, boxing, swimming and sailing. This enterprise, not without its ironic nature, led to the establishment of Eton Manor Boys' Club and eventually Eton Manor FC. The Boys' Club was formed in 1901 by a group of wealthy Old Etonians led by Sir Edward Cadogan, Arthur Villiers and Gerald Wellesley. In 1921, the group used their influence to acquire 30 acres of waste ground in Leyton, on the northern edge of the Marsh, and rapidly turned it into,

> *... one of the most conspicuously beautiful recreations in the metropolitan area.*
> *- M. Johansen (2008), Adventure in the Wild East: The Early Years of the Eton Manor Boys' Club, lecture to the Villiers Park Educational Trust (www.villerspark.org.uk)*

'The Wilderness', as it became known, was seen as a sporting 'Eden', with nine football pitches, two rugby pitches, a cricket square, six tennis courts, a squash court, a running track, a bowling green and a swimming pool. Not content with this galaxy of sporting facilities, the benefactors later erected floodlights alongside the 440 yards running track.

The Eton Mission, which grew out of the old 'Rough Boy' clubs in Mallard Street, Hackney provided a range of activities for young children, but the benefactors believed that those with the most pressing needs were boys over the age of 18. As Wellesley himself commented,

... the alternative which presented itself to the boys on leaving the Mission, was whether to make the street corner once again their meeting place of an evening ...
- M. Johansen (2008)

In 1909 the Old Boys' Club opened in a coal shop in Daintry Road, Hackney, exclusively for ex-members of the Eton Mission Boys' Club, but kept a polite distance from their more church-oriented Mission pioneers. In 1913 the Old Boys' Club moved into a magnificent, purpose-built clubhouse in Riseholme Street, Hackney. The new clubhouse, close to Victoria Park Station, was built on the land of the old Manor Farm, hence the famous name, Eton Manor. We can tell from photographs taken at the time that the Riseholme Street centre was the most extraordinary achievement. The June 1913 edition of Chin-wag, the club magazine, includes a description of the gleaming new facility:

The Hall ... the finest of its kind in the world, has been admirably fitted up as a gymnasium with various appliances for making you grow taller, fatter or thinner at a moment's notice ... There are all kinds of parallel bars, ladders, rings, poles, ropes and other devices for hurting yourselves all over, which should prove wonderfully beneficial to the healthiness of the club.
- Johansen (2008).

As Michelle Johansen tells us in her 2008 lecture to the Up the Manor Project,

Everything to do with the Eton Manor was carried out on a grand scale, the emphasis on excellence. Great men of the day ... would be invited to Riseholme Street to meet with and inspire the boys. When the Boys' Club took part in sporting activities the expectation was that they would be the best. It was an expectation that was often realised.
-Johansen (2008).

There is no question that Eton Manor was intended to be an

elite club and only accepted ex-Mission members. It was not uncommon for young men to train four or five nights each week, even though many had physically demanding jobs or school commitments. Discipline and dedication were key founding principles of the Mission. It taught the boys that they could achieve, and their success must have given them confidence in their lives outside football. If the Old Boys had high expectations of their members, the Mission was an inclusive organisation set up in one of the toughest and most deprived parts of London, and the lives of hundreds of local boys were transformed as a result.

From the early 1920s, the boys at the Old Boys' Club had use of the excellent indoor facilities at the Riseholme Street centre and the acres of playing fields at The Wilderness. But it is clear from accounts at the time that the Manor was more than a sports club; it was, as Johansen says, "a way of life". In a time of high unemployment, the staff would find the boys jobs and offered their families houses at low rents or provided no-interest loans. The Manor Charitable Trust provided financial help to other projects in the area, and virtually bankrolled the Eton Manor Club. In recognition of his tireless work to improve the lives of young people in the area, one of the Manor's founders, Lord Villiers, was created a freeman of the boroughs of Hackney and Leyton. As Johansen writes,

Joining Eton Manor meant much more than simply gaining access to a fine sports ground and a well-equipped clubhouse ... Being part of Eton Manor gave boys growing up in one of the poorest areas of East London purpose and structure in their daily lives ... and an enduring notion of belonging ...
- Johansen (2008).

The Eton Manor project grew out of the 300 or so boys' and girls' clubs set up in London in the late nineteenth century. As the wealthy beneficiaries of the industrial revolution began to find ways to ease their consciences, the youth of the poorest parts of the capital became an obvious target for their philanthropy. There is little question that the motives of the new philanthropists were benevolent, but many also harboured a fear of social unrest, even insurrection, by the proliferation of boy gangs in the east of the City. One Westminster churchman couched the problem in biblical language:

> *The youth of both sexes ... are yearly turned loose, without aid, without sympathy, without exercise, without amusement into the fiery furnace of the streets of our growing and densely crowded cities.*
> *- Johansen (2008).*

Gang culture is no new twenty-first century phenomenon. It has been a central part of the life of Western cities for at least 300 years, and the Eton Manor initiative was, arguably, the first to try to tackle the problem in a systematic and organised way, and with a serious financial commitment. The project achieved most of its aims and continued to prosper in the 50 years from the end of the nineteenth century up until the Second World War.

The 1930s saw further consolidation of the individual rugby, football and cricket clubs. As the constituent clubs began to go their separate ways, Eton Manor FC, in particular, enjoyed a long period of success that continued throughout the post-war period. Famous names such as Sir Alf Ramsey and Len Wills had spells at the club as players, while undertaking some coaching duties. Most amateur footballers from the area would have played at the Eton Manor FC ground at one time or another. Located at the edge of Hackney Marshes at the top of the Eastway and surrounded by a high brick wall, the ground was regularly used as the venue for local Cup finals and it was also known for its running track, which encircled the football pitch. The track, infamous for its tight bends, opened in 1949 and was one of the first in East London. Interestingly, the track was constructed with the original cinders used at Wembley Stadium for the 1948 London Olympic Games.

The Eton Manor ground, the old Wilderness, has long been developed and built over, and the individual clubs have either folded or moved away. The football club, following a spell in the Greater London League, transferred to the Essex Senior League in 1975, where they remain to this day. For some years the club were homeless, as a result of the development of their ground, and currently they share with Barking FC out at Dagenham. The first home match of the 2009/10 season saw Eton Manor FC, with its illustrious and historically important past attract a 'crowd' of just 38 people to watch the once proudly worn dark blue and light blue colours. I doubt if any of the 38 souls in Dagenham that day sang the Old Boys' songs like 'Eton Boys', 'Manor Boys' or 'Dear old Hackney Wick', or their signature tune, 'Down on the Wilderness', with its evocation of 'green grass and glories of the air'.

Perhaps the saddest story in the denouement of Eton Manor is told by a local youngster, Terry 'Tosher' Bell when he wrote in 2008:

The Rev Piggot ... arranged for us to visit the Eton Mission Club which sadly has fallen into disrepair ... The only inhabitants are three squatters ... who have utilised one small room on the first floor as their sleeping accommodation ... one has made a bed on the snooker table.
- T. Bell (2008), 'Wiggy's Walkabout around Hackney Wick Saturday 3rd May 2008', from the Up the Manor Project (published by Villiers Educational Trust and held in the Bishopsgate Institute).

To Tosher's horror, many of the original books, artefacts, snooker tables and old photographs are still in the derelict building, and he writes:

Why oh why these items of history are left abandoned and not collected for the manor archives I will never understand as clearly if not rescued soon they will be lost forever.
- Bell (2008).

Tosher Bell was a member of the Up the Manor Project of George Mitchell School in Leyton. In 2009 the Heritage Lottery Fund (HLF) acknowledged the local importance of Eton Manor Boys' Club to the sporting and social heritage of an area undergoing dramatic change ahead of the 2012 Olympics. The HLF awarded a grant of £50,000 to Villiers Park Educational Trust to create a permanent oral history of the club. This inter-generational oral history project brought together young and old East London when a group of Year 10 pupils from George Mitchell School in nearby Leyton interviewed former Manor players and others involved with the club over the past 50 years. The boys filmed and recorded some of the interviews and hosted a visit to the school by some of the Manor old boys. (A

52-page project booklet and DVD have been made available to the general public and a project exhibition was held in the Vestry Museum in Walthamstow). Over 40 interviews were recorded, transcribed and deposited in the Eton Manor archive at the Bishopsgate Institute in London. The Up the Manor project ended in July 2008 with an event in the Bishopsgate Institute's Great Hall, when over 140 invited guests heard a moving testimony to the profound impact made by the club on the lives of its members. The Eton Manor Club is just one of a number of memorable and moving stories of the hallowed turf of Hackney Marshes.

It is easy to say that the heritage of the Eton Manor project has been carelessly squandered. The athletics track was moved to Temple Mills at Leyton, before finding a permanent and superior home at the Lea Valley Sports Centre. There is now nothing left of the unique social and sporting experiment that was Eton Mission and the Eton Manor Sports Club. For 50 years the project was a central part of the life of East London and formed a vital element in the history of Hackney Marshes. Without the Mission there would probably have been no Hackney Marshes and no local football for several generations of East Londoners.

Death by tarmac?

Despite its long and honourable contribution to the local sporting culture, Hackney Marshes is facing a real threat to its future. An article in *The Times* newspaper stated:

> *... the LDA (London Dockland Agency) let slip that some of the most important and fertile football pitches in the country are to be turned into an Olympic car park ...*
> *- Martin Samuel, 'Death by Tarmac: the sorry fate of Hackney Marshes in pursuit of our Olympic Dream',The Times, 28th September 2005.*

Samuel's article describes the decision to turn a large area of Hackney Marshes into a car park. The 'death by tarmac' of the Marsh in the cause of the 2012 Olympics will further reduce the football opportunities for hundreds of local youngsters and will threaten the future of clubs, despite the LDA promise to reallocate. The LDA claim that the lost pitches will be fully reinstated 12 months after the Games have packed up and moved on. Samuel continues:

> *Of the 34,000 playing fields that have been lost since 1992 ... how many do you notice being turned back into football pitches?*

With the number of pitches being reduced since the late nineteenth century from the original 120 to 88, the Marsh can ill afford this threat to its future. The Lammas rights accorded to Hackney Marshes guarantee recreational use in perpetuity. The Olympic challenge to these rights includes a connecting bridge from the Marsh to the main Olympic Park and a huge coach park on the East Marsh. This will result in the loss of a stand of lovely old ash trees, a line of 150-year-old poplars and dozens of old flowering cherries. Trees, wildlife, shrubs and grassland will suffer permanent loss in this ruthless land-grab and denial of centuries-old Lammas rights.

The London Olympics presents a huge challenge to the defenders of the Marsh. Those of us who were excited when the 2012 Games was awarded to London face the prospect of a difficult irony. Priceless local sports facilities and the opportunities they have provided for generations of Londoners are under threat in the service of the most elite sports event on the planet. Locals are extremely sceptical that football will return to the Marsh as they have known and loved it. As we move towards 2012, a vital and historic part of East London's sporting culture is under threat.

Olympics or no Olympics, as we have seen there has been a huge shift in the sporting tastes and habits of local people over the past 40 years. Hackney Marshes has been diminished, not only by the selling off of some desperately needed green spaces, but also because the culture of local sport has altered dramatically, and Hackney Marshes has been struggling to adapt to the new world of what is now called 'sport and leisure'.

TEA AND CAKES AT LOW HALL FARM

On any winter Saturday afternoon, if you leave Walthamstow Central underground station and at the end of the Victoria Line turn into the high street, you will enter the longest street market in Europe. The market is bustling, busy and full of noise. This is lively, multicultural London where you can buy wonderful

Asian sweets and exotic vegetables, or enjoy pie and mash at Manzies pie shop, complete with the original green sauce. In the 1960s the record shop on the corner opposite Woolworths would have filled the market air with the sounds of The Beatles and The Stones. The record shop is gone, of course, and in its place rap music and banghra blare out of the stalls that sell cheap CDs to the crowds of young people who hang out in the market on Saturday afternoons. Sadly, 'Davy Crocket's' remnants stall has gone, and you can no longer buy fine lace from the old lady opposite Manzies. But, mercifully, the offal stall outside Rossi's ice-cream shop was finally forced out of the market in the late 1970s.

Leaving behind the noises and smells of the market at the end of the high street, and after a short stroll through quiet back streets, you arrive at the end of Markhouse Road and at the gates of Low Hall Farm. Go through the gates and carry on past the Victorian Pump Station built in 1888 and lovingly preserved by a group of local residents, and you enter a part of Walthamstow with an extraordinary history. A large seventeenth-century farmhouse dominated the farm until it was obliterated by a Nazi bomb in the early part of the Second World War. When developers excavated part of the area in the 1990s they discovered the remains of the fourteenth-century Low Hall Manor, which is now covered by 'affordable' housing. Low Hall Farm was acquired by the local council in the mid-nineteenth century with full Lammas rights. These were extinguished in the 1930s as Walthamstow Council took part of the farm for the N&E railway and an extension of its sewage works. Fortunately, the playing fields on the farm are protected under old common land rights and cannot be used for development.

Once past the Pumping Station, you will be struck by the sight of at least 20 hard-fought games of football being played out around the central pavilion of this delightful sports ground. Low Hall Farm is close by the Walthamstow Reservoirs and part of a string of similar facilities along the banks of the River Lea, which takes in the marshes of Walthamstow, Leyton and Hackney. The ground is now surrounded by a housing estate, a couple of factories, and dozens of neat, lovingly cared-for allotments. All of these park grounds have football pitches, and some accommodate rugby, cricket and hockey on their grass and artificial pitches. In the 1960s Low Hall Farm was used almost exclusively for local amateur football. There were 20 pitches of varying quality, including the two on the Arena reserved for important League clashes and Cup finals. In 2008, within the ground's 18 hectares, our traveller will find 16 grass football pitches (two for mini-football), two all-weather floodlit multi-sports areas, two artificial cricket pitches, five tennis courts and a designated area for the local cycling club.

Before choosing which game to watch you can buy a hot cup of tea in the ground's elegant pavilion, which has been home to successive generations of local sports clubs. This gem of a ground is the home ground for a number of Walthamstow schools, and a range of junior and senior clubs train and play on the ground's dry and springy turf.

The ground is known for the quality of the pitches – something it shares with Hackney Marshes and Wanstead Flats. Having said that, I remember that one or two of the pitches were a little undersized, which made life difficult for an easily marked centre forward. An opposing centre half used to enjoy a pint before the game to "get me psyched up", as he used to say. He also told me that he wouldn't shave for five days before a match because he thought it made him look 'hard' for Saturday's match. With his beery breath and sharp whiskers he wasn't the most pleasant of opponents, and he would hit you like a ton of bricks once or twice during the match. He was not easy to escape on one of the smaller pitches.

Low Hall Farm has a distinguished history. Bobby Moore and Graham Gooch both played football on the ground for their schools and junior clubs, as did Teddy Sheringham and David Beckham. The latter may even have represented the Waltham Forest District team on one of the Arena pitches in their school days back in the 1989/90 season. Over the years scores of senior amateur players would have graced the old ground, including Jimmy Lewis, Doug Insole and Frank Rist. Nationally known local Sunday sides such as Britannia, Mount Athletic and Buxton, with their international players, all played on Low Hall Farm in the 1960s and 1970s. Forest District Sunday League, often attended by 500 to 600 noisy spectators, played most of their senior Cup finals on the Farm's Arena pitch. Forty years later it is difficult not to overstate the excitement generated by these Sunday morning matches. Standing in front of the pavilion on an Autumn Saturday afternoon, with around 15 games just about to start, there was a real feeling of excitement around the ground - a distinct sense of theatre and history.

Today the quality of the football played at the ground is a little disappointing, and Saturday afternoons in particular lack the tense atmosphere of the games in the 1960s and 1970s. But with its Pumping Station, allotments and sports field, Low Hall Farm is a priceless and irreplaceable element of the local culture. Walthamstow people make good use of the place, and the nearby Douglas Eyre Indoor Centre is a hive of activity. With places like the Kelmscott Centre, the borough's superb pool and track facility, and Low Hall Farm, the young people in Walthamstow are well served for sports facilities and the local authority are to be congratulated on their commitment to local sport, or leisure and recreation as they like to call it (In 2009 Waltham Forest Council submitted a £3.5m bid to the Lottery for an upgrade of the sports facilities at Lloyd Park, Walthamstow, home to the William Morris Museum).

CIRCUSES, FAIRS AND FOOTBALL

A few miles to the north of Walthamstow High Street, along the North Circular Road, is the borough of Wanstead. It could hardly be more different than its London neighbour. Less obviously multi-ethnic, the borough boasts a private golf club, Wanstead Cricket Club and a high street full of designer bars, pavement cafés and expensive dress shops. There is no evidence of allotments or street markets in this place. Wanstead is posh in the Essex kind of way, almost as though it can't forget that it is still only a couple of miles away from the dangers of Forest Gate and Stratford. Wanstead is protected from the inner city by the buffer of Wanstead Flats. The Flats is a wonderful 150-acre green oasis pressed on all sides by the clamorous urban sprawl of Leyton, Leytonstone and Manor Park, with Wanstead safely located just to the north.

The thought of Bobby Moore walking out as a young lad to play football and cricket on Wanstead Flats, close to his birthplace in Leytonstone, is an intriguing one. But both the Leytonstone lads, Moore and Gooch, and David Beckham later, graced the Flats as young hopefuls playing for their schools and junior clubs. Historically part of the southern section of Epping Forest, Wanstead Flats was secured for public use by The

Epping Forest Act of 1878, following a series of strong protests by local people. Managed by the City of London Corporation since 1878, organised sport has been played on the Flats since 1957, but it was used for casual sport between the wars. The Flats, known to generations of local footballers, is located at the southernmost tip of the Forest and spreads across the London boroughs of Waltham Forest, Redbridge and Newham. It shares borders with Wanstead Golf Club and the City of London Cemetery and is surrounded by residential housing on three sides. Interestingly, the Flats is dissected by four major roads, although the busy traffic fails to disturb the essential peace of the place.

The Flats was used as a prisoner of war camp in the Second World War, and there are stories of the grounds staff digging up motorcycles and other wartime debris when the grass was reinstated after the war. In 1957, under the Defence of the Realm Act, prefabs were built on the Flats to ease the acute housing shortage. These were finally demolished in the early 1960s and the old football pitches were fully reinstated. The Sandhills, as the development was known, was typical of hundreds of such projects across East London. Prefab 'villages' tended to be neat and tidy and were well maintained by their occupants. There were vegetable patches, fruit trees and garden plots, and residents even kept a few animals. But the prefabs were all demolished as other, more permanent, if problematic, solutions were found to address the housing shortage in the East End.

Hands off the Flats

Once done this cannot be undone; if the Flats go, they for ever, and the future generations will condemn the folly of those who permitted it to happen.
- Hands Off the Flats, leaflet, 1946.

At the end of the Second World War East and West Ham were desperately short of housing. Thousands of houses in the area were damaged or destroyed in the war, not to mention the substantial loss of life, as we saw in Chapter 1. West Ham alone lost 14,000 homes. The bombing made an already difficult situation worse. Both boroughs had chronic housing shortages in the inter-war period and the existing stock was of poor quality, and this was accompanied by unemployment and extreme poverty. Enemy action had destroyed around 100,000 houses across London and nearly two million were in need of urgent repair. The scale of the problem in 1945 was immense in the capital and was exacerbated by the 'baby boom' of 1946.

During the war, as we have seen, Wanstead Flats was pressed into use for military purposes and became a transit point for the D-Day invasion force. All this military activity made the Flats a target for enemy bombing and its north-west side became known as Hell Fire Corner. Civil Defence records state:

The wail of the siren opposite the Post announced at 8.15 the arrival of the raiders. The Flats were a sea of flame. Thousands of incendiaries were burning in an open space. The guns roared.
- Quoted in M. Gorman (2009), Homes for Heroes or Space to Breathe: The Struggle for Wanstead Flats 1946-47, Leyton & Leytonstone Historical Society.

Unfortunately, for years after the war, and some have argued before the war, the City of London Corporation neglected the Flats to the point where it began to be completely unusable:

By 1945 Wanstead Flats were in a poor state – large areas were covered with barbed wire, bomb and rocket craters, the remains of gun emplacements and building ... or churned up by vehicles and military boots.
- Gorman (2009).

West Ham Council saw their opportunity and applied for a Compulsory Purchase Order (CPO) in 1946 to acquire large areas of the Flats to rehouse local residents made homeless by the bombing and to build much-needed shops, offices and schools. The council had previously been granted permission to build 10,000 temporary homes on the Flats, which had to come down within a ten-year period, and proposed to make these permanent. In a story that has contemporary echoes, West Ham Council's plan met with ferocious opposition, as local people objected to any potential damage to sacred city greenbelt land. A petition was signed by 60,000 people and presented to the Epping MP, and the council received 379 formal objections to their proposal. Broadly the protestors were in two camps: the Wanstead middle-class property owners who were keen to protect the green spaces around them; and a number of what might be called 'green' groups, sports clubs and the Playing Fields Association. But they were sufficiently united to establish a highly effective Defence Committee.

West Ham Council played up the factions in the protest groups as a case of Blue Tory Wanstead against the socialist East End, 'the haves' and 'the have-nots'. How could the affluent folk of a leafy suburban borough deny thousands of homeless war heroes the right to decent housing? In other words, they played the 'class' card. Hard as they tried, however, the council failed in their efforts to discredit the protestors, who succeeded in securing their demanded public enquiry. The enquiry, at the old Stratford Town Hall, lasted four days and was a test case for similar proposals across the country. The Town Clerk, E.E. King, expressed the council's concern at the time:

... because the land was an open space and they knew the type of English mind which said that because a thing had been used for years for a certain purpose it was always wrong to change it.
- Gorman (2009).

But he fought in vain and the council's CPO was rejected on the grounds that valuable open spaces in a densely populated area should be protected and that West Ham Council did not have access to the materials needed to realise their ambitious housing scheme. The council were left to find other ways of meeting their housing needs, which in any case required national attention and support. The Flats became a part of the Abercrombie Plan for London, along with Richmond Park, Hampstead Heath, Victoria Park and Hackney Marshes, which included establishing key open spaces in the capital for leisure and recreational purposes. The Flats was saved because local people cared enough, and perhaps the last word on the episode should go to a local bus driver who, when giving evidence to the committee, pointed to his own experience of the magic of the Flats:

... he told a graphic tale of his dismal progress through Hackney, Homerton and Leyton to the point at which the houses ended and he

and his bus emerged into the light and air of Wanstead Flats, with their trees, grass and grazing cattle.
- Gorman (2009).

The Flats was saved and, following an initial period of neglect by the Corporation after the war, in the 1950s this glorious East London open space was restored and once again became the hugely popular facility that it had been back in the nineteenth century. Without the stout resistance of the Defence Committee to West Ham Council's plans to develop the Flats, we can only imagine what it would look like today. We do know that this glorious crescent-shaped ribbon of woods, heaths and grassland would have been lost to generations of young footballers in the area, including our two sporting heroes from East London, Bobby Moore and Graham Gooch. The Flats' golden years were in the 1960s and 1970s, but it is now undergoing a minor renaissance, as we shall see.

In addition to sport, the Flats has been used for a host of community activities for the past 200 years. Fairs and circuses have been held there since the late eighteenth century. The early fairs tended to be cattle markets, but they slowly evolved into what we know today - raucous Bank Holiday entertainment for hordes of East Enders. In later years the fairs reflected the multicultural nature of the area, and in 2000 a Hindu religious festival attracted thousands of people from across the East End. But sport has been the bread and butter of the Flats since 1945. Buildings housing changing and showers blocks have been added over the years, and today there are three much-needed car parks to serve the 60 pitches currently available. Sadly, the bandstands are gone, along with the underground Local Government Command Centre, but the Flats now proudly boasts a brand new, well-used children's playground, and in September 2009 a new changing facility, complete with offices, a kitchen and a community room, was opened by the Mayor of Newham.

As on other London playing fields, sport on Wanstead Flats has constantly evolved and been reshaped over the past 40 years. Traditionally, schools have used the Flats on Saturdays mornings, while the afternoons were reserved for the serious business of adult League football. Clubs from the Forest and District League, the SW Essex League, the London Business

Houses League and others played on the Flats, producing football of varying standards but always executed with unbridled enthusiasm. With 60 pitches available at least 1,000 local footballers would have used the Flats every Saturday afternoon through the season.

Sunday football was first played on the Flats in 1967. There had been an increase in requests for Sunday play in the early 1960s, and 'illegal' Sunday games had been played on the Flats for years. Sunday morning football was a huge success, to the extent that in the 1971/72 season play was extended to the afternoons. But Sunday morning football was overwhelmingly popular at this time, as Saturday use began its long decline. The 1971/72 season was the most successful season in the long history of the Flats, mainly as a result of the popularity of Sunday football.

Sunday morning matches would have been played on the same pitches used for Saturday games. This was not usually a problem, but unfortunately Sunday footballers would find themselves changing in rooms full of cigarette butts, empty lager cans and other discarded rubbish from the previous afternoon, and the showers were invariably freezing cold. Parking the car was always a problem when playing at the Flats and often meant a ten-minute walk to the changing rooms. But we always enjoyed games there, and the pitches were good and less cramped than Hackney Marshes. In addition, if you played on Sundays, after the game there was a wonderful stall selling tea, whelks and jellied eels on Aldersbrook Road, and the Eagle pub in Snaresbrook would always welcome thirsty Sunday footballers.

In the 1960s and early 1970s there was a full programme of league football played on the Flats on Wednesday afternoons. The clubs were made up of fireman, night workers, porters from Covent Garden and Smithfield markets, postmen and cab drivers. The games were of dubious quality, with no nets or corner flags and only the occasional referee, but they were great fun and the laughter almost lifted the roof of the changing rooms. The Nightingale at Wanstead used to open early on Wednesdays for the footballers, and the noise in the pub could be heard 200 yards away in High Road. The landlord, a real old cockney, used to provide sandwiches and chips and, best of all, a huge cauldron of broth, which went down a treat on cold winter afternoons.

The 1960s and 1970s were the heyday of football on Wanstead Flats in terms of both the quality and the sheer number of people and clubs involved every weekend. Demographic changes and shifts in cultural sensibilities have left their imprint on the provision of sport on the Flats as they have everywhere else in London. Very few schools use the ground during the week or on Saturday mornings as they used to, and weekend mornings are now the preserve of junior clubs with their loud coaches and even louder partisan parents. Senior teams continue to use the Flats on Saturday afternoons, but they are few in number and empty pitches are now the most obvious sign of the sad demise of serious Saturday afternoon local football in the area.

A more positive development on Wanstead Flats over the past few years has been the encouraging number of girls' and women's clubs enjoying the improved facilities now available at the weekend. The standard of women's football is improving rapidly and the clubs and leagues are well organised. People who run the Flats expect women's football to continue to grow and to provide an increasingly influential voice in the development of local league football.

In 2008 the City of London Corporation submitted a bid to the Heritage Lottery Fund (HLF) for ecological and environmental improvements to the Flats. This will be welcome, but unfortunately the bid does not include plans to develop the sports provision on the site. This is disappointing and would appear to be a lost opportunity. It is to be hoped, with the 2012 Olympics in sight, that the authorities will recognise that unless the Flats is improved as a sports facility the slow decline in popularity will continue. But the HLF project will aim to preserve wildlife and to conserve the rich natural resources of the Flats, itself designated a Site of Special Scientific Interest. An interesting detail of the plan is to protect skylarks from the attentions of local dogs - and, presumably, the cruder language of some of the footballers skylarking on the pitches below.

In October 2008 the City of London Corporation, recognising the slow decline of sport on the Flats, created a new post of Football Development Officer in its Epping Forest Open Spaces Department. The new post signalled a shift in the way the Corporation viewed sporting activities in the Forest. In previous years football on the Flats was perceived as a bit of a nuisance by the Forest wardens, who saw their primary aim, not unnaturally, as forest management. But the Corporation has a responsibility for sport on the Forest's grounds, and it is to its credit that in recent years it has begun to take this responsibility seriously. The person appointed to the new post was Sinem Cakir, and her appointment represents a major step change in the aims and objectives of the Corporation. Sinem has a real understanding and passion for sports development in East London and, in particular, removing cultural barriers to participation. This is clearly stated in her *Football Development Action Plan* (Sinem Cakir (2009), *Football Development Plan*, City of London Corporation, Open Spaces Department – Epping Forest) published a few months after she took up the new post. The report provides a useful snapshot of the current state of grassroots football in the area and a clear indication of the Corporation's plans for development.

At the heart of the Corporation's thinking about sports development is that the days are gone when the staff at Wanstead Flats could simply sit back and take bookings for the many clubs and leagues that needed pitches, season after season, as they did through the height of its popularity in the 30 years between 1960 and 1990. Today managers are determined to be proactive in their planning and are keenly aware that the decline in Saturday use is a disappointment, because it means that Wanstead Flats is no longer the thriving centre of park football in East London that it once was. They are similarly aware that in the current season, 2008/09, there are no schools using the Flats, a staggering thought when we know that London schools are starved of outdoor facilities. Sinem Cakir has admitted that there has been a trend for local clubs to fold in recent years; more clubs folded in 2008/09 than in any other previous year (interview with Sinem Cakir, 4th March 2009). The collapse of traditional Saturday afternoon football is an indication of a significant cultural shift in the area and is further proof that the increase in popularity of Sundays, and indoor and all-weather floodlit provision, is at the expense of the old organised local league-based 11-a-side game. Sinem and her team are keenly aware of the reasons why the number of people using the Flats each weekend slowly decreased from 6,800 in 1965 to 4,300 in 1995. Weekend usage further declined to about

3,000 in 2008.

There is now no midweek competitive football played on the Flats. Waltham Forest and Newham began to withdraw in 1986/87, booking fewer and fewer pitches and causing a serious loss of income for the organisers. But Wanstead Flats is resilient. In 1985 and 1986 30,000 people attended May festivals organised by Newham Council, and in 1989 there was a massive uptake of casual bookings for recreational soccer on Sunday afternoons. In 1991 7,000 people attended a summer sports festival, involving football, athletics and kabaddi, and in 1993 35,000 local people attended the Newham Mela and an Inner City World Cup. Then in 2000 60 teams entered a charity tournament held by East London Mela. Demand for mini-soccer for young people has increased, and in 1998 the Flats was approached by the London FA to provide a facility for this new style of youth football. The East London and Essex Youth League was formed at the Flats in 1999.

Today there are 150 acres of recreational facilities on Wanstead Flats, attracting 75 adult and 40 youth teams on Sundays and 19 and 25 respectively on Saturdays, much lower than in previous years as we have seen. But it remains a vital recreational facility for people of the area despite the seeming decline in the demands for pitches, with the encouraging exception of youth team football and its new variant, mini-soccer. Women's and girls' football are also healthy and are likely to feature prominently in the future.

We saw in Chapter 1 how much the population of East London has changed over the past 40 years. Such a demographic revolution is bound to have an impact on the local sports scene. Oddly, research shows that the downturn in the use of the Flats has not been accompanied by a fall in demand; on the contrary, demand is strong. But today local people want to use the Flats on a much more flexible basis. The job of the new Football Development Officer is to develop a programme to meet this new demand, ensuring that it is sensitive to the changing needs of multicultural East London.

The Flats' Action Plan has set some interesting and challenging targets. A structure of high, medium and low priorities indicates what Sinem Cakir and her team wish to achieve. The high priority targets in the plan are centred on helping clubs and individuals achieve the following:

• Meeting the FA Charter Standard;
• Introducing new boys and girls teams to the Flats;
• Developing work with partners, including West Ham United, Leyton Orient and local schools;
• Establishing mini-soccer leagues;
• Training and development of more coaches;
• Recruiting and training referees;
• Training ground staff to develop more flexible working patterns;
• Developing facilities, including new changing rooms for girls and women;
• Working with local faith and community groups, including the Asians in Football and the Asian Football leagues;
• Introducing a whole programme of courses and events for the Flats.

These targets and priorities represent a radical new philosophy in sport and leisure provision and they are being driven by politically aware practitioners such as Sinem Cakir and funding bodies who will expect to see these kinds of priorities written into funding bids. Accessibility, cultural sensitivity and participation are at the heart of this new philosophy. The philosophical premises that underpin the Flats' Action Plan are common to all sports development projects across the UK and meet the criteria set by central and local government policy. If sport and leisure projects fail to meet the required criteria, they will simply not be supported. All of us want to see improved opportunities for disabled people to participate in sport and leisure. Similarly, the huge success of girls' and women's football, in terms of sheer numbers and improved skill levels, has proved that target setting can achieve significant increases in participation in sport. However, not everyone agrees that public bodies should take account of people's ethnic and cultural background when developing policy.

Kenan Malik argues against local authorities' use of ethnic monitoring as the basis for policy initiatives. Malik's central point is that ethnicity and culture should not be the most important labels we place on each other. There is no doubt that in East London ethnic groups are over-represented in poor housing, while black young people are under-represented in higher education, and people from ethnic minority groups are less active in sport and leisure. But, for Malik,

> *... this is not a consequence of belonging to a particular racial group. Minority groups are not homogenous and are as likely to be divided by class, gender and age as the rest of the population.*
> *- K. Malik, 'Race obsession harms those it meant to help', The Sunday Times, 29th March 2009. Malik's argument is developed more fully in his book, From Fatwa to Jihad, Atlantic Books, 2009.*

To illustrate his claim about social class being more important than ethnicity, Malik makes the point that pupils of Indian origin tend to do well at school, Bangladeshis and Pakistanis perform at more or less the same level as black pupils, while bottom of the class come white working-class boys. His point is that using people's ethnic identity as the basis for policy overlooks people's real needs, in poverty, employment, housing and health, which are determined by class rather than ethnicity or gender.

Warming to his theme, Malik argues that the greatest error of multiculturalism has been labelling people of Bangladeshi and Pakistani origin as 'Muslim'. This has had the effect of disguising important differences between groups, which would be helpful to policy makers. For example, failing to recognise similarities between groups across cultures has had a damaging effect on educational policy. Malik argues that,

> *To improve the educational possibilities of all these groups – Bangladeshis, Pakistanis, African Caribbeans and working-class whites – we have to understand what they have in common – which derives less from their race than their class.*
> *- Malik, Sunday Times.*

In this argument ethnic monitoring, which underpins current policy in education and sport and leisure provision, produces misleading data. Public funds are given to ethnic-based groups, and in this way people begin to identify themselves in terms of ethnicity, where previously they did not. The cultural theorist, Raymond Williams, believed that if we only see people as fixed identities or, even worse, 'masses', we fail to see them as people. It would be a tragedy if local and central government policies designed to help people from ethnic backgrounds had the effect of creating divisions by virtue of this lazy thinking. As Malik points out, Muslims are British citizens with a variety of views and beliefs, whose primary loyalty is not necessarily to their faith. A consequence of multiculturalism is that many Muslims may come to see themselves as 'semi-detached Britons'.

In local authority centres and schools throughout East London, current sports development policy may create divisions when the opposite is intended. In the race riot-torn 1970s and 1980s many of the teams who played on Wanstead Flats and Hackney Marshes were made up of Greeks, Italians, blacks and whites. Difference was generally respected and no special favours were expected or given. It is true that there were few women's teams in East London and it was rare to see an Asian footballer among the thousands that played every weekend. Today exclusively Asian teams and separate Asian leagues are encouraged and supported. Of course, this is a complex and sensitive area, but it feels that by promoting separation something has been lost. It is much easier to accept separation and division, and much harder to find solutions to bring communities together. Local sport and recreation is one area of life in which people can come together with a common purpose. A failure of will in this area on the part of policy makers has meant that this opportunity could be lost.

Despite reservations about the way in which important issues of ethnicity and culture have been handled, if the Wanstead Flats' Action Plan works then it could become the model for urban playing fields of the future. The Plan is timely. With the Olympic Park close by in Stratford, there is a clear opportunity for the Flats to become a vital part of the 2012 Games legacy development programme – that is, if the Games planners haven't earmarked this jewel in the crown of London's playing fields as a gigantic coach and car park. You wouldn't put it past them.

Wanstead Flats is in good hands and will continue to provide a welcome place for the people of East London to play sport for the foreseeable future, Olympics or no Olympics! There are plans to upgrade some of the facilities, and this is long overdue. But somewhere out on one of the 60 pitches one Saturday morning, perhaps the new Bobby Moore will be dominating play for his school team, just as the real one did 50 years ago.

But today he is more likely to be seen displaying his skills in 5-a-side games in an indoor centre, or on a plastic surface under floodlights, before moving on to the West Ham Academy.

The local sports grounds of East London and Essex that survive are in better shape than they were 30 years ago. They have modern changing facilities, all-weather surfaces and floodlights. This is heartening and due in most part to the efforts of local activists and dedicated recreation staff, who have worked hard and with imagination to secure their future. However many, such as Salisbury Hall in Chingford, have been lost altogether to provide space for supermarkets and shopping malls, where local people are encouraged to exercise their credit cards rather than their bodies. Hackney Marshes has been reduced in size over the past 30 years and its future is now threatened by the spreading 2012 Olympic project. Wanstead Flats, like the Marshes, has seen a massive reduction in Saturday play over this time and, arguably, this has resulted in a sharp decline in the standard of local league football. The rise of all-day Sunday football is welcome, but the standards are not high and the games are more recreational than competitive. The current agenda set by funding bodies and controlled by central government is largely political and is much more concerned with addressing social inequalities and disadvantage than in the provision of high-quality local grounds designed to raise standards.

CHAPTER 3
ESSEX: STRONGHOLD OF AMATEUR FOOTBALL

There is a real sense today, in both amateur and professional football, that something precious has been lost, perhaps even stolen. Inevitably, this loss is linked to wider social and political trends. The economist, Paul Ormerod, believes that the economic recession of 2009 will have a positive impact on professional football. He argues that the values on which sport were traditionally derived were corrupted during the economic boom times of the 1990s and the first few years of the twenty-first century. His argument is particularly persuasive when applied to professional footballers who, for Ormerod, flaunt their wealth and celebrity, revelling in the distance they have achieved from sports lovers and fans. He writes,

> *The recession may bring an end to the gross excesses in professional soccer. Players have become distanced from the fan base.*
> *- P. Ormerod (2005), Why Most Things Fail: Evolution, Extinction and Economics, Faber and Faber.*

Bobby Moore understood that he was part of a close-knit, hard-working community and, despite his huge fame and celebrity, he never wanted to distance himself from his roots. The evidence is overwhelming that Premier League footballers see the world differently today, and many embrace the culture of celebrity. The English Premier League has become the richest in the world, and as such it can attract many of the world's greatest players. In 1975 West Ham United were the last club to field a team composed entirely of English-born players in an FA Cup final. Supporters of today's Premier League clubs must wonder just what it is they are supporting – probably only each other. Ormerod's blast is aimed at the rapacious but now bankrupt capitalism of Premier League football, with its grubby, wide-boy agents and dodgy sponsorship deals, which have had a near disastrous effect on local amateur football, particularly in East London.

The shrinking of Hackney Marshes and the loss of dozens of other local London sports grounds can be attributed to the commercial and business values so beloved of the football authorities and, in 2009, so utterly discredited in society at large. Ormerod's argument is no nostalgic purist's rant, but a thoughtful and accurate assessment of what has happened to the sporting culture of the UK over the past 20 years. The loss has been severe. The unique experience of Hackney Marshes, deeply felt by generations of players up until 1970, has been sadly diminished. Wanstead Flats is a pale shadow of the vibrant focus of East London football that it once was. Along with the vandalism done to our local sports grounds there has been an accompanying squandering of the social and cultural life of local communities. We can test this argument by examining the current state of local sport in East London and Essex.

A rich tradition

After a Sunday game on any of the sports grounds in Essex and East London players head for their local pub, perhaps inviting their opponents to join them for an after-match pint or two. Clubs would use the same pub after matches, and the grateful landlord would often lay on some welcome hot food. In the early 1970s there used to be a pub down on the estuary at Leigh-on-Sea, the Rose & Crown, which is now a posh gastropub frequented by out-of-town hedge-fund managers and media people from the Docklands. When we played down there, the opposition used to invite us back to the pub after the game. The landlord, an old East Ender from Canning Town, laid on one of the best after-match spreads you would ever see – almost the full Sunday roast. But there was just one small problem: the pub was the headquarters of the local National Front outfit, still very active in the 1970s. At 2.00 p.m. sharp, after he had called time, the landlord rolled out a huge Union Jack across the bar and led a rousing cockney version of 'God Save the Queen'. We always had a few black, Italian and Greek lads in our team, but far from taking offence they took great pleasure in watching these idiots play out their prejudices in time-honoured Leigh-on-Sea fashion. Ironically, up until the 2.00 p.m. flag-waving ritual everyone was mixing fine – nothing personal lads!

In the 1960s and 1970s most local park teams in the area had a friendly landlord who would open early on a Saturday afternoon to let in groups of thirsty and hungry young footballers. In midwinter, games would begin at 2.30 p.m., which meant that the teams were ready for the pub around 5.00 p.m. Generous landlords would lay on steaming cauldrons of broth, hot roast potatoes, bowls of chips and sandwiches. Pubs have changed today and food is frequently available all day, but the tradition of free hot food for freezing footballers after a game on Hackney Marshes, or elsewhere, still continues, even though a lager shandy or a couple of cokes are today's post-match drinks of choice rather than the four or five pints of light and bitter before driving home of the 1960s.

There were 'football pubs' all over East London in the 1960s and 1970s, where players from different clubs gathered on Saturdays nights to swap stories about their game that afternoon and celebrate or commiserate with each other about how West Ham or Leyton Orient were performing that particular season. These pubs had no plasma TV screens; in fact they had no TV at all. These were traditional old boozers, usually with a public bar for bar skittles or a quiet game of dominos, a lounge for a peaceful pint, and a barn of a room reserved for live music and loud and animated conversation.

The Prince Albert in Chingford was arguably the best of the football pubs in the area. The Albert had live music most nights of the week, and Saturdays were special and featured some of the best jazz musicians in London. The resident band, the Rex Cull Trio, supported some wonderful soloists, including the great guitarist Terry Smith and singer Norma Winstone. Around 200 people would descend on the jazz bar at the Albert to hear some of the best live music in London. The Albert, known throughout East London, was founded in 1873 and the first landlord, a Philomen Lodge, had 12 children and in 1900 became one of Chingford's first local councillors. He died in 1920 and was buried, not without some irony, up the road from the pub in the same cemetery that later accommodated late members of the Kray family. One of Lodge's daughters went on to run a successful forge and taxi company in Chingford, and when her horses were lost to the war effort she opened one of the first motorised taxi services in London. A taxi firm still exists on the site and is much used by regulars of the Prince Albert.

In the 1960s people dressed up to go to a pub like the Albert. Then men wore suits - not just off-the-peg 'whistles' from Burton's, but handmade suits from local tailors. A three-piece suit would take two fittings and the choice of cloth was crucial: a Prince of Wales check, a navy blue worsted, or the height of fashion (nobody used the word cool in those days), a blue tonic mohair from George the tailor at the top of Walthamstow market. This would be the required dress at many of the 'smart' pubs across the East End, including the Prospect of Whitby and the Blind Beggar further into town. The atmosphere at the Albert on Saturday nights was electric, fights were rare, and the only disturbances to the evening's entertainment were the weekly visit of the Salvation Army selling *War Cry* and the whelk stall man and his tray of 'fresh' seafood.

Perhaps the greatest night in the Albert's history, as with most pubs in London, was the night of 30th July 1966 – just hours after England won the World Cup for the first and only time, captained by the saintly Bobby Moore. That night customers had the time of their lives, and they sang 'When the Reds go Marching In' at the tops of their voices until the landlord finally called time. Many of us left the pub at closing time and headed west to Trafalgar Square to continue the celebrations into the night – and what a night! Sadly, Bobby Moore was not in the Albert that night, as he was being royally entertained elsewhere. However, famous footballers, including the England captain himself, could be seen in the pub some Saturdays having a relaxing drink with their wives and friends, enjoying the music and unmolested by the locals. It was just an ordinary thing to do. Professional footballers in the 1960s remained close to their community, and locals were yet to be overwhelmed by their celebrity.

Waiting to get into a music pub in Stratford one evening in mid-1963, I recognised The Beatles' manager, Brian Epstein, directly ahead of me in the queue. The Beatles had played up the road at Leyton Baths the night before. When Epstein told the doorman who he was, drawing himself up to his full height, the old boy replied, "I don't care if you're f***ing Charlie Drake, you're not getting in 'ere without paying."

John Lennon would have enjoyed the 'jobsworth' reply and appreciated the lack of deference shown by the pub doorman to this particular national celebrity. Epstein duly paid and went in to see the band he had heard about – if memory serves me correctly they were a young group called the Small Faces (who later came to fame with such songs as 'Itchycoo Park').

Just across the road from the Albert in Chingford there was a branch of Burton's, the menswear store. Burton stores in East London occupied the prime position in the local shopping centres. The first floor of Burton's almost always housed a snooker hall, with several good-quality full-size tables. 'The 'all', as it was known, had a tea bar in the corner which sold hot pies and steaming mugs of tea till about 2 o'clock in the morning. All the well-known local footballers used to meet up in the 'all at Chingford when the pubs shut. Very occasionally a scrap would break out over a disputed shot or someone's turn on the fruit machines. Nostalgia is not always blameless. On one occasion in the late 1960s I was walking past Burton's in Chingford late one Saturday night, when a bloke came crashing through the entrance after being booted down the long staircase. He lay on the ground, half in and half out of the doorway. I watched two policemen doing their Saturday night rounds and, as they strolled past, one of them with his boot gently rolled the unfortunate victim back inside the doorway, closed the door and carried on his nightly patrol.

The wonderful old Victorian building that housed the Albert was demolished in the late 1970s and was replaced by a shopping arcade and a soulless underground bar, which the planners had the temerity to name – you've guessed it - the Prince Albert. The demolition of the Albert in Chingford was the first of many acts of planning vandalism in the area perpetrated by lazy, incompetent architects and complicit councillors. The old-style football pub has gone, replaced by licensed outlets for Sky Sports selling freezing cold lager, microwaved lasagne and cling-filmed sandwiches to bored and hungry shoppers - yet another example of the collapse of a culture, to be replaced by what? An architectural gem? A thoughtful contribution to the improvement of the area? No, a cynical, money-making slap in the face of the local community.

The thriving culture that existed around football and pubs in the 1960s and 1970s was rich and deep and much more than just after-match hospitality for both teams, designed to drive out the cold. And it can get bitterly cold on Wanstead Flats on a

January Saturday afternoon with a biting wind and freezing temperatures that cut right through a flimsy nylon football jersey. I remember captaining a side during one such game and begged the referee to abandon the game (we were 4-0 down after 60 minutes) because our 18-year-old outside right, unable to get into the game, was developing early signs of hypothermia. The caring referee agreed and we quickly got the young lad out of the wind into an ice-cold dressing room, where he was unable even to hold a hot cup of tea that the café staff rushed down to him. Fortunately, he recovered quickly and later proudly took his place with his teammates by the pub fireside, fortified by hot sausage rolls and baked potatoes. The club held raffles in the pub after the game and also ran a much more lucrative '200' club scheme, and throughout the season they held fundraising evenings in the local, and elsewhere. It was all part of the rich culture of local football.

Counting the cost

It costs money to run a local football club. Pitch and referees' fees have to be paid, a new strip is required every couple of seasons, which will include shirts, shorts, socks and, these days, substitutes' cold-weather gear, top of the range footballs, corner flags, nets and energy-giving health drinks. Pitches can be extremely expensive to hire. Some clubs get lucky and a local plumbing firm or bookmaker might sponsor the kit, but most are likely to meet their costs through club fundraising and the players' reluctantly handed-over £3/5 match sub. This has always been the case. Clubs have to be exceptionally well organised to survive, season after season.

Today Lottery funds are available through the FA and Football Foundation to help clubs improve their facilities and junior sections. To gain access to grant aid for nets, new regulation goalposts, improved changing rooms, pitch upgrades, etc., local clubs have to meet FA Charter Standards, which requires complying with a bewildering number of criteria. These include compulsory attendance for officials, helpers and coaches on FA coaching and 'awareness-raising' courses, including one called 'Goalpost Safety' – book early to avoid disappointment. This is tough on local clubs run by volunteers. Most clubs meet their increasing costs by raising the funds themselves to avoid the FA's bureaucracy test. A growing number of others simply fold.

The selling of sports grounds, the destruction of local amenities, shops and pubs, and the drive to turn active citizens into passive consumers are all having a negative effect on the sporting culture of the area, once so rich and vital to community cohesion – think of what now binds young people in the area to their neighbourhoods? Someone once used the phrase 'private wealth and public squalor' to explain the past 20 years of social and community decay, and nowhere is this more true that in East London and Essex. But all is not lost and there are many dedicated individuals and groups who are committed to regaining what has been lost.

No ordinary county

Essex is no ordinary county. Essex County FA, formed in 1883, is the largest in the country, with around 5,000 teams playing across an area that includes five London boroughs (Redbridge, Waltham Forest, Newham, Barking & Dagenham, and Havering) and nineteen local authorities. Counter to the popular view, it is an extremely diverse area, stretching from the Olympic borough of Newham, along the Thames Gateway regeneration project, and out through the more prosperous towns of Brentwood, Chelmsford and north to Colchester. Essex FA covers hundreds of rural villages like Braintree, the Rodings and Peshey, and if one adds to this diverse mix the less prosperous towns of Basildon, Thurrock and Canvey Island in the south-east one can begin to grasp the nature of the challenge facing the Essex County FA in encouraging enough opportunities to meet so many different needs and demands in its rural and urban catchment area. The current staff and committee members should gain heart from the record of their distinguished predecessors.

In a study of football in East London and Essex it would be rude not to mention the five League clubs in the area: West Ham United, Dagenham & Redbridge, Southend United, Leyton Orient and Colchester United. This is not the place for a full discussion of the relative merits of these clubs or to dig deep into their respective histories; however, it is interesting to look at the League clubs in relation to local football in the area. Dagenham & Redbridge are a relatively recent addition to the Football League and their history is covered briefly later in this chapter. Leyton Orient and Southend are much-loved clubs with a devoted local following.

All five Essex League clubs have grown out of local amateur football, as we have already seen with The Hammers and their association with the Thames Ironworks. Dagenham & Redbridge's history stems from the Ford Motor Company, and Leyton Orient has equally colourful origins. Formed in 1881, Leyton Orient are the second oldest professional club in London after Fulham and joined the Football League in 1905. The club emerged as the footballing arm of the Eagle Cricket Club and became Clapton Orient FC, before becoming the club we know today. Legend has it that one of the early Orient players worked for the Orient Shipping Line and suggested the club took the name. The club's golden years were in the 1960s and 1970s, despite the severe financial problems at that time. I can remember attending one home match in the late 1960s, played on a Sunday morning to increase the gate, when a collection was organised by passing plastic buckets among the crowd. The dire financial situation would have been improved by an FA Cup semi-final appearance at Stamford Bridge in 1978, where the combined vocal support of the Orient faithful and thousands of Hammers fans failed to lift The O's sufficiently for them to reach their first ever FA Cup final. It is ironic that in their only season in the old Division One, Orient cheekily managed to beat their big brother across East London, West Ham, both home and away.

Successive boards of directors have managed to steer the club to its current stable position. The present Chairman, Barry Hearn, is the owner of the Matchroom snooker stable, and the future of the club, if not rosy, at least looks hopeful. The club did have something of a senior moment in the 1970s when rather foolishly they changed their name from Leyton Orient to The Orient, but they quickly changed it back under protest from the fans. Some wonderful footballers have graced the excellent Brisbane Road pitch over the years, including the late Laurie Chamberlain, who died tragically in a road accident in Spain, where he was playing for Real Madrid, the ex-Hammer Peter Brabrook, legendary forwards Dave Dunmore, Tommy Johnson and Mickey Bullock, and excellent defenders in the elegant Glenn Roeder and the less elegant Terry Mancini. Among the club's managers in recent years have been the fearsome Dick Graham, John Carey, Frank Clark, Tommy Taylor and Martin

Ling.

Bobby Moore, of course, managed Southend for a short while, and the club have been served by successive former West Ham players seeing out the last years of their careers. The club seem destined to slide between Divisions One and Two, although the town deserves better. With a thriving town centre, a County Cricket Ground and the famous Kursaal Stadium, now remodelled, the town could easily accommodate a Championship club. Sadly, the famous pier no longer exists, and the most recognisable features of the town are outrageous stag and hen parties, plentiful cockles and whelks, and an unlovely oil refinery across the estuary.

Perhaps the club with the most interesting history in the local area are Colchester United. Set in the northernmost part of Essex, Colchester is an agreeable old market town set around Castle Park, one the most delightful city parks in the county. Within the park's grounds sits the County Cricket Ground, home to the Essex Cricket Festival, usually played late in the season when footballers are completing their pre-season training. If you stroll through Castle Park down from the high street on a clear summer's morning when Essex are at Colchester for the week, you begin to catch the halting sound of announcements over the loudspeaker. At this point, sensing play is about to begin, dozens of small boys equipped with everything they need for the day begin to sprint down towards the entrance gates, caught up with the excitement of a day's cricket ahead. The rest of us, equally excited, approach the gates in a more orderly manner.

Colchester has a proud history as a garrison town and local girls swarm into town on Friday nights hoping meet the soldier of their dreams. Colchester United have had a complicated history, but it is safe to say that the club emerged from an amalgamation with Colchester Town and moved to the Layer Road ground in 1909, where they played until very recently, when the stadium was demolished to make way for the splendid, if unimaginatively named, Weston Homes Community Stadium in 2008. In 1950 the club were accepted into the Football League and they have enjoyed mixed fortunes since, dropping out of the League in 1990 for a couple of seasons. The club's best performance was in season 2006/07, when they finished as runners-up in League One, but this bald fact disguises a remarkable and exciting history (B. Webber (2004), The Way U's Were: A Personal History of Colchester United, Tempus Publishing). Colchester United have had a direct influence on West Ham United and their famous purist playing style, which at its best, in the 1960s, could raise the hair on the back of your neck. Ted Fenton left The Oysters to join West Ham and instituted a philosophy of football that produced the three 1966 World Cup heroes as well as exciting, gifted players like Johnny Byrne, Harry Redknapp, John Sissons, Trevor Brooking, Alan Devonshire, Tony Cottee and Joe Cole. Fenton, the sharp-dressing, tactical genius, played 176 games for The Hammers before returning to succeed Charlie Paynter as the club's manager. He was in charge of the West Ham side that won the Division Two Championship in 1957/58. Fenton eventually left Upton Park to end his career in Scotland, where he was tragically killed in a road accident. Benny Fenton, Ted's brother, played for The Oysters in the 1950s until he reached the age of 40 and pursued a career in football management.

The best years for Colchester United were in the 1950s under Fenton, but several sublime moments have punctuated their otherwise steady progress. An FA Cup tie against Arsenal in 1958/59 attracted 16,000 people to Layer Road to see the home side hold out for a 2-2 draw, only to lose the replay 4-0 in front of 62,686 people. Newcastle were the Cup visitors in 1960 and again in 1982, when Colchester lost the tie in a replay at St James Park to a goal by the young Chris Waddle. The Oysters have all been involved in classic Cup ties with Huddersfield Town, Leeds United, Blackpool and West Ham over the years. Among the outstanding footballers who have played for Colchester United are Vic Keeble, whom Fenton claimed could take penalties with his head and who later left for Newcastle; goalkeeper Dick Graham, later manager of Leyton Orient; locally born John Bond, affectionately known at West Ham as 'Muffin the Mule', who enjoyed a distinguished career in club management; striker Bobby Hunt, who scored 39 goals in the 1961/62 season; and, arguably the most famous of them all, centre forward Ted Phillips, who later enjoyed an illustrious career at Ipswich Town. In the summer months Phillips turned out for Colchester CCC and was known as a devastating fast bowler. In addition to the Fenton brothers, The Oysters were once managed by Jock Wallace and the great England centre half, Neil Franklin.

The purpose of including this sketch of the five Essex and East London League clubs here is to illustrate the close historical connection they have with the local football community. All five clubs emerged from local football, apart from Leyton Orient, whose origins oddly lie in a cricket club. The five clubs have developed a network of close working relationships over a 100-year period that has seen players, coaches and managers moving between them to the mutual benefit of all. Today all the area's professional clubs operate successful community schemes involving girls' and women's football, multi-ethnic projects and educational schemes. These schemes are generally distinct from the elite Academy structure and help the clubs to maintain close links with the communities they serve.

A go-ahead county

Essex has a proud reputation as a football area and a strong record of participation, and it encourages progress up through the different levels of the game, often bucking national trends. In 1952 the FA produced a bulletin that included the following tribute to the county:

> *... the county of Essex, with its densely populated boroughs along the Thames, has throughout the present century played a leading role in the progress of the amateur side of the game. Why is this?*
> *- Essex – A Stronghold of Amateur Football, FA Bulletin, December 1952.*

The bulletin points to the fine record of the County XI in the Southern Counties Amateur Championship (SCAC) and the success of its clubs in the FA Amateur Cup. In 1899 the County Association had no fewer than 100 affiliated clubs compared with 800 in 1952. In the very early days Fred Pelly, of the Old Foresters FC, had been capped by England against Scotland, Ireland and Wales. Pelly eventually became President of the County Association and was reputed to be the richest footballer in the country when it was discovered that he had left £472,000 in his will. As far back as the late nineteenth century the Essex footballer had an eye for money.

Essex owed its prominence as a footballing county to a number of outstanding players and administrators. The first of these was Vivian Woodward (VJ), who played for Clapton Town FC before the First World War, served an apprenticeship with Chelmsford and went on to represent England in full and amateur internationals. VJ also played as an amateur for Tottenham Hotspur before finishing his career with Chelsea, where he was made a director. Other famous players at that time were Andy Ducat from Southend Athletic FC, who gained several England caps as well as an FA Cup winner's medal, and Harry Hasle from Wanstead, Southend and eventually Manchester United. At Old Trafford he partnered the England legend Billy Meredith on the right wing when United won the Cup in 1909. It is worth noting here that all three of these distinguished players learned their game in the modest South Essex League. Players from the area who were selected for the England Amateur side in the 1960s, before the amateur/professional distinction was abolished, included Brian Adams and Peter Green from Leyton, Les Tilley from Leytonstone, and Jim Lewis and Brian Harvey of Walthamstow Avenue.

As the bulletin states, it was not until after the 1914-28 war that Essex "really began to shine in amateur football". Essex made ten appearances in the final of the SCAC from 1921 to 1952, winning on eight occasions. In addition, Essex clubs appeared in nine Amateur Cup finals in the period between the two wars and in four out of the seven finals from 1945 to 1952. The FA suggests, with unexpected historical understanding, that "the roots of the present lie deep in the past", and points towards the reasons why Essex was the dominant County Association in amateur football over such a prolonged period. These include:

1. The early influence of ex-players from the universities and public schools who formed the Old Boys' Clubs network.
2. The establishment of the headquarters of the famous Corinthians at Leyton.
3. The development and stability of a string of strong clubs in the Metropolitan area of the county, including Leyton, Barking-Woodville, Clapton, Ilford, Romford and, further north, Harwich, Colchester and Chelmsford, who had begun to engage professionals.
4. The presence of large open spaces in the metropolitan area

like Wanstead Flats and Lea Marshes.

Of course, Essex 'metropolitan' would have incorporated large tracts of land along the Thames, which would have included Stratford, Forest Gate, East Ham and West Ham, right up until 1965. The FA describes the structure of Essex amateur football as a "soccer ladder", which begins in the schools at primary level and moves up to the town and district representative level organised by the English Schools FA and the Essex and London Schools FA. The Bulletin states:

The work of the officers of the Schools FA for over 30 years is now being rewarded by the very high standard of amateur football to be seen every week in the County. Over 350 boys have represented the Essex County Schools FA in various games since 1922.

These are the foundations that produced the likes of Bobby Moore, David Beckham, Teddy Sheringham and a host of other modern-day international footballers. Perhaps crucially, and in contrast to today,

On leaving school these boys are not forgotten and the Minor Association carries the process a step further up to the age of 18 by organizing all manner of League and Cup competitions for boys who join Youth Clubs.

One of the reasons for the success of the county over a sustained period is the continuity of training and guidance from junior to senior amateur football. The FA offers a delightful tribute to the stalwarts of the Essex model:

... in the late Sir James Slade and the present Sir Herbert Dunnico, Essex has been blessed with two Presidents who have never missed the opportunity of going all over the county, even to the remoter wilds of North Essex, to preach good sportsmanship.

Today's Colchester fans may object to the "wilds of North Essex" description of their charming and unexpectedly modern town but will understand the sentiment expressed by the FA in 1952. The bulletin describes the process by which boys could progress through the different levels, receiving a thorough grounding in the game and benefiting from a small army of FA-qualified coaches. It was the Essex FA's intention in the 1950s to have an FA coach in every one of the county's schools. It is to be hoped that they were a more restrained and considerate group of coaches than the present bunch of overenthusiastic zealots of the professional game.

As the FA points out, Essex had an abundance of clubs under the "more scientific and skilful play associated with the Isthmian and Athenian Leagues," and players of all abilities could find a club with players at their own level:

In South West Essex particularly, one finds Leagues covering every possible grade within a 10-mile radius of Ilford - schoolboy, old boy, junior, and intermediate: with senior amateur leagues operating everywhere.

In addition to the existence of a whole network of clubs and leagues at every level, the FA highlights two other reasons for the county's outstanding record in amateur football. Firstly, many Essex clubs, despite their long history, have never been interested in achieving senior amateur status, but their very stability has contributed to the success of what the FA describes as this "go-ahead county". Saffron Walden, Maldon, Coggeshall and Halstead have been affiliated to the FA since the 1880s and have never reached full senior status, but they have inspired generations of players to play according to the highest traditions of the game. Secondly, there has been a decisive influence on the game by a number of Essex sporting families, who have raised the standard of football in the county over the past 150 years, including:

The five Farnfields of Woodford, the four Porters of Ilford, the four Russells of Leyton, the three Chalks of Barking-Woodville, the three Kings of Coggeshall, the Groves of Leytonstone, and finally, the father and son Earles of Clapton and Lewis of Walthamstow Avenue.

It is difficult to overemphasise the positive influence of the Lewises on the borough's sporting history. With their distinguished playing career and Jim Senior's sports shop opposite the Palmerston pub, just down the road from the

Avenue's ground in Green Pond Road, the much-respected family was an inspiration to thousands of local sports-mad youngsters. To ram home the point of the success of the Essex County FA in the twentieth century, the FA points to the playing excellence of the clubs, stating that:

> *... of eight amateur clubs which played in the FA Cup last month (1952) four came from Essex – Leyton, Grays Athletic, Leytonstone and Walthamstow Avenue - can be traced to the advice and instruction given to players both on and off the field by Mr JW Bowers, a member of the FA Amateur Selection Committee ... It is this valuable advice which has stood many a prominent Essex player in good stead over the years.*

The tribute to the Essex County FA concludes by referring to the tremendous work of J.T. Clark in guiding the Association since 1908, stating that in the 70-year history of the County FA to 1952 there had been only two secretaries, Clark and the legendary Robert Cook. These were the early pioneers of Essex amateur football and they were succeeded by a host of similarly dedicated local sporting heroes who have continued their good work. Of course, out of the four clubs who played in the FA Cup in 1952 only two, Leyton and Grays Athletic, remain in existence.

A thoroughly modern association

A modern County FA has a very different set of challenges from its predecessors and it is required to serve many masters, often with conflicting demands, but the good news is that the legacy appears to be in safe hands. Officers at the County FA are serious people, and former County Development Manager of the Essex County FA (now Chief Executive of Hertfordshire FA), Nick Perchard writes:

> *Essex is doing extremely well. In other parts of the country, open age football has been declining at such a rate that it's difficult to see how it will ever recover. In Essex we are aiming to expand further through initiatives such as the North Essex Veterans' League, which has already increased participation.*
> *- N. Perchard, 'Build, Create and Expand. Essex County FA Strategy 2008-12: Shaping Football in Essex,' E.C.F.A Magazine, Issue 13.*

This increased involvement in local football in Essex extends to women's leagues, the newly introduced Under 21 men's small game league and also five-a-side football, now available twelve hours a day, seven days a week. Table 1 illustrates both the level of participation in the county and the rate of increase.

Table 1: A sample of male participation in local Essex football taken from the Essex FA website in 2009.

	2006/07 %	**2007/08** %	**Change** %
Barking & Dagenham	5.5	6.9	+1.4
Rochford	11.7	13.0	+1.3
Havering	2.6	3.6	+1.0
Braintree	5.4	6.2	+0.8
Southend	7.5	8.3	+0.8
Waltham Forest	4.5	5.3	+0.8

This is an encouraging story and illustrates clearly the level of interest and commitment to sport in the county, and the County FA's powers of organisation. However, despite the upbeat note, if we dig a little deeper we see some more worrying figures. Participation rates in the five London boroughs are below the national average in all forms of the game – some seriously so. An Essex County FA strategy document, *Shaping Football in Essex: 2008-2012*, makes the following claim:

> *The story is a fine one, with all areas of the game at worst retaining participation levels.*

This is only partly true. The document tell us that nine out of eighteen leagues in the county have fewer teams than five years ago, with two of those leagues now defunct. These are alarming figures. Given the diversity of the area, it is also worrying that 93 per cent of all the players registered with the county's Charter Standard clubs are 'white British'. Essex FA is working hard to increase participation among ethnic minorities, women and girls, older men, and people with disabilities. It is a huge challenge, and £20,600,000 (yes, you have to look twice, but these are the sums available) has been invested in developing the infrastructure of local football to support the strategy, but the real challenge lies in the London boroughs rather than out in the heart of the county.

The Essex County FA claims that participation rates have, at worst, been maintained in both the five-a-side and the more traditional eleven-a-side game. This goes against national trends, which show a dramatic fall in participation. Essex FA is to be congratulated on its efforts, and it is not complacent. However, there are concerns about future of the traditional game in East London, based on the availability of fewer grounds, the lack of interest or encouragement of ethnic-based teams and, perhaps most worrying of all, the effect of wider trends in society on playing and watching football. It is not surprising that visits to the Lakeside Shopping Centre on Saturday afternoons have become habitual at the same time as participation rates in local football have dropped. The sporting culture of East London and Essex, alive and kicking in the period from 1950 to 1980, does appear to be in decline and, despite the energetic efforts of the County FA, this downturn could be terminal. One area of the local sporting culture illustrates this problem with worrying clarity.

Factory football

In the post-war period up to about 1980, there were amateur football clubs in East London and Essex that were in the privileged position of not having to worry about money. Most had superb private pitches and their own groundsman, warm and spacious changing rooms, and usually their own private bar with extensive catering facilities. These clubs were subsidised by their paternal owners, to the extent of providing everything from the pitch to the team strip – complete with company logo. These were the so-called 'firms' clubs, the grandest of which was the Ford Motor Company based at Dagenham. There were a number of such clubs in East London and Essex and they tended to be in two groups: 'white-collar' clubs, which entered a team in the Old Boys' or Southern Olympian League – combined in 2002 under the new Amateur Football Combination; and teams that represented industrial firms in working-class areas. Class distinctions in work were reflected in local league football, as in most other areas of life. In the early days, to play for these clubs it was compulsory to work for the firm or company. This rule became more relaxed as playing standards dropped or when clubs struggled to put out teams of sufficient quality.

Together with Ford's, venues such as the Metropolitan Police Sports Ground in Chigwell, the London Hospital ground in Chingford and Tate & Lyle's in Newham had high-quality playing surfaces and facilities. There were others, but Ford and Tate & Lyle provide the two most interesting case studies of a sporting culture centred on local industry in East London and Essex – now lost forever.

The Tate & Lyle sugar company has been a major employer in the East End since 1878 and, as such, was central to the working life of the area. The company's factories and refineries suffered extensive bomb damage in the war. My mother told a story of molten sugar running down the streets following direct hits on the Plaistow works during the Blitz. With these kinds of shared experiences local people gained an attachment to companies such as Tate & Lyle, not only for the employment opportunities they offered generations of East Enders but also for the sport and leisure facilities they provided for their staff, even if this paternalism could be viewed as a tactic to encourage staff loyalty and drive up productivity (For a detailed argument on this point, see Phil Mosely, 'Factory Football: Paternalism and Profits', Sporting Traditions, Vol.2, no.1, Nov. 1985, University of Sydney). So what if it did?

Tate & Lyle had two refineries in East London – Thames Refinery and Plaistow Wharf, which in 1950 employed between them around 6,000 people. Today this number has been reduced to just over 500. Just outside the Thames Refinery was the Taste Institute built by Henry Tate and donated to the people of Newham as a library and community centre. In time, this facility effectively became the firm's social club. 'The Tate', as it became known locally, had a large function hall, a bar and a billiards room. The place flourished throughout the 1950s and 1960s, being used for meetings, social evenings and wedding receptions. The Sports Club had a number of sections, including cricket, football, tennis, swimming, golf, shooting and fishing. All activities were subsidised by the company, as was the Sports Club itself. The company had its own sports ground, about one mile east of the Thames Refinery, with a cricket pitch, tennis courts, pavilion and bar. In addition, the Sports Club rented a local football ground from British Gas to accommodate all those that wanted to play. In the mid to late 1980s, the Sports

Ground was subject to a compulsory purchase order to make way for the proposed East London River Crossing. The Tate was finally closed in 1995, following a long period of steadily declining membership.

Sadly, there are no written records of the history of the Tate & Lyle Sports Club, or of any other similar factory sports provision in the area. Indeed, there is little record of any kind relating to participation in sport in the area, from this or any period. We can only imagine the level of activity and the quality of the facilities available to the employees. We do know that the firm had its own internal football competition. This was a serious league founded in 1911, comprising eight or nine departmental teams. The staff team (probably the office workers), captained by Albert Buckeridge, won the league in 1913/14 and was a mixture of Mincing Lane and Plaistow staff. Teams continued to play for the original cup into the 1960s. Between the wars, boxing was a flourishing sport and the local champion, Billy 'Kid' Brooks, proved a great help in training and promoting enthusiasm among the younger members. The annual inter-refinery boxing match gradually became an occasion of intense rivalry, with "hordes of bloodthirsty girls" cheering on their men – not good for inter-departmental relations (I am grateful to Michael Grier at Tate & Lyle Co. Ltd for his summary of the history of the firm's Sports & Social Club in Newham. For more background detail, see Oliver Lyle (1960), The Plaistow Story, Tate & Lyle). Lastly, we can say with confidence that one of the first examples of organised sport in Plaistow was the Tate & Lyle Swimming Club. The club was formed in 1909 and members competed for a cup presented by Leonard Lyle. The cup could be seen in the Sports Club's trophy showcase up until its demolition in the late 1980s. There is no longer any sport in the area associated with the Tate & Lyle company.

Fun at Ford's

Further east, out in Essex, the Ford Motor Company provides a very different example of factory football to the sugar producers in the East End. Whereas Tate & Lyle was involved with the local, grassroots game, Ford has had a long, if complicated association with senior amateur football in the area. Ford's car plant was established in Dagenham in 1924, the company having acquired a large area of marshland down by the Thames.

The car plant became a staple industry in the area and provided employment for generations of East London and Essex people. In 1952 the firm employed 40,000 workers at its Dagenham plant alone. If we add the thousands of individuals and small companies that supplied Ford, we can begin to imagine the importance of the company to the economic and cultural life of the area. After 50 years at Dagenham the plant closed in 2002, and today the Ford operation in Essex is limited to two small factories in Newbury Park and Basildon. The company now employs just 14,000 people in the whole of the UK, and in early 2009 it announced a further 850 redundancies (I am indebted to John Nevill of the Ford Motor Co. Ltd for providing background information and access to the firm's Warleigh archive).

Following the example of Tate & Lyle and others in providing sports facilities for their staff, Ford was unusual in that it helped to form two senior amateur clubs, Briggs's Sports FC and Ford Sports FC, both established in 1934. Briggs Motor Bodies (BMB) provided car bodies for Ford (later the two companies merged their operations), and Briggs Sports FC became one of the finest amateur sides in England. Subsidised by BMB, they regularly won the London and Spartan League titles and enjoyed success in County Cups, reaching the later stages of the FA Amateur Cup on a number of occasions but never actually winning that grand old competition. In 1952 the club moved from their original Victoria Road location, now the home ground of Dagenham & Redbridge FC, to the Rush Green site within the Ford factory complex. As many as 6,000 people used to crowd into the old Briggs's sports ground with its rustic stand and earth terraces. But when the club were invited to share Ford's new football facility, the temptation was too great. Briggs's shared the Rush Green ground with Ford Sports FC and continued to compete in amateur football at the highest level. Ford Sports FC were members of the London and Spartan Leagues but remained in the shadow of their more famous rivals, and never matched Briggs's crowd appeal – Briggs's were very much the team of the people. I don't suppose I will ever know why, but my dad followed the fortunes of Briggs's Sports FC even though he never saw them play. When I was a boy, in the early 1960s, it was the first result we looked for in the old pink classified edition of the *London Evening Standard*. People just did that then without really needing any tangible allegiance.

Ford's Rush Green sports ground occupied 28 acres within the company's factory gates at Dagenham, with facilities for a whole range of sporting activities. Alongside its two-storey, luxury clubhouse was a first-rate 'arena' pitch for the first team, with other pitches stretching out to the perimeter of the ground. With just a rope around three sides of the main pitch, the arena lacked the atmosphere of other senior amateur grounds, despite the quality of the clubhouse. But sport comes a poor second to business, and a development of the factory site swallowed up an area of Rush Green in the late 1950s, forcing the company's own team, Ford Sports, to take up residency at Old Dagenham Park. Ford did develop an alternative site off the A12 at Goodmayes, but not before the club finally decided in 1958 to throw in their lot with Brigg Sports. Ford United was the result of the merger of these two great amateur clubs.

There is evidence to suggest that the higher echelons of senior amateur soccer never really accepted what they saw as vulgar works teams that largely operated outside their control. Perhaps due to this, the newly merged club went into slow decline through the 1960s and 1970s, playing on inferior pitches and in front of small crowds. But I suspect that the decline had more to do with the running down of the company at Dagenham. Ford United later lost their identity entirely when they changed their name to Redbridge FC in the 1990s, aiming to gain support from the club's host borough.

The demise of Ford United occurred largely because the Ford Motor Company refused to grant the club more than a 12-month lease on the Rush Green ground. The Isthmian League (currently sponsored by Ryman) ruled the ground ineligible and demanded a more secure tenancy. The company refused to change its position (no business case) and to stay in the Isthmian League the club were forced to leave the home of their founders. Ford ceased its activities at Rush Green at the end of 2008 and leased the ground to West Ham United to use for training.

Briggs's Sports and Ford Sports football clubs are now no more than a fond memory, and we can only recognise their achievements and remember their distinctive contribution to senior amateur football in the area. Their successor, Redbridge FC, were rescued from their own financial difficulties by Sky

Sports in 1995, and they are known to this day by the old Briggs's Sports nickname 'The Motormen'. The greatest player to have played for Ford United was England international Peter Brabrook, who signed for Chelsea in 1954 and later played for West Ham and Leyton Orient. Brabrook played for England three times, including a match against Russia in the 1958 World Cup. He was a contemporary of Moore, Hurst and Peters at West Ham, and after retirement he returned to the club to prepare The Hammers' young star players, Frank Lampard, Joe Cole, Michael Carrick and Rio Ferdinand for careers with Chelsea and Manchester United.

Local clubs with windswept and muddy grounds and freezing changing rooms loved to be drawn away to the works clubs in Cup matches, just for the opportunity to play on the best grounds in grassroots football. Some of these clubs had their own industry national Cup competitions. One among them was the CMA Cup, a tournament for teams representing firms in the cable and wireless industry. I had the privilege of playing in this competition on a number of occasions, and not only were the pitches of Premier League standard but also we had both a referee and linesmen – unheard of in local football. The players were treated to a plunge bath, a sumptuous meal and free beer after the match rather than the cold-water troughs and hot tea of Wanstead Flats and Hackney Marshes. Sadly, most of these private grounds have been sold for development and only a small number remain, a further example of the collapse of a once thriving and proud sporting culture. We can only imagine what it was like.

In memoriam

The names of the old amateur leagues in the London area reveal the kinds of values that inspired their founders. The Isthmian, Spartan, Delphian and Athenian leagues conjure up images of a classical world of manly virtue, while their replacements, such as the Beezer Homes or Romford Roofing and Scaffold leagues, suggest a wholly different sporting ethic, but at least the league is no longer sponsored by the Rothman's tobacco giant. The original motto of the Isthmian League, founded in 1905, was 'honour sufficit' (honour suffices), and for many years they refused to award any trophies or medals to either League or Cup winners. With the onset of professionalism in the amateur game the League has lost its independence and has been restructured several times since the 1970s, and it is now part of the FA pyramid structure introduced in 2004.

Leytonstone FC were for nearly a hundred years stalwarts of the Isthmian League. Formed in 1886, the club's record is one of the most impressive in the long history of English amateur football. Always close rivals of their neighbours, Walthamstow Avenue, Leytonstone, in the course of their distinguished history, won the prestigious FA Amateur Cup in 1947, 1948 and 1968. Between the years of 1933 and 1952, in addition to winning the Amateur Cup twice, the club were Isthmian League champions a remarkable seven times. The club's ground on the high street was adjacent to the Midland Railway station and on Saturday afternoons you could watch the match from the station for the price of a platform ticket, so a small crowd would gather on the platform for every home game. The ground had one covered, corrugated-iron stand and three terraces that were open to the elements, and as 16-year-olds we paid the princely sum of 2d admission and a further 2d for a bag of Percy Dalton peanuts. The 5,000 or so loyal supporters were entertained by the Leyton Silver Band, and at half-time they were encouraged to throw their loose change into a stretcher carried round the pitch by willing club officials.

The Leytonstone pitch was always in excellent condition and was lovingly cared for by groundsman Alf Walters, who owned the flower shop next door to the High Road police station. In some ways the club were a breeding ground for Leyton Orient and produced many of the professional club's local players, including Frank Neary and Bunny Groves of the footballing Grove family. One of the great characters in the history of the club was Leon Joseph, who had a menswear shop under the arches near the railway station. With his good looks and fine singing voice, Joseph was a local heart-throb who sang regularly at the club's Saturday night socials. Much to the delight of the fans, the film star Jayne Mansfield made an appearance at the ground in 1962. It is said that she had an 'association' with one of the players, and it just might be that the player was young Leon Joseph.

My cousin Kenny married into a strong Leytonstone FC family. His wife Kath's father, Ernest Morgan, was club treasurer from the immediate post-war period up to the late 1950s. He was heavily involved in all the club's activities, which included children's parties, 'beanos' (day trips) and holidays. There were regular Bank Holiday outings to Dimchurch, Bognor Regis and Walton-on-Naze. Over Christmas 1954 the club stretched to a trip to Margate and an overnight stay at the delightfully named Kittiwake Hotel. From her account of her family's involvement with the club we can see just how much Leytonstone FC were part of the local community, much like their close neighbours, Walthamstow Avenue. Sadly, both of Kath's parents died when she and her siblings were quite young, so her memories of her parents' connection with Leytonstone are understandably sketchy. But one story stands out above all others. The club had a real live goat as their mascot. The goat lived in the back garden of the Morgans' house not far from the ground, and before every home match Kath's parents would walk the proud mascot along Leytonstone High Road to the ground, where it would be paraded on the pitch. The goat would be escorted back home after the game, much to the delight of local children out shopping with their parents. One of these youngsters might well have been Graham Gooch, who as a boy lived just up the road from Leytonstone's High Street ground. Later the Morgans moved a couple of miles up the road to Forest Gate, closer to the East End, but loyally continued the Saturday match-day ritual with, perhaps, the most curious club mascot in senior amateur football (I am grateful to Kath Emberson for passing on her childhood memories of Leytonstone FC and for kindly allowing access to some wonderful photographs of the club's activities during the 1950s).

Sadly, Leytonstone FC, these once proud bastions of amateur football, closed their doors in 1979 and their ground, full of rich football memories, was sold off for development. Leytonstone collapsed because they could not cope with the financial demands imposed in the 1970s by the introduction of player contracts, which signalled the end of senior amateur football in London. When Leytonstone FC perished so did the vigorous social life that had developed around the club. For many, the collapse of Leytonstone, Walthamstow and Ilford football clubs, along with many others, presaged the end of a rich and vibrant culture in East London.

Up the Avenue

Just like the vast majority of players in local league Saturday and Sunday football in the 1960s and 1970s, it is interesting that none of the teams in the works and companies leagues used to be paid 'boot money'. Today London's Amateur Football Combination (AFC), one of the largest leagues in Europe with over 100 clubs and 350 teams, prides itself on its pure amateur ethos and proudly promotes its strapline, the true 'Spirit of Football'. But all senior amateur clubs in the area made under-the-counter payments to their best players.

Illicit boot money disappeared when the professional/amateur distinction was finally abolished in the 1973/74 season. From then on, highly skilled and committed amateur footballers were able to enter into contracts with non-league clubs and be paid a legal wage. The biggest senior amateur clubs in East London and Essex - Walthamstow Avenue, Brentwood, Leyton, Leytonstone, Chelmsford, Dagenham and Barking - officially became non-league and, by implication, professional. These clubs became legitimate employers able to attract lucrative sponsorship deals both for the club and their players. Professional coaches were recruited and players became fitter and more professional in their outlook. One casualty of this long-overdue development was Sunday morning football, as most non-league contracts included a clause forbidding contracted players from playing on Sundays, to the detriment of the quality of the Sunday game.

The abolition of the amateur/professional distinction marked a fundamental difference between the laissez-faire attitude to amateur football of the 1960s and 1970s and the more hard-headed, commercially driven values of the 1980s and 1990s. In many respects the ending of boot money acts as an illustration of the differences between the careers of Bobby Moore and Graham Gooch, as we shall see. But first let us have a closer look at just what this mysterious boot money was in the senior amateur game.

Contrary to popular legend, clubs did not actually place brown envelopes in players' boots at the end of a game, but brown envelopes full of various amounts of cash were distributed discreetly, following midweek training or at some stage on the Saturday of the game. The better the player the greater the sum received and nobody complained, as players were delighted to supplement their weekly wages outside football with some welcome 'beer money'. In the 1960s the amounts would have been fairly modest - £30 for the best players, £5 for the rest. Win bonuses were awarded to players in the more successful teams, and this would boost a player's seasonal income considerably. The awarding of win bonuses often had comic consequences. An unexpected victory over one of the league's top teams would catch club directors by surprise, and envelopes were often distributed minus the well-earned win bonus, as there were no cash machines at that time from which to make urgent withdrawals. This left players seriously cheesed-off, taking the shine off an otherwise memorable performance. All the promises about being paid the following week in training came to nothing as players began gearing up for Saturday night. As always in the East End, cash was king.

This relaxed attitude to senior amateur football, with a charm all its own, was really too good to be true, and dramatic change came with the hard commercial values of the Thatcher-inspired 1980s, when greed was good. A consequence of lucrative player contracts was that, overnight, decent non-league players in top senior amateur football were faced with the decision to give up their day jobs as plumbers, cab drivers or city clerks and become full-time professionals, which some did. But most players continued to supplement their wages and salaries with the extra money they now earned legitimately from football.

Now legally professional, the bigger clubs were able to attract serious sponsorship and raise cash, either through fundraising or bar takings, and began to attract the best players, with disastrous consequences for the less well-positioned clubs. In the late 1970s and early 1980s many senior amateur clubs in East London and Essex followed the national trend and either folded altogether or, where there was a will, amalgamated with a neighbouring club in a similar plight. The strongest survived and prospered, while the weak or ill-managed went to the wall. Clubs in the area with national reputations and distinguished histories disappeared. FA Amateur winners Walthamstow Avenue FC, Leytonstone FC, Ilford FC and Brentwood FC, among others, all folded, their grounds bulldozed to make way for inhospitable and barren housing estates and soulless supermarkets, often involving very shady deals between estate agents, local developers and planners.

There ought to be an annual minute's silence at all local park matches in Walthamstow in memory of the Avenue. Walthamstow is in the London Borough of Waltham Forest, a place that sits neatly on the cusp of East London and Essex, comprising the formerly independent Essex County boroughs of Chingford, Walthamstow, Leyton and Leytonstone. Peter Blake, who designed the cover of The Beatles' *Sgt. Pepper* album, was born there, as was the nineteenth-century philosopher William Morris; Johnny Dankworth, the great jazzman, is a local and went to the same school as Doug Insole; Andrew Lloyd Webber hails from Leyton; and Ian Dury attended Walthamstow Art College. The 1990s pop band East 17 (later regrouping as E-17), named after the borough postcode, are perhaps the borough's most famous citizens, and they even named their debut album *Walthamstow* – you can't get much more local than that. But in 2009 the band's status as the borough's biggest name received a challenge from an unlikely source. The celebrated contemporary artist and Turner Prize winner, Grayson Perry, completed his new work, 'The Walthamstow Tapestries'. Grayson, whose studio is based in the borough, was born into a working-class family in Chelmsford and attended the prestigious King Edward V1 Grammar School in the town. To add to his local credentials, Grayson was recently appointed as Professor of Fine Art at the University of East London. Perhaps Walthamstow will become the new London centre for the arts as a result of Grayson's new work. Somehow I doubt it, however, and it is more likely that Grayson will choose to stay close to his roots. But it is a sign of the times that a working-class London borough famous for its greyhound-racing stadium and Walthamstow Avenue FC is now at the centre of the international art world.

Walthamstow is a perfect case study for looking at the kind of social and cultural change that enveloped London in the years between 1960 and 2000. Bobby Moore and Graham Gooch were born and raised nearby and practised their skills in the local school playgrounds. Later David Beckham and Teddy Sheringham followed their peerless predecessors. Waltham Forest is a diverse borough and parts of Leyton and Leytonstone can be described as 'inner city' and have all the attendant problems associated with poverty and alienation. The inhabitants of the east of the borough must look with envy at the relatively affluent folk to the west in Chingford, still simmering for being dumped out of Essex in the 1965 local government reorganisation. Chingford is perhaps best known for its former MP, right-wing Tory ideologue and Thatcher enforcer, Lord Tebbit, and National Front supporting tennis player, Buster Mottram – not much to be proud of there. Actually, the real virtues of Chingford are found in its broad avenues out by Epping Forest, lined by lovely old Edwardian houses - the jewel in the borough's crown. If Leyton and Leytonstone are tough, multi-ethnic and inner city, Chingford is all fast-fading gentility and seething resentment.

Walthamstow is caught somewhere in the middle and is rightly proud of its heritage. The great Victorian socialist and reformer William Morris was born in the streets around the Avenue ground, and William Morris House, a museum dedicated to his life and work in Lloyd's Park, is a cultural highlight of East London. In 2009 the Williams Morris Society was successful in attracting a substantial grant from the Heritage Lottery Fund for a full refurbishment of the house and grounds, so visitors will soon be able to take in the 'Beckham Trail' and experience the aesthetic delights of William Morris House all in the same day.

Some of us were sent to William Morris School in Walthamstow back in the 1960s as a reward for passing the 11+ - some reward. A consolation for an otherwise miserable experience, including the more vicious forms of corporal punishment handed out by staff, was the annual school Christmas Carol Service in the delightful twelfth-century St Mary's Church in the heart of Walthamstow village. The village is now a conservation area - a delightful mix of fifteenth-century timber-framed houses, a group of seventeenth-century almshouses and the wonderful Vestry House Museum, known locally as the 'Ancient House', a former workhouse that has been a local history museum since the 1930s.

The borough's football club, Walthamstow Avenue FC, was founded in 1900 and played most of their football in the amateur Isthmian League. An urban myth states that to qualify to play for the club you had to prove that you actually lived in an 'avenue'. Who knows! In 1946 the Avenue marked the return to football at Green Pond Road with a match against a Soviet side called the Russian Dynamos, a certain sign of the ambitious nature of the club. They won the FA Amateur Cup twice, in 1952 and 1961. The 1952 final was the first match at Wembley to be played in front of 100,000 spectators. In 1952/53 the club reached the fourth round of the FA Cup, beating Watford and Stockport County on the way, before drawing 1-1 with Football League champions Manchester United in front of 80,000 fans at Old Trafford. They lost the replay at Highbury 5-2, with Jim Lewis Jnr scoring twice, and the old Arsenal ground was adorned with the Avenue's black and blue colours on what was undoubtedly the greatest moment in the club's long and distinguished history, and in front of 53,000 fans.

The Avenue goal at Old Trafford was scored by the incomparable East London football legend Jim Lewis, an immensely talented centre forward – it was unthinkable that it could be anyone else. In two periods at the club, Jim scored 423 goals in 522 appearances. Now 82 years old and living out in Essex, Jim Lewis was the most successful amateur footballer of his generation, and he also played cricket for Chingford CC. Born in Hackney in 1927, Jim signed for Chelsea soon after the Manchester United replay, following a telephone call from the Chelsea manager, Ted Drake. Lewis never did turn professional, unlike his Avenue former colleague and distinguished Chelsea teammate, Derek Saunders. It is important to remember that the financial disparity between professional and amateur in the 1950s and 1960s was minimal. Lewis combined the duties of his day job as a salesman with the not inconsiderable commitment of playing in the 1954/55 Championship-winning Chelsea side. These were the days of the maximum wage for professionals, with a sizeable reduction in off-season. Lewis's father, Jim Lewis Snr, also played for Chelsea, and he gained a full England cap in 1939, later opening a successful and locally renowned sports shop in the borough. The shop was just down the road from the Royal Standard in Forest Road, famous in the 1960s and 1970s for hosting residencies by the likes of Danny Le Roux, Ray Martine and Mike Reid. Of course, back then there was live entertainment of high quality somewhere every night of the week in Walthamstow and in every East London borough.

With the great Roy Bentley installed as the regular Chelsea centre forward, Lewis played as a goalscoring outside or inside left and scored 40 goals in 95 appearances for Chelsea, where he stayed until 1958. Perhaps the most enduring tribute to this greatest of amateur footballers of the 1950s and early 1960s was his 49 caps for the England amateur side and his appearances for the Great Britain teams in the 1952, 1956 and 1960 Olympic Games. It is an extraordinary sporting story by any standards. It is to be hoped that Jim Lewis will be one of many, largely forgotten, real East London sporting heroes whose achievements will be celebrated at the 2012 London Olympic Games. There ought to be at least a blue plaque – a statue would be better - dedicated to the memory of Jim Lewis on the impressive approach road to Walthamstow Town Hall.

Other notable Avenue players include Vic Groves, who played for the club in the early 1950s before signing for Arsenal in 1955 for the princely sum at that time of £23,000. Groves had a solid career in the professional game as a goalscoring winger. His nephew, Perry Groves, played for Arsenal in the 1980s and 1990s, again as a penetrating left winger with a decent goalscoring record. Vic Groves was never awarded a full England cap, but he played several times for the England Amateur side during his time at the Avenue, where he was a key player in the Isthmian League championship wins in the 1950s.

The great Essex and England cricket all-rounder, Trevor Bailey, played for Leytonstone and the Avenue in the early 1950s. With Leytonstone he won the Essex Senior Cup, the Thameside Cup and the London Senior Cup, but he failed to win the greatest prize, the FA Amateur Cup. He achieved his dream with the Avenue, where his determined wing play was a vital part of the side's success in 1951/52. In his first season with the Avenue they won the FA Amateur Cup at Wembley, and in the following season they reached the latter stages of the FA Cup. Born in Westcliff-on-Sea, Trevor Bailey was one of the last international cricketers to play football at a senior level. Sadly, the injuries he picked up while playing football began to threaten his cricket career, and he gave up the winter game the season after the Avenue's great FA Cup run. Bailey's great friend and Essex teammate, Doug Insole, a Cambridge Blue from 1946 to 1949, played for the Avenue in 1943 and went on to have a distinguished playing career, first with Pegasus and then with the Corinthians for 12 seasons. The Corinthians' home ground was the Surrey Oval, where the FA Cup final was played for several seasons. Insole remembers crowds of 6-7,000 people turning out for games at the Oval and over 12,000 for

Cup ties. Insole had England amateur trials, but up against the likes of George Robb, Bill Slater and Jimmy Bloomfield his opportunities were always going to be a little restricted.

Insole's reminiscences of his playing days at the Avenue are interesting. He recalls that the team never had a manager, even in its most successful period. Senior players such as Jim Lewis or Danny Groves gave the team talk and left the rest to the good sense of the players. These memories of one of the greats of East London and Essex sport are priceless. Insole regarded Leslie Compton as the greatest centre half in the country after the war, while his brother, the more famous Denis, played professionally for Arsenal on the left wing, earning £8 each week plus a £2 win bonus. Compton, claims Insole, would have made more money playing cricket in those days, earning £945 for a five-month tour of Australia in 1948. Insole reveals that he regularly captained a football team in the 1950s for his old friend, the Walthamstow sports legend Arthur Sedgewick. Regular players for the Doug Insole XI included Essex cricketer Gordon Barker, Ron Greenwood, John Lyall, the Spurs inside forward Tommy Harmer, Trevor Bailey, Jimmy Bloomfield and George Curtis, who had a distinguished career at Coventry City.

Jim Lewis Jnr and his Walthamstow Avenue teammates, including Trevor Bailey, were certainly celebrated back in their day. Avenue's home games at their wonderful old Green Pond Road ground regularly hosted over 10,000 (Trevor Bailey confirms this in his autobiography, Wickets, Catches and the Odd Run, Willow Books, 1986, p.199) people in the late 1950s and early 1960s and was used as the football venue for the 1945 London Olympic Games. Locals loved the club and football was not the only attraction. The cavernous space under the stadium's main stand accommodated the dressing rooms, a spacious area with four full-size snooker tables, numerous dartboards and a bar stretching the length of the main stand. The ground was open seven nights a week for darts and snooker matches, or for members to enjoy a quiet pint or two in the evenings. Sociologists could tell us about the permanent damage done to the local community when the ground was demolished in 1988, the club being dissolved and amalgamated into what became known as Redbridge Forest FC. Leytonstone and Ilford went the same way and followed the Avenue into football oblivion. It would not have mattered one jot to

Walthamstow people that Redbridge Forest was to become Dagenham & Redbridge FC, later promoted to the Football League. If anybody thinks that this particular kind of football hooliganism, driven by greed and envy, is simply just business, it is worth pointing out that on Christmas morning 1963 20,000 people crammed into Leytonstone FC's High Street ground to watch the local derby between the home side and Walthamstow Avenue, on a day without buses or trains, and at a time when few people owned cars (Bailey (1986), p.199). Sadly, Walthamstow Avenue FC died a slow and painful death, playing their last game in 1989 in, of all places, Borehamwood.

Losing your local football club is bad enough, but the fact that the Avenue had such a distinguished history and enthusiastic following, and was such a fundamental part of the life of the borough, compounds the loss. However, things do change, for whatever reason, and move on – it happens. The real frustration lies in what replaced this: a callous, commercial culture that preached the idea of community and neighbourhood but in reality had a very different set of values and imperatives, largely driven by shadowy people intent on quick profits who rode roughshod over the lives of local people. This was happening in most cities across the UK in the late 1980s and 1990s and continues to the present day.

We see this in what happened to the second great stage of sport in Walthamstow, the famous greyhound-racing stadium. Both made a huge contribution to the community life of this hard-pressed, working-class London borough. 'The Stow' was sold for redevelopment in 2008, and in 2009 the iconic dog stadium will be razed to the ground to be replaced by yet another desperately needed retail park, designed to empty the pockets and credit card accounts of local people. It is to be hoped that eleventh-hour attempts by activists to save the old place will succeed. But the loss of this stadium is a further example of how the sporting heart and soul of this honest and hard-working area of East London has been torn out.

Londoners, however, are not easily defeated and some responded bravely to their loss. At the same time as these acts of wanton destruction were being perpetrated on the community, some local councils in the area were reacting positively to the consequences of commercial greed. Six new indoor sport and leisure centres were opened by the London Borough of

Waltham Forest in the 1980s, usually with all-weather, floodlit multi-sport pitches and new, modern, indoor swimming pools. This trend of local councils taking the lead in the provision of high-quality community sports facilities was replicated all over East London and Essex, and probably throughout the UK. Gradually in the 1980s participation in sport and leisure became accessible and affordable for all members and sectors of the community. Disability and age awareness increased, and gender and ethnic sensitivities were respected and incorporated into the design of leisure programmes. The result was an expansion of provision that runs counter to the presumptions contained in discussions about obesity in the young and young families.

The democratic impulse behind the increased offer of leisure provision by local authorities is laudable. But did this impressive expansion of local authority leisure provision from the 1980s have the desired effect of increasing participation in a range of sports and put sport and leisure at the heart of the community where it once proudly stood? Well, in Waltham Forest I'm afraid to reveal that the answer is probably, no! Research by the borough in 2005 (LBWF, Sports & Physical Activity Strategy 2006-12) showed that fewer people in Waltham Forest took regular exercise than anywhere in the country as a whole. Just 25 per cent of local adults took 30 minutes' exercise at least five times a week, the national figure being 32 per cent. Despite these disappointing figures, leisure centres in the borough are well used, with 1.37 million visits in 2004/05, above average for the capital. Satisfaction levels were acceptable. The only conclusion we can draw from this is that the same highly motivated people are using the shiny, well-equipped new centres more often, and the policies of accessibility and widening participation have been resisted by people in the borough who would benefit most. Perhaps without the unifying and community-oriented local institutions like Walthamstow Avenue FC, Briggs's Sports and others, which in their day attracted tens of thousands of spectators to home games, people will resort to more sedentary activities. The descendants of people who once at least watched live football now sit in the 'modernised' Prince Albert in Chingford watching Sky TV and eating pizza, or alternatively are to be seen strolling the gilded halls of the Bluewater Shopping Centre, further widening the gap between fans and the players that Paul Ormerod has identified. There is a hole in the heart of society that a vibrant sporting culture once, at least partly, filled. This culture is in danger of collapse and it is to be hoped that the Olympic planners have factored this into their thinking for 2012.

CHAPTER 4
ON THE SIDE OF THE ANGELS

Bobby Moore attended Tom Hood Grammar School in Leyton in the mid-1950s, after duly passing his 11+ at the primary school near his home in Barking. He would have had a longish journey to school from home, but it wasn't unusual at the time for bright young people from working-class areas to travel up to an hour to and from school, either by school bus or public transport. Grammar schools were generally situated a few miles from the kind of neighbourhood from which Moore and others emerged at the time. The alternative for those who either failed or didn't take the 11+ in the late 1950s would have been the local secondary modern, but Moore, being a bright and willing lad, was spared this particular educational experience.

Graham Gooch attended Norlington High School in Leyton, a decent comprehensive with dedicated and highly skilled teachers. By the time Gooch reached secondary school age the borough's grammar schools had been abolished, and the young Graham and his parents were spared the stresses of the 11+. Although a useful schoolboy footballer, Gooch was clearly an even better cricketer and he received support and encouragement in this direction from his teachers and his father. Like Ravinder Bopara, another East London cricketing prodigy, Gooch's talent was developed in club cricket rather than at school.

It was natural, as a supremely gifted young footballer, that Moore would sign for his local professional club West Ham United and, as a promising young batsman, be courted by Essex County Cricket Club. Doug Insole recently said that he thought Moore was a better cricketer than Geoff Hurst, and offered the 16-year-old future England football captain a contract with Essex. Everything appeared very simple in those days, but much has changed since our two sports-mad youngsters attended their local schools in Waltham Forest, unaware that both would progress to captain their school, district and national teams in their respective sports.

In July 1966 Moore demonstrated, perhaps more than anyone before or since, that sport is at the heart of British culture and society. We should not be surprised then that sport provides one of the cornerstones of school life. Perhaps this is understating the role of sport in schools, as, rather than merely forming an important part of the curriculum, sport in most schools is fundamental to the ethos and purpose of the institution. Time allocated to physical education on the national curriculum has gradually been reduced since Moore lifted the World Cup, but schools continue to value sport as a way of reinforcing their ethos and for promoting the institution itself. Schools also provide most young people with their first experience of playing sport, and it is where their ability and enthusiasm first emerge. Clubs always come later.

Over the past 40 years, a period of accelerating social and cultural change, schools have been used as an instrument of social policy. Inner-city schools have become an ideological battleground, and school sport has suffered more than most at the hands of overzealous policy makers. Depending on your political perspective, school sport is either too competitive or not competitive enough, elitist or an occasion for innocent healthy exercise. We all have our own memories of PE at school; the cold showers and muddy fields and the embarrassment and pointlessness of it all. But schools are required to provide all young people with the opportunity for healthy exercise and developing their fitness. Good schools and sympathetic PE teachers who handle vulnerable youngsters with sensitivity will succeed in providing an experience that all can enjoy.

Representing your school at sport used to be regarded as an honour. If you were selected to play for the school football or cricket team you felt a sense of pride. A headteacher colleague of mine used to say that schools were ten years behind the times. By this he meant that the values schools promote are out of step with those of the communities they serve. In this view schools are not the pioneers of social and cultural change but the last defenders of a discarded morality. Of course, as with all such broad claims, there is some truth in it and also much that is wide of the mark. Schools usually have a clearly defined set of ideals, including non-negotiable principles such as equality, tolerance and fairness, but these are seen by some parents and commentators as feeble, and worse, trendy. In refusing to betray these principles, teachers would claim to be ahead of the culture, and it is not always obvious to teachers that the world outside their gates supports them in defending their liberal instincts. During the 25 years I spent working in schools and other areas of education, it certainly seemed as though we were defending something that no longer interested students, parents or the wider community. We thought we were leading but in actual fact had fallen behind, and in this sense my old headteacher was right.

The recent history of sport in schools illustrates how difficult it is for teachers to hold to a set of values that they know to be right but that are regularly challenged by students, parents and others. I would not want to overstate the case, because in my own professional experience the majority of young people and parents get behind their school, trust the staff, and accept, often reluctantly, the rules and regulations that schools are obliged to impose. However, there is mounting evidence to suggest that the authority of schools is coming under increasing pressure, and teachers are beginning to feel under siege, particularly those involved in running school football teams. In his 2008 New Year message, George Fry, Chairman of the London Schools' FA, felt obliged to take a stand against the current problems facing school sport:

> *At the recent Committee Meeting, I was appalled and saddened to hear about a number of serious incidents, which had occurred at our Individual Schools' Competitions matches. Some of the reported disturbances resulted in serious injuries and the involvement of the police. These unacceptable incidents occurred not only on the field of play but also involved extremely bad behaviour after matches around dressing rooms, social areas and team transport.*
> *- London Schools' FA, Chairman's Message, published on the LSFA website, December 2008.*

Serious injuries, appallingly bad behaviour and police involvement are not the kinds of things that we normally associate with school sport. The London Schools FA (LSFA), in existence for over 100 years, is having to deal with these worrying incidents with increasing frequency in games under its jurisdiction. A further example reinforces Mr Fry's concerns.

The English Schools FA's (ESFA's) Under 15 semi-final

between Plymouth and London Blackheath in May 2008 was abandoned following a brawl between players and spectators, which left a linesman unconscious. Both teams were thrown out of the competition and replaced by the two losing semi-finalists. The ESFA has banned both Plymouth and Blackheath from its national competitions. An FA investigation found both teams equally responsible for the outrage ('Schools teams kicked out after brawl', Sunday Independent, May 2008). This occurred on a peaceful spring afternoon in Tavistock, a delightful market town in rural Devon. The area of London around Blackheath is a place of contrasts – expensive villas owned by wealthy bankers with huge mortgages sit close by housing estates blighted by drug use and violent crime. Plymouth has the latter, but not the former. The irony of the young representatives of Plymouth and Blackheath taking out their anger on a quiet rural town in Devon is not lost.

These incidents are far from rare today and are on the increase, but it is shocking that this is happening in schools' football. As George Fry pointed out in his message,

> *... sportsmanship .... has been the byword for schools' football for more than 100 years.*

So why is this happening now? It would be easy to blame our old friend Margaret Thatcher and the way she promoted selfishness and individualism as virtuous values in our culture. But that was a long time ago and, like all major shifts in social behaviour, the reasons are more nuanced and complex. There has been a flurry of reports over the past couple of years on the state of childhood in the UK in the early part of the twenty-first century.

A UNICEF report on child well-being, published in early 2007, looked at a number of indicators from 2000 and 2003, including poverty, family relationships and health. The report concludes that underinvestment and a 'dog eat dog' society are to blame for Britain's underperformance against other countries such as Sweden, Denmark and Finland. The report states:

> *By comparing the performance of countries we see what is possible with a commitment to supporting every child to fulfill his or her*

potential.
- UNICEF Report Card 7, 'Child Poverty in Perspective: An Overview of Child Well-being in Rich Countries', 14th February 2007.

In response to the report Bob Reitemeier, Chief Executive of the Children's Society, said:

We simply cannot ignore these shocking findings. UNICEF's report is a wake-up call to the fact that, despite being a rich country, the UK is failing children and young people in a number of crucial ways.
- B. Reitemeier, Chief Executive, Childrens' Society, 'Response to UNICEF Report' Children's Society website, www.mylife.uk.com, 14th February 2007.

Professor Sir Aynsley-Green, the Children's Commissioner for England, responded in a similar way:

We are turning out a generation of young people who are unhappy, unhealthy, engaging in risky behaviour, who have poor relationships with their family ... who have low expectations and don't feel safe.
- Professor Sir Aynsely-Green, 02/14/2007) 'UK is Accused of Failing Children', www.news.bbc.co.uk

Those of us who have been involved in the education of children over the past 30 years will recognise some of these findings but find others more difficult to accept. Such overgeneralised reports lack any depth of understanding of the individual lives of children at home and at school, and many teachers and parents won't recognise the picture of childhood that is being painted in the report. However, despite some initial scepticism, the evidence begins to mount.

A Good Childhood

A Good Childhood, a Children's Society report published in February 2009, supports the UNICEF findings. The report looked at what it described as "massive changes in our way of life" over the past 20 years (such as increased parental break-up), and the "excessively individualistic ethos" of contemporary British society, both of which are key factors in the increased difficulties faced by children today. Jill Kirby from the Centre for Policy Studies points out that

> *90 per cent of children born in the UK in 1958 were still living with both parents at 16. Now fewer than 65 per cent do so. In 1958 only 5 per cent of children were born outside marriage. Now the figure is 43 per cent.*
> *- J. Kirby, 'Childrens' lives harder today' The Sunday Times, 8th February 2009.*

By any standards these are significant and will have had a profound effect on the lives of children. Other changes in the period from 1960 include the fact that 70 per cent of mothers now work, compared with 25 per cent in the late 1970s. One out of every three 16-year-olds now lives apart from their father. The Children's Society's report claims that young people's lives are now more complex and difficult and this is the largest survey into childhood conducted in the UK, with over 35,000 contributors. The report's findings appear counter-intuitive. Children today are better educated, have more possessions and, in many senses, are given more freedom than previous generations of young people. And yet it is stated that too many are unhappy and feel unsafe. The report's authors conclude that children should be loved within a framework of discipline and support, and sets out recommendations to parents, teachers and the government on how they can better care for children.

If we take these two reports to be, in large part, an accurate picture of childhood in the early twenty-first century, can we assume that a link exists between their findings and the increasing violence in school football and the concerns expressed by the Chairman of the London Schools FA in his message? In other words, is school sport contributing to the problem identified by UNICEF and the Children's Society, or does it provide an effective means of support for children in the way the reports recommend?

We have some evidence to identify the time that children today spend playing sport or taking some form of exercise. In summer 2008 the Department for Children, Schools and Families (DCSF) commissioned an independent research survey to track the take-up of sporting opportunities by 5 to 16-year-olds (DCSF, PE and Sport Survey 2008/09, online publication, www.publications.dcsf.gov.uk). The survey was conducted among all schools in the School Sport Partnership Programme – a club/school links initiative. By 2007 all 21,727 maintained schools were in the programme. The survey had a 99.6 per cent response rate. The survey findings show that real progress has been made since a similar survey in 2003/04. For example, the earlier survey recorded that 62 per cent of pupils participated in at least two hours of PE and school sport per week. The 2008 survey shows that this level of participation has increased to 90 per cent. The greatest improvements have been in Years 1 to 4, while Years 10 and 11 have shown only a modest increase from a low baseline figure.

Pupils spent an average of 103 minutes per week doing PE and school sport in 2003/04, and 118 minutes in 2008. The report shows that an impressive 78 per cent of pupils participated in at least 120 minutes of curriculum time, compared with 34 per cent in the first survey. Schools have developed more effective links with clubs, which will be discussed in more detail later, and the number of sports available to all pupils has increased. Despite these positive figures the survey highlights these worrying trends:

- The best performing schools in terms of PE and school sport tend to be in more affluent areas.
- The best performing schools have a low participation of children from ethnic minorities.
- There is a disappointing decrease in participation within the age range of 14 to 16.

The survey report concludes that much has been achieved in the five-year period, particularly at primary school level, where links between schools and local clubs are most effective. Progress in secondary schools has been more modest and this will need to be addressed. An underlying assumption behind these figures is that there is no necessary link between participation in PE and school sport and the selling of local authority and school sports grounds for development, which has occurred in schools throughout London. But we get nothing from the survey about the excellence or otherwise of school sport, teachers' current views on competition, the quality of facilities, the qualifications of staff, or issues about discipline. There is nothing either about participation rates when young people leave school. How many continue to play sport after 16?

The survey's results, which appear encouraging, are at odds with the reports by UNICEF and the Children's Society regarding the state of children's lives in twenty-first-century Britain. More physical education has not resulted in improved health or behaviour among children in working-class urban areas, and there is a worrying drop-out among the 14-16 age group. We do know that school sport has changed radically since Bobby Moore and Graham Gooch represented their Waltham Forest schools. In some senses school sport today has improved beyond recognition. Schools today have well-equipped indoor sports facilities and all-weather, floodlit playing areas, and PE as a subject is taught much more sensitively and fairly than in the past. The causes of the problems relating to the health of young people, violent and intimidating behaviour in team sports, and gang culture on the streets, will not be found in schools themselves but in the world that begins outside their gates.

Teachers would have gained encouragement from a report published in early 2009 and based on the findings of a group of Oxford University researchers, which argues that, contrary to the 'broken Britain' thesis, family life is actually becoming more cohesive and will continue do so for the next 20 years:

> *You've got parents devoting more time to their children, parents and adult children staying close, and husbands and wives supporting each other more than ever – the closeness of the family is helping to draw society together.*
> *- Michael Moynagh (2009), Changing Lives, Changing Business, Economic and Social Research Council/Oxford University.*

This revival of the nuclear family has occurred as a result of women achieving greater equality in the workplace and by better informed parents deciding to concentrate harder on bringing up their children. The report's findings run counter to the claims that Britain's children are among the unhealthiest and unhappiest in the Western world. According to the report. working fathers are spending half an hour a day more with their children, compared with 40 minutes in the mid-1980s. In addition, working women are with their children for nearly three hours each day, a significant increase over the past 40 years. As well as greater mutual support between husbands and wives, grandparents are playing a greater part in family life.

The report goes on to claim that fathers are increasingly more involved with their children, contributing to childcare, cooking, cleaning and shopping. Moynagh explains the reason for this:

It makes economic sense for the domestic chores and childcare to be shared more equally because, increasingly, the woman's earnings are equal to or higher than the man's. ... the popular view is that families are not spending time together, but the number of families eating a meal together every night doubled from 12 per cent in the 1960s to 20 per cent in 2002.

You only have to visit Hackney Marshes' and Wanstead Flats' playing fields on Sunday mornings throughout the year to see that the authors of this report have got it about right. Across both grounds you will see family groups either watching junior games or, as a family, watching their mothers and fathers play football. The family unit is not as broken as the doomsayers claim; on the contrary, as the report shows, families are spending more time together. However, the Oxford University research does not contradict the findings in the UNICEF and Children's Society research. What all three reports show is that British society is not crumbling but is growing increasingly polarised. As the Oxford reports warns us:

Households that do not stay together will be increasingly likely to fall victim to poverty, benefit dependency and unhappiness.

This pretty much hits the nail on the head and shows very clearly that the problems in school football highlighted by the Chairman of the London Schools FA are the result of sharp divisions in our urban centres rather than a more general malaise in society. Bobby Moore and Graham Gooch grew up in a time when family life in East London was more settled and conventional, with parental roles more clearly defined. School catchment areas would have been less volatile and more stable, allowing schools to be clearer in what they needed to achieve. In many primary schools in East London there is a huge turnover of children from Year 1 to Year 6. In one school I am familiar with, out of the 75 pupils who started together in Year 1, only 25 completed all five years. This level of instability makes life very difficult for both teachers and pupils, and makes teaching sport particularly difficult.

In the 25 years I was involved as a teacher in football and cricket in schools most problems associated with bad behaviour or ill-discipline were caused by parents and not by the players themselves. Referees regularly had to calm partisan parents, and on many occasions teachers received a hail of abuse when substituting a child that was thought by his parents to be the next Bobby Moore. It was not uncommon for scuffles to break out between parents 'supporting' opposing teams, and this kind of parental indiscipline has been increasing over the past ten years. I cannot recall a single incident of such behaviour in London in the 1970s and 1980s. Teaching in East London at the time, I regularly took football and cricket teams on Saturday mornings. Almost always school football on Saturday mornings meant Hackney Marshes. Fleets of coaches appeared in the car park at around 10.00 a.m., although my teams used to appear in fleets of taxis – not because the school was in a particularly affluent area but due to the fact that many of the boys' parents were cab drivers. Teachers were always greeted with respect and were allowed some distance. I can remember one taxi-driving parent remarking to our Head, who took the First Year third team, that he must have the best job in the world running his school. Today you might hear a different parental view about teaching. The FA's current 'Respect' campaign, designed to improve both player and spectator behaviour, is particularly aimed at parents of children representing school teams. Respect for players, teachers, other parents and referees is what the FA's campaign is seeking to achieve.

In his foreword to the 2008/09 handbook of the Essex County Schools FA, Chairman Mike Spinks asks colleagues to draw up Codes of Conduct for parents who attend matches to sign and makes various recommendations for sports teachers regarding behaviour:

> *... consider having all supporters on one side of the pitch and the coaches and substitutes on the opposite touchline. ... Within the family of schools football I guess we do not have so many problems with our players ... as teachers we should be able to exert control over*

our teams ... we have all sorts of sanctions we can apply if behaviour falls below our personal levels of expectation. ... Spectator behaviour, however, is a different matter and, if we are honest, an increasing cause of concern.

It is sad to report that recent incidents I have heard about or have witnessed personally were almost always at football matches. During the 20 years that I coached cricket and basketball to all age groups I cannot remember a single parental problem. In 2005 my Plymouth school's Under 19 team played St Bonaventures of East London in the quarter-final of the All England Championship. Our school sports hall was packed to the rafters and the atmosphere was electric. We lost the game by two points and it is difficult to imagine a more competitive match at that level. The behaviour of both players and parents was exemplary, as it always was, and the players socialised after the game, mixing together comfortably. What is it about football? Society's problems seem to haunt our national game.

The DCSF very clearly believes that its policies on participation in sport at school are working and, moreover, that sport is a positive factor in children's lives. The school sports survey report concludes:

PE and school sport play an increasingly important role in school life. They help to raise standards, improve behaviour and health, increase attendance and develop social skills.

I doubt that civil servants at the DCSF attend school football matches, have ever carried out weapon searches, or have taken a group of 16-year-olds 200 miles from East London to an away match in Devon. Neither will they have read the 2009 'New Year Message' from the Chairman of the London Schools FA. However, despite Mr Fry's concerns, most staff involved with school sport believe passionately that they are making a positive, even decisive, difference to young people's lives. They would accept the DCSF's findings, although recognising the force of the claims made by UNICEF and the Children's Society. Primary teachers will be encouraged by the increased participation while secondary teachers will be more sceptical of the report's conclusions.

The *Wolfenden Report*

Back in the 1950s a government-commissioned report was published that had a deep and lasting effect on the way we provide sport and leisure opportunities for young people. The *Wolfenden Report* of 1960 laid out a set of recommendations that form the basis of local authority policy on sport and leisure (Central Council of Physical Recreation (CCPR), Wolfenden Report, 1960). The report was commissioned partly in response to the Notting Hill riots in 1958, and by the growing perception that a fundamental review was needed on the cultural, leisure and sporting opportunities provided by local authorities for young people outside of school. The report was largely aimed at the youth service, as was the later *Albermarle Report*. Today most if not all cash-strapped local authorities have reduced their youth service to skeletal proportions, leaving only a few heroic individuals to deal with the increasing issues associated with young people in the twenty-first century. But the *Wolfenden Report* continues to influence current practice in three major ways:

1. in changing the way that local authorities think about sport and leisure provision;
2. in influencing the way in which schools, clubs and governing bodies structure their provision; and
3. in forcing schools, clubs and sports bodies to think about the ways they could work together.

The report identified weaknesses in post-school provision and in the relations between schools and clubs. In accepting the importance of play, the report recognised that sport could have a positive impact on the lives of young people. It identified a "clear need for more playing facilities, especially for indoor games and sports, including women's teams," and recommended that local authorities open at least four new indoor centres for multi-sports activities for young people. Now all local authorities have leisure departments and leisure teams that, in many ways, are acting like specialist youth workers. The number of local authority-controlled leisure centres has increased 20-fold since 1960. It is interesting to note that Newham Council has four local authority-controlled leisure centres offering a broad and accessible programme for young people and adults. All young people in the borough receive free entry to the centres through Newham's 'Gold Card' scheme. In some respects, the 1980s-inspired drive to sell off school and council playing fields has been offset by new indoor facilities and all-weather, floodlit pitches.

The other significant influence on sport and leisure in schools, clubs and local authorities was the setting up by the new Labour Government in 1989 of the Priority Action Team (PAT 10) and their policy document, *Sporting Futures for All*. In its own way, this lesser-known initiative may have far more influence on school sport and the relationship between schools and clubs than the *Wolfenden Report*. PAT 10 took sport in the community to another political level in an attempt to drive up participation rates among young people. More than this, sport was identified by the Blair government as having a unifying role in society. It was vital for policy makers that sport should contribute to a number of their key policy objectives which linked to other PAT priorities, in the interests of 'joined up' political thinking. These general priorities included neighbourhood renewal, social inclusion, crime reduction, health awareness, educational improvement and youth unemployment. This was a real departure from previous thinking about the role between schools, sport and society. The Blair government decided that Lottery money could be used for the development of sport in the UK. Sport England was set up to administer and share the Lottery funds directed to sport, and successful applications had to show that their projects satisfied the necessary criteria. These included disability access, increased participation across gender and ethnic-based groups, community benefit and a sports development policy in every bid. Successful projects had to be researched thoroughly, show evidence of need and be supported by their local authority, which was required to have a sports development plan of its own. The Lottery funding scheme was hugely ambitious and tough on applicants. Lottery funding was also channelled through sport governing bodies like the FA and its offshoot, the Football Foundation, which also received money from the Premier League. Grassroots sports did benefit in the first few years of Sport England, before the demands of elite sport began to get the lion's share of the money. The 2012 Olympics should see this trend continue, although there should be considerable benefits for community sport in East London, providing the Olympic heritage issue is properly managed.

Schools do not operate in a social or political vacuum and are subject to the policy whim of national local government. Sport in schools is no exception to this rule, and in many respects the changes have been welcome. PE teachers are much more sensitive to gender and cultural differences and similarities, and, crucially, to the physical development and performance of all children. The training of PE teachers today is centred on the question: how can we get the best out of each and every child? One of the great skills in teaching is to balance the needs of the less able and the most gifted of our children. With careful preparation and a determined approach, the best teachers can achieve the right balance. This kind of teaching can make modern PE departments lively and welcome places, so different from the Brian Glover teacher stereotype figure in the film *Kes*. Bored with watching the class's feeble attempts to play football, he decided it was time for his Bobby Charlton impersonation, and the Glover character proceeded to score goal after goal, turning his kids off sports for the rest of their lives.

Local heroes

Arguably the greatest authority on the state of school sport in East London and Essex is Dave Playford, General Secretary of the Essex County Schools FA. Dave, now retired, taught in Redbridge and Essex schools for many years, and ran District sides in most age groups. Fittingly, Dave lives in Wanstead, adjacent to the renowned local sports ground in Nutter Lane. Dave Playford is one of a group of legendary teachers in East London and Essex who have dedicated their careers in the interests of school sport in the area. John Smith, now sadly deceased, Dave Agass in Newham, Hayden Davies in Newham and for Essex, and Del Steward and John Edwards in Waltham Forest have with persistence and skill built a structure of school and district football and cricket in East London and Essex that has served generations of young people, including our two local heroes, Bobby Moore and Graham Gooch. I met Dave Playford in the Spring of 2008 at his home in Nutter Lane and asked him what he thought were the major issues facing sport in schools in the area. His answers helped to bring into clearer focus just what challenges teachers face today.

Firstly, Dave exuded a sense of optimism when revealing that in the 2008 cricket season more schools had entered teams in cricket competitions than for some years, while football has remained fairly constant over the past few seasons. There were far fewer district sides than in previous years in both sports, which have effectively removed a level, and is a concern when we remember that for players like Moore and Gooch and others the district team was the next step up the ladder from school. There are a number of reasons for this decline in the first level of representative sport. Firstly, teachers are less well-disposed to take district teams which involve additional work and the inevitable travelling at weekends. There is another more insidious reason why there is little football played at school district level today, and it can be described in two words – Club Academies.

The top London professional clubs all run soccer academies and centres of excellence which scoop up the best local players, and often the best players from Europe, even Africa, which has led some to accuse the clubs of dealing in child trafficking. In 2009 Chelsea FC was banned from buying any foreign players for two seasons for gross misconduct in their handling of very young players from abroad. At home Academy Clubs can and do refuse permission for their registered school-age players to represent their school and their district, neither do they allow them to play any other sports at school. This practice has weakened school football and terminally weakened the game at district level. This would not be so bad if the clubs didn't discard 95 per cent of their centre of excellence and Academy youngsters at 16 years of age. Many of the rejected young players become disillusioned and leave the sport altogether.

As Dave Playford pointed out, the professional clubs employ a small army of part-time FA qualified coaches who boost their wages by coaching in schools. Some of these are very good and some are win at all costs merchants who do more harm than good. School and district football teams led by coaches rather than teachers, tend to be the teams that have discipline problems with players and spectators, because coaches are club-minded and do not posses the same value system as teachers, nor do they have the authority good teachers command. This is a huge problem in English football at school level, and as long as professional clubs persist in abusing their privileged position and influence over impressionable youngsters and their parents the problem will continue.

Catching cradles and playground pitches

When I was at school in Walthamstow and Chingford we had grass cricket pitches, as did most others in the area in the 1960s, as Graham Gooch confirms. There were grass pitches in the borough sports grounds at Salisbury Hall, Parmiter's Sports Ground in Highams Park, at the Bluebell Wood ground in Highams Park, and the Britannia ground in Billet Road, Walthamstow. Just behind the Britannia, close to the birthplace of the great nineteenth-century socialist polymath William Morris, was the intriguingly named 'The Gunshot', a huge field with football pitches and a cricket square that ran down to Walthamstow Marshes. Graham Gooch remembers clearly playing his school cricket on the grass wickets at Draper's Field in Leyton. If you were good enough to be selected for the school district team, like Gooch and Bobby Moore, there were cricket matches against Hackney, Bethnal Green and other London boroughs. At school, in the early 1960s, we had a grass square for matches, decent outdoor nets and an old, wooden, slated catching cradle for fielding practice, which I am sure would be banned today for health and safety reasons.

A friend of mine attended Stepney Green Comprehensive School and has fond memories of playing cricket for his school back in the late 1960s. The school, opened by Harold Wilson before he became Prime Minister, had decent outdoor nets and the school teams played their fixtures against other schools out at Fairlop in Redbridge. He remembers that the boys had to find their own way to the games, which would have involved several buses and a fair bit of walking. One of the feeder schools for Stepney Green was Old Palace Primary, which had its own nets in the playground and played matches across at Victoria Park. At Stepney Green at the same time as my friend was Tony Green, now the youth coach at Upton Park, who was the school's football captain and cricket captain.

Apart from one or two rare exceptions, all the school cricket grounds in Waltham Forest fondly remembered by generations of local youngsters have gone, along with the opportunities for young people to play cricket on good wickets, or even to play cricket at all. It is little wonder that Robin Hobbs was the last

Chingford boy to play for the county. Admittedly, there are one or two artificial strips placed between football pitches where the odd school game is played in the early summer before football begins again. But these are just a token gesture. This laying to waste of some of the best school cricket facilities in London is not a new phenomenon. When I taught at Highams Park School in the 1980s we would take teams to other schools and play controlled matches on tarmac playgrounds, making up our own rules as we went along. We usually managed to contrive an exciting finish, generally ending in a draw with 11 or 12-year-olds, as older pupils wanted a more competitive experience. Playground cricket never really bothered the kids, who, for all they knew, might have been playing at Lord's, such was their enthusiasm. Highams Park regularly played matches against Bobby Moore's old school Tom Hood, and once or twice against Gooch's Norlington High, all on playgrounds rather than the old grass wickets our sporting heroes would have remembered.

Both Tom Hood and Norlington High have been extensively redeveloped in recent years. Tom Hood is an 'all through school', which means that not only does it cater for children from 0 to 18 but also the premises will house nursery provision, social services, youth workers and a sport and leisure centre. This type of school is designed with the purpose of serving inner-city, multi-ethnic communities and providing support to parents and children at every turn. Interestingly, Tom Hood has a new all-weather facility that also serves the local community, but it is primarily intended for football. Cricket is considered a very poor relation indeed, so there isn't much prospect of a new Ravinder Bopara or Charlotte Edwards emerging from this part of East London in the near future, I'm afraid.

Football is now all-consuming and the old traditions of school football have been hijacked by the professional clubs. But there is hope for school cricket largely thanks to the England and Wales Cricket Board's (ECB) initiative 'Chance to Shine'. Essex's Doug Insole revealed to me one quiet afternoon watching Essex play Middlesex at Castle Park in Colchester that he thought that this project was beginning to work. You could hear the relief in his voice.

'Chance to Shine': educating through cricket

Established in 2005, 'Chance to Shine' is the Cricket

Foundation's campaign to bring cricket and its educational benefits to at least two million children in England and Wales by 2015. Backed nationally by £50 million, each individual project provides a structured coaching and competition programme designed for groups of around six primary and secondary state schools. Over one-third of state schools are registered for scheme, with a potential for involving over two million young people. The ECB's actual estimate is that 3,000 schools are signed up to Chance to Shine, with about 350,000 primary school pupils taking part. These are immensely encouraging figures (For full details of the Chance to Shine project, see the ECB website, www.ecb.co.uk).

How does it work? The heart of the scheme is developing effective links between schools and local cricket clubs. There is nothing in the scheme designed to provide schools with cricket grounds and make them the centre of cricket. The onus is very much on the clubs to make the initiative work. Groups of schools are supported by professional, qualified coaches engaged by one local cricket club. The scheme provides the clubs with the necessary equipment, as well as training for teachers and coaches. Each project is funded for a minimum period of five years and once it has ended the project teams will work closely with schools and clubs to help them make their partnership sustainable.

Taking their lead from previous similar initiatives, Chance to Shine also has what we might call non-cricket objectives. The ECB website states:

> *All competitive team sports can play a vital role in the education and personal development of young people, offering opportunities to lead healthy, purposeful lives.*

These are laudable sentiments and the project leaders believe strongly that cricket has special attributes because it:

- Promotes leadership, teamwork and strategic awareness;
- Teaches respect, how to win, to lose and cope with setbacks;
- Is the ultimate team game, demanding both individual and collective responsibility;
- Insists on high standards of conduct and provides good role models;
- Is wholly inclusive, drawing together people from all cultures

and backgrounds and giving opportunities to boys and girls, as well as to those with special needs; and
• Is able to reach all of our major ethnic communities in a way no other sport clearly can.

Tracey Miller, a teacher at St John's Primary School, Bethnal Green, London, describes how cricket helps her in class:

If you can convey different ideas using something that interests them then that's half the battle. Because of the sessions they love cricket and I've found it a great vehicle to help with maths and literacy. They listen more because they find it interesting and it gives them concrete examples.
- Dr R Jeanes and Dr T Kay, Evaluation of Chance to Shine Phase 1, for the Cricket Foundation 2007/08

The project claims to have pioneered special, web-based educational resources to support innovative, cricket-themed lessons that have proved very popular with teachers involved with the scheme. The material from Chance to Shine has been used across the curriculum, enhancing pupils' literacy, numeracy and IT skills.

In 2008 the ECB commissioned a piece of research designed to evaluate the effectiveness of the scheme. The research reportmake some very bold claims; for example, in schools where the project is operating, cricket is "improving the 'social well-being' of thousands of state school pupils". The report by the Institute of Youth Sport (IYS) found that pupils involved in the Chance to Shine initiative displayed increased fitness levels, greater social skills and improved sportsmanlike behaviour.

The research also includes evidence to show that cricket is improving the behaviour of young people both on and off the field, particularly in deprived areas, and the so-called 'gentleman's game' is helping girls to overcome "restrictive gender beliefs" and gain confidence in playing sport. The report goes further and says that the project may also be helping to cut down truancy as

... more pupils look forward to and enjoy attending school when Chance to Shine is taking place - 53 per cent - compared to 36 per cent when it is not.
- Jeanes and Kay (2007-08)

Dr Ruth Jeanes of Loughborough University, who led the research says:

Whilst Chance to shine is undoubtedly having a positive impact on general cricket provision and the development of opportunities for young people, its contribution to improving the social wellbeing of many of its participants illustrates that it is much more than just a cricket development initiative.
- Jeanes and Kay (2007-08)

The potential of cricket for supporting young people in developing friendships and support networks was illustrated by one of the cricket coaches cited in the report. He describes how a child had been severely bullied all his life to the extent that he was "quite psychologically damaged" and required a psychiatrist. It was only when he joined the local cricket club, through Chance to Shine that he started to make friends and according to his consultant "cricket had been his saviour".

Dr Jeanes claims that cricket sessions have contributed positively to the development of pupils' social skills, such as teamwork. One cricket-mad 9-year-old told her:

We've all, like, bonded a bit more. We've realised that we've got to work as a team ... because there's no point in just trying to be selfish and barging other people and catching the ball so you get all the pride, but if someone catches it's the whole team's pride.
- Jeanes and Kay (2007-08)

'Fair play' is a reoccurring theme in the report, with pupils saying that winning is not the most important thing when playing cricket and that the sport is great fun in itself. "You learn sportsmanship, you can work together and help people out," says one Year 5 pupil, while a Year 6 female pupil interviewed says that cheating in cricket was uncommon:

With football they (the boys) sometimes kick you and things but with cricket no one really tries to trick you and cheat. And we clap when someone does well.
- Jeanes and Kay (2007-08)

There is more good news for the future of youth cricket.

Earlier this year the Cricket Foundation charity teamed up with the MCC for a nationwide drive to encourage fair play by introducing a two-hour 'MCC Spirit of Cricket' session to 3,000 state schools during the summer term. Teachers highlighted how taking part in the programme has encouraged positive changes in pupils in the classroom. They say the cricket sessions have been effective in reducing "disruptive behaviour during class" and encouraging pupils to "act more responsibly". Teachers working in special schools also praise the scheme:

For children with behaviour difficulties, you know they're wanting to turn themselves around ... and we take them out of school and I know that I can trust their behaviour within those situations to play the cricket matches ... a lot of our best players are the ones who do have some behaviour difficulties.
- Jeanes and Kay (2007-08)

The value of the cricket sessions for improving girls' confidence was notable and they were especially successful at encouraging Asian girls to become involved in cricket. For at least one of the pupils Chance to Shine has helped some girls to gain a new-found status in school:

It's like everyone says girls can't do cricket, they are no good at boys sports but we are doing it and we are really good. We keep winning all the time and it has made the boys realise we can be as good as them.
- Jeanes and Kay (2007-08)

One 13-year-old, Caitlin Byrne from Durham, had never played cricket before Chance to Shine arrived at her school. She discovered she was a good left-arm seam bowler, developed further at South Shields Cricket Club and now plays at her age group for Durham County.

Wasim Khan, Chief Executive of the Cricket Foundation, says about the project:

The news that Chance to Shine is having a major impact on our schools, teachers and pupils is extremely encouraging.
- Jeanes and Kay (2007-08)

The success of the project will certainly gladden the heart of 85-year-old Doug Insole, as well as the teachers who have given so much to developing school cricket in East London and Essex for the past 30 or 40 years.

In the interest of English cricket it is to be hoped that Chance to Shine produces another Graham Gooch down in East London, but, perhaps more importantly, cricket will once again become the sport of choice for thousands of young people in the area. In East London and Essex, schools have traditionally played the leading role in both identifying and developing outstanding young sporting talent, largely through the efforts of outstanding individual teachers. This has not been the case for some years. Cricket in state schools in East London has died a slow death over the past 20 years, although cricket in public schools out in Essex has survived and prospered during this time. At Brentwood, where the grammar school has survived and there are a number of private schools within a short distance of the town, cricket is thriving. The Colts organiser at Brentwood CC, Ken Hobbs, and his team have over 200 boys and girls at the junior coaching evenings at the Old County Ground. This is a clear indication that Chance to Shine is working, but it does help that the club enjoys a good working relationship with the local schools, which have their own grass pitches. The real challenge is whether projects such as Chance to Shine lead to a renaissance of cricket in the inner city, where there is huge untapped potential but few clubs, no grammar or public schools and no cricket grounds.

In football the situation is different. The professional clubs bully schools into submission, and the outstanding inter-district programme that existed in the area for many years has been run down to a shell of its former self. London Academy clubs call the tune and the parents dance. As we have seen, without the restraining influence of good teachers, violence involving players and parents is on the increase, threatening the very fabric of youth football. School football and cricket in inner-city East London that nurtured the talents of Bobby Moore and Graham Gooch to such good effect has, in part, been betrayed by the councils selling precious green spaces, and by the increasing commercialisation of professional football. Projects such as Chance to Shine, with its crucial partnership between clubs and schools, and the initiatives introduced by Newham and Tower Hamlets councils to encourage more young people from all backgrounds into sport, are commendable and timely. The 2012 Olympics offers a once-in-a-generation opportunity to rebuild school sport in East London and beyond. It is critical for the area that the opportunity is not wasted and that youngsters like Caitlin from Durham have the opportunity to fulfil their potential.

CHAPTER 5
BOBBY MOORE, PEERLESS PRINCE OF FOOTBALL

And the glow from that light can truly light the world
- J.F. Kennedy

I could never take my eyes off him. There is a photograph of Moore that beautifully encapsulates the man and the footballer. He is standing in the goalmouth in front of the North Bank at Upton Park, right hand against the near post, defending a corner for his beloved West Ham. His face betrays his feelings. His look is intense but imperious, displaying complete control of everything around him. He is entirely caught up in the moment – in his element and master of his universe. Moore had supreme confidence, but this never strayed into arrogance. He always knew where he came from – completely at home in the mud and rain on a winter's night in the East End of London, doing what he was born to do. This picture stayed in my mind for many years and inspired me to look more closely into the life and career of this incomparable legend of post-war British sport.

There is another photograph of Moore, instantly recognisable, which shows him in an embrace with the great Pelé following England's defeat against Brazil in the 1970 World Cup in Mexico. Both players are smiling, shirts off in the Mexican sun, both at the height of their considerable powers – the two greatest footballers in the world. Here is the Moore that everybody knew and respected - the great international sportsman and the only England captain to lead his team to World Cup glory. Of course it was Moore - who else would lift the Jules Rimet Trophy for England? However, the Bobby Moore known to West Ham supporters and people in East London and Essex was not the international superstar, but the person in the first photograph, in claret and blue, playing for his club in front of his adoring fans. I want to find out where he fits in with the sporting story of the area, and what were the values that sustained and nourished him to achieve such a level of greatness? What is it about the place and its sporting culture that enabled him to become the best he could be? Lastly, does this culture remain strong enough to produce another Bobby Moore, as the world prepares to come to East London in 2012?

Firstly, a few bare facts to put Moore's achievement in clear perspective. He won two FA Cup winners' medals, one European Cup Winners' Cup medal and, the highlight of a truly glittering career, a World Cup triumph at Wembley in 1966. Of course, he was captain of the winning team on each of these occasions. Between 1962 and 1973 he was awarded 108 England caps, 90 as captain of his country, which he proudly represented at every level. Moore made 544 appearances for West Ham and was the club captain for ten years. Towards the end of his career he played 124 games for Fulham, including an FA Cup final against - wouldn't you know it – West Ham United. He was Footballer of the Year in 1964, BBC Sports Personality of the Year and World Cup Player of Players in 1966, and in 1967 he was awarded the OBE. A BBC *This is Your Life* tribute followed. After his sad early death, in 2007 a statue was erected to his memory at the new Wembley Stadium, and for many of us, as we will see later in the chapter, this was the most fitting and lasting tribute. The old stand on the south side of Upton Park was eventually demolished to make way for the new Bobby Moore Stand. As a further mark of respect, West Ham finally withdrew the No. 6 shirt from the team numbers as a tribute to their greatest son, but not until 15 years after his death and after much pressure from the fans.

Jeff Powell's updated biography (J. Powell (1998), Bobby Moore: The Life and Times of a Sporting Hero, Robson Books). is the most detailed account of Moore's life, although Tina Moore's later autobiography (T. Moore (2005), Bobby Moore: By the Person Who Knew Him Best, Harper Sport) is far more compelling. There is some inconsistency between their two versions of the great man's life, with Tina's version only obliquely referring to Powell's quickly compiled account of his friend's life. Sixteen years after Moore's death we may able to look at Moore's life and career a little more dispassionately. Is there anything new to say about our greatest football hero? My aim is to set Moore's legacy within a local context, and to try to identify the values that shaped and informed his career. What did he actually mean to the people of his area? Why was he held in such high regard? How did this East End footballer - in the end that was all he was - become such an iconic, stand-out cultural figure in his time? With the Olympic Games being staged in Moore's own backyard in 2012, there is an opportunity reconsider his legacy.

An unpromising start

Robert Frederick Chelsea Moore did have one advantage, and it was an accident of birth. He was a wartime baby, born in 1941 into an East London that had withstood the horrors of the Blitz with such stoic courage. There is no question that the young Moore inherited his parents' qualities and values. After the war Moore's parents' generation set out to rebuild East London by restoring their neighbourhoods, renewing their community networks and resurrecting their sporting culture. Churches, allotment societies, Christmas clubs, sports clubs, adult education groups, and so on, were all re-established as local people began to build some kind of social and cultural infrastructure from the wreckage left by the Nazi bombers. The job of rebuilding was formidable and took nearly 20 years, but by the early 1960s they had largely succeeded in their task.

Within a few years local playing fields were back in full use, football and cricket leagues in East London and Essex came to life again, swimming clubs held their galas and boxing clubs reopened their gyms. By the end of the 1950s a rich amateur sporting culture had literally re-emerged from the ashes of war. This required a Herculean effort by local enthusiasts, as grounds had to be prepared, changing rooms renovated and equipment acquired. Many of the football pitches and golf courses had been dug up to prevent enemy planes from landing, or were used for growing vegetables as part of the war effort. Although still in the shadow of the war, East End and Essex people had the will and tenacity to restore to their area the things they cherished most – and their local sporting facilities and institutions were very near the top of their list. Out on the edge of Epping Forest, the golf course and football pitches on Chingford Plains and the facilities at Wanstead Flats were reinstated, following their wartime use as prisoner of war camps. The open ground of Chingford Plains was 'corrugated' during the war to stop Nazi planes from landing in East London and, although the football pitches at Chingford were lost years ago, the corrugated fairways of the golf course remain to this day, leading to some rather difficult shots for local golfers (There are two golfing facilities on the site of the old prisoner of war camp on Chingford Plains: Chingford Golf Club and Royal Epping Forest Golf Club. Members of both clubs are required to wear red clothing on the course to distinguish themselves from members of the general public, who are entitled to roam freely across the plains).

If football was a song ...

The generation of Moore's parents worked to build a new world on the graveyard of the old one. They had to cope with loss, hunger, unemployment, rationing and homelessness to a degree that we can barely imagine today, but they were determined to rebuild the sporting culture that had meant so much to the East End. C.L.R. James stresses the importance of sport to communities such as those in East London:

> *A glance at the world shows that when common people were not at work, one thing they wanted was organised sport and games. They wanted them greedily and passionately.*
> *- C.L.R. James (1963), Beyond a Boundary, Stanley Paul, p.150*

By the end of the 1950s much of the local sporting infrastructure in the area was re-established. The stage was set for the emergence of an extraordinary local hero who was to conquer the world of sport and become a central figure in the social revolution of the 1960s. It is fitting that the nation's hero of 1966 came out of this forward-looking culture of renewal.

If East London and Essex was a place of reconstruction in the 1950s, by the early 1960s local people began to enjoy the benefits of all their hard work and self-sacrifice. This was the positive environment that nourished one of the greatest careers in international sport. Moore grew up in this time of high activity, imagination, independence and cooperation. The community values that nurtured Moore and his generation meant that he was able to make the most of his talents. The world into which he was born created the conditions for him to succeed. In West Ham United FC he found a club that encouraged skill, creativity and forward thinking – it was not called 'The Academy' for nothing.

To paraphrase an American saying, 'If football were a song, Bobby Moore would be the singer'. But, in truth, Moore transcended sport in the way that Stevie Wonder transcends music or Nelson Mandela transcends politics, except with Moore the transcendence occurred after his death rather than during his lifetime. The image of him carrying the Jules Rimet trophy aloft on 30 July 1966 is one of the most enduring, not only in sport but also in British culture more generally. Tom Geoghegan, writing in the *BBC News Magazine*, commented:

Every time England crash out of a football tournament, the reputation of the late Bobby Moore is fortified just a little bit more.
- T. Geoghegan, BBC News Magazine, online publication, 11 May 2007,www.news.bbc.co.uk/nolpda/ ukfs_news/hi/newsid_6645000/ 6645619.stm

There were, of course, other great players in his time, and in a BBC Radio interview with Neil Durden-Smith Moore was asked to name the best players of his generation. He said the players he respected most were Pelé, Eusebio, Beckenbauer and Cruyff. Moore said that Pelé had no weaknesses, and he recounts the conversation he had with the Brazilian team manager, Mário Zagallo during the 1970 World Cup, when Zagallo told Moore that he could play the great forward in goal, at full back or centre forward and he would still be Brazil's best player. But, great as these players were, they have not yet achieved the kind of iconic status accorded to Moore by the world of football following his sad death in 1993.

The 1960s, the years of Moore's greatest achievements, appear in retrospect to be a carefree time compared with the grey and austere 1950s. I remember driving along Oxford Street in my old Ford Popular (bought in the Barking Road for £75) one sunny summer afternoon in the mid-1960s, when a police panda car pulled me over. Fearing the worst I wound down the window only to be greeted by a kindly copper who offered me £100 to take the car off my hands there and then. It turned out that he was a Ford enthusiast and had taken an instant liking to my three-gear version of the old classic. Imagine that happening in the often tense and hostile atmosphere of today's London streets? The copper and his mate may have been on duty the previous weekend trying to control the riots at the American Embassy in Grosvenor Square. This decade was a time of increased political tension between the Soviet Union and the USA, which reached a climax in the Cuban Crisis of 1962, when many of us thought that a nuclear war could break out at any moment. Then there were the horrors of Vietnam. So much for the carefree 1960s – but somehow, despite the perilous international situation, the sixties did feel like a time of hope and high optimism.

The early 1960s felt like a transition period between two very different times. For example, the designers of the official programme of the 1964 European Cup Winners' Cup final between West Ham and TSV 1860 München at Wembley – price one shilling and printed in black and white – seem not have caught the swinging sixties creative design bug. The Hammers captain is listed as a left half and the centrefold sets out both teams in 2-3-5 formation. The programme itself is interesting as a historical document. It includes four full-page advertisements – the *Radio Times*, Double Diamond ('the beer men drink'), the Hot Bovril Supporters' Club ('drink your health in Bovril') and Yardley ('a man's talc'). The last is appropriate since the Yardley factory was situated on Stratford High Road in East London and was responsible for the sickly smell of sweet perfume mixed with the pungent aroma of ground bones, its principal ingredient, which hung over the streets of the area for many years.

If the FA programme design for the match belongs solidly in the 1950s, the notes do pay a generous tribute to the East London club. Peter Lorenzo of the *Daily Mirror* writes that West Ham have established themselves as among the sport's finest ambassadors Britain has ever sent abroad, and they have been a credit to themselves, their sport and their country. Those who are familiar with West Ham's purist playing style over the past 40 years will appreciate Lorenzo's comments when he wrote:

> *From all aspects, talent, intelligence, tactical ability and overall approach, there are few, if any, better-suited flag carriers than West Ham United.*
> *- Peter Lorenzo, 'Official Programme', 1964 European Cup Winners' Cup final, 1964, p.11.*

It is difficult to see how West Ham could have acquired this proud reputation without the presence in their side of their incomparable No. 6 – he fully exemplified the football intelligence that was at the heart of the club's football philosophy. Through his own example Moore was to lead both his club and his country into a new, if brief, period of great excitement in English sport and culture.

The post-war generation needed an ideal, as most of us do, and the communities of East London had reason to need one more than most. Bobby Moore became an idol, a symbol of achievement, firstly for his own 'manor', and then for a nation grateful for his skills and commanding leadership. His personal qualities reflect well on a part of London whose people have been much derided in their history as feckless, hostile, even ungovernable, but whose true qualities are a fierce independence, a heightened sense of fairness, a strong work ethic and a fine sense of humour.

A close look at these communities reveals a culture that is as richly nuanced and complex as any other. We see this in the history of Moore's own family, set out for us in the autobiography of his first wife, Tina. We know that his paternal grandfather, like many East End young men, died in the First World War. His father, Bob, was a gas fitter from Poplar, a genuine cockney, who had an extremely tough childhood. He was a popular and kind man, plain-speaking and with an impish sense of humour. Moore's mum, Doris, known in the family as Doss, was the dominant character in the family and perhaps the most interesting. Doris's family were devout Salvation Army people, who visited the pubs of East London on Saturday nights selling the War Cry and on Sundays marched through the East End streets with their bonnets and tambourines. As Tina Moore writes:

> *... she and Big Bob were very upright. God-fearing people.*
> *- T. Moore (2005), p.46.*

Bobby's mum, although God-fearing, resisted the temptations of the Sally Army, although she neither smoke nor drank and never quite understood her son's taste for a few glasses of lager after a match. There are stories of Mrs Moore fishing Bobby out of a pub one Christmas when Tina's pleas for him to return home were ignored. But, clearly, both parents adored Bobby and were extremely proud of his growing list of accomplishments. His mother regularly attended West Ham home games, and on one occasion she took her future daughter-in-law to Upton Park for her very first visit.

One of the most striking things when looking at the life of Bobby Moore is the strength of the women around him. His mother, Tina's mother and Tina herself were all intelligent, strong-willed women who knew how to keep a house and home together in difficult times. They also had interests and abilities in their own right. I am sure this strength of purpose and will is rooted in the experience of the Second World War and the deprivations of the 1950s. East London women quickly learnt to become independent and develop strategies to cope with hardship, loss and bereavement. They did this while working in factories, shops and offices and at the same time bringing up their families. My own mother brought up seven children on a council estate in Chingford. As a young mother during the war, she looked after three young children at home while my father was away in the armed services and was imprisoned for three years in the death camps of Auschwitz. Experiences such as these were not uncommon in the area and they taught local women to be resourceful and emotionally strong.

The Moores were a hard-working, decent, 'salt of the earth' family; good people who often struggled to adapt to the new world breaking around them. But for the young Moore, Tina's fun-loving family must have seemed like a breath of fresh air.

Ilford is an area of flatland on the East London/Essex border. It is largely middle class and conservative, with a few pockets of poverty concentrated on the standard appalling local authority housing estates. In the 1960s Ilford was upwardly mobile, its high street being a Mecca for East End families on Saturday afternoons before the Bluewater Centre at Thurrock destroyed the prosperity of many Essex town centres in the 1990s. Families from all over the East End aspired to live in Ilford. Many achieved their dream, transforming the nature of the town from a settled, largely white community to the more transient, multicultural place of today. Ilford's high street was famous locally for its coffee bars, where young people could meet and plan their Saturday night excursion to the local Palais just up the road. In the 1950s Tina Wilde lived with her mother in a ground-floor flat in Christchurch Road, while other members of her family occupied the first floor. The flat had an outside toilet and a tin bath, which hung from a nail on the outside wall at the back of the house. When mother and daughter tired of the tin bath, they took themselves down to the local public baths, as many families did. Tina writes:

I can still remember those shouts of, 'More hot for Number Six'.
- T. Moore (2005), p.23.

Tina's mother was one of seven children and, like her daughter, won a grammar school scholarship, but sadly her mother refused to let her take it up. Her maternal grandmother played the piano, and her aunt and uncle were European professional ballroom dancing champions and owned a small dance hall close to where Bobby Moore grew up in Barking. As Tina points out, ballroom dancing was hugely popular in the fifties. There were small private dance clubs all over East London. Back in the early sixties my own parents used to attend King's Dance Club in Chingford two or three nights a week and became wonderful dancers. They would dance all evening, refreshed by a mid-session cup of tea, and then get the bus back home across Chingford. As a 15-year-old I often had to cycle miles up the North Circular Road to Bobby Shearer's shop in Palmer's Green, where my dad had had his dance shoes repaired, and then cycle all the way back – I loved it.

In many ways Tina Wilde was part of a typical East London close-knit family, with the all the usual good and bad times. And she remembers her childhood with real affection:

I remember my years in Christchurch Road as full of laughs and a lot of fun. I had good manners and politeness drummed into me gently but fairly. I was a well brought up girl.
- T. Moore (2005), p.24.

'Well brought up' extended to being sent to elocution lessons as a young girl, something that lots of East End girls were subjected to in the fifties and early sixties, boys probably being seen as beyond redemption. Of course, in the late sixties it became acceptable, even desirable, as a career move to speak with a working-class accent, even on the BBC. Michael Caine,

Billy Cotton and David Bailey were pioneers in this respect.

Bobby Moore seemingly inherited some of his mum's more complex personal traits. According to Tina, Moore shared his mother's repressed but strong personality. He was very critical of himself, tidy in the extreme and obsessive about his appearance – he wasn't the only one back in the sixties to have the latter personality trait.

Moore also symbolised mastery over his own fate, and as such he became an inspiration to a generation intent on creating a new world based on optimism and hope. C.L.R. James, writing about W.G. Grace, seems to encapsulate perfectly both the man and his time:

> *There he was … building as much of that old world as possible into the new, and fabulously successful at it. The more simple past was battling with the more complex, more dominant, present … In any age he would have been a striking personality and vastly popular. That particular age he hit between wind and water. Yet, as in all such achievements, he could conquer only by adopting the methods of the new.*
>
> *- James (1963) p.176*

James could just as easily have been describing Bobby Moore. He did have the guidance and counsel of modern football thinkers to help him, but more than anything it was his own personal qualities, nurtured in post-war East London, that enabled him to "hit between wind and water" in his incomparable career, to give a nation the hero it craved. Moore came to represent a world at the point of transition when anything seemed possible, as Britain arrived at a high point in its cultural history. London became the world centre of popular culture and, despite his more or less conservative appearance and conventional values, nobody represented this exciting and creative new world more than Bobby Moore. He was able to carry with him the virtues of hard work, good manners and plain decency that he was taught in the 1950s to the liberated decade of The Beatles, pirate radio, flower power and Carnaby Street. Nobody connected two such dramatically different decades more than the England football captain. He would have been equally at home in the Essex coffee bars of the 1950s, the pubs of East London or the splendour of the Royal Kensington

Hotel, scene of the celebrations of the England squad in July 1966. He symbolised the more stoic qualities of the earlier period, but somehow came to represent the best of the sixties. In many respects he was the 1960s in the form of a footballer. Jim White of the *Daily Telegraph* neatly encapsulates this sense of Moore as an iconic figure for his time:

The 60s was a time of great forward-thinking. They were washing away the austerity and grime of the 50s in culture, music and fashion. Bobby Moore was an easy symbol for that. He was one of the figures of the 1960s, the easy way in which modernity was washing away the grit of the past. He looked handsome and elegant in that kit and he smiled modestly.
- J. White, 'The Making of an English Gentleman' BBC News Magazine . 25th April 2009

Tina Moore describes the early days of her relationship with the man she met at the Ilford Palais at the age of 17, dancing to the music of Ambrose and young singers, Kathy Kirby and Gerry Dorsey (later Engelbert Humperdinck). Tina Moore writes:

Bobby and I were not complete hicks ... we were living in an age when working-class people were starting to make a lot of money in fashion and showbiz. Football was part of their roots, so naturally he was one of their heroes. We'd already started to rub shoulders with some of his up-and-coming East London contemporaries – Terry Stamp and Kenny Lynch.
- T. Moore (2005), p.58

There was a sense of real excitement at the extent of cultural change in the sixties. The young wife-to-be goes on to recall her excitement at the new kinds of food available at the time:

It was, after all, the start of the sixties when the most luxurious kinds of food were just becoming available after the dreary diet and relative deprivation of the post-war period. We were getting a taste of melon, avocado, French cheese and Italian wine at last.

Blue Nun wine, T-bone steaks and Black Forest gateau were just around the corner for aspiring young East Londoners who were beginning to leave behind the "relative deprivation" of their parents' generation. Now that's not a phrase that trips off the tongue of today's footballers' wives. Clearly, Tina was an intelligent young woman alert to the social revolution that she and Bobby were about to be swept up in.

Following the 1966 World Cup, football and footballers became enormously fashionable. The media began to discover the advertising worth of top footballers as far back as 1962 when Terry O'Neill's photograph of Moore, surrounded by pretty young models, appeared in an edition of *Vogue* magazine. The great sixties photographer David Bailey, an enthusiastic young talent as a teenager, was a neighbour and friend of Tina Moore's family. But, despite the escalating glare of publicity he received as one of the great figures of the 1960s, Moore never forgot the values he acquired from his family and local community growing up back in Barking. The grime may have been washed away, but his personal values - dignity, sportsmanship, generosity of spirit, grace under pressure, modesty and an insatiable work ethic – stayed with him. With one or two notable exceptions, such qualities appear thin on the ground in the football culture of 2010 (At the time of writing, the funeral was held at Durham Cathedral for the recently deceased former England manager, Sir Bobby Robson, one of the last figures in the game to hold to the values of Moore and his like).

In the Neil Durden-Smith BBC interview Moore explained how, along with other young players at the club, he cut the grass, prepared the pitch for match days, swept the terraces and cleaned the senior players' boots. He thought nothing of this. He believed that it taught youngsters respect for older players and it provided an insight into how a professional football club works. Moore described to the listeners, with a hint of excitement in his voice, that a new fully indentured apprenticeship scheme had been recently introduced to the English game. The new scheme would teach young players about all aspects of professional football and provide them with educational opportunities and some sort of security of employment. No more cleaning boots and sweeping freezing terraces. True to his generosity of spirit, Moore saw this development as wholly positive, with no hint of the 'it wasn't like that in my day' mentality you so often get with older professionals.

For much the same reason as Graham Gooch left school to start an engineering apprenticeship, the young Moore supplemented his football earnings by working in the factory where his mum was employed. Young professional footballers from the area often had summer jobs in the 1960s and early 1970s, often in a factory or, if they were lucky, as lifeguards on the beaches of the south coast. I remember one less fortunate young apprentice professional folding searing red-hot sheets at a Chingford laundry for £6 a week during the summer, but at least he had a few of his mates to keep him company and in good humour. The factory work did Moore no harm and allowed him time to think about his future as he prepared for first team football, and marriage.

The first family of football

Bobby Moore from Barking and Tina Wilde from Ilford became engaged on Christmas Day 1960. At the age of 19 Moore was in his first full season with West Ham and two years away from his first England cap. Like Bobby, Tina had passed her 11+ and duly attended Ilford High School for Girls, close to Valentine's Park, home of Essex County Cricket Club's annual festival. On leaving school, like generations of East London and Essex folk before her, Tina made the short journey to Liverpool Street to work for Prudential Insurance in Holborn. At the time of their engagement she was actually earning more money than her professional footballer fiancé, the former England Youth captain. In 1960 the young Moore was paid just £8 a week, £3 less than his future wife. At this time professional footballers were still on the Football League's maximum wage of £20 a week, until the Professional Footballers' Association (PFA), under the leadership of Jimmy Hill, forced its abolition in 1961 after threatening a players' strike. Just like any other couple from the area at the time, things began to improve rapidly for the young couple as Moore began to establish himself in the West Ham side and push for an England place.

Expecting to leave with his West Ham teammates for the club's pre-season tour to Africa in the summer of 1962, Moore was informed by Ron Greenwood that he should pack his bags for South America. He had been picked for the England squad for the 1962 World Cup in Chile. Moore returned from South America in high spirits, which received a further boost when the couple were married on 30th June at St Clement's Church in Ilford, just a few miles from Upton Park. Noel Cantwell was the best man and the wedding was a real Hammers event, with hundreds of fans swarming around the church to witness the occasion. The couple held their reception at the Valentine's pub in Gants Hill and left the following day for their honeymoon in Majorca - where else for a young Essex couple. In her book Tina remembers that the best man and his mate Malcolm Allison, by sheer coincidence of course, were also in Majorca that week with their families. To her horror, they both turned up at the couple's hotel and in true West Ham tradition managed to prise the bridegroom away from his honeymoon for long enough for Bobby to get into serious trouble with his new wife. Not a good start.

Bobby and Tina returned from their honeymoon to their new marital home, a three-bedroom terrace in Gant's Hill, for which they paid the princely sum of £3,850. Tina describes the new home of the future England captain:

The house had French doors at the back which opened onto a pretty garden where Bobby and I planted a magnolia tree – our favourite. Indoors, the lounge had a green carpet patterned with pink roses and a plate rail going round the walls where we put Bobby's memorabilia.
- T. Moore (2005), p.64.

Moore was brought up in a small house close to an industrial estate and Tina's family lived in an Ilford flat with an outside toilet, so the couple were on their way, although the young housewife found their new life difficult at first:

I found the first year of our marriage a bit uncomfortable. It took a long time to adjust to such a change in my life. Bobby didn't want me to work, because he trained in the mornings only and came home for lunch.
- T. Moore (2005), p.65.

But the new Mrs Moore was soon to adjust, and the couple later moved to the sought-after Manor Road in Chigwell to a house that was more fitting for an England football captain. Manor Road was the Moore's family home where they raised their children and enjoyed the fruits of their success. But, as with most families, the good times were balanced by difficult ones, as we will discover. The Moores had come a long way, and in the early years of their married life together the two youngsters from Barking and Ilford grew from strength to strength. The newly married Tina now did her shopping in Bond Street rather than Ilford High Road and had the daily help of an au pair. The golden couple appeared to have it all.

The Moores were very much of their time, enjoying the fruits of the sixties social revolution. The dull, austere East London of the fifties that they lived through as children would have seemed like a different planet to them, despite both of them keeping close to their roots. It is difficult to imagine even the most famous footballers of the fifties making the front cover of *Vogue* magazine or being invited to parties at the home of film stars.

By the late sixties the Moores had become a celebrity couple, with a luxury home, beautiful children and celebrity friends, but in 1964 their world came crashing down around their ears. For Moore, three events had marked out the 1963/64 season. He had led West Ham to FA Cup victory at Wembley in May, and at the end of the season he was elected Footballer of the Year by the Football Writers' Association. In addition, if that wasn't enough, Tina became pregnant. Everything seemed to be going to plan.

However, in the summer of 1964 Moore noticed a swelling on one of his testicles. He mentioned this to the West Ham physiotherapist, who assumed it was caused by a knock in training. But the swelling grew and became extremely painful. Something was clearly wrong. The Moores went to see their family GP in November and within 24 hours Bobby was on the operating table. The surgeon informed Tina that the diagnosis was. At the age of 22 and six months pregnant Tina had to think through how she was going to cope with this devastating news. Would her husband live through it? Would he be able to play football again? Should he be told?

In the 1960s the medical authorities dealt with cancer patients and their families very differently. Today medical staff at West Ham would have immediately referred Moore to a doctor. Secondly, once the consultants had identified cancer they would be obligated to inform the family and the patient. It is now their right to know. The club would also have handled the player's absence in a more sensitive way. Today the press would want to know every detail, and in any case would find them out. Back in 1964 Tina Moore had to cope alone. She spoke to her Catholic priest, and then after a few days she shared the awful news with her mother. Tina's mum had given up her job to run the sports good shop that Moore had opened opposite the Boleyn ground in Green Street, and she was very close to her son-in-law. The family was devastated.

In due course the surgeon removed the affected testicle and Moore returned home desolate. He was self-conscious by nature and worried about his teammates and the public discovering his problem. He had to draw on all his considerable personal resources to get through the next few months. West Ham United attributed his prolonged absence to a groin strain picked up in training. The patient continued to undergo regular hospital checks, while his young wife researched the disease in the local library. With her personal strength and intelligence she clearly possessed the ability to cope with this sudden shock to her now famous family. Tina was convinced by her research that her husband would come through it and be able to lead a full and normal life. Bobby, trying desperately to put his life back together, began to suffer from the insomnia that affected him throughout his career.

Roberta Christina Moore was born on 24 January 1965, and the Moores began to recover from the shock of Bobby's illness. Moore returned to training and within a few weeks he was playing as well as ever, leading his West Ham side that May to victory in the European Cup Winners' Cup final at Wembley Stadium. Life was back to normal and a year later the couple had their second child, a baby boy. Dean was born on a Saturday afternoon shortly after West Ham's home match against Chelsea. Tina attended the game, accompanied by the family doctor in case of emergency. Bobby was at the birth, dressed in his West Ham kit, fresh from the match. To add to the growing family's sense that things had now turned around for them, Bobby Moore was awarded the OBE in the New Year Honours List in January 1967. Throw in the World Cup final in 1966 and life was good again and the cancer a painful memory, but a memory nonetheless. The Moores had coped well with the crisis. Bobby had recovered from his illness and the couple had two young children, emerging from the crisis stronger and closer.

Football – 'a smaller world'

A simple remark that Tina Moore makes in her book reveals much about football in the mid-sixties, particularly at Upton Park. She says, "Football was a much smaller world in those days". What she means by this is that players, wives and girlfriends were free to meet in East End pubs like the Black Lion in Plaistow, where they would socialise with the locals and the Redknapps and Lampards, and Alan Ball and his wife. Their children all grew up together. She tells a story about the groundsman at Upton Park, who was rather fond of a drink. Around the Christmas festivities he regularly needed help keeping the white lines straight for match days, something he often failed to do, much to the amusement of the Hammers players and fans in the know. There were no posh hotels on the ground, no executive boxes and no all-seater Boleyn. The infamous Chicken Run stand was a drab terrace, although Tina Moore recalls this particular West Ham institution with some fondness:

> *... the back row was used as a pissoir so it wasn't the sweetest smelling place in the world, but it teemed with the most fervent ... and good-humoured fans. Bobby loved them ... the whole place was great. It had a lovely, familiar feel. It wasn't slick and business-oriented like it is now.*
> *- T. Moore (2005), p.89.*

The Chicken Run was demolished following the *Taylor Report* and was replaced by a modern, soulless structure much like any other across the English Premier League. Most of the seats in the all-seater stand are reserved for season ticket holders. When you arrive at the match now, you enter the new stand, not through the old turnstiles where you handed over your fiver, but by swiping your membership card. We would not want to go back to the days of the old Chicken Run, but something has been lost forever as a result of what Tina Moore describes as the new 'business-oriented' West Ham United. Somehow, 'business-oriented' doesn't sound quite right at Upton Park. Back in the 1970s three blocks of high-rise flats appeared behind the

Chicken Run; they seemed an intrusion but sparkled like Chinese lanterns during night matches. The comedian James Corden, a loyal Hammers supporter, once said that when he first saw the flats as a youngster he thought they must be the poshest flats in London because they had a view over the Upton Park pitch. In fact, they were council flats erected for the poorest families in the area.

Chicken Run or not, in the late 1960s Moore was playing some of the best football of his life. The couple had a host of good friends, many from the old days, and also many new ones like Jimmy Tarbuck and Sean Connery. Professional footballers had come a long way from the soggy leather ball and inch-thick shin pads of the fifties. And of course, Bobby Moore became a household name. Even in the 'Age of Aquarius', where anything was possible, the Moores led extraordinary lives. But they were not spared the worst features of family life. Tragedy touched their lives again in 1968 when Tina's mother died of cancer at the age of 51. The family were very close and Nanny Wilde was clearly very dear to Bobby, as well as to her daughter.

A low and dishonest decade

Despite the fame and adulation after 1966, the Moore family had times when their courage and close bonding were tested to the full. As the sixties came to a close, things began to change. The seventies were a bad time for football, with the worst kind of violence and intimidation both on and off the field. West Ham fans were some of the worst offenders, although the team didn't forget the ideals of Ron Greenwood even if their results never quite matched those of previous years. John Lyall, Trevor Brooking, Billy Bonds and Alan Devonshire would continue to fly the flag for the Academy, but the seventies were a bleak period in Britain's social history, characterised by racism, class war and violence. In the late seventies punk rock blasted away the last fragile remnants of the hippie culture, and Queen and Pink Floyd ruled the charts – bleak times indeed.

The dark times were made worse in the early part of the decade by the three-day working week introduced by Ted Heath's Tories. The oil crisis raged on, sending the West into the deepest recession since the 1930s. In the 'winter of discontent' of 1978/79 the streets around Upton Park, and all other cities, were piled high with rotting rubbish for weeks during the long public sector unions' dispute with Callaghan's Labour Government. At the height of the economic difficulties of this miserable decade inflation reached a staggering 26 per cent. The seventies ended with a 1979 General Election victory for Mrs Thatcher, whose class-based politics exploited the deep divisions in British society and won her three successive elections. If there ever was a time that Britain was broken it was during the late 1970s and the years under the Thatcher government. I can remember my mother throwing her slippers at the TV whenever Mrs 'no such thing as society' Thatcher appeared on the screen. She dearly wanted to outlive the Iron Lady, but sadly her wish was denied.

Despite the grim and often desolate times, the seventies did provide some signs of hope. Led by Hammers' supporter Billy Bragg and others, the Anti-Nazi League, Red Wedge and Rock Against Racism fought back against the growing influence of the National Front on white working-class young people in our urban centres. The legendary Ian Drury, from out on the estuary, gave us many 'reasons to be cheerful' at the time. Throughout the decade the civil rights movement continued to gain ground against prejudice and inequality in social and political life. It is a pity that David Bowie and Eric Clapton, from rock music's less socially aware school of fame, chose to side with Enoch Powell and other racists who inhabited the seamier side of our political culture in those days. This was the background for the worst examples of football violence to be seen on the football grounds, railways stations and streets of our major cities.

For Bobby Moore the beginning of the seventies was a time of the most extraordinary emotional highs and lows. In the 1970 World Cup in Mexico he played the football of his life against a background that tested every ounce of his personal strength and courage. The bracelet incident at the Green Fire gift shop in the Tequendama Hotel in Colombia is well documented. It caused an international incident and deep anxiety and stress in the Moore family. The incident occurred while the England party were in Bogotá to play Colombia in a warm-up friendly. Moore and Bobby Charlton had gone into the hotel shop to look for gifts for their wives. After they left the shop they were approached by the hotel staff and informed that there was something missing from the shop. The police were called, but the matter appeared to have been resolved and the squad left Bogotá to play Ecuador in another warm-up game three days later. Following the Ecuador game, the team were due to fly out to Mexico to start their defence of the Jules Rimet Trophy. Unfortunately, they had to change planes back at Bogotá, where the police were waiting. Moore was arrested on suspicion of stealing the 'missing' bracelet and was taken to the house of Alfonso Senior, Director of the Colombian Football Federation, where he was held under house arrest pending a full investigation.

The rest of the England team flew out to Mexico without their captain, and one can only imagine how Alf Ramsey and his squad were feeling, with only a few days remaining before their first group game. On 27th May Moore was taken back to the Tequendama Hotel, where a re-enactment of the incident was staged in front of a judge. A witness came forward claiming to have seen the England captain pocket the bracelet and Moore, for the first time, began to think the worst. Up until then he had been confident that he would join his teammates in Mexico for the start of the tournament.

Moore was worried about his physical condition and the following day Alfonso Senior found a local pitch where Bobby could train. The England captain training on his own on a park pitch in Bogotá was a cause of great local interest, as Tina Moore remembers:

> *The jungle drums had been beating and, by the end, Bobby's work-out had turned into a kick-about friendly with a bunch of barefoot local kids in front of a media posse.*
> *- T. Moore (2005), p.119.*

A final appearance in front of the judge followed, and to great relief all round he ruled that Moore had no case to answer. So on 29th May Moore flew to Mexico City en route to Guadalajara, where his England colleagues were waiting. By this time Moore had become a hero to ordinary Colombians and hundreds of them were there to cheer him off at the airport. They knew only too well that he had been the innocent victim of an extortion operation aimed at visiting celebrities. On his way to catch up with the England squad Moore made an overnight stop in Mexico City and stayed at the home of the

British Ambassador's Information Officer. Bizarrely, Moore had a visit that evening from his great friend Jimmy Greaves, who was in Mexico for the World Cup Car Rally. Moore would have been greatly cheered up to see his intrepid friend, proof at last that he was back in the real world. Nobody was more pleased to see Moore arrive in Guadalajara than the England manager. Alf Ramsey had said all along that there was nothing more he wanted to see than his captain walk down the steps of a plane and be reunited with his teammates. Sir Alf had got his wish. Moore had to wait until 1975 before the Home Office finally informed him that the case was closed. The Colombian police had eventually uncovered a plot to frame the England captain. As Jimmy Greaves might have said - well done, Bob, end of story, fancy a lager?

We can only imagine what the media would have made of the bracelet incident today. For Tina Moore the incident refuses to go away completely, as she reveals in her autobiography. The effect on the family would have been profound, particularly on Moore's mother Doss. The children were young at the time, although Roberta had just started school. The parents were worried what the other children at her school might have said to Roberta. They needn't have worried too much, however, as the only thing she remembers was a friend saying to her, "Your daddy's found a bracelet." Today the media would be camped outside the school for days.

Not content with every East Ender's dream of living in Manor Road, in 1972 the Moores bought a plot of land in Stradbroke Drive, the most desirable street in Chigwell. They built a house that was true to the specifications of the Chigwell faux Georgian villa, with six bedrooms, numerous bathrooms and Bobby's very own bar. What else could they call it but 'Morlands'? As the proud Mrs Moore says of her new house in her autobiography, "... it was a million miles away from the tin bath that hung on a hook in Christchurch Road". The home of their dreams had cost them £80,000, an astronomical sum in 1972. In the best traditions of East End folk made good, they had made it to the 'promised land'. Having seen off cancer and coped with family bereavement, and with the stitch-up in Bogotá firmly behind them, what could possibly stop the golden couple now as they appeared to defy the prevailing mood of seventies depression and disappointment?

There ought to be a law against him

Secure in his new family life Moore was able to concentrate fully on his football, and boy did he focus. A study of Moore from a local perspective should not forget that the crowning glory of his career will always be his 108 England caps and that he was the youngest ever England captain at the age of 22. Writing in the *Sunday Times*, journalist Hugh Mcllvanney makes a comparison between players who achieved their England caps in the 1950s and 1960s and those who have represented their country in more recent times. It comes as a surprise to discover that brothers Gary and Phil Neville have more England caps between them than Jack and Bobby Charlton. The incomparable Stanley Matthews gained just 54 caps during his long career. We should not forget that in every one of his 108 matches for his country Moore would have been on the pitch for the whole 90 minutes. In other words, he started every game and finished every game. In comparison, David Beckham, who equalled Moore's 108 caps in February 2009, played for the full 90 minutes only 55 times, having appeared as a substitute on nine occasions. He was taken off 42 times in his 108 caps and was sent off twice. So, in effect, Moore played the equivalent of 19 matches more than Beckham. Mcllvanney concludes from these figures that

> *David Beckham deserves warmest congratulations for an outstanding accomplishment but caps are devalued currency and no longer a genuine measure of a career's worth.*
> *- H. McIlvanney, Sunday Times, 15th February 2009.*

Moore earned every one of his 108 caps and all his achievements were hard won. He also experienced disappointments in his seemingly benighted career, as we shall see. For example, he never won a First Division Championship medal, which nagged away at him and was the source of conflict with his managers and the club directors. His post-playing days were a disappointment both to Moore himself and to those who idolised him and wanted the best for their hero. There can be fewer contrasts, even ironies, in sport than that between the glory of Moore's playing career and the anticlimax of his tragically shortened retirement. This is an issue that remains unresolved for many football lovers, and not just the Hammers faithful. But, before we examine this sensitive and delicate issue, we should return to the beginnings of this best of all sporting careers.

Bobby Moore was not born a natural athlete, although he played football from a very young age. On the football pitches of Flanders Fields, his school ground, he was known by the unflattering nickname 'Tubby' and was regarded as a hardworking rather than a skilful young footballer. Later Moore was to show the same courage and coolness under pressure that characterised the spirit of soldiers who fought in the French fields that shared the same name as the primary school ground. As a youngster Moore regarded himself as "sound rather than spectacular". But he tasted glory early when his school, Barking Primary School, won the prestigious Crisp Shield two years running, with Moore as captain in the second year. At his secondary school, Tom Hood, there is some confusion over his academic ability, although Moore himself remembers gaining 4 O levels, which is pretty much average for a young East London boy who is mad keen on football. He failed to attract early interest from professional clubs and wondered about a career as a draughtsman, or perhaps as a hedge fund-holding city boy. But the inevitable did happen and the young Moore was spotted playing for the Leyton Boys District side by Jack Turner, a West Ham scout, who recommended him to the West Ham manager, Ted Fenton. The rest, as they say, is history.

It was inevitable that an outstanding young footballer, selected under-age for the East London schools' representative side, would be spotted by the local professional club. West Ham had a good scouting set-up, which was much more thorough than the other London clubs. In the 1950s and 1960s professional clubs relied on a regular supply of young players from local schools for their youth teams, who perhaps one day would join their first team. Having said that, even a club with as good a scouting system as West Ham couldn't expect to pick up the future England captain and arguably the greatest defender the world has ever seen, from the Leyton Boys Schools District team.

It was not uncommon for managers from the old Division One clubs to be seen at Saturday morning school matches, hoping to spot the next Jimmy Greaves or Johnny Byrne. I remember one Saturday morning in the early 1960s at the George White Sports

Ground close to the Walthamstow dog track standing close to the old Spurs manager, Bill Nicholson. We were watching the Walthamstow Boys under-16s side, which in 1962 came very close to winning the English Schools Trophy. Billy Nick, as he was affectionately known, was enjoying a warming beverage outside the ground's old tea hut. In the Walthamstow side that day were Ian and Roger Morgan, Denis Bond and Mick Leach. Roger Morgan and Denis Bond eventually signed for Tottenham, after spells at Queens Park Rangers and Watford, respectively. Bond, an England Schoolboy international, was perhaps the most gifted of an outstanding quartet of young footballers on show that Saturday morning. Ian Morgan and the late Mick Leach had distinguished football careers and were regulars in the great QPR side that comprised Rodney Marsh, Don Masson, Terry Venables, Bob Hazell and Phil Parkes. Bill Nicholson must have enjoyed that particular Saturday morning and in his own quiet way would have been excited by the football served up by the best young players of their generation - much in the way that West Ham scout Jack Turner would have been after first seeing the 15-year-old Bobby Moore play just a few miles across East London in Leyton.

Outstanding schoolboy footballers, held in awe by their contemporaries, often fail to achieve their potential and the transition to the professional game. Moore was never going to make that mistake. Clubs in the 1950s and 1960s knew that local boys were the future of the club and gave them every opportunity to succeed. However, things have changed. The West Ham team that won the FA Cup in 1964 were the last to consist totally of English players, most of them from East London and Essex. Since the advent of the Premier League and Sky TV cash in 1992, clubs have less need for extensive scouting systems designed to spot the best local youngsters. The scouting systems today are worldwide operations, but sadly not always operating with the highest ethical standards, or any standards at all. English football owes a debt to West Ham United FC for not only spotting the schoolboy Moore but also for providing a standard of coaching that was rare in the professional game at the time, and which ensured that his rare talent was not lost to the professional game.

So, together with his genuine talent and despite his own initial doubts, Moore was able to prosper from his ethos of hard work, diligence and willingness to learn by applying it within a coaching structure whose principal virtues were wit, imagination and tactical flair. Noel Cantwell and Malcolm Allison were the West Ham coaches who took this no more than promising young defender under their wing. Allison was one of the original members of the Academy who gathered at the old fifties-style Casserati café close to the Boleyn ground to discuss the finer points of football for hours on end. The café sessions began after manager Ted Fenton arranged for the club to provide the players with vouchers for Casserati's, known in the area for providing two types of bubble and squeak – one with a soft, creamy top and the other toasted, hard and crispy. Tea and an old-fashioned fry-up would be frowned on by today's club dieticians but they seemed to work for the growing Moore. Harry Redknapp, himself a member of West Ham's old café society, recently described these pasta and broccoli obsessed characters as "the 'elf professionals around the club". Dear old 'Arry.

If we look at the original members of the West Ham Academy we can only imagine the kind of football conversation that occurred at Casserati's. Together with Cantwell and Allison, there were Dave Sexton, Jimmy Andrews and Frank O'Farrell, all of whom went into club management. Bobby, eager to learn, would sit in on these meetings, listening to the heated debates on technique, tactics and training methods. Allison would give the youngster a lift home to Barking from the café, providing an opportunity for the young defender to benefit from Allison's one-to-one tuition. It was an opportunity he would not waste.

If we add the name of Ron Greenwood to this distinguished list of coaches, we can begin to understand how West Ham United gained a reputation for technical innovation and a free-flowing, close passing game, so beloved of The Hammers' passionate supporters down the years. Who will ever forget Hurst's flicked header by the near post against Argentina in the 1966 World Cup, from a measured cross by his club teammate Martin Peters? This was a move dreamed up and practised on West Ham's training ground at Chadwell Heath. The author of many of these characteristic moves was Ron Greenwood, Moore's coach at England Under 21 level and finally club manager following the departure of Ted Fenton in 1961. Greenwood was a complex character and was later to fall out with his most famous player. He was a genuine student of the game, whose views on football were heavily influenced by Puskas's great Hungarian side of the early 1950s, which took England apart at Wembley in 1954 – a defeat that shook the English game to its roots. Bobby Moore himself was to lead the full recovery of the England team 12 years later. Greenwood had learned his lesson well.

Greenwood selected Moore for his West Ham debut on 8th September 1958 at the age of 17, a few months after signing his first professional contract. To the great surprise of the fans, he was selected for the game against Manchester United ahead of his mentor Malcolm Allison, who had recently recovered from tuberculosis. Greenwood clearly had complete confidence in his young defender. Later that season Allison regained his place, but the young 17-year-old had made his mark and a lasting impression - his promotion to the permanent West Ham No. 6 was simply delayed.

If Greenwood was to prove a decisive early influence on Moore's career, Sir Alf Ramsey was to provide the finishing touches. Ramsey was a Dagenham boy, born just a couple of miles away from his 1966 World Cup captain. He was the last of a line of forward-thinking coaches who would guide Moore's exemplary career and influence the way he thought about the game. Without the level of tactical ingenuity provided by Ramsey, Cantwell, Allison and Greenwood at his most formative stage, Moore may not have fulfilled his early promise and become one of the greatest players in the world. It helped that Moore was an enthusiastic listener and quick learner.

Ramsey had developed his own ideas about the way football should be played during his years as a stylish fullback at Tottenham and in his England career under the tutelage of the cerebral Sir Walter Winterbottom. When his playing days ended, Ramsey became a thoughtful and highly successful club manager with Ipswich Town, playing a style of football that was to become the hallmark of his World Cup winning side of 'wingless wonders'. With Martin Peters and Geoff Hurst also playing a decisive role in the 1966 World Cup final, West Ham fans love to boast that West Ham's technical innovations were central to England's victory. In fact many of them believe that West Ham actually won the World Cup.

The influence of the young West Ham coaching staff

permeated into the raw environment of local park football. Back in the late 1960s I played for a Sunday club in East London whose 'manager' was close friends with several West Ham players. He persuaded the club to allow Roger Cross, a promising young centre forward, to take us for training on Wednesday evenings. Something that Cross said to us has stayed with me down the years. He told us that West Ham professionals always trained "on their toes". This seemingly simple idea helped them to be alert, respond quickly to teammates' decisions and, most importantly, encouraged forward movement and quick passing, all at the heart of West Ham's purist style of play. I am not sure that the 'train one your toes' mantra worked with our mustard keen but half-fit bunch of amateurs on Wednesdays evenings on Wanstead Flats, but at least we didn't put our young professional off coaching forever, as he is currently coaching in the Premier League.

Bobby Moore was to flourish in this hotbed of progressive coaching methods and tactical innovation, uniquely practised at Upton Park and later introduced to the England team by Sir Alf Ramsey. Perhaps the most decisive of these innovations for Moore's career was the 4-2-4 system or its variations. Defensively, zonal marking required two centre halves, a big 'stopper' and a more skilful reader of the game, who was positioned just to the left of the No. 5. This system suited Moore to perfection. His 'stopper' partner at Upton Park was Ken Browne, as solid as they come, and of course later with England, Jack Charlton. Other players famous for gracing the 'sweeper' or 'libero' role in Moore's time were Germany's Beckenbaeur, Moore's famous adversary in the 1966 World Cup final, and Baresi, the great Italian No. 6. Whereas Baresi and his team used the sweeper role to build a stone wall defence, Moore used it to liberate his team without losing the solid defensive qualities for which he is best known. Before non-West Ham football fans laugh at the thought of 'solid defensive qualities' as one of the team's virtues, it had to be said that the concentration on an attacking game over the years, at the expense of all other virtues, is the main reason for the club's famous inconsistency and reputation as a 'soft touch', particularly with some of the more hairy-arsed clubs in the north of England. It continues to this day, and Hammers fans wouldn't have it any other way – I think.

But in Moore The Hammers had the perfect No. 6. The position allowed him to apply the key qualities that set him apart from other players. His coolness under pressure inspired confidence in the players around him and made him the ideal captain. One example stands out. In the dying seconds of the 1966 World Cup final, with England protecting a 3-2 lead, for the final time that afternoon Moore broke up yet another German attack. With the crowd and the rest of the England players, except one, screaming for him to blast the ball into the North Circular Road, Moore drilled an inch-perfect pass to his other switched-on teammate, Geoff Hurst, who ran on and fired a left foot shot into the top corner, breaking the German resistance and their hearts in one sweetly executed movement. His display of that kind of composure in such a pressure-cooker atmosphere at the age of 25 is one of the qualities that set Moore apart from the rest. In those few seconds he showed us all why Ramsey had such complete trust in his captain. In that moment he made certain that England won the World Cup.

Ramsey's 'wingless wonders' were not strictly in 4-2-4 formation, but a version of it that kept Nobby Stiles in a holding position in central midfield in what is known today known as the 'Makélélé role', after Claude Makélélé of Real Madrid and Chelsea, who is the best modern exponent of this tactically crucial position. Like Makélélé, Stiles shielded the back four by watchful interceptions and incisive tackles, before hitting short, precise passes to an England midfield colleague, usually Bobby Charlton. Ramsey's back four of Cohen, Charlton, Moore and Wilson hardly needed protecting, but his deployment of Stiles in a holding role gave full rein to Bobby Charlton's attacking instincts and allowed Peters and Ball to push forward from wider positions. Ramsey chose Ball and Peters because they were versatile footballers who fitted into his preferred system, much like the roles played by Collison and Behrami, the young wide players of the current Gianfranco Zola West Ham side, of which so much is expected and so little will be achieved.

In his wonderful book on the history of football tactics, Jonathan Wilson writes:

> *Martin Peters was like Ball and Hurst, a modern multifunctional footballer, capable of both creativity and of doing his share of leg-work.*

- J. Wilson (2008), Inverting the Pyramid: A History of Football Tactics, Orion Books, p.149.

There lies the description of the modern footballer, although today you might add pace and physicality. Moore in the sweeper role was also perfect for Ramsey's pragmatic approach. With Moore and Stiles consistently breaking up opponents' offensive play, the team could switch quickly to all-out attack, with Charlton, Ball, Peters, Hunt and Hurst all likely goalscorers. Both Moore and Stiles absolutely thrived in the roles that Ramsey gave his key defenders, and his team had the balance that the coach was seeking.

In his book Wilson cites the two great European coaches, Michels and Lobanovsky, as having a clear recognition of just how football should be played. Ramsey had his moment of epiphany during the 1966 World Cup. He worked out, given the players he had at his disposable, just how his team should play to win the tournament. Wilson's description of the Michels and Lobanovsky tactical method should be equally applied to Ramsey's misunderstood 'wingless wonders':

The game, as they saw it, was about space and how you controlled it: make the pitch big when you have the ball and it is easy to retain it; make it small when you do not and it becomes far more difficult for the opposition to keep it. ...
Both encouraged their players to interchange positions, both relied on teammates being able to cover, and both produced sides that were capable of exhilarating football. ... Pressing was the key, but it was probably only in the mid- to late-sixties that it became viable.
- J. Wilson (2008) p.218

If only some of the West Ham managers over the years had realised that winning football matches requires more than pretty passing in neat triangles. Here we have in a nutshell why Ramsey felt he had to ditch two of the most skilful players in his squad, neither of whom could possibly fit into the England manager's ideal system. Peter Thompson was a highly talented winger in the great Liverpool side, while Jimmy Greaves was arguably the greatest English goalscorer of all time and was also a close friend of the England captain. By the time England had reached the last eight in the 1966 World Cup, both of these gifted individuals had been sacrificed in the cause of victory. Neither could or would track back or press, and Ramsey needed players that could do this.

Ramsey was in a privileged position vis-à-vis previous England managers. He became the first England manager to enjoy complete control over team selection and tactics, and he was free to make the kinds of decisions that sidelined the likes of Thompson and Greaves without worrying about offending committee members. Ramsey was a strong character and deep tactical thinker, and there was no question in terms of allowing blazered FA committee men to pick his team. He was also a winner, as he had shown at Ipswich. Moore was ambitious and keen to build on the personal success he had achieved at West Ham, and the two formed a football marriage made in heaven. As Ramsey said at the time:

If people say England would have won the World Cup without me as a manager, I can say it would have been impossible without Bobby as captain. In so many ways he was my right hand man, my lieutenant on the field, a cool, calculated footballer I could trust with my life.
- J. Powell (1993) p.272

This is an extraordinary tribute to his captain by a successful England manager. When Moore was under arrest on the trumped-up charge in a Colombian jail in 1970, Ramsey told the press that he just wanted to see his captain walk down the steps of a plane in Mexico City; then, and only then, would he be able to get on with his job of preparing his team to defend the World Cup. A little like Moore, Ramsey was an austere, often aloof individual, who was conscious of his working-class background. However, he was tactically astute and shaped a winning team in his own pragmatic image. He knew what it took to win important games, and it helped that he had a number of world-class players at his disposal, three of whom - Ball, Peters and Hurst - were well on their way to becoming among the best in the world.

Moore and Ramsey were born a couple of miles from each other in what is now known as the London Borough of Dagenham & Redbridge. The crucial difference between their characters was that Moore was proud of his roots whereas

Ramsey did everything he could to forget them. The West Ham crowd, with their rough music, can be as intimidating as any in the world. Moore loved the atmosphere created by the North Bank at Upton Park, while Ramsey would have found it a little beneath him – a bit too undignified for this most self-possessed of men. Fortunately, their differences never affected their professional relationship, which was perhaps the best manager/captain partnership in the history of international football.

Form or function?

To say that Ramsey, England's most successful ever football coach, was a pragmatist raises one of the most interesting debates in the game and one of the most compelling in sport generally. It comes down to a question of aesthetics. Should we always go for the guile, grace and sheer beauty of Jimmy Greaves over the more powerful, utilitarian muscle of Geoff Hurst? Is the essence of sport more about beauty than function? Is the point of play to aspire to the beautiful? Or is it actually about achieving a result first and foremost? In his incomparable book, *Beyond a Boundary*, the cultural analyst and great sports lover C.L.R. James argues that sport and art are part of the same human quest for beauty and aesthetic perfection. It would be tempting to think that James was right about this, but his argument is unconvincing. Art works, or should work, on a more elevated level than sport and invokes an altogether different level of meaning and allusion, even if both art and sport are concerned, at least partly, with beauty. In sport the ideal is to combine beauty with success, as in football with the Real Madrid side of the late 1950s and early 1960s, the Brazilians in 1970, Puskas's great Hungarian side of the 1950s and the West Ham side of 1964 – well, at least the first three.

Although Ramsey was a pragmatist, primarily interested in success, and perhaps influenced by the FA staff coaches Charlie Hughes and Adam Wade, his players were not robots fitted into a rigid system. His players' footballing instincts and skills were not stifled and 'dehumanised', as suggested by Lars Arnesson, coach of the Swedish national team in the 1974 World Cup. For one thing, it would have been extremely difficult for a coach, however strong a personality, to impose himself on Bobby Moore, Bobby Charlton, Alan Ball or Martin Peters, all of whom were wonderfully creative players but whose instincts were to tailor their abilities to the benefit of the team. Here we have strength, beauty, industry and resilience, not just organisation and energy, which would not have got them past the group stage. Ramsey's team of 1966 was of its time. The Real Madrid side of Di Stephano and Pelé's Brazil would have known how to adapt to the systems and levels of fitness of the modern game. Bobby Moore's game was perfect for its time: a desired balance of skill, aesthetic qualities and strength, combined with a will to win. Ramsey had found a soulmate.

Ramsey admired his captain's calm but inspired leadership qualities. Playing on the left of a zonal defence enabled Moore to control the way his team were playing. He liked to play the ball quickly, as he did with the free kick that set up England's opening goal in 1966, and he could read the pattern of a game and work out his opponents' next move. This usually resulted in an intercepted pass, or perfectly timed tackle, allowing Moore to do what he loved most - get his team going forward again, with a defence-splitting pass, a run with the ball deep into the opponent's half or a measured pass out to one of his fullbacks. As his team moved forward he liked to switch the point of attack with an accurate cross-field pass to unbalance the opposition's defence. He once said that his perfect pass would result in his teammate taking the ball forward without breaking stride. In the 2009 Premier League season you will almost always see players passing the ball either directly at a teammate, or more likely a metre behind, a much more cautious approach to attacking play. This might be because defenders are fitter than they were in Moore's day, quicker over five yards, and are able to turn simple forward passes into bone-crunching collisions. It is tempting to think that Moore's football intelligence would have enabled him to make the necessary adjustment. Unlike Rio Ferdinand, Moore had no pace, but he had quick feet and a quicker mind.

This intuitive football intelligence enabled Moore to reach soaring levels of skill game after game. The most obvious of these were his tackling and passing, which could, and often did, turn games. Sports journalist Mike Langley describes one of Moore's tackles perfectly:

The right leg stretches out and Bobby, echoing the opening batsman

Essex so keenly wanted him to be, sinks onto his left knee like Denis Compton about to sweep the ball through fine leg. But Moore's knee doesn't touch the ground. Somehow, marvellously athletic, he rises with the ball now completely filched from Charlie Cooke of Chelsea and Scotland.
- M. Langley, quoted in 'Bobby Moore' International Football Hall of Fame (www.ifhof.com)

Chelsea were one of the most feared teams in England in the 1960s and 1970s, largely due to their dangerous pair of brittle geniuses, Peter Osgood and Charlie Cooke. These two could destroy any team within minutes. Stealing the ball away from Cooke in such a manner would not only inspire his team but would also lift the Upton Park crowd. Of course, every football lover knows about the tackle on Brazil's Jairzinho in the 1970 World Cup – it's simply part of the folklore of the game and has been immortalised in song – "but I still see that tackle by Moore" ('Three Lions' sung by the Lightning Seeds, with lyrics by David Baddiel and Frank Skinner, which was England's Euro '96 anthem). It is said to have been the greatest tackle ever made and just cannot be improved upon. Of course, it had to be against a Brazil team that were said to be the greatest ever, and in a World Cup competition. Also that year East End punk band, The Business, recorded a tribute song to their idol called 'Viva Bobby Moore', which showed the breadth of affection in which he was held. The latter was an ironic tribute, as Moore himself preferred Sinatra to the Sex Pistols, but he would have enjoyed the compliment.

The year 1970 was in some ways a triumph for Moore, a time in which he built on his already considerable reputation. The Jairzinho tackle against Brazil in Mexico was in a group game that would have graced any World Cup final, with both teams playing to the limits of their considerable ability. Moore's tackle, Gordon Banks's astonishing reflex save from Pelé's sharp downward header and Alan Ball hitting the bar with minutes to go were just some of the highlights. Unfortunately, the highly fancied England went out of the competition in the quarter-finals, losing 3-2 to Germany in a game in which they had dominated and led 2-0, before the England substitutions gave Germany the encouragement they needed, with Peter Bonetti and Gerd Müller doing the rest.

Ambition and an honourable man

Prior to the start of the 1966 World Cup tournament Moore was having a difficult and frustrating time with his club, West Ham United. It is important to remember the extent to which clubs controlled their players, who, once registered, were actually owned by the club, in or out of contract. Moore's existing contract was due to expire on 30th June, but he was in dispute with his club and had refused to sign a new contract. As every player in the World Cup had to be contracted to a club in order to play in the competition, there was huge doubt hanging over Moore's participation. Without a club contract he would miss the World Cup opener against Uruguay.

By this time Moore was convinced that he would become a Spurs player the following season. The principal issue in the dispute was a £10 pay rise, a miserly sum by today's standards but enough to cause a grievance, as the England captain was poorly paid in comparison with his colleagues in the England squad. For Ramsey and millions of England fans this was unthinkable. When it became apparent that there was a problem, Ron Greenwood was hastily summoned by the England coach to the England team's headquarters at Hendon Hall. At a very short meeting with Greenwood, Moore quickly signed a month-by-month contract with the club and the matter was resolved. He was free to go on and win the World Cup for his country, as well as achieving a personal triumph in the shape of the Player of Players award at the end of the tournament. Moore was entitled to harbour a high level of resentment against his club, although he disguised this magnificently during the course of the tournament.

Fours year later Moore returning from Mexico in a rather restless and unsettled mood, and his former disenchantment with West Ham returned with a vengeance. Moore, now around 30 years old, hungered after a First Division Championship winners' medal and had become frustrated with his club's apparent lack of ambition, and his relationship with Ron Greenwood quickly reached breaking point. It is worth reminding ourselves that by this point in his career Moore had acquired an FA Cup Winners' medal and a European Cup Winners' Cup medal, and had captained his country to the ultimate triumph, a World Cup victory on home soil. Moore's frustration may have been rooted in his relatively modest wages (as they were still referred to in the 1970s) of around £200 a week - enough to own a substantial house in Chigwell but lower than players with lesser ability were earning at other clubs. But it is more tempting to believe that it was a desire to win a League Championship medal, probably with one of the London glamour clubs of the time, Arsenal or Spurs, although the glamour of both was based on past rather present glories.

We can trace Moore's disillusionment with his club and manager back to 1966. He remained unhappy that Greenwood had missed the opportunity to sign players that would have given Moore the team he craved. As ever, the England team gatherings provided the opportunity for players to voice their personal frustrations to eager listeners, and close friends of Moore were in a position to help persuade him that it was time for a move. One of these friends was Terry Venables, a real influence in the game, particularly in London. After a successful period at Chelsea, Venables' spell as a player at Tottenham was not especially distinguished, and neither were the Spurs fans convinced about his commitment to their cause. Perhaps his mind was on his managerial and business future at QPR, Crystal Palace, and later Barcelona. Venables was an Essex boy, born in Dagenham down the road from his great friend. He was a football celebrity in the 1960s and early 1970s in the way that footballers were beginning to be figures of popular culture back in that most democratic of decades. He was a product of his East London upbringing and it was there that he acquired his famous wheeling and dealing skills, much in the way that Harry Redknapp did more or less at the same time. It is hard to believe that Moore had the taste for such East End ducking and diving. Certainly, his post-playing days show no evidence of any natural instincts for this way of working, and this is probably the reason why he later failed as a club manager.

In the late 1960s Terry Venables bought a pub for his dad in Essex, out on a bleak stretch of road that runs from Chingford to Waltham Abbey, adjacent to a kosher abattoir and a few hundred yards from what was left of the Royal Enfield small arms factory. A little later Venables bought his mother a corner shop a mile down the road from the pub, on the edge of the council estate where I grew up. My family and all the neighbours used the shop on a daily basis, and Venables was often there in his sheepskin coat, always friendly and quick with a joke. My mother worked in the pub for a spell and spoke fondly of Terry and his young family. It is hard to imagine today's multimillionaire, celebrity international footballers staying this close to their roots and local community.

Moore and Venables were mates but had different instincts and personalities. Venables was the shrewd, sharp business-oriented operator, but no spiv. Moore was the ingénue, and despite his undoubted intelligence he became an easy target for sharks and local duckers and divers. He lived for playing football, and when it was gone he was left rudderless and lost. He once said that on the football field nobody could get to him; it was where he belonged and was his whole identity. This explains Moore's football ambitions, for himself, for West Ham United and for England. So when Venables suggested to his friend that his ambitions would be better served at Tottenham rather than with the more modest aspirations of West Ham he was bound to be tempted. Moore put it this way:

Spurs were supposed to be above these things, but the fact remained they wanted me and I was itching to go there. Tottenham would have suited me down to the ground. They were the team of the sixties, no trouble.
- Powell (1993), p.88

In the days before players' agents tapping was routine, Jeff Powell points out in his biography of Moore, that Greenwood was at home in the dark arts of the football transfer system – and this was in the days before brown envelopes, 10 per cent for managers and other examples of corruption and near-criminal transfer activity. Powell uses the example of the way in which Greenwood lured Johnny Byrne from Crystal Palace as evidence that he was not above sharp practice. Moore himself remembers Greenwood as the England U23 manager and then Arsenal youth coach suggesting to him that Arsenal were very impressed with the young defender and would love to see him at Highbury. Moore's loyalty for Greenwood was definitely compromised by this memory.

West Ham fans could accept that Moore was unhappy at the club's lack of ambition - but Tottenham? They may have been the team of the sixties, but they were in decline by the end of the decade. However, much to the relief of the West Ham faithful, the transfer to Tottenham never materialised for one reason or another. The sight of their beloved England captain in the white No. 6 shirt of Tottenham would have been too much to bear. Fortunately, Tottenham hesitated and West Ham dug their heels in.

A further test of Moore's ambition in the domestic game was to come in the early 1970s, in the unlikely figure of the legendary Brian Clough. The incomparable Clough, who cared little for FA rules and regulations, was manager of Derby County when, at the end of the 1972/73 season, West Ham went up to the Baseball Ground and drew 1-1. By his admission Moore played at the very top of his majestic game. Moore spoke later of his own performance:

I played more than well. Derby paralyzed us but they only got a draw with a penalty in the 84th minute. Even Ron Greenwood came up to me and said well done. Praise indeed.
- Powell (1993), p.90

Clough took careful note of Moore's performance and made what is now called an 'illegal approach' for Moore through a mutual friend. The two men met at a top London hotel - and who wouldn't have paid a great deal of money to have overheard that particular conversation? Clough was a world-class motivator and Moore felt he needed someone with the great man's enthusiasm to lift his game and help him to continue to perform at the highest level. The West Ham and England captain believed that self-motivation and his own sense of pride had carried him to the heights he reached in the 1960s. But now he needed a boost. However, not even Brian Clough could cut the umbilical attachment that Bobby Moore seemed to have to West Ham United.

Moore was told by his club that he could go to Derby for a fee in excess of £400,000 in a treacherous deal that involved the young Trevor Brooking joining him at the Baseball Ground. It appears that Greenwood later blocked the deal, explaining to Moore that it was in his best interests not to go to Derby, far away as it was from everything that Moore knew and loved in London. Greenwood had a point. It has to be said that the thought of the England captain sitting down to Bakewell pudding for tea and putting away pints of dark mild after a match did seem a little bizarre at the time. Greenwood argued that Moore should think carefully about joining Clough at Derby because he would be out of contract at the end of the season and would be able to negotiate a good deal for himself on a free transfer. Moore was refused permission by West Ham to speak to the Derby manager, who in any case was soon to leave the Baseball Ground for Nottingham Forest, where he was to achieve managerial greatness by winning two European Cups. Moore and Clough never did join forces, and in the meantime Moore's Championship-winning ambitions were over, although there remained several twists and turns in the latter part of his career.

That Moore neither signed for Tottenham nor joined forces with Brian Clough was due to the intransigence of his club and manager and their not unsurprising unwillingness to lose their captain to a rival club. The tensions between Bobby Moore and West Ham United are often forgotten in the image of his benighted career. Older West Ham fans do not forget that they almost lost their idol to Spurs at a time when they had their most successful team and their greatest chance of winning the First Division Championship. Not for the last time their passion for the club was thrown back in their faces. Moore signing monthly contracts for his club in 1966 was the ultimate insult to the fans.

Moore was awarded a testimonial by West Ham at the end of the 1970 season and Celtic came to Upton Park as the Boleyn paid tribute to their greatest ever player. But the relationship with Greenwood further deteriorated and entered the public domain. West Ham fans found it hard to accept when their beloved captain and haughty, academic and aloof manager fought out their differences in public. Moore criticised Greenwood's ambition and man management. Greenwood could not accept what he believed was his captain's disloyalty and, on the odd occasion, unprofessional behaviour. Even harder to accept for the club's fans was that Greenwood did have a point. Despite being an iconic figure with a profound influence on Britain's national game, Moore had his moments. He was just a footballer from East London after all. There was also the Blackpool incident in 1971, which is buried deep in West Ham folklore. Moore, along with Brian Dear, Clyde Best and Jimmy Greaves, gaily attended boxer Brian London's nightclub in the city. This would have been okay, but it was the night before an FA Cup tie which, in time-honoured fashion, West Ham proceeded to lose 4-0 to a team keen to put one over on their 'soft southern' opposition. The captain out drinking into the early hours with younger players, in the case of Clyde Best, would have profoundly disappointed Greenwood rather than angered him. All four players were fined a week's wages, and for Moore it was the beginning of the end of his career at the club he had joined as a teenager, his local club. In Moore's defence the weather was so bad on the Friday night that it looked unlikely that the game would go ahead. In addition, the merrymakers were all back at the hotel, perfectly sober, before 1.00 p.m. But Moore knew that what he had done was wrong and apologised for his actions. With exquisite timing the BBC screened its This is Your Life tribute to Moore the night before the infamous Blackpool incident.

That Moore liked a drink and a night on the town, almost always after a match, is well documented in Jeff Powell's biography. But Powell is careful to balance his description of Moore's extra-curricular activities by reminding us that he was often seen in the gym, out running or working off the night on a Sunday morning, alone on the Upton Park pitch. Greenwood would have probably lived with this. Moore was an East Ender and had the spirit and verve for life characteristic of people from the area. However, despite his occasional lapses from grace, Moore knew what it took to get to the very top of the professional game and trained as hard as any of his England teammates. But, for Greenwood, Moore had crossed a line at Blackpool, largely because he had involved a young and impressionable professional in Clyde Best.

Greenwood was recognised as a talented and innovative coach who was able to bring the best out of top players. He was able to turn an ordinary wing half, in Geoff Hurst, into one of the most effective forwards in the modern game. Similarly, he was the inspiration behind the kind of football that West Ham played in the early 1960s – Blackpool notwithstanding – which had the purists purring with pleasure. The breathtaking forward play of Moore, Johnny 'Budgie' Byrne, Martin Peters and Hurst, supported by wingers Johnny Sissons and either Peter Brabrook or the young Harry Redknapp, is today generally regarded as the best ever seen at Upton Park. Greenwood is also credited with the football development of Trevor Brooking, and his influence extends to the Cole, Lampard, Ferdinand generation of young Hammers of the 1990s and can be seen today in the skills of West Ham's local youngsters Noble, Collison, Tomkins, Stanislav and Sears. Hammers fans will fervently hope that the promising new generation will not be squandered like Lampard and his young teammates. Frank Lampard Jnr cannot be blamed for leaving the club that his father played for with such distinction, although the repeated kissing of the Chelsea badge after yet another goal from midfield is guaranteed to inflame even the mildest-mannered Hammers fan. However, the blame for the loss of the Lampard generation lies solely with the club's board of directors, a particularly spineless and over-promoted bunch of incompetents.

In his 1993 biography of Moore, Jeff Powell recalls the occasion when Moore, at the age of 23, was elected Footballer of the Year by the members of the Football Writers' Association. The award ceremony was held at London's Café Royal just a couple of days before West Ham's 1964 Cup final against Preston. Moore later reflected on the occasion:

> *I made my way over from our hotel alone. Yet even though Ron had refused to let the lads come, I couldn't believe the club wouldn't support me. I looked around the Café Royal and I couldn't see a soul from West Ham. Not a single face. Not even a director. Did the directors think they were playing on Saturday? That hurt deep down. I still left early enough to help win the bloody Final for them.*
> *- Powell (1993), p.37*

Moore admits to making a conciliatory gesture towards Greenwood after the final, which West Ham won 2-0. Moore went to embrace his manager but was rebuffed. By this time Greenwood thought his captain's aloof personality – so much like his own – indicated that Moore no longer respected him as manager. Moore did believe that Greenwood's technical team talks went over the heads of the players, but he felt that his manager should get the credit for winning the FA Cup and Cup Winners' Cup. For Moore, Greenwood signed the wrong players in 1967 in his attempt to strengthen the heart of his brilliant, if brittle, team. For some reason Moore wanted the tough defender Maurice Setters to supplement the more cerebral skills of Peters, Byrne and the others. Greenwood, not without some justification, thought that Setters was a troublemaker and so he settled for John Cushley and Alan Stephenson, neither of whom was able to impose himself strongly enough to radically change the Hammers' habit of flattering to deceive.

There is little doubt that Moore sought Greenwood's approval and would have appreciated a more emotional response to some of his great deeds. Their difficult relationship was not helped by both men's seemingly aloof and detached attitude. Greenwood visited Moore during his stay in hospital following the discovery of his cancer in 1964. The visit, according to Tina Moore, demonstrated Greenwood's lack of sensitivity towards his players. The West Ham manager told his stricken captain that he need not worry as the team were doing perfectly fine without him. What Moore wanted to hear was, "Bobby, the team desperately need you back and we will do everything we can to support you and the family until you are back where you belong." Greenwood's insensitivity hurt the young Moore and their relationship never really recovered.

Feeling the wrath of Sir Alf

The England captain was also at the heart of a confrontation with his England manager, Alf Ramsey. Prior to a prestige international against Lisbon in Portugal in 1964, Moore and six other members of the squad left their London hotel for a stroll along Bayswater Road. Then the inevitable happened and one of them suggested a couple of pints before bedtime. Footballers being footballers, Ramsey's not ungenerous curfew was broken. When the players returned to their hotel they were greeted by the shocking sight of passports on their pillows. However, Ramsey, showing his talent for man-management and his strength of purpose, let them stew, took them all to Portugal and said nothing about the incident until the day before the match. He then read them the riot act, leaving the players in no doubt who was the boss. All seven played in the game against Portugal, which England won 4-3, and all were at the top of their game. Against the iron-fisted Ramsey, Greenwood may have appeared a soft touch, as he preferred to believe in the innate common sense and decency of players and credited them with being capable of managing their own behaviour. Oh dear.

In the late 1990s the Manchester United manager clearly struggled with the A-list celebrity of David Beckham and his wife, despite the player's reputation as a consummate professional. The impression is that Ferguson would have been better able to handle the odd drunken night out than Beckham's red-carpet, celebrity lifestyle. Like Greenwood, Ferguson was - and still is - old school, but he shares Ramsey's belief in the necessity of discipline. The idea of Bobby Moore emerging from the West Ham changing room with a plaster over one eye after a disagreement with his manager, as David Beckham did from Old Trafford after the hairdryer treatment from Sir Alex, is as unlikely as it is amusing. Greenwood would no more kick a loose football boot in the direction of his captain than Ferguson would put a consoling arm around Beckham when his wife's latest single failed to make the No. 1 at Christmas.

Moore's finest moments

Bobby Moore respected Greenwood's principled approach to the game and his innovative coaching methods and tactical awareness. The England captain, along with thousands of fans both at the club and up and down the country, loved the open, free-flowing football that is Greenwood's legacy. In the late 1960s and early 1970s, while Leeds United and other sides felt it necessary to supplement their obvious skills with intimidation and sheer thuggery, West Ham stood alone in championing the values of the 'beautiful game' at club level in the UK. Moore was proud to be part of a club that refused to give up their principles. West Ham's proudest moment was England winning the World Cup in 1966, with three Hammers in the side, one the captain, and all four England goals scored by West Ham players. Others argue that the 1965 Cup Winners' Cup final win at Wembley against TSV Munich was the highlight. My own personal favourite moment was the 1-0 victory over Arsenal in the 1980 FA Cup final, with Billy Bonds lifting the trophy after Trevor Brooking had scored the winner with a rare header. Whether the header was intentional or not is still debated among West Ham's older fans.

Fans steeped in West Ham's football culture still debate which game was Bobby Moore's greatest for the club. There were hundreds of matches where Moore stood head and shoulders above any other player on the pitch. Like Graham Gooch after him, Moore was able to deliver his best when it really mattered. But two stand out in particular as times when his technical skill, football intelligence and sense of occasion came together in performances that were as awe-inspiring as they were effective. In both games Moore's contribution ensured victory. In the semi-final of the 1965 Cup Winners' Cup competition West Ham had been drawn against a very good Spanish side, Real Zaragoza. The Hammers were drawn at home for the first leg, which they narrowly won 2-1. Neither the fans nor the players really felt that a one-goal lead would be enough against a Zaragoza side with a star-studded forward line. The return leg in Spain turned out to be a classic. Moore said about the game:

We put a brave face on it but none of us believed deep down that that it would be enough. They called the Zaragoza forward line the Magnificent Five and we knew they would give us a real going over in Spain. Sure enough they wiped out the lead early on and we were left trying to contain them for the rest of the match. Suddenly John Sissons and Brian Dear broke away and knocked in a goal between them, and we'd got a great result.
- Powell (1993), p.67

These modest words disguise a performance by the West Ham captain that reached a new level of technical excellence. The basketball fraternity in the USA describes defensive perfection as "shutting every door and window on defence". This sums up the level of Moore's performance that evening in Spain perfectly. In Jeff Powell's words,

... the Magnificent Five had foundered on the Magnificent One.
- Powell (1993), p.67

Ron Greenwood argued that Moore's greatest performance for the club was in the final of the Cup Winners' Cup, scheduled that year for Wembley Stadium. West Ham brought their A game with them that evening, playing their quick passing game with a fluency and freedom that the Germans struggled to match. But Munich had their moments in a breathtaking encounter with The Hammers at their irresistible best. The Hammers' captain remembered this moment in the club's history with typical understatement:

We benefited from the experience of the previous year and took part in what many people believe was one of the best matches ever played at the old stadium. There was a lot of good football and we played really well against a good side with a lot of good players. We felt lucky to get the chance of satisfaction at Wembley so soon after the FA Cup Final.
- Powell (1993), p.67

West Ham's victory over Munich was the highlight of Ron Greenwood's management career and he later admitted his debt to his captain with untypical clarity:

This was Bobby Moore's greatest game for West Ham. Technical perfection.
- Quoted in Powell (1993), p.68

The complicated relationship between Moore and Greenwood continued for years and the two never had the kind of bond at West Ham that John Lyall later enjoyed with Billy Bonds. The frustration on Moore's part ran deep. He believed that Greenwood simply did not have the motivational skills and sheer determination necessary to be a successful as well as principled manager. Greenwood's insensitivity surfaced again when he was asked by a reporter if he was sorry to see the former England captain leave the club. Greenwood answered coldly, "I'm sorry when all players leave the club." (T. Moore (2006) p.178). Ironically, Moore believed that nobody had more knowledge of football than Greenwood, and despite their deep differences they usually presented a united front. After all, Moore could not deny his manager's achievements in the FA Cup and in Europe, but his club's commendable if limited achievements and their purist reputation were simply not enough. Oddly, a further nine years at Upton Park slipped away after the FA Cup Winners' Cup triumph in 1965, years in which the club seemed to lose their way. Greenwood's complex football brain failed to adjust the club's quick passing philosophy to the demands of the modern game's emphasis on hard tackling, uncompromising defence and direct tactics. This complex and decent man, a practising Christian, could not compromise, made poor signings and despised the thuggery and violence into which his beloved football descended in the 1970s both on and off the field.

In many ways Greenwood and Moore created the old tradition despite their differences. They were also gentlemen in a kind of 1950s way in terms of resisting the temptation to air their differences in public and keeping their counsel. But for Hammers fans the sight of the England captain on the substitutes' bench following his return from a suspension imposed by the club after Blackpool signaled that the writing was on the wall. Moore believed that the West Ham team of the mid- to late 1960s was good enough, with one or two additions, to dominate the English game in the way that Leeds United did in the 1970s. Greenwood's signings, with the notable exception of Bryan 'Pop' Robson, weakened rather than strengthened the team. As they had come to do in the late 1990s, the club lost an opportunity to build a great side. For most players, winners' medals in the 1964 FA Cup, the European Cup Winners' Cup the following year and the World Cup in 1966 would have been enough. But Moore wanted the League Championship and sustained success at club level.

I was at the Boleyn the day that Moore's suspension was lifted and it was a real shock when, following the pre-match warm-up, Moore strolled past the British Legion band and took his place on the substitutes' bench. There can be no more bizarre or bewildering sight than Bobby Moore on the subs' bench at Upton Park. (We were later to witness the sight of Bobby Moore on the substitutes' bench again on the night of England's infamous World Cup qualifier against Poland in 1973). How had it all come to this? Following a spell of sustained crowd pressure in the second half, Greenwood finally brought his club captain off the bench. The cheer when he jogged onto to the pitch to join the action was loud and heartfelt – their hero was back where he belonged – but the end of his West Ham career was in sight.

Moore never asked too much of Greenwood and West Ham United: a little more money in line with other top players of the day, signing high-quality players as a commitment by the manager and the club to winning the First Division Championship and recognition of Moore's great achievements. If Moore were playing for West Ham these days he would have been transferred long ago, in the manner of Ferdinand, Carrick, Cole and Lampard. We were fortunate to have him when we did and there is little doubt that with more sensitive handling he would have stayed and finished his career at the club he loved the most and which gave him his first chance.

Ron Greenwood was from a different generation to his captain and this might go some way towards explaining their differences. Moore's celebrity was probably at the heart of his increasing distance from his manager. Greenwood had experienced the hardships of the post-war period and was a conventional man who never felt comfortable with the emerging football celebrity culture. He had served with the RAF in the Second World War and returned to play out a modest career with Chelsea, among others; ironically, like Moore, he ended his career at Fulham. He learnt his managerial skills as assistant to George Swindon at Arsenal and played under Ted Drake at Chelsea, as a member of the team that won the First Division in season 1954/55. He joined West Ham as manager in 1962 and won the FA Cup and European Cup Winners' Cup in true Hammers style. He would have taken great pride in having three of his team representing England in the 1966 World Cup final and scoring all four of their team's goals. He became the England team manager in 1977, following the departure of Don Revie. During his time as the national coach England qualified for the European Championships in 1980 and the World Cup in 1982, performing modestly in both competitions. In his 55 games in charge of the national side he won 33 and lost 10 – a decent record. He died in 2006, at the age of 84, after a long struggle with Alzheimer's disease and there is a blue plaque to his memory at Upton Park and another at Loughton in Essex where he lived during his years with West Ham and England.

Despite the unwelcome friction between Moore and Greenwood, the 1960s was a great time to be a West Ham supporter. These were the years when the foundation of the club's purist philosophy was established. The often breathtaking football, particularly when Trevor Brooking later joined the party, was accompanied by a deserved reputation for fragility, resulting in humiliating defeats against teams that should have been swept away in a couple of flowing forward movements. In truth, the golden years did not last very long. The humiliating defeats continued while the joyful football, so beloved of the club's followers was seen less and less, as the club bounced backwards and forwards between the old First and Second Divisions.

A long goodbye

Moore's invincibility as a player began to show signs of weakening during his last season at West Ham, and his long occupation of the England No. 6 shirt was coming to an end at this time. The moment that signalled the beginning of the end of his peerless international career was the World Cup qualifying match against Poland in Katowice in the summer of 1973. The England captain was undone by the skills and pace of the Polish forward Lubanski. The great Pole stole the ball from a dithering Moore early in the second half and raced on to score, putting the Poles ahead. Later in the game Alan Ball was sent off and the following day the two heroes of 1966 were crucified in the press for their errors. As Tina Moore states in her autobiography, "that night in Katowice was the low point of Bobby's footballing life". Early the next morning Moore was spotted by FA officials asleep on a park bench close to the team's hotel. Plagued by insomnia, he had tried to escape the heat and humidity of his hotel room by a taking a pre-dawn walk in the local park. As a result he fell asleep on a bench, only to be woken by the horrified by FA functionaries, who were not amused at the sight of the England captain apparently sleeping rough. Today, of course, Moore's condition would have been diagnosed and treated by the England medical team, but back in 1973 the FA staff were completely unaware of their captain's insomnia problems. Tina Moore is convinced that the Katowice incident was instrumental in the FA's subsequent shunning of Moore in his retirement.

The disastrous qualifier in Poland was followed by a defeat to Italy, with a further Moore mistake leading to one of Italy's goals. Moore was inconsolable, haunted by his mistake against Lubanski and deeply hurt at letting his country down. After the Italy game he revealed to his wife:

> *I think I've blown my chances of ever playing for England again … I should have been in control of the game and I wasn't. I feel I've let everyone down – Alf, the lads, the country.*
> *- T. Moore (2005), p.165.*

In October Poland were due at Wembley for the return group game. Before this crucial World Cup qualifier England had arranged a friendly against Austria, which they won 7-0. The England team that evening were captained, not by the great Bobby Moore, but by Martin Peters. Alf Ramsey had informed Moore prior to the Austria game that he intended to play Norman Hunter at No. 6 in the Poland game and that Hunter would be playing in the Austrian friendly in order to get the team settled. Ramsey had assured Moore that if England qualified for Germany then he would name him as captain. Bobby Moore was on the bench during the disastrous game against Poland, which England had to win to qualify, with Poland needing only a draw.

The Poland goalkeeper, Tomaszewski, had the game of his life and huge slices of luck, and the match ended in a 1-1 draw. Ironically, Hunter made the mistake that led to Poland's goal, and England's forwards contrived to miss chance after chance to put England through to Germany. The Poland game was effectively the end of the international careers of both Moore and Ramsey. A few weeks later, in November 1973, England were scheduled to play a friendly against Italy, and Moore was brought back into the side by Ramsey for his 108th cap and the opportunity to play his last game for his country at Wembley. Six months later Alf Ramsey was summarily sacked by the FA. The end of Moore's England career stands in stark contrast to the stage-managed final appearances of David Beckham in an England shirt. Moore did not have the 'benefit' of publicists and image-makers back in 1973 - perhaps it would have been better if he had. There was a kind of sadness in the way that Moore finished his England career. His contribution to football and the national life of this country failed to be recognised until after his early death in 1993. After a further period of prevarication by club and country, finally proper memorials were erected in his memory at the Boleyn and Wembley.

From East to West

Moore played his last game for West Ham in an FA Cup tie against Hereford United in January 1974. In March that year he was allowed to leave the club that had nurtured and supported him in the early part of his career. Allison, Cantwell and Greenwood had developed his talent and taught him well.

But all West Ham fans knew that he had left feeling frustrated and a little bitter, despite the respect, love and affection he always received from the club's supporters. After more than 15 years with West Ham, he had achieved the club record for appearances (later surpassed by Billy Bonds) and had brought the World Cup to Upton Park. He didn't get the free transfer that he was half-promised by the club. Unbelievably, West Ham demanded £25,000 from Second Division Fulham for Moore's services, who at that time was the most capped player for England.

Along with some old Hammers friends, I went to see Moore play for Fulham in a Second Division match at Luton Town. Again, I couldn't take my eyes off him. Gone were the surges into midfield of his younger days and the quickly taken free kick to the near post. Instead he strolled around, directing the game and giving a lesson in positional play to his younger colleagues on both sides. Bizarrely, Rodney Marsh and George Best were in the Fulham side that afternoon, but it was Moore who took the eye and gave the most polished display. Despite his semi-retirement at Fulham, the football gods had not finished with Moore. In the 1974/75 season Moore helped Fulham to reach the FA Cup final against, of course, West Ham United. The Hammers won 2-0 in a disappointing game, as is so often the way with FA Cup finals. Wembley pre-match rituals involve both sets of players strolling around the pitch in club suits, giving interviews and taking in the atmosphere of the great old stadium. This final was no different, except that Fulham's No. 6 was not out there with his teammates. One of the Fulham players was interviewed on TV and was asked where the great man was and why he wasn't out there on the Wembley pitch breathing in the atmosphere and enjoying the moment. After all, it was going to be his last Wembley appearance. Moore's teammate replied, "Where is he? He is laid out on the treatment table in the dressing room fast asleep. It's just his way of preparing for this game." Oh well, at least it wasn't a park bench. Moore would have known that this would be his last Wembley appearance and he wanted to experience it in his own way.

Moore played his last game for Fulham in the Second Division on 14th May 1977 against Blackburn Rovers. Fulham lost the match, but their star player played well, organising the defence, knocking quick balls out to his fullbacks and generally keeping his team in the game. The Blackburn match was an important milestone for the former England captain: it was his 1,000th appearance as a professional footballer. As Jeff Powell recalls for us, *The Times*, aware of the poignancy of the event, sent their senior sports journalist, Geoffrey Green, to Ewood Park for Moore's final game in English football. Green wrote:

> *By his masterly reading of the game, his uncanny anticipation, his temperament, his coolness under pressure and his ability to turn defence into counter-attack by the accuracy of the long pass, Moore dominated all.*
> *- Powell (1993).*

Green comes as close as anyone could to capturing Moore's technical ability in these few words. He could easily have been writing about Moore captaining England against Germany in the World Cup final at Wembley in 1966 rather than about his playing for Fulham against Blackburn in his last game in English professional football in 1977.

Welcome to the fear factor

In the 1970s, influenced by the success of Juventus and AC Milan, English football became preoccupied with negative tactics and direct play. It was as if the free-flowing game exemplified by the Brazilians and Rinus Michels' Holland had never happened. Fear began to grip the national game both on the pitch and on the terraces. Jonathan Wilson refers to a remark by the great Brazilian coach and philosopher of football, Jorge Valdano, to illustrate the extent to which the professional game had succumbed to this most unappealing and corrosive aspect of sport:

> *Coaches ... have come to view games as a succession of threats and thus fear has contaminated their ideas. Every imaginary threat they try to nullify leads them to a repressive decision which corrodes aspects of football such as happiness, freedom and creativity.*
> *- Wilson (2008), p.307.*

Ron Greenwood and Bobby Moore, if not Sir Alf, would have fully endorsed Valdano's analysis of what had happened to football after the 1970 World Cup, which, despite the 1966 World Cup victory, was Moore's finest hour. Valdano warms to his theme:

At the heart of football's great power of seduction is that there are certain sensations that are eternal. What a fan feels today thinking about the game is at the heart of what fans felt fifty or eighty years ago. Similarly, what Ronaldo thinks when he receives the ball is the same as what Pelé thought which in turn is the same as what Di Stefano thought. In that sense, not much has changed, the attraction is the shame. (Wilson, p.307).

Valdano articulates what every fan feels: a heightened sense of expectation when you pass through the turnstiles. The triumph of results-driven football over the natural style advocated by Valdano has distorted the experience of both fans and players and bent it out of shape. Valdano denies that results are the only thing that matter and that people remember:

What remains in people's memories is the search for greatness and the feelings that engenders … it's about the search for perfection. We know it doesn't exist, but it's our obligation towards football, and, maybe, towards humanity to strive towards it. That's what we remember. That's what's special.
- Wilson, p.307.

This would have resonated with Moore and Greenwood and the West Ham fans, even if they might have used slightly less elevated language. The 'results only' brigade might respond by saying, "Well they would say this wouldn't they, never having won anything much." But it remains true that West Ham fans would never want to surrender their passing game for negative football, even if the latter might reward them with a place in the top six in the Premier League at the end of each season. This is precisely why the appointment of Gianfranco Zola in 2008 aroused such excitement and hope at Upton Park, because his ideas about the game are sympathetic to the West Ham tradition. If he is to succeed he will need all the courage and skill he showed as a player if he is to succeed. I'm afraid the signs are not good.

What's wrong with Bobby Moore?

San Antonio is a beautiful city in Southern Texas, famous in the

USA for the Alamo Centre, its delightful Riverwalk and the all-conquering San Antonio Spurs basketball team. In the summer of 1976 the old Spanish town was to be graced by the appearance of the former England soccer captain, Bobby Moore. Moore had agreed to spend the summer that year playing for the town's North American Soccer League (NASL) franchise, San Antonio Thunder. Football was given a huge boost in the mid-seventies when Pelé, Best, Beckenbauer and others decided to commit to playing in the NASL. When Moore was invited to join San Antonio as player/coach he could barely conceal his delight. The Moores had visited New York with West Ham early in Bobby's career and had fallen in love with the place, and they thoroughly enjoyed the time they spent in San Antonio, far away from all the financial troubles they had run into with Woolston Hall and other similar disasters. The football was enjoyable for Bobby, as there were few expectations and for once he could relax and enjoy the summer. The family spent time over the Mexican border in Corpus Christi, a three-hour drive from San Antonio.

The NASL operated in much the same way as the National Basketball Association (NBA). Imagine a situation in England where the FA decided at the end of each season which clubs would receive the best young players. The objective is to keep the playing standards at the clubs across the USA as even as possible. This arrangement eliminates the possibility of any club(s) dominating the competitions for long spells, as they do in the English Premier League. In essence the clubs are subservient to the NBA. Tell that to Sir Alex Ferguson. Of course, the Soccer League in the USA has always been a poor relation to its basketball counterpart and has never really captured the hearts of the average American sports fan. But the Moores enjoyed the experience, before they had to return to the UK for the worst kind of reason. It is tempting to think that Moore and his family had found peace in America, away from the pressures of football in England, the media and his increasingly troubled business life. However, if he did find peace, it was short-lived. Their trip was cut short when, back in London, Moore's father was rushed into hospital after a stroke, which robbed him of most of his speech and part of his sight.

At the same time as attending to his father, Moore began his final season in English football. Like George Best and Rodney

Marsh, but for different reasons, he was facing the end of his long and incomparable career. Best and Marsh were drawn to Fulham by the presence of Bobby Moore, the charm of Alec Stock and the money of the chairman, Ernie Clay. Former chairman, Tommy Trinder, had been replaced by Clay after the club got into financial difficulties over the building of their new riverside stand. What is it with professional football and financial irregularities and double-dealing? Tragically, one of the Fulham directors, Sir Eric Liddle, committed suicide in 1976, only two days after visiting the Moores at their home in Chigwell.

Marsh was an old friend of Moore and their time together with Best must have been hugely enjoyable, but the season was disturbed when Alec Stock left the club. Stock was highly respected in the game and, like Ron Greenwood across London at Upton Park, he was old school and highly principled. Stock was to be immortalised later by Paul Whitehouse in *The Fast Show* as the model for their 'small boys and coats for goalposts' football manager sketch. Stock had a good career, having managed Moore's personal hero Johnny Haynes and characters such as Alan Mullery, Tosh Chamberlain and, of course, Jimmy Hill.

The 'Rocket Man'

In May 1977 Bobby Moore was approached by the pop star Elton John, then chairman of Watford Football Club, with a view to Moore becoming the new Watford manager. A meeting was held in London, which appeared to have reached a satisfactory conclusion. Moore was offered the job on a three-year contract with an annual salary of £15,000 - not an extravagant offer, but acceptable for a first managerial post. On the surface it looked a likely partnership: Elton John, the international superstar, and Moore, glamorous former-England captain, with an exemplary name in the professional game. Watford had ambitions and they were situated close to the capital. It seemed a golden opportunity for the first step on Moore's managerial career ladder – why wouldn't he accept? I am sure that he was thrilled and excited by the prospect of working with Elton John and the Watford players.

A further meeting was arranged between the two for later that week so that Moore could sign the contract drawn up by

Watford's legal people. However, when the day came Moore received a call asking for the meeting to be postponed to give the Watford chairman time to discuss the matter with his fellow directors. Presumably, he could not find time in the previous five days, given his hectic schedule, to inform his directors of his intention to appoint a new manager. Moore, of course, agreed with what he thought was a reasonable request and the meeting was duly postponed. The Moores went to Majorca for a break and on the way back from his usual run one morning he stopped to collect a newspaper. There on the back page was the headline "Graham Taylor appointed new Watford manager". Moore was deeply shocked. He had mistakenly believed that a handshake with the Watford chairman meant the deal was closed. He learnt a hard lesson about English football that day – in a newspaper headline.

The Watford affair was the first example of many opportunities denied to the former England World Cup winning captain. Graham Taylor, one of many adherents to the direct, pressing game admired by the England staff coaches and exemplified by Dave Bassett's Wimbledon FC, was eventually offered the job. Moore, true to form, wished Taylor well in his new post. The English FA admired Taylor's methods so much that they later appointed him as manager of the national team, with disastrous results.

Why Watford changed their minds we may never know. We would like to think that if Moore had been the Watford manager he would never have resorted to the ugly, negative methods adopted by Taylor and his followers. Moore subscribed to the 'beautiful game', and we cannot know if his more purist instincts would have been as successful as Taylor's pragmatic approach. We would rather the shabby incident with Elton John had never taken place and need not be mentioned. The tacky episode was not worthy of the great footballer, but it was indicative of the way he was to be treated when he had finished playing. At the end of his career Moore applied for several jobs in football, including the England manager's post. Nobody had the courtesy to reply, not even staff at the FA, who might at least have acknowledged a job application from England's World Cup winning captain and their greatest ambassador for the game – just ask Pelé, Cruyff and Beckenbauer.

The late seventies was a difficult time for many people in

Britain. The economy was in a mess, rubbish remained uncollected on the streets, social unrest was in the air and Prime Minister Callaghan was staring defeat in the face. It was not a good time to be looking for a well-paid job in football. Without his player's wages, with his business interest in trouble and with an expensive house and lifestyle to maintain, Moore became desperately worried about providing for his family – an old-fashioned virtue left over from his East London upbringing, which he never abandoned. To put in bluntly, the state of Moore's family finances meant that Bobby needed to get a job. At Pelé's invitation the couple flew to New York to be guests of honour at Pelé's farewell game for New York Cosmos. At the retirement dinner that followed the Moores were in the celebrated company of Andy Warhol, Henry Kissinger and Robert Redford. In his farewell speech the great Brazilian looked towards Moore and described him, with great respect and affection, as

... the English gentleman who is my friend.
- T. Moore (2006) p.199

Here was the great irony. The Moores were rubbing shoulders with rich and famous celebrities, and Bobby himself was still regarded with great respect and admiration throughout the world. But he continued to be ignored in England by the game he loved and which he had graced for so long. It is not an exaggeration to say that, with the possible exception of Bobby Charlton, nobody represented English football more than Bobby Moore. In the sixties he single-handedly transformed the image of professional football in the public imagination. Together with Bobby Charlton and Gordon Banks, Moore restored the image of England as a top football-playing nation, destroyed by the Hungarians in 1953. But still no offer came his way, and the sense of rejection made this great hero of 1966 increasingly despondent.

In the spring of 1978 Moore had a brief and abortive spell as player/coach with Third Division Danish club Henning, before a call from his old West Ham pal Harry Redknapp, then managing Seattle Sounders in the USA, restored some hope. The Moores enjoyed their time in Seattle, with Bobby playing a few games and helping the manager with the training. But it wasn't meant to last, and at the end of the season the couple were back in the UK. Tina Moore admits in her book:

Those two years, 1978 and 1979, were terrible for Bobby. They were such a painful contrast to the golden days of success, of being lauded and feted everywhere and of being the most famous, glamorous England player of them all.
- T. Moore (2005), p.201.

Financial problems began to bite. The children were in private school and the Moores' expensive Chigwell villa and lifestyle ran away with the money. But a huge part of the problem for Moore remained his sense of self and well-being, Tina writes:

By then, I could see that a very big part of the problem was that he was trapped by what he had achieved. He was a very proud man. How was he going to be able to cope with being a mere mortal?
- T. Moore (2005),p.203.

Late in 1979, after being out of work for 18 months, Moore received an offer from the chairman of Oxford City FC to become their new manager. Oxford City were a non-League, part-time outfit with no supporters and little money. But it was a job. What was interesting about Bobby Moore was that he would accept a job like the Oxford City one, not in a resigned and cynical way, but with a positive outlook and an almost naïve enthusiasm. He saw the offer as an opportunity to make his mark on the English game and quickly invited his former Seattle boss, Harry Redknapp, over from the USA to join him. Moore believed that the former speedy West Ham outside right had real management potential. How right he was. Redknapp was persuaded to give it a year. In his 1998 autobiography Redknapp registers his surprise at the whole situation:

It's hard to imagine Bobby Moore, captain of England's World Cup winning team in 1966 and one of the most respected men in soccer, struggling to eke out a living in the twilight world of non-league football.
- H. Redknapp (1998), My Autobiography, Collins Willow, p.55.

Redknapp also reveals that one of the reasons he took the job was because he thought the club was Oxford United, not Isthmian Oxford City. Redknapp and Moore were stable mates. They were East London boys who had grown up in the shadow of the Second World War and had made it as professional footballers. Like Moore, Redknapp played at international level as a youngster and they were both part of an exciting West Ham team. But there the comparison ends. Redknapp was to prove to be a tough and durable character who knew what it took to be a manager and became skilful in his dealings with agents and players. But he loved and respected Moore and agreed to join him at Oxford. According to Redknapp, Moore's wages were £500 per week and a brand new Daimler, while the assistant manager accepted £120 a week plus a second-hand Ford Fiesta.

Neither of them knew anything about non-League football and had no knowledge of players at that level. They found it difficult to adjust to working with part-time players who only trained in the evenings. Redknapp admits that the year was a real struggle as Redknapp:

> *I used to sit there saying to myself, what the hell am I doing here? Then we would play someone like Tilbury away in the pouring rain and I'd look to Bobby and think. What am I doing here? What is he doing here?*
> *- Redknapp (1998), p.56.*

The pair soldiered on for a year or so before the Oxford chairman agreed to let them go. Aspiring young managers often use non-League football to gain experience in management before moving on to the next level. But Moore failed at Oxford; perhaps it was a lost cause, but it was a failure nonetheless. Redknapp secured a job at Bournemouth, where he went from strength to strength until he became a managerial fixture in the Premier League. But it was another three years before Moore found another job in football and during that time his family began to be concerned about his mental state. What was happening was tragic. He just didn't seem to have the personal resources necessary to make a success of life after being Bobby Moore.

During those difficult years in the early 1980s while Bobby was effectively out of work, Tina started to show the qualities of resilience and courage that she inherited from her mother. She began to work for The Samaritans and did some voluntary work with The Probation Office and thought she might train to become a social worker. She also took a part-time job at Harrods, which provided some welcome financial independence. Relief came for Bobby when he was offered a part in the 1981 prisoner-of-war film *Escape to Victory*. Astonishingly, the dreadful film was directed by the great John Huston and starred Michael Caine and Sylvester Stallone. Moore loved the involvement with the celebrity pair and the friendship he made with Caine. The money he earned from the film helped to boost the family finances, but once the filming was over everyone else turned to the next thing, while Moore returned to Chigwell to face reality.

If being without work didn't bring Moore down to earth, the behaviour of the FA certainly would have done so. In what seemed at the time a personal rebuke, the FA invited Bobby Charlton to lead the England contingent in the opening ceremony's parade of past champions at the 1982 World Cup in Spain. Nobody would deny the right of Charlton to be included in the parade, but surely the 1966 World Cup captain should have been at the head of the party. To be completely ignored must have been hard to accept and understand. It does seem as though the English football establishment had deliberately turned its back on its greatest asset. Why? Tina Moore writes:

> *What had he done? … My own feeling is that Bobby was too much his own man for their liking. English football was still run by the old network and they probably expected a certain deference which he was unable to give.*
> *- T. Moore (2005), p.215*

In his autobiography Redknapp expresses his anger at Moore's treatment by the FA and English football in general. He believed that Moore should have been given a job at West Ham involving a combination of representing the club and looking after the young players. Bobby would have loved working with the youngsters while learning what it takes to run a major football club. The club would have had at their disposal the services of the most respected player in their history. And the fans would have their hero back. But it never happened.

What did happen was more like serendipity. In 1983, with the children now teenagers, the Moores were relieved when Bobby received a welcome offer of a six-month coaching job from Hong Kong-based club, Eastern Athletic FC. Moore appointed his close friend Alan Ball as his assistant. The club made an apartment available in Hong Kong and the Moores considered letting out Morelands for the length of the contract, as the 'ideal home' was proving to be a financial burden. However, for reasons which we will come to, Tina couldn't bring herself to give up her home, but the couple did spend time together in Hong Kong before Tina returned to the UK to support her daughter through her A level exams.

Eastern was always going to be a tough job, with a chairman who wanted instant results and a culture that was difficult to adjust to, even for a much-travelled international sports star like Bobby Moore. He returned home at the end of his contract, only to walk head-on into yet another football manager's job from hell (With sincere apologies to the many devoted supporters of Southend United FC). But before taking the managerial plunge again he accepted an offer from his old friend Rodney Marsh of a few weeks' coaching in the USA. So Moore spent the summer of 1984 in the Carolinas recharging his batteries and enjoying America again.

Paddling down Southend

While in the USA with Rodney Marsh Moore received a call from England. Would he be interested in managing the Third Division club Southend United? Unlike Oxford City, The Shrimpers were in the Football League – just. Moore, aware that the school and gas bills had to be paid, gladly accepted, although one would like to think he did so with some misgivings. Hard times mean hard choices. Moore became team manager and chief executive of the club down on the Thames estuary. The inevitable Essex football fiasco played itself out, as the club were threatened with bankruptcy after a local businessman nearly brought the club down with his dodgy business interests. Moore paints a very graphic image of his time at Southend:

> *... we've got so many bailiffs knocking on the door that every night I go round collecting all the televisions, lock them in my office and keep the keys in my pocket.*
> *- Powell (1993), p.241.*

Moore was two years at Southend before he handed in his keys and left. It was to be his last job in football. The retirement of Bobby Moore was now becoming a tragedy of Sophoclean proportions. After leaving Fulham in 1977, he made 24 appearances for San Antonio Thunder and 7 for Seattle Sounders. He tried his hand at management of a sort, with brief spells in Denmark, Hong Kong, and in England at Oxford and Southend – not a great CV for a former England captain with 108 caps for his country and a World Cup winning medal. His retirement was tragic in the sense that he was such a key figure in the life of the nation in the 1960s and early 1970s. Somehow, despite his only too human flaws, Moore came to represent something deep and inexpressible in the British culture.

The end of a dream

We know from Tina's autobiography that the family ran into financial difficulties after Bobby finished playing. Business ventures collapsed, often with Moore picking up the bills. Their new house in Chigwell was expensive to run and the couple were determined to keep the children in private schools. Work was sporadic and, in today's terms, poorly paid. Moore was finding it increasingly difficult to adjust to life after playing, and it must have disappointed him deeply when no offers came from the FA or West Ham United. And then, on leaving Fulham in 1977, he had written to the FA to express his interest in the England manager's job when a vacancy became available, and they never had the decency to reply.

Tina Moore admits that Bobby was showing signs of depression in the late 1970s and it was around his time in Hong Kong that Moore began an affair with the woman who was to become his second wife. Accounts of Moore's personal life in Tina's autobiography and Jeff Powell's book reveal a man who fell in love but struggled with the lies and deceit involved in having an affair and the guilt in leaving his wife of 25 years. The feelings of guilt were compounded by being estranged from his children, whom he clearly adored and who revered and respected their father. Moore would also have to explain himself to his mother, who would not have been used to divorce in the family and was also close to Tina and the children. Over time Moore's guilt would have been eased by the close and loving relationship he continued to enjoy with his children. His mother, probably reluctantly, accepted his new life, desperate as she would have been for the son she worshipped to be happy again. Tina admits that Bobby was extremely generous in the divorce settlement; "He gave me everything," she said, including their luxury Chigwell home. The dream marriage of the celebrity couple from East London with the dream house, the Jaguar in the drive and the famous friends was sadly over.

What is striking in the two previous accounts of Moore's life, although there is a clear tension between them, is how supportive the family members were to each other at this difficult time. At the death of Bobby's mother Doris of cancer and during Bobby's own losing battle with the disease, the family closed ranks. This closeness would have sustained Moore during his illness. The desperate nature of the situation would have been extremely difficult for Tina as she sought to bring a degree of normality to the lives of her children.

In January 1986 Tina divorced her husband and set out to make a new life. She sold Morelands and bought a small house nearer London in the pleasant Essex town of Loughton. She began to travel as the children became more independent, enjoyed her voluntary work and embarked on a counselling course, while continuing to dabble in the property market. Most importantly, she had her family and friends close by her. Roberta and Dean were now young adults and were becoming successful in their own right, Roberta with her company and Dean working with his father for the *Sunday Sport*. To Tina's delight, Dean produced her first grandchild, Poppy, and later proudly gave away his sister at her wedding in New York.

However, despite having this important network of emotional support around her, after a couple of years Tina decided to start a brand new life in America. She loved the USA and the time she had spent there with Bobby in San Antonio, New York and Miami. But she had to draw on all her courage and strength of character to make a new life in a new country where she had no family and few friends. In Florida she took Spanish classes and worked in a local hospital and a graphic design shop. She kept up her interest in property development and later started a management company with Roberta, which included organising events for the Kennedy family and Bill Clinton. She even had plans to write a novel.

The days of high celebrity and constant media attention for the golden couple from Barking and Ilford, who began their married life in a modest house close to their East London roots, were now a thing of the past. Reconciled with his children, Bobby's new life brought him renewed happiness. He relished new experiences, travelling, attending concerts and enjoying nights at the opera. Why shouldn't he appreciate these things? He was a bright former grammar school boy enjoying an exposure to a life that was far removed from the brash, boozy culture of the world of professional football.

The one person who will never be forgotten

Towards the end of his life Moore began to turn things around. In 1993 he joined Capital Radio as a match analyst working with the BBC TV commentator, Jonathan Pearce. He seemed to enjoy this work, which put him back in touch with the football public. I would like to think that he had mixed feelings working with the appalling *Sunday Sport*, an association that stood in stark contrast to his new cultural interests, encouraged by Stephanie. His media work would have eased any financial worries that Moore might have had at this time, while providing a means to communicate his immense knowledge of the game to his listeners. But, and there is a huge but, despite the happiness he found later in his life there is a real sense in which the greatest footballer of his generation was sidelined and ignored, not by the football public but by those who are responsible for running football in this country. The English public loved him. The immense outpouring of emotion following his early death was an indication of the affection they had for the hero of 1966. More than that, he represented something they admired and needed and thought was lost forever with his passing. Dignity, courage, coolness under pressure and inspirational leadership may all be qualities they admired in the man, and he was not to deny the English people what was for them the greatest prize in sport. His cancer returned when he was the happiest he had been in years.

He had an operation for suspected cancer of the colon in April 1991 and the news was devastating. But, of course, he fought hard, showed no self-pity and continued trying to live as normal a life as possible, including running and swimming on most days. He married Stephanie at Chelsea Registry Office on 4th December 1991. In February 1993 the couple, concerned about rumours of Moore's deteriorating condition, issued a public announcement about his illness, which made headlines all over the world and was the leading news item on all radio and TV channels.

Bobby Moore died on 24th February 1993 at the age of 51, at home surrounded by his family, having turned down the offer to spend his last hours in hospital. His wife Stephanie said later:

> *Bobby left us with a lasting image of his dignity and courage. I want it to be known that there was no pain and that when we announced that he had died peacefully surrounded by his family, it was absolutely true.*
> *- Powell(1993) p.263.*

The couple had enjoyed a holiday that January in Florida, where Bobby swam and played golf. On his return, aware of his worsening condition, Moore made the short journey across London to visit the Royal Garden Hotel in Kensington, scene of wild celebrations on the night of 30th July 1966. At the hotel he had arranged to meet his friend, the *Daily Mail* football reporter, Jeff Powell. He wanted Powell to compose the statement about his health that was shortly to be released to the public. Powell and Moore had been friends from the days when Powell was a football reporter on the *Walthamstow Guardian* back in the sixties. The statement agreed, Moore courageously completed his final assignment for Capital Radio for the England game against San Marino on Wednesday 17th February, to be held where else but at Wembley Stadium. It was very sad that he couldn't make it back to Upton Park for one last time. For West Ham supporters and East London and Essex people who had grown up with him and followed him through all the good and bad times, he was their hero who remained one of them. The close-up TV shots of him that night were unbearable to watch, as the seriousness of his condition was cruelly exposed to the world. We were soon to show the depth of our affection, respect and gratitude.

Moore's daughter Roberta, with her father to the end, knew she had to call her mother in Miami. Tina had already said her goodbyes to Bobby's mother, who had lost her own battle with cancer in 1992. The funeral was held on 2nd March at Putney Vale Crematorium and was a very private family occasion. Tina returned to England to be with her children for the memorial service at Westminster Abbey on 28th June. Moore was only the second sporting figure to be honoured in such a fashion, the first being the great cricketer, Sir Frank Worrell. It was a fitting tribute to the great footballer.

When the famous nineteenth-century novelist Thomas Hardy died he was buried, with full honours, in Poets Corner in Westminster Abbey. Hardy's novels were set in his beloved Dorset countryside where he was born and grew up. At the request of his family Hardy's heart was removed from his body, placed in a biscuit tin and buried in the graveyard of Stinstead Church, scene of one his greatest novels. Following Bobby's family funeral service in Putney, where Moore lived and found happiness with his second wife Stephanie, his remains were rightly returned to his own 'manor' next to those of his father, in the City of London Crematorium at Newbury Park in East London, just down the road from Wanstead Flats and close to Upton Park. Mick Geoghegan is a Hammers fan whose late wife is buried close to Bobby's memorial. On his regular visits to the crematorium Jim often walks over to pay his respects to Moore, and he wrote recently:

> *There are always flags and nicks-nacks on his grave and the tree next to it. He is one person who will never be forgotten.*
> *- This quote is taken from a letter to the author from Mick Geoghegan 14th October 2009.*

God bless, Bobby, sleep well

The public response to Moore's death was frankly unexpected. Nobody could remember such an emotional show of public affection for a sporting figure. At West Ham the response was immediate, as thousands of fans and well-wishers made the pilgrimage to the Boleyn Ground to pay their respects and say goodbye. Shirts, scarves, messages, wreaths and flowers adorned the gates to the ground, which became a shrine to his memory. Moore died on a Wednesday, and later that week visitors to Upton Park stood in stunned silence at the sight of the gates, which by this time were a sea of claret and blue. Complete strangers wept in each other's arms, overcome with emotion and a profound sense of loss. As one fan said at the time, "Bobby's death rocked the country ... you just don't see scenes of public unity like this today."

To achieve this kind of emotional outpouring there had to be something about Bobby Moore that transcended football. Certainly, he was hugely popular during his life, but the level of grief surprised his wife, Stephanie, who said:

What was very supportive was that the entire nation mourned and it was only then that I realised what a legend he was.
- J. Geoghegan, 'The Making of an English Gentleman' BBC News Magazine, 11th May 2007

After Bobby's death Stephanie put all her formidable energies into setting up the Bobby Moore Cancer Fund, for which she has raised over £10 million to support bowel cancer research. The Fund is now the official charity of West Ham United FC.

In his time Moore achieved things he could only have dreamed about as a boy playing football in the back streets of Barking. His legend has grown with every pathetic display of the England football team, with their millionaire players and their incompetent coaches, who believe they are doing the country a favour by turning out for the national team. The extreme emotional response to Moore's early death was driven by feelings that we had turned our back on him in his retirement years. Jim White of the Daily Telegraph suggested that his talents were "scandalously squandered" and wrote:

I think there's a lot of guilt involved in our relationship with Bobby Moore, and a realisation that we should have treasured him at the time, so maybe we are compensating for that now.
- J. White, quoted in T. Geoghegan, BBC News Magazine, 11th May 2007.

Why should we have felt guilty? Moore led a rich and full life, achieved fame and enjoyed a degree of wealth denied to most of his fans. He travelled the world and made friends with film stars. He was a household name. Moore had a family who adored him and who never faltered in their support. Of course, we were all saddened by his early death. His mythical status is guaranteed and his hold on the nation's affection will never diminish. The public outcry that his abilities were wasted is based, as Jim White suggests, on the image of our handsome blond hero, which evokes a,

Above: The Eton Manor Hall of Fame 1921, by courtesy of the Villiers Educational Trust

Right: True spirit of Eton Manor Boys Club, the Chinwag cartoon 1929, by courtesy of Bishopsgate Institute, London

Above: Children's party at Leytonstone FC in the late 1950s, with photograph of the club's FA Amateur Cup-winning side on the back wall

Right: The much-loved mascot of Leytonstone FC with his adoring owners

Left: Players and supporters of Leytonstone FC stop for a quick one on the road – late 1950s

Below: Cricket at Walthamstow in the 1920s, by courtesy of Vestry House Museum

Above: The Walthamstow CC team for their centenary match in 1962. The team includes the legendary John Welch and the West Ham's Alan Sealey, by courtesy of Geoff Sherman

Right: Walthamstow captain John Welch hits out in typical belligerent style, by courtesy of Geoff Sherman

Left: Walthamstow players on the pavilion steps during a home match in the 1960s, by courtesy of Geoff Sherman

Above: Friday evening Colt's cricket at Brentwood CC, 2009.

Left: Ken Hobbs - unsung hero of Brentwood football and cricket

Above: Ravi Bopara on his way to a double century against Surrey in 2009, at a very sunny Colchester Festival

Left: An ecstatic England captain saviours the greatest moment of an illustrious career, courtesy of Mirrorpix

Right: A happy Hammer celebrates after West Ham win the 1964 FA Cup Final, courtesy of Mirrorpix.

Below: Graham Gooch in typically majestic mood

... lost age of innocence, humility, grace, a sense of purpose, hard work and, above all, sporting success.
- J. White, BBC News Magazine,11th May 2007

His contemporaries were given public roles commensurate with their talents and abilities: Pelé became an ambassador for Brazil and the world of football in general; Beckenbauer practically ran football in Germany; and Bobby Charlton had his Manchester United directorship and the honour of being appointed a UN ambassador. Moore, on the other hand, was allowed to struggle in his post-playing days. He had desire and ambition in his playing days, which seemed to evaporate when he hung up his football boots. The football authorities at West Ham or the FA should have embraced him and put his talent at the disposal of the national game. Instead we had to watch while he moved from one lost managerial cause to another, and his innocence in business enabled unscrupulous 'friends' to use him for their own sordid purposes. Harry Redknapp spoke for many of us when he wrote in his autobiography:

One of the most saddening sights was seeing Bobby Moore sitting in the back of the stands at Grimsby, eating fish and chips out of a newspaper and freezing his nuts off, just to earn a couple of bob helping out a radio station. This was the England captain who lifted the World Cup but no one gave a shit.
- Redknapp (1998) p.186

Redknapp's graphic description of Moore in his retirement sums up the feeling of the nation: anger that we didn't make enough of his abilities and neglected him in retirement. He was not perfect, he liked a drink, but as his managers and teammates tell us he was a model professional and the first into training every day. He wasn't an establishment man like Bobby Charlton. He was independent-minded and really had no time for the 'suits' in the FA. He had some dodgy business connections, but no real taste for the wheeling and dealing culture of East London. Moore himself would not have wasted a second worrying about being neglected by the FA or anybody else. In his heart I think he knew that the public loved him, perhaps even more when the arc of his life took a downward turn. As Tony Fowles said at the time of his death, "The fact that he was human was maybe the thing that made him so special." (www.bobbymooreonline.co.uk) Moore was the East End boy made good. Fowles, the editor of the West Ham fanzine *Ironworks Gazette*, wrote this moving and honest tribute:

> *... if you were going to a job interview and had an East London address you used an address of an aunt or uncle who lived outside the East End. Why? Because the rest of London looked down on us. When one of us came good, usually through singing, boxing or football, it was one in the eye for the rest of London.*
> *- T. Fowles, bobbymooreonline.co.uk*

For the moment the East End has become a fashionable place to live and work, mainly because of cheap rents and property prices. But ordinary East Londoners have a different feeling about their 'manor':

> *Bobby earned us respect ... and with a team of mostly local lads we went to Wembley three times, the FA Cup, the European Cup Winners' Cup, and then ... the Jules Rimet Trophy. If you love West Ham and you love the East End ... Bobby did that for all of us.*
> *- T. Fowles.*

And that's it. We loved him for what he did for us, and for what he was. His memory evokes the values that English people have lost but not forgotten. He was proud, dignified and successful, as the country had been in the 1960s before the deep divisions and harsh realities of British society were exposed and exploited by one government after the other through the next 30 years.

A fitting tribute

In their preparations for the design and construction of the new Wembley Stadium the planners agreed that a statue of a sporting hero should be placed at the top of Wembley Way to represent all that is good in football. Who should it be? To assist in making a decision the FA carried out a survey among England supporters and they overwhelmingly chose Bobby Moore. There really was nobody else. A 'super' committee, including architect Sir Norman Foster, the FA's Brian Barwick, Sir Geoff Hurst and Bobby's widow Stephanie, was then set up to commission the work. The commission was won by the royal sculptor, Philip Jackson, who had created the *Champions* statue of Moore, Hurst, Peters and Ray Wilson, which stands proudly and vandalism-free in the Barking Road close to Upton Park. Jackson is a world-renowned sculptor whose commissions have included statues of Queen Elizabeth II (London), Sir Matt Busby (Manchester) and Mozart (London).

Jackson had the difficult job of depicting the late England captain in a way that would satisfy a number of different audiences. These included his clients, the English football public and, most importantly for Jackson, Moore's widow Stephanie. The sculptor's research included photographs, videos, books, newspaper articles and discussions with Moore's colleagues in the England team. So thorough was his research that he asked the studio technicians to walk around in the England football kit so that he would have an accurate 3D perspective of his subject. Jackson's research revealed that Moore was a very special footballer. He was strong and opposition forwards feared him, and he was a thoughtful and serious player with immense powers of concentration. As England captain he was dignified and restrained, leading by example rather than by screaming and shouting at his teammates. Jackson concluded that in 1996 Moore gave the England side something extra: "His sheer presence made the team play beyond itself." The statue needed to embody these essential characteristics of the great footballer. Jackson wanted a still image just about to move, not an artificial action pose, and he felt a smiling Moore might trivialise the image, so he worked on creating a more thoughtful and contemplative figure. But it also needed to have emotional appeal, and Jackson focused on the intimate details of his anatomy, his face, neck and shoulders, which had to be represented fully in the round. At 12 feet high, the bronze figure had the necessary elevation to represent a hero.

When he was happy with his design, Jackson invited the committee down to his studio in West Sussex to view the provisional clay model in full scale. Crucially, he allowed Stephanie Moore to see the sculpture a few days before the committee. The model was full size and stood on its own in Jackson's main studio. When he unveiled the figure to Stephanie the response was immediate. He had wanted to create the statue through her eyes, and for the response to be "an emotional punch in the chest". Jackson achieved his aim, as Stephanie burst into tears at her first sight of the epic work. Stephanie's approval meant that the committee would accept the design and the work could begin. The sculpture was completed in 33 weeks, but it remained in the studio for a further 12 months while work on the stadium was completed. The statue of Bobby Moore at the new Wembley Stadium acts as a constant and eloquent reminder to us of everything that is good in football. It is a fitting tribute indeed (Philip Jackson comments here are taken from an interview with the author at Jackson's studio in East Sussex on 26th October 2009).

Captain of all of us

Geoff Hurst's first goal in the 1966 World Cup final stays in the memory. As the ball hit the back of the net, Hurst turned to his teammates, raised his arms momentarily and trotted back to the centre circle where Moore quickly shook his hand before returning to his position. After all, we were still only halfway through the first half. No wheeling celebration, no mindlessly running to the corner flag, ripping off shirts or brainless faux dancing. Top footballers today, for many of reasons, have lost touch with their fans. A young Hammers supporter tells a story of how he knocked on Moore's door in Chigwell, having been sent there by his workmates on a wind-up. Moore answered the door, took one look at the boy's astonished face and invited him in, and then signed his ball and sat chatting with him for 20 minutes. There are hundreds of stories like this. If the great man's star shined a little less brightly when he stopped playing, who are we to judge?

Moore was not a typical 1960s type of popular imagination. As a young man, he narrowly missed National Service and we can only speculate how different his career might have been after a spell in Aden, Germany or Suez, but he just seemed to be from that kind of generation. His appearance was conservative, with his short cropped blond hair, and he inherited the good manners and humility of his parents' generation. His dramatic gesture in the Royal Box in 1966 when he wiped his muddy hands on his shirt before shaking hands with the Queen was pure Bobby Moore. The gesture was instinctive, made amidst the frantic euphoria of England winning the World Cup final.

I want to believe that Moore led an exemplary life outside

football, but he was an East End boy to his fingertips and became surrounded by the kinds of chancers, wide boys and second-hand car dealers who pretended to be businessmen running pubs and nightclubs, but who you wouldn't trust to run a whelk stall on Hackney Marshes on Sunday mornings. The Barking Road was full of these people in the 1960s. They thought that if they drove a Jag and bought their mohair suits from showbiz tailor Douglas Hayward rather than old Joe, the Jewish guy at the top of Walthamstow High Street, they were entitled to boast about their so-called business interests. There was nothing they liked more than bathing in the reflected glory of someone like Bobby Moore. Modern footballers such as Beckham, similar to his predecessor in many ways, would have avoided these people at all costs. Moore was simply too trusting a character; a case of a personal strength becoming a commercial weakness, as one after another of his acquaintances let him down or, in some cases, robbed him blind. The Woolston Hall Country Club in Chigwell (where else), Moore's pub in Stratford and the leather goods firm he part-owned all collapsed, the first two actually burning to the ground.

Today's top footballers have glamour lifestyles and show business friends. Moore had a few of these but kept characters close to him whose motivations were, to say the least, questionable. Compare Moore's business experience with the outside interests of two England football captains in recent years, both London boys, David Beckham and Rio Ferdinand. Beckham, born a short bus journey from Moore in Leytonstone, is a multimillion brand with a global reach. Ferdinand, the 'new Bobby Moore' at West Ham in the late 1990s, has remained in touch with his Peckham roots but has always kept them at a distance. It is difficult to imagine the young Moore launching a free online magazine for young people called *5Magazine* at the age of 30, as Ferdinand has done, featuring a personal interview with the world-famous US rap star 50 Cent. Even as young as 25 Moore was much more likely to have been listening to Johnny Mathis or Frank Sinatra, when he probably ought to have been listening to The Beatles or The Rolling Stones. His taste in music was as conservative as the clothes he wore and the way in which he conducted himself. Both Beckham and Ferdinand have prepared for their non-playing days in ways that were not available to Moore in the mid-1970s. Today's footballers, such as

Ferdinand, like to be seen as cool and down with the street, but this can make them as exposed to criminal elements as their predecessors of the 1960s. In April 2009 the brother of the young Tottenham forward Jermain Defoe was murdered in London after being attacked in the street. At least Moore's 'dodgy' East End friends were less inclined towards violence than the young street kids of today. In their wildest dreams they may have seen themselves as the new Ronnie and Reggie Kray, but in reality they were a pathetic imitation of those infamous East End brothers. They did have their moments, however, as Tina Moore tells us in her autobiography. One of Moore's partners in the Woolston Hall debacle pulled out of the project after "someone fired a shotgun at his house from a passing car". The FA would not have been impressed by this kind of notoriety.

Moore kept close to his neighbourhood and the East End kept close to him. It is tempting to believe that his abortive business ventures and gang of dodgy mates were the reason that the FA failed to honour its greatest player while he was alive, much in the way that his friend Terry Venables was snubbed by the football elite. Jonathan Pearce, a close friend of Moore, has his suspicions:

He was neglected ... because the establishment was suspicious about his business connections and there were lingering doubts about his arrest for allegedly stealing a bracelet in Colombia in 1970. That accusation was later to be found groundless.
- J. Pearce, quoted by T. Geoghegan, BBC News Magazine, 11th May 2007.

"If the world had played Mars, Moore would have been man of the match"
- G. Hurst, Powell (1993) p.272

Perhaps we ought not to linger too long on Moore's life after football. In his playing days he was an astute and inspirational captain, and when you add tactical awareness to supreme skill you have the perfect No. 6. Moore was a great student of the game and a very attentive listener. Early in his career as a teenager he listened carefully to the excited technical discussions between Malcolm Allison and Noel Cantwell. Later he benefited from Ron Greenwood's innovative thinking, and finally he was a willing graduate student at the Sir Alf Ramsey finishing school for international footballers. Ramsey's version of the 4-2-4 system used in the late stages of the 1966 tournament allowed Moore to move from the best defender in England to the best in the world.

Moore played his last game for England in a friendly against Italy in 1973, his last for West Ham in 1974 and his final match in the English professional game for Fulham in 1977 at the age of 36, 19 years after his West Ham debut in 1958. In the years between 1958 and 1977 he acquired 108 England caps (90 as captain), winners' medals in the FA Cup, the European Cup Winners' Cup, and, so memorably, the World Cup. In addition Moore was the FWA Footballer of the Year in season 1963/64, World Cup Players' Player in 1966 and BBC Sports Personality of the Year in 1966. He was also voted Hammer of the Year on four occasions. The boy from Barking was awarded the OBE in 1967 and exceeded by miles every expectation that school teachers, club coaches, friends and family had of him as a teenager.

Bobby Moore enriched the lives of a generation and continues to inspire respect and affection. He has a safe and warm place in the heart of a nation. In the words of C.L.R. James, again in the context of a discussion of the role in history of W.G. Grace, but which seem to fit Moore perfectly,

> *He enriched the depleted lives of two generations and millions to be born. He had extended our conception of human capacity and in doing all this he had done no harm to anyone.*
> *- James (1963) p. 183*

Moore found a proper home at Upton Park, while Wembley Stadium became the ultimate stage for his talent. Anyone who saw him play at the old national stadium would happily endorse the sentiment that Bobby Moore belonged to Wembley, and Wembley belonged to Bobby Moore. Sports stars rarely figure in social history. C.L.R. James points out that the social histories of the nineteenth century fail even to mention the name of W.G. Grace. For James, Grace was one of the greatest, if not the greatest Victorian, with an influence reaching far beyond his own century. James argues that social historians do not begin to understand what inspires ordinary people and what rouses their passions. It is to be hoped that our age is more democratic and that heroes of popular culture like Bobby Moore will be given the place in our history that their achievements and stature merit. How we miss him.

CHAPTER 6
CRICKET, LOVELY CRICKET

In the spring of 1959 Trevor Bailey gave a talk to the second-year pupils at William Morris School in Walthamstow. Sitting in rapt attention in the front row, I hung on every word uttered by our local hero. Bailey had recently returned from England's disastrous Ashes tour of 1958/59. As a makeshift opener he had bagged a pair in the final Test, as England's batsmen collapsed yet again to the Aussie bowling of Davidson, Lindwall and Benaud. Bailey was in good company, as a batting order of May, Cowdrey, Graveney and Dexter failed to cope with the Aussie combination of extreme pace and leg spin. None of this mattered to the assembled pupils on that day as they listened spellbound to their guest recalling his experience of the previous winter. From the day Trevor Bailey walked into our school I was hooked on cricket, and in particular Essex cricket.

If Bailey's appearance at our school made a lasting impression on a sports-mad youngster, then a rather painful event that occurred two years earlier left a more physical mark, still visible today. Yardley Lane Primary School was about a mile and a half from our house, set on the edge of a large post-war housing estate on the edge of Epping Forest. On summer lunchtimes I ran home from school as fast as I could to catch the last 30 minutes of the morning session of the Test Match on TV. After a hurried sandwich and half an hour watching Trueman, Statham and Laker bowling, or the batting exploits of Peter May and Ted Dexter, I would sprint back to school and arrive moments before the bell sounded for the afternoon classes. But on one particular day I failed to negotiate a sharp bend in the road and crashed to the ground, smashing two front teeth against a low stone wall. Fifty years later I still have two stumpy front teeth as evidence of a young boy's passion for cricket.

I played a bit of cricket at primary school and in 1958 I was chosen to represent Chingford Under 11s against Walthamstow in the annual district match. But Trevor Bailey's personal appearance at my secondary school was the spark that ignited a passionate 50-year affair with Essex County Cricket Club. Many years later I was privileged to teach cricket at Highams Park School on the East London/Essex border, and in the early 1980s I enjoyed a few seasons coaching Waltham Forest Schools U13 district side. The coaching experience convinced me that youngsters, brought up today on a diet of uninterrupted football, adore cricket and enjoy learning about its intricate, often arcane rules and techniques. Their enthusiasm for the game reveals what could be achieved in junior cricket given the right leadership and half-decent facilities. Sadly, many thousands of potential club cricketers, particularly in our urban areas, are lost to the game as a result of poor coaching, rubbish facilities and a lack of effective communication between schools and clubs.

Beach cricket

Despite the inspirational example of Trevor Bailey I failed to become an even moderately decent cricketer. I was a much better footballer, but at the end of a long football season I was either too exhausted to contemplate playing serious cricket, or preferred to spend weekends indulging in less strenuous pursuits, in my case playing golf. The highlights of my cricket career remain my two outstanding bowling performances in the late 1960s. I hasten to add that these were not first-class fixtures, or even club games, but matches played with great energy and enthusiasm on the beaches of Bournemouth and Newquay. I was there on holiday with a gang of sports-mad young Essex lads, who because of the wonderful weather became known locally as The Sunshine Nine. I remember the matches were always between The Fats and The Thins and involved pitch rolling, marking and the setting of boundaries. Beach cricket was a serious affair enjoyed by the other holidaymakers on the beach, despite the noisy interruptions to their activities and hard-hit tennis balls raining down on them all day. Even Graham Gooch in retirement succumbed to the joys of beach cricket, although the Caribbean was his preferred venue rather than the cold and windy beaches of the south coast of England.

Sport always figured prominently at home. My dad was not a great football and cricket lover, but he adored tennis and athletics. His personal heroes were Bobby Wilson, whom we followed at Wimbledon each year with his deft touch and graceful play, and Derek Ibbotson, England's gritty sub-four-minute miler. Dad regularly took me to the White City Stadium, home of British athletics in the 1950s and '60s. Before their events the athletes warmed up under the cavernous stands, which made autograph hunting a relatively simple affair. Ibbotson, Gordon Pirie, the incomparable Australian world mile record holder Herb Elliott, the great English sprinter Peter Radford, and Woodford Green's own David Jones, were all prized signatures acquired deep in the bowels of the old stadium. But cricket and football became my personal passions, together with the occasional game of golf.

Chingford Golf Club was located a few miles from our house, on the edge of Epping Forest, just a few hundred yards from Chingford CC's Forest Side ground. The golf club with its corrugated fairways was a municipal course where young people were made welcome and were given every encouragement by the members. Golf was so popular in the 1970s that a queue began to form outside the clubhouse at 5.00 a.m. on Saturday mornings. The early morning golfers were fortified by hot tea and toast provided by the sympathetic professional and his young assistants. My brothers and I became members and played to a decent standard. As soon as I reached the age of 17 I bought a Honda 50, which we meant we no longer had to carry our clubs on the bus. The sight of my brother and I sat on this low-powered vehicle, creeping up the steep hill leading to the course, each with a set of golf clubs on our back, must have amused passers-by. My eldest brother went one better and travelled to the course on his motorbike with his clubs sticking out the top of his sidecar.

Nowhere else I would rather be ...

Members and supporters across the country will claim that their county club is somehow special. The Yorkshire faithful will point to their history and the fierce, if misdirected, loyalty of the Western Terrace. Surrey members are proud of their successful past and their Oval Test Match ground, while Warwickshire supporters can boast Edgbaston and a hugely successful and benevolent fund-raising operation, from which Essex CCC among others have benefited. But Essex are special in the same way that West Ham United are special, in that they are the two mother ships of a vibrant sporting culture. Both clubs have hard won reputations for a carefree, attacking style of play and fiercely loyal sets of supporters. And both clubs, until recent years, acquired unwanted but reliable reputations for losing in style.

I have many fond and priceless memories of watching cricket in the 1960s. A very young Keith Fletcher edging nervously out to bat at the Ilford Festival was a particular highlight, and the sight of a youthful Graham Gooch lofting the Kent bowlers over the old oak tree at Canterbury in the mid-1970s remains a vivid image. But the most enduring memory has to be that glorious July day at Lords in 1979 when Essex won the first trophy in their long history. At the time my sister worked in the offices of a large Oxford Street store and she managed to get two corporate tickets for my brother and I to watch the final. We had great seats close to the pavilion where we sat glued to the cricket for the whole day. In honour of the solemnity of the occasion, and wanting to savour every minute, we refused the temptations of the all-day bar. However, I think that we probably more than made up for the day's abstinence during the course of the long evening celebrations.

I later asked my brother what gave him the most pleasure, West Ham beating Arsenal in the 1980 Cup final or Essex winning the 1979 Benson & Hedges final at Lords in 1979. His answer revealed precisely what it means to be an Essex supporter. "The Essex victory every time," he answered. "It was much more personal." Every Essex fan will identify with the sentiment. Football may be the beautiful game, but it will never attract the same kind of personal attachment.

The 1980s were a glorious time to be an Essex supporter. Despite the success, the atmosphere at the home games remained relaxed and friendly. All through the 1980s my wife and I used to take our places on the hard wooden members' benches outside the pavilion at Chelmsford with the Bassett Hound sleeping peacefully under our feet. Players and their families would mix easily with the members, helping to create the special feeling at the club for which Essex are associated. Sometime in the 1980s, as we settled down for the start of a Gillette Cup semi-final at Chelmsford on a glorious summer's day, I remember hearing a fellow member declare quietly to his friend, "There is nowhere else on earth I would rather be today." He spoke for every Essex supporter on the ground.

Organised loafing or intense sporting conflict?

Cricket is a very special game. The great Trinidad writer, C.L.R. James, goes as far as describing cricket as an art. In James's Introduction to *Beyond a Boundary*, Mike Brearley puts both sides of the case for the role of sport in society. On the one hand, he states that sport

> *... reduces people rather than enlarges them; it fosters aggression, or at best channels it in relatively harmless ways; it is peripheral and wasteful.*
> *- James(1963), p.9*

On the other hand, as Brearley observes, James has a very different view of the role of sport in society:

> *James demands that cricket, far from being apologised for, should take its place as an art, 'not a bastard or poor relation but a full member of the community'.*
> *- James (1963), p.9*

James further argues that sport has been undervalued, not only aesthetically but also socially and historically. For instance, he questions why there is no statue of W.G. Grace. Both these opposing views about sport exist today, although 40 years after James wrote *Beyond a Boundary* there is little doubt that sport is more popular than ever, despite its regular descents into violence and intimidation. Sport today has become very big business and even the once benighted game of cricket has succumbed to the temptations of crude commercialism, to the point where England cricketers turn down contracts with their country to play 20/20 cricket in the Indian Premier League, and the ECB is seduced by corrupt American financiers.

Long gone are the days when cricket could be described as "organised loafing" as it was by William Temple in 1942, although you might be excused for thinking that the England team might occasionally subscribe to this view, with their fluctuating performances in recent years. Actually, I'm not sure there is much wrong with organised loafing at village level, but G.M. Trevelyan, writing in 1942, took cricket much more seriously:

If the French noblesse had been capable of playing cricket with their peasants, their chateaux would never have been burnt.
- GM Trevelyan, quoted in D. Pracy A Social History of Essex Cricket (unpublished) p.252

It's a bold claim to say that cricket saved the English ruling class from losing their heads, but many would argue that it has had a unifying role in English society over the past 200 years, even if its heroes, as James argues, have not received the public recognition that their achievements justify. In the end cricket is just a game that cannot seem to throw off completely its class-ridden 'Gentlemen v. Players' image of the first half of the twentieth century. Certainly, the language of cricket has been used for many years to express the essential characteristics of English people. 'It's not cricket' and 'playing with a straight bat' are phrases known to everyone. But before making further bold claims for our 'summer game' we ought to note that the Zimbabwean dictator, Robert Mugabe, once said, without irony, "Cricket civilises people and creates good gentlemen." However, cricket lovers make no claims about the game other than that it is their passion. They love the statistics, the averages and the complexities of the Duckworth Lewis method, and they endlessly discuss the state of pitches and the quality of the teas at club matches. In 2010 first-class cricket is at a crossroads. As Graham Gooch warned recently, a balance has to be achieved between the traditional form of the game and the commercially driven 20/20 cricket. County cricket is a shambles, a puzzling mishmash of competitions that even the most devout follower finds difficult to comprehend. But in Essex, at least, club cricket has never been stronger. Sadly, cricket in the inner city is a mere shadow of what it was 40 years ago: school playing fields have been sold for development, clubs have lost their grounds and folded, and the number of young players being introduced to the game has been reduced to a trickle. However, as we shall see, against all the odds there are some encouraging signs of a cricket renaissance in East London. I have been immersed in cricket, particularly Essex cricket, at all levels for 50 years. In this time Graham Gooch has emerged as the central figure and his story gives a fascinating example of how developments in cricket and society are inextricably linked and confirms James's view: "What do they know of cricket who only cricket know?"

CHAPETR 7
ESSEX, MY ESSEX

We know that cricket was first played in Essex during the early part of the seventeenth century. A cricket match took place between Chingford and Mr Edward Stead's XI, probably at Chingford, in 1724. (D. Lemmon and M. Marshall (1987), Essex County Cricket Club: The Official History, Kingswood, p.12). Over the next 150 years several clubs playing in the county have been referred to as 'Essex', notably Hornchurch CCC, but it is clear that Essex County Cricket Club were formed on 14 January 1876 at a meeting in the Shire Hall at Brentwood, a town that was to become close to the heart of cricket in the county, and were finally accepted as a first-class county in 1894. What is undisputed is that Essex CCC failed to win a single trophy during their long history until 21st July 1979. The club captain on the long-awaited day was K.W.R. Fletcher. Keith Fletcher was appointed Essex captain in 1974 on the retirement of the previous club skipper Brian 'Tonker' Taylor. Essex CCC and their members and supporters owe Keith Fletcher a huge debt. He turned the 'Cinderella' county, at least in cricketing terms, into the side that dominated English county cricket between 1979 and 1985. Not content with leaving an indelible legacy for the county's history, Fletcher carefully groomed his successor, Graham Gooch, to carry on the new winning tradition.

Lemmon and Marshall's superb official history of Essex CCC takes us up to 1985. In addition, there are autobiographies by such Essex luminaries as Doug Insole, Trevor Bailey, Keith Fletcher, Graham Gooch and Nasser Hussain, the latter being by far the best cricket autobiography of the past ten years. This chapter should not be seen as an attempt to provide a detailed, match-by-match description of the club's activities since 1985. What follows is a more impressionistic account of this very special county club over the past 40 years, highlighting the deep connection they have with the rural metropolitan communities across the county of Essex and in East London. I am particularly interested in exploring the thinking that inspired an extraordinary change in the club's fortunes after 1979.

Essex's fortunes began to change for the better in the 1970s when the county received praise from an unlikely source. Ted Dexter wrote in his column in the *Daily Mirror* that Essex was "an up and coming cricket force East of London". He continued:

> *Major Brown, the secretary-cum-major domo of Essex, who is quite likely to be seen putting on the covers, marshalling the cars, doing the books and cajoling the team all in the space of one hour, is confident of another good year. "We are off to a good start," he said. "The present formula of fixtures is working out well for us. Though it is hard keeping up with all the innovations, far be it from me to complain if they continue to bring the lively cricket we have had so far".*
> *- Quoted in Lemmon and Marshall (1987). P.281*

Major Brown was referring to the introduction of limited-over cricket, which Essex took to with real enthusiasm and a sense of purpose when other counties were shunning the one-day game introduced into English cricket in the 1960s. One-day cricket gave Essex the ideal platform for their expansive, attacking style. As the Gillette Cup and the John Player League became an established part of the English summer, Essex grew stronger, but the side still continued to fail despite the sense of optimism around the club. This was particularly frustrating, since the club believed that this was their best team for many years.

At the end of the 1970s, both Graham Gooch and Keith Fletcher were acutely conscious that Essex had never won the County Championship, and they had a reputation as a talented, good-natured but ultimately ineffective bunch of underachievers. The club chairman, 'Tiny' Waterman spoke for everyone at Essex when he said at the end of the 1977 season:

> *Enterprising cricket, unstinting effort, superb fielding, outstanding individual performances, promising young players – nothing to show for it all. Nothing that is, if the winning of a competition – any competition – is the over-riding consideration in the support of a side which, year in, year out, provides entertainment unsurpassed by any other county.*
> *- Lemmon and Marshall (1987), p.306*

I am keen to explore the reasons why, in the late 1970s, Essex changed from being a happy bunch of professional cricketers content to jog along from game to game with little expectation of winning anything, to dominating English cricket through the 1980s and '90s. The dramatic turn in the county's fortunes at this time occurred because a talented group of players were turned into a winning team, by the desire and sheer willpower of Keith Fletcher, and later Graham Gooch, to change the course of the club's history. The first thing Fletcher knew he had to do in his quest for success was to instil a sense of self-belief in his players. He writes of his thinking at the end of the 1978 season:

> *It had been … a question of self-belief … we were all convinced we were good enough and that if we played even equally well we would not be denied again.*
> *- K.W.R. Fletcher (1983), A Captain's Inning: An Autobiographys, Hutchinson, p.85*

If self-belief was a necessary precondition for success for Fletcher, the second was for the team to develop a winning mentality. He continues:

> *There is a way of forming the winning habit. I am sure of that now.*
> *- Fletcher (1983), p.85*

Fletcher was a perceptive and intelligent cricketer who thought deeply about the game and had a profound desire to turn Essex into the best side in county cricket. Self-belief, will and desire are necessary qualities to succeed in any sport, and it is to Fletcher's credit that he understood this and that their absence was the reason for Essex's long years of failure. He wrote:

> *I wanted to prove to everyone that we now had the best team Essex had ever seen, and the only way I could do that was by winning the title they had waited for for so long.*
> *- Fletcher (1983), p.85*

Fletcher had a real sense of place, adored his county and wanted Essex people to be proud of their cricket team. But even he could not have imagined how proud they would become over the next 20 years. I like to believe that, for Fletcher, success for Essex was more important than success for England. He wrote of the great day at Lord's in the B&H final of 1979:

> *Even taking all my England experiences into account, it was the greatest day of my career.*
> *- Fletcher (1983)*

Fletcher's mentor and successor as captain of Essex, Graham Gooch, equipped with his predecessor's qualities of will and desire, expressed similar sentiments about his true loyalties. Gooch was Essex through and through and had a passion for the county that may even have surpassed that of Fletcher, who was actually born in Cambridgeshire. Ivo Tennant, in his biography of Gooch, wrote:

> *His devotion to Essex was such that his vice-captain, Derek Pringle, reckoned he would play for them without being paid, so well did he feel he had been treated down the years.*
> *- I. Tennant (1992), Graham Gooch: The Biography, Gollancz/Witherby, p.149*

Gooch would have thought it perverse to see things any other way. As Tennant writes:

> *... he did not see anything unusual in his devotion to his county. 'Some players think they can save their best performance for Tests – I see it the other way round', he said.*
> *- Tennant (1992), p.149*

For Fletcher and Gooch then, Essex was their first love. This deep affection for their home county, together with a drive and ambition for their home club to become a major force in English cricket, was to prove a powerful combination. It did help, of course, that both were exceptional cricketers, and in Gooch's case one of the greatest batsman in the post-WW2 period. This gave them the natural authority they needed to inspire the Essex team of 1979 and their winning successors. The side quickly developed the self-belief, desire and winning mentality that both Fletcher and Gooch believed to be necessary for success at the highest levels of the game. In this chapter we will discover more about the philosophy of Essex cricket, the extent to which both captains received leadership and support from the club's hierarchy in their quest to conquer the English game, and how a county that won nothing in over 100 years uniquely produced three England captains in 20 years in Fletcher, Gooch and Nasser Hussain, and a likely fourth soon in Alistair Cook.

Like many Essex supporters I tended to lose interest in the England team's fortunes for a few hours when Fletcher or Gooch were out, or when Robin Hobbs or John Lever were taken out of the attack. This feeling continues today when either Alistair Cook or Ravi Bopara loses their wicket playing for their country, which seems to happen with surprising regularity. Essex supporters are desperate for their England players to perform well for their country. This is probably because following the county has been such an emotional roller-coaster ride, or at least it was until that glorious day in the summer of 1979. Since that unforgettable year when the club won the Benson & Hedges Cup and the County Championship under Keith Fletcher, following Essex has been a much less bumpy ride.

The road to success began in 1967 when the club wisely adopted New Writtle Street at Chelmsford as their permanent home. It was a further 12 years before Peter Edwards was appointed as General Manager. With the appointment of Edwards in 1979 came the recognition that to become competitive it was essential for the club to become a professional and commercially successful business. In his thoroughly candid and hard-hitting autobiography, Keith Fletcher cites the appointment of Edwards as crucial to the modernisation of the club. Edwards was in all but name a chief executive officer (CEO) of a growing business enterprise, with a team of staff able to look after the administration while the CEO was free to ensure the smooth running of the club. Essex had recruited Edwards from his job as company secretary of the John Laing construction group, and it helped that he was a passionate supporter of the club. His appointment allowed the faithful Ronnie Cox to concentrate on the commercial and sponsorship activities. Fletcher argues that getting the business side of the club running efficiently was crucial if Essex were to challenge Yorkshire and Surrey at the top of the English game. There was a realisation on the part of the Essex management that the administration and business aspects of the club had to support the hunger and desire of Fletcher and Gooch to win cricket matches. For too long Essex had been a cricket backwater. It was 1979 when the club gained the respect of the other county sides as serious contenders for honours. But, despite becoming more professional and efficient in all aspects of their approach to professional cricket, from links with schools and clubs to marketing and public relations, Essex players never lost their legendary ability to enjoy their cricket. As David Lloyd of Lancashire once said of the 'new' Essex,

> *They would turn up, joke around a bit, and suddenly you found you had lost in two days.*
> *- I. Oxborrow and R. Pritchard (2009) Fletcher's Aces and Jokers: Essex County Cricket Champions 1979, Desert Island Books, p.44*

Frank Henry Rist: A Local Hero

Frank Rist was one of the great unsung heroes of Essex cricket and he personified every quality that the club and their supporters hold dear. He is not an obvious choice as a local hero, but he was a key character in the narrative of Essex CCC that takes us right up to the end of the successful season of 2009. He joined the club in 1932 at the age of 18 and developed from a solid county cricketer to the club's chief coach, helping to bring on some of the young players who became the backbone of the all-conquering team of the 1980s. In the club's official history, Lemmon and Marshall wrote of Rist:

> *... Frank Rist...had been for some years in chargeof Essex young players followinh his retirementfrom the first-class game. The club could not afford a coach ... and there was talent to be spotted, fo Frank Rist agreed to work for next to nothing, and continued to so for a number of seasons... many young Essex players..remain indebted to him for the start he gave them.*
> *- Lemmon and Marshall (1987), p.267-68*

David Pracy, archivist at the Vestry House Museum in Walthamstow, interviewed Rist for a project involving the Waltham Forest Oral History Workshop. He came over as a cheerful and uncomplaining man who appreciated the opportunity to have a long and happy association with the game that he loved. As a boy Frank Rist had always wanted to play football and cricket. His father was a CID inspector who ran the station cricket team, for which Frank was always guaranteed a game. The young Frank left school at 14 to work for a rubber company at nearby Hackney Wick, and he recalled his early experience of work:

The Guv'nor called me in his office, I thought I'm in trouble here and he asked me if I'd go down and play cricket for his firm … against Welwyn Garden City. We won the game … and he sent his chauffeur to pick me up and bring me back home and … on the Monday he called me in his office and said, 'I was very pleased with what you done '… He gave me a couple of pound for playing which was more than I got in a month and he said, 'I know you're very interested in becoming a cricketer and a footballer. Now while you're here you can have as much time off as you like to play.' Well, I was made, wasn't I?
- I am very grateful to David Pracy for allowing me to use his unpublished paper 'Social History of Essex Cricket' as the research material for this discussion of Frank Rist.

With such a benevolent employer, Rist had made a dream start to working life. As a youngster, Rist was sport-mad. He watched the Essex and England players Jack O'Connor and Stan Nichols play at the old County Ground in Leyton, who took time out to encourage the youngster. Knowing that he wanted to become a professional cricketer, they recommended that he join the Essex grounds staff. Working under Dick Brewer, he did all sorts of jobs around the ground, including mowing the outfield on a motor mower, cutting and rolling the pitch, and covering the ends of it when it rained.

Rist played for the Essex Club & Ground side and remembers scoring a century against Buckhurst Hill in his last game at Leyton:

These two policemen were standing watching me and they knew me and I think I hit the ball out the ground about six times and they scarpered, because they saw me later and said, 'Well, we thought you were going to injure someone so we left you to it …

Rist recalls that amateurs and professionals dined separately during matches, although the visitors' dressing room was shared, and he remembers:

> *The Essex pros had a little place that was sort of attached to the Pavilion while the amateurs had their own dressing-room. 'We were treated like pros and they were treated like amateurs [but] we got on all right on the field, obviously.'*

He particularly remembered Ken Farnes, Hopper Read and Leonard Crawley. Rist revealed that members of the committee were mostly retired amateurs, who did not always turn up at matches. He accepted the situation because as he put it, "It was all we knew, wasn't it?" He believed that the amateurs were wealthy and could afford the time to play a game that could take up to three days of their time "depending how they batted and bowled". After the war, "they got paid [and] weren't amateurs, they were pros," because they were able to claim for travel expenses and other items. In his autobiography Trevor Bailey recalls that the professional/amateur distinction was less visible at Essex than at other counties, where the two groups of players were kept strictly apart.

It is interesting to compare the financial position of players today with those like Rist, who grew up in a very different time. Rist was paid £4 a week during the season and £3 in winter, with an extra £2 if he played in the first team. In winter he played soccer, initially for Clapton Orient but then with Charlton Athletic. He was Charlton manager Jimmy Seed's first signing for his new club and was part of a highly successful Charlton side. Rist was the club's centre half when they made their unprecedented rise straight from the old Third Division to the First in successive seasons. He later joined Colchester United.

When Rist eventually made the Essex first team his pay went up to £8, with £6 in winter. Essex "were not bothered" about his playing football, because the cricket and football seasons didn't overlap in those days and it was not unusual for people to play both sports at a professional level. In a revealing comment on the financial situation of cricketers at the time, Rist pointed out that professionals in the 1950s had to "pay for their own bats, pads and other gear". In those days Essex cricketers bought their equipment from Breeden's, the bat manufacturers, who had a shop under the arches at Leyton Midland Road station, just down the road from the County Ground. Players' equipment has changed a great deal since Rist's time, with lightweight pads, coloured clothing and heavy bats all assembled in huge wheeled coffins: "We had great big heavy [boots], leather things, but now they're like slippers what they play in." When Rist first started playing he would have had to pay two guineas for a top-price bat, but later he found a sponsor and was given all his gear by Gray-Nicolls, the sports goods firm, although he was not required to display their logo.

In the 1950s if players were sick or injured they only received their basic pay but no appearance money, although "no one ever seemed to get sick or injured in my day ... not like they are now". There was not as much protective gear as in the modern game, but Rist was rarely injured, perhaps because he was "a big lad" who had "always played with big fellows like policemen".

When Essex played at Leyton, Rist lived in digs at Francis Road, close by his father's police station. Younger players usually stayed in digs, but it was a nomadic existence for a professional cricketer. For a while he lodged in Chelmsford, where his landlady was the wife of a former Essex cricketer. The club decided to leave Leyton to reduce costs and because of a lack of local support, as Trevor Bailey confirms in his autobiography. Crowds improved when the club left Leyton to play around the county because, as Rist explains, "we spread ourselves out so that members didn't always have to travel so far". The improvements to the new headquarters at Chelmsford had made it into "a very nice ground now".

During the war Rist was stationed in Blackpool, where he played Lancashire League cricket and encountered some northern class prejudices. Younger cricketers had great respect for capped professionals – "you almost stood to attention, you know". He was greatly honoured to play against Harold Larwood who, as a professional of the old school, thought that amateurs should be addressed formally as 'Mr', as Rist recalls:

He was coming down the steps before the game and I went after him and said, 'Hello Mr Larwood'. He said, 'My name is Harold, not Mr Larwood. Remember that, OK?' ... The ground was packed ... I went in first, scored a hundred, mind you he wasn't the bowler that he was in his prime ... I can always remember our captain, he was a wing commander, playing for Somerset. You stood to attention when you spoke to him. They suggested that I should have a collection, 'cos professionals in those days had collections in the league, and the captain said no, he's a service player, he's not entitled to a collection. I could have done very well …

After the Second World War Rist captained the Essex Club & Ground XI and joined the sports outfitters in Walthamstow owned by his father-in-law, Arthur Sedgwick. Essex asked him to become their coach, which at the time was an unpaid job: "They couldn't afford the money, but I was in a position where I could have what time I liked off, and all they did was pay for me petrol." He also had a testimonial that raised just over a £1,000, which was "quite good". His work at Sedgwick's ensured that Rist was never unemployed. After retiring, some of his colleagues "got decent jobs, but some of them didn't". He kept in touch with some of his former footballing colleagues who became managers and then "came in the shop and bought their gear". Anyone who played sport in the Walthamstow area knew Sedgewick's sports shop. Local parents bought their children's school PE kit and games there, and it was a kind of meeting place for all those involved in sport in the borough.

During an interview at the Colchester Festival in 2009 Doug Insole remembered Frank Rist with some fondness. He pointed out that Rist's only first-class wicket was against Northamptonshire when he dismissed the England captain, Freddie Brown. Warming to his task, Insole further revealed that in 1948 Rist played in the Essex match against Yorkshire in which Len Hutton made his first-class debut. Rist was keeping wicket in the match and in the second innings took the catch that ensured that Hutton was out for nought in both innings, in an unpromising start to the great batsman's career.

Frank Rist is very much in the tradition of local Essex heroes. Much like Graham Gooch he came from humble beginnings and achieved his schoolboy dream of becoming a professional sportsman. He was popular with the club's supporters and was respected by teammates and opposition alike, both in cricket and in football, and he never let the class prejudices that beset cricket in the 1950s hold him back. How he must have enjoyed dismissing Freddie Brown. He was a much-loved feature of the local sports scene in my schoolboy days, and I must have bought dozens of pairs of laces and tins of dubbin in the shop, mainly because it was just a great place to be on Saturday mornings.

Frank Rist is in a long line of great Essex cricketers after the war that includes the Smith cousins, Peter and Ray, who played for the MCC in the late forties and early fifties. Indeed, Peter Smith played for England in the 1946/47 season and was a Wisden Cricketer of the Year in 1947 for his excellent batting and leg-break bowling. Going back further, the legendary all-rounder Johnny Douglas was the Essex captain between 1911 and 1928 and played for England and the MCC in this period, captaining his country when they lost the 1921 Ashes series 5-0. Douglas was a Wisden Cricketer of the Year as far back as 1915. He was known as a strong disciplinarian and was keen on his players being physically fit, much in the mould of Graham Gooch and Nasser Hussain in modern times. Even further back in the dynasty is the remarkable Charles Kortright, who deserves a biography of his own. Born in South Weald, close to Chelmsford, Kortright captained the county in the 1903 season and represented the MCC in 1893. A fearsome fast bowler and useful batsman with a highest score of 131, Kortright played regularly for Brentwood CCC, as we will see in the following chapter. Bunny Lewis, Tom Pearce, Denys Wilcox, Ken Farnes, Bailey, Insole, Taylor, Fletcher, Gooch, Hussain and Cook are all part of the long lineage of wonderful Essex cricketers. Frank Rist stands out as a local East London boy who 'lived the dream', as they say today. In that sense he paved the way for Graham Gooch, himself a local hero, and is part of the success story of Essex CCC.

Hearts and minds

Essex's belated success in the 1980s was not achieved overnight. Throughout the 1960s Brian Taylor, Trevor Bailey and Doug Insole had been thinking about a 'philosophy of Essex cricket' that might produce a winning team without losing any sense of the joy of the game. But this was a 'hearts and minds' job, and such aims are notoriously difficult to communicate, let alone achieve. However, they did try, and to their great credit they almost succeeded. Firstly, they had to convince the players. John Lever, who in the 1970s combined his fast-medium bowling responsibilities with the job of Essex fitness trainer, provides some clues to the way that Insole cleverly communicated his ideas to the players:

Pre-season training in those days saw us go for a sandwich in the local pub and the committee would pop in and Doug Insole would put his head round the door and say "good luck" and encouraging words like "If it means winning the game or walking off if you have nicked it, we as a committee would rather you walked off."
- I. Oxborrow and R. Pritchard (2009), Fletcher's Aces and Jokers: Essex – County Cricket Champions 1979, Desert Island Books, p.43

For Lever these were strong words indeed, but they were put in a way that took the pressure off the players. There was no direct criticism. Lever continues:

They were very much for playing the game in the right way and producing England players.
- Oxborrow and Pritchard (2009), p.43

Arguably, from the days of Nasser Hussain and central contracts, to the point today when Alistair Cook and Ravi Bopara are now England players who play for Essex, rather than the other way round, producing England players has had a negative effect on the club's results. But no one at the club, then or now, sees this as a problem, even though the financial cushion fails to compensate fully for the runs and wickets of the club's best players. This aside, Insole and his team did communicate a framework of what kind of cricket they wanted Essex to play, and Fletcher and Gooch did the rest.

Doug Insole MBE
One of the greatest servants of Essex cricket was, of course, Doug Insole. Insole scored 2,477 runs in the summer of 1955, and in 1956 he was selected for the 1956/57 tour of South Africa as vice-captain to Peter May. To cap a wonderful year for the Chingford man, Insole was also chosen as one of the Wisden Five Cricketers of the Year. On retirement Insole became an England selector and in 1982 he was appointed manager for England's tour to Australia and New Zealand. An established and respected international figure in the game, Insole never lost his love for Essex and served the county in two spells as chairman, the first of which entailed the daunting task, for a

relatively young man, of succeeding another Essex cricket legend, the redoubtable T.N. Pearce.

It would be difficult to be more Essex than Doug Insole CBE. Chingford born and bred, Insole could often be seen wandering around the Co-op in Station Road on Saturday mornings, where you might also bump into the legendary local leg-spinner, Robin Hobbs. Insole attended Monoux Grammar School in Walthamstow (now a Sixth Form College), whose alumni include Johnny Dankworth and Teddy Sheringham, before going up to Cambridge University in 1946. Insole was at different times an Essex player, captain, manager and, of course, chairman, and he has been the single most consistent presence at the club since the war. He played in nine Test matches for England and in retirement became President of MCC and Chairman of the Selectors. He famously dropped Geoff Boycott from the England side after the Yorkshire opener scored 246 not out in his previous innings for his country. A serious man, Insole would have been very proud to see Fletcher and later Gooch gain the success for the club that had eluded him and his contemporary Trevor Bailey. Insole could be an awkward character. During a match against Northamptonshire in the 1950s, Freddie Brown, the England captain, instructed Northamptonshire to bat on against Essex rather than making a sporting declaration. A furious Insole brought himself on to bowl at Brown, threw down a combination of underarm and other illegal deliveries and, for the first and only time in his long career, was called for throwing. Now in his eighties Insole remains an enthusiastic supporter of the club and can often be seen around the various county grounds. Doug Insole did more than most to drag Essex kicking and screaming into the last 30 years of the twentieth century.

'Barnacle' Trevor

Trevor Bailey captained Essex from 1961 to 1967. With the possible exception of Doug Insole, there is no greater figure in the history of Essex cricket than the man who became known to all cricket lovers as The Barnacle or The Boil, depending on your preference. The story goes that Bailey acquired the 'Boil' nickname when his surname was mispronounced as Boiley and, cricketers being cricketers, this was quickly shortened to Boil. However, Bailey is better known by his other nickname,

Barnacle, acquired as a result of his particularly obdurate batting for England in the 1950s. Not only did Trevor Bailey captain the county during the late fifties and through most of the sixties, he was also secretary and looked after the club's rather fragile finances. In addition to this daunting workload he continued with his role as England's first-choice all-rounder. Like Graham Gooch in the 1980s, Bailey never let his England duties affect his performances for his club. He achieved a remarkable double of 2,011 runs and 100 wickets in the 1959 Championship season, and scored a total of 21,460 runs for his county, with a highest score of 205. His bowling was equally valuable, with 1,593 wickets at 21.99. It is no wonder that the county's fortunes continued to falter when such a heavy responsibility was entrusted to one member of staff, even one as hardworking and accomplished as Trevor Bailey.

The talented Essex all-rounder Barry Knight was a companion of Bailey and Insole on England tours. Knight was something of an Essex legend, and he was a good enough batsman to score two Test centuries and complete the domestic double of 1,000 runs and 100 wickets for Essex four times. But his bowling was not quite fast enough to earn him the new ball for England ahead of the likes of John Snow and Ken Higgs. Sadly, Knight had a falling out with Essex and left to join Leicestershire, where he spent three seasons, leaving them in 1969, the year of his last Test appearance. After running into some business problems Knight left the UK for Australia, where he set up a successful indoor cricket school in Sydney and developed into a successful coach, for a time acting as mentor to the young Allan Border. To this day Barry Knight remains one of the very best players to have played for the county.

Coaches and coaching

Self-belief, a winning mentality, intensity and desire, combined with a few laughs to ease the pressure of the modern game, were the essential ingredients of the Essex recipe for success. This was to change their world. But these things, noble and vital as they are, will not in themselves win championships or turn good players into internationals, even England captains. Technical coaching is essential in any sport to enable players to reach their potential. Great individuals such as Gary Sobers, Roger Federer, Michael Jordan, Tiger Woods or Kelly Holmes will all have received advice and technical help from their coaches. Cricket, like golf, is a very technical game, and the right kind of coaching can make a difference; however, it will never turn a good player into a great one, whereas developing the right mental approach just might. This has certainly been the belief at Essex over the past 30 years.

Keith Fletcher was never properly coached until he joined the Essex staff, apart from the odd bit of advice from the players at his club, Royston. Fletcher writes:

> *I developed a style and technique by endlessly studying a book called The Art of Cricket by Don Bradman. I tried to copy his shots from pictures, and stood for hours with a bat in front of the mirror, frequently cajoled and corrected by my father.*
> *- Fletcher (1983), p.17*

During his career Fletcher may not have reached the dizzy heights of the great Australian, but his boyhood 'coaching' served him well. With typical good sense, Trevor Bailey told the young Fletcher to play as much cricket as possible and no one at Essex ever tried to make changes to his technique or style. In any case Fletcher would probably have objected to any undue interference. He writes:

> *Too often, I have seen players who succeed without suiting conventional styles, and suffering total lack of confidence as a result. I was left alone, apart from tips which concentrated more on tactics and attitude than technique.*
> *- Fletcher (1983), p.17*

Recently Graham Gooch revealed that he received very little coaching as a boy, apart from tips from his dad and some guidance from the older players at Ilford CC. Gooch is a very different character and believes strongly that if a young player has personal qualities such as self-reliance and positive thinking then they are much more likely to succeed. Gooch received encouragement from his schoolteachers and older players at his club. Bill Morris, Gooch's coach at Ilford, wisely decided to leave well enough alone when he first saw the young hard-hitter from Leytonstone for the first time:

I didn't have a lot to do with his technique or his mental approach, which is difficult for young cricketers.
- Tennant (1992), p.30

Gooch valued encouragement more than anything else and, fortunately for Essex and English cricket, he received more than his share. As we have seen, both Fletcher and Gooch, and earlier Doug Insole and Brian Taylor, believed strongly that providing encouragement to young players and instilling the right kind of mental approach were better suited to their development than precise technical coaching. But there was a further, more subtle element in the philosophy of Essex cricket that helps to explain the club's continued success and the fact that within the space of a few years Essex produced three England captains. Fletcher puts it this way:

I have always encouraged players to chip in with their own thoughts on any particular situation ... At least a player who puts forward an idea is thinking about the game, which usually means he is mentally right for the job. I try to instil in youngsters coming into the side that they must think about their cricket ... an alert mind is essential.
- Fletcher (1983), p.83

During an interview with Gooch at Fenner's in June 2009, he outlined his thoughts on young players and their progress, to make his point dividing them, perhaps a little crudely, into two types: 'receivers' and 'tellers'. (Author's interview with Graham Gooch at Fenner's Cricket Ground, Cambridge (June 2009). When youngsters are in 'receive' mode they will come to the coach or senior player seeking advice on different aspects of their game. If the player is in 'teller' mode, he or she will always need to be told if there is a problem, which then makes it difficult to correct a fault because the player is unlikely to be as receptive to advice as the first category. Gooch put Alistair Cook and Ravi Bopara firmly in the 'receiver' camp. He believes that a coach is halfway there with this type of player. Learning from his own experience as a youngster making his way in the game, Gooch goes out of his way, as Cook and Bopara have testified, to welcome and encourage youngsters. In this way they will feel more confident and more able to ask for advice. But more than anything it is personal drive and ambition that Gooch looks for in a promising player, as without that, in today's intense and pressurised professional game, even a very gifted youngster will struggle.

In Fletcher and Gooch Essex had senior players and later coaches who believed strongly in encouraging young players to think about their cricket. They were looking for players who were confident enough to seek advice and who wanted passionately to move forward to the next level as they progressed through the junior and senior ranks. Their aim was to see young talent maturing and able to look after themselves in cricketing terms, moving smoothly from one level to the next. For Gooch at least, this is part of a 'life process'. Clearly, Cook and Bopara of the current generation have these qualities in abundance, as did Fletcher, Gooch himself and Nasser Hussain. Gooch makes it very clear that, although he could tell when they were first spotted by Essex scouts that Cook and Bopara were outstanding young prospects, both are very strong characters and mature young men who are ready to test their ability at the highest level.

Desire, self-belief, a winning mentality and a particular way of bringing on young players have been the main building blocks for a philosophy of cricket that has served Essex so well from the mid-1970s up to the present day. This philosophy, designed by Brian Taylor, Keith Fletcher and Graham Gooch, has been the cornerstone of the club's success over the past 30 years.

A home at last!

Throughout the 1960s Essex CCC continued its nomadic, if not actually hippy, existence, travelling from festival ground to festival ground, usually losing more matches than they won. However, the 1960s were not without some playing highlights. In 1962 Essex beat the touring Pakistan side by nine wickets at Leyton, and in 1964 they famously defeated the Australians at Southend, with Keith Fletcher scoring 125 and Gordon Barker 123. In 1966 Essex began their long haul to become a serious club by purchasing the Writtle Road ground at Chelmsford, thanks to the financial generosity of the Warwickshire Supporters' Association. That same year, while Bobby Moore was lifting the Jules Rimet Trophy, the club staged their first Sunday fixture, with 6,000 spectators turning up at Ilford to watch the match against Somerset, who were to be Essex's closest rivals in limited overs cricket during the 1980s.

As the decade of flower power drew to a close, Essex continued their tradition of success against touring sides. In 1969 the county defeated New Zealand by 15 runs at Westcliff, home club of the county and England all-rounder, Trevor Bailey. Essex's spin attack was too much for the tourists, with Ray East and Robin Hobbs taking 8 for 68 and 6 for 88 respectively. There were several notable developments in the history of the county in the late 1960s, with Romford, Clacton and Brentwood hosting their last festivals, while Purfleet was added to the list of occasional county grounds for the newly introduced John Player League. The changes to the itinerary were mainly designed to facilitate their return to Chelmsford, firstly as a festival ground and later as the club's headquarters.

Insole and Bailey were loyal, talented and distinguished servants of Essex CCC during the 1950s and 1960s, but the team's performances continued to disappoint during their respective times as captain, with the state of the club's finances a contributory factor to their failure to win a major trophy. Essex's highest finish in the County Championship in the sixties was sixth in 1962 and sixth again in 1969. The intervening years saw the club finish no higher than tenth. The catalyst for a change in the club's fortunes came with the appointment of Brian 'Tonker' Taylor as captain in 1967. Brian Taylor played 539 matches for Essex between 1949 and 1973, scoring 18,240 runs at 21.92. His highest score for the county was 135. A wicketkeeper for most of his career, Taylor contributed 1,040 catches and 191 stumpings to the Essex cause and was an energetic and competent 'keeper, taking eight catches in a match an impressive five times. All of this amounts to a considerable 24-year career. However, it will not be his figures, modest in some respects, for which Taylor will best be remembered at Essex, but rather the manner in which he began the process of modernisation at the club, later taken forward by Keith Fletcher, Graham Gooch and Peter Edwards. Keith Fletcher writes:

The 'germ' of Essex's success in the late seventies had been planted ten years earlier. Although we never won anything under Brian Taylor, the mental approach of the side improved beyond recognition.
- Fletcher (1983), p.75

A democracy of ideas – a successful leadership style

The return to Chelmsford, a move that signalled the end of the county's nomadic existence over the previous 100 years, could not have come sooner. At last the conditions were in place to stage a recovery, both in financial and cricketing terms. The recovery, when it came in the late 1970s, created the platform from which Essex were to produce cricketers of real international quality such as Graham Gooch, Keith Fletcher, Derek Pringle, Neil Foster, Nasser Hussain and latterly Alistair Cook and Ravi Bopara. Success on the field was bound to follow. In retrospect Brian Taylor's succession to the captaincy coincided with a turning point in the attitude and approach to playing professional cricket, not just in the insular County Championship but also across the world. The introduction of the John Player League (JPL) marks that point. Fletcher likes to emphasise the mental approach of the game, and the JPL, if not the Gillette Cup introduced a few years earlier, forced counties into accepting that they needed to acquire a new mentality, a brand-new professional mindset, if they were going to be able to compete.

In his autobiography Fletcher reveals how senior professionals in the Essex side, and for that matter in all county sides, resisted the innovation of the Gillette Cup. Fletcher points out that in the sixties pre-season training consisted of a few gentle nets, and even on match days the team would turn up an hour before the start of play and then sit around drinking tea till play began. There were no structured warm-ups or systematic fielding practice, let alone health drinks, personal trainers and team huddles beloved of today's über-professionals. Fletcher reveals that life was extremely relaxed under the captaincy of Trevor Bailey, to whom, given his natural gifts, everything came so easily. But it was the attitude to the Gillette Cup that mystified the aspiring young batsman. Fletcher writes:

> *I saw the amateurish Essex outlook most clearly when the Gillette Cup began its illustrious life in 1963. This, surely, was an exciting new chance for honours, and the opportunity to win through to a Lord's final ... most of our staff did not see it that way. Instead, they regarded this new competition as an unwanted intrusion on their free days.*

- Fletcher (1983), p.19

The Essex teams of the seventies and eighties, under Fletcher's astute and purposeful leadership, took to the one-day game like a duck to water, and as a consequence their fortunes were miraculously transformed. But it was Brian Taylor that began the process of sweeping the old cobwebs away and instilling in his players the need to change their whole approach to playing professional cricket. As Fletcher says, the club attacked the Sunday League with relish. Taylor quickly realised the potential of the competition, and with a young fit side at his disposal he set about introducing new training methods, including intense fielding practice, getting the bowlers to adopt a plan suited to one-day cricket and encouraging the whole side to begin thinking more carefully about field placings. Training specifically for one-day cricket clearly paid off, as Essex finished second to Lancashire in the opening season of the JPL in 1969. The young Fletcher admired Taylor's attention to detail and applied it as an essential element of his own ideas on captaincy.

Essex, like many counties at the time, stopped treating one-day cricket as a joke. Taylor, then Fletcher, quickly realised that the Sunday League and the Gillette Cup would not only improve playing standards but also, in particular, would take fielding to a level never seen before in the first-class game. Fletcher sets out his ideas about playing one-day cricket in his autobiography:

> *Containing bowling was the first advance; pacing an innings rather than slogging indiscriminately was another. From a captain's point of view, field placing became more crucial, bowling changes could be decisive and a switch in the batting order could turn a tight game.*
> *- Fletcher (1983), p.77*

Certainly one-day cricket made the Essex players think about their approach to being professionals. They trained harder, became more athletic in their movement and developed a greater competitive edge. The introduction of the one-day game in the 1960s added a new dimension to county cricket. For the first time cricket became a pressurised sport. As each county raised their playing standards, the competition and pressure intensified. The Gillette Cup and the JPL were often played in front of large crowds and, crucially, were televised. Live TV and packed grounds week after week throughout the season brought huge financial benefits to the game, and in a few years the financial fortunes of the clubs were transformed. Cricket had joined other professional sports in becoming pressurised, intense, highly competitive and financially sound. Brian Taylor understood this in his time as captain and began to prepare his players for the new challenge. In the 1970s Keith Fletcher took up this challenge with considerable relish and with unprecedented success. Taylor's successor was a thoughtful and determined cricketer who understood that his first responsibility as Essex captain was to the club's long-suffering supporters. Fletcher knew how much winning a first trophy would mean to them and set about building on the solid start established by Brian Taylor. Fletcher's experience of Essex's appallingly complacent approach to the Gillette Cup when he first came into the side under Trevor Bailey left him in no doubt as to the magnitude of the task.

On taking over the captaincy from Taylor, Fletcher set himself clear objectives: firstly, to improve the players' fitness and attitudes to practice; and secondly, to work on his team's mental approach to the game. In his book *The Art of Captaincy* Mike Brearley wrote:

> *It was (Keith) Fletcher who told me that in his view the most crucial aspect of captaincy is treating individuals differently. …*
> *… I know Fletcher has made a point of having dinner with one of his players who tends to feel depressed and lonely.*
> *- M. Brearley (2001), The Art of Captaincy, Channel 4 Books, p.266*

Brearley was writing about Fletcher's captaincy of the England team and his handling of individual international players. However, this was also Fletcher's style of leadership at Essex and this was shared by his successor, Graham Gooch. Sensitivity to different individuals' needs and temperaments was an element of Fletcher and Gooch's wider aim of increasing motivation and fitting each player into an effective team unit. The approach certainly worked for Essex, as the team of the late 1970s gradually began to evolve into the most powerful force in English cricket. Providing individual attention and encouraging players to contribute creatively on the field of play are signs of respect and can be hugely motivating. Players feel well regarded and develop self-confidence as a result. An important effect of Fletcher and Gooch's leadership style was that it created a positive teamwork ethic and a heightened sense of morale. With this approach cliques and cynicism on the part of individuals are unlikely to develop; if they do, it is unlikely that the team will be successful, particularly at a time when teams are operating in relentlessly pressurised situations, under the glare of publicity and the constant scrutiny of statisticians.

Brearley compares the job of a cricket captain to that of a senior nurse on a hospital ward, where everyone is working under intense pressure and in stressful conditions. In these kinds of situations individuals become anxious and deal with their anxiety by developing a hard-nosed cynicism. The task of the ward sister is to create conditions in which a spirit of cooperation and high morale can flourish, thereby achieving a good team ethic with shared aims and objectives. The analogy is a good one, because individual players will harbour anxieties under the constant scrutiny of the media and this can damage the team's efficiency. A further useful analogy is a headteacher of a large school, where high levels of anxiety are present. A good head will work to develop a spirit of cooperation and teamwork among colleagues and students. He or she knows that without this the institution will not succeed. As Brearley writes:

> *… it is up to the captain and coach to help players with self-defeating attitudes that arise individually or collectively as a result of their anxieties. It is also up to them to create an atmosphere in which players feel safe enough to offer their own diagnosis or point of view …*
> *- Brearley (2001), p.5-6*

Anybody who has worked in a leadership team in a school or hospital will identify with Brearley's views. I once observed a colleague preparing a group of lively 14-year-old girls for a PE lesson when she noticed a member of the group sitting on her own, in tears and looking extremely anxious. The teacher sat down beside the distraught youngster and took a minute to reassure and encourage her. Her intervention had two results: firstly, the girl enjoyed her lesson; and secondly, it brought the whole group together. In effect the teacher took on the girl's anxieties and found a creative solution to her difficulty. Brearley claims that

> *The need for such qualities is universal, applies to all walks of life … there is no substitute for the leader's capacity to bring people together in a common task, so that people come to take pleasure in their joint and individual work.*
> *- Brearley (2001), p.7*

Our teacher was a natural. She was intuitive and just knew what to do. Brearley argues that the leadership style of the likes of Fletcher and Gooch comes naturally or, if you like, is intuitive. I think this is true in the case of Fletcher, although he was a deeply reflective thinker about the game and was driven to succeed, much in the way of that very different successful Australian captain, Steven Waugh. But if Fletcher was intuitive, Gooch was heavily influenced by his mentor, and in that sense his style was derivative but strongly felt. Like my teacher friend, Fletcher's intuitive sense derived from the fact that he cared. Gooch was the same: it mattered so much to him that Essex were successful.

Both Fletcher and Gooch were keen to develop young players, preferring to mould them into the right kinds of professionals that would benefit the team. They both enjoyed helping young players to mature both technically and in terms of their emotional intelligence. Essex young players who succeed are likely to have acquired mental strength, increased maturity as individuals both inside and outside the game, and a concern for their physical fitness as professional athletes. Fletcher had strong individuals in his successful side of the 1980s. If you think of the likes of Gooch, Ray East, Ken McEwan, Brain Hardie, Stuart Turner, J.K. Lever, David Acfield, Neil Foster and Derek Pringle, then you can guess the size of Fletcher's task. That he was able to turn a group of highly talented but potentially disparate characters into a powerful, highly motivated unit is an indication of the quality of his leadership skills. Fletcher tolerated different opinions, indeed welcomed them, because they were no threat to his authority and would only strengthen the team.

Both Fletcher and Gooch were an inspiration to young

players, gave them respect and listened to them. Both were hugely determined characters who understood what success meant to the club's members and supporters. Fletcher succeeded in creating a winning mentality at Essex because he was crystal clear in what he wanted to achieve. He had the desire necessary to succeed at the top level and communicated this to his players. Graham Gooch, like his predecessor, wanted nothing more than to continue Fletcher's legacy.

In 1979 Keith Fletcher achieved his aim of developing a winning mentality among his players. The team had acquired a desire to win and had developed self-belief and personal pride as a first-rate group of professional cricketers. The only thing left was to know how to win, and it was soon to become a habit.

Winter jobs and sponsored cars

In the world before players received relatively large sums of money from central contracts, sponsorship, ghosted books and advertising, they relied on winter jobs to supplement their meagre income from cricket. While this was the case it was difficult to instil in players the professional outlook that the modern game required for success. Keith Fletcher's Essex team of the late 1970s and early 1980s all had winter jobs if they were not involved in an England tour. Fletcher himself, countryman that he was, worked during the close season as a part-time gamekeeper and agricultural oil salesman well into his career. David Acfield was a qualified teacher and taught at Brentwood School for two terms each year. Stuart Turner and John Lever had school coaching work, while others did a variety of jobs, including window cleaning rounds and selling second-hand cars. From time to time contracted players would sign on the dole if winter work was not available.

Once upon a time cricket and football were much more closely related than they are today. Many cricket clubs started out as football clubs. The Kennington Oval hosted 22 FA Cup finals between 1872 and 1892. One of Essex CCC's original grounds, Leyton, has for many years been the home of local amateur soccer clubs. Yorkshire's Bramall Lane and the County Ground at Northampton were both three-sided grounds that hosted first-class cricket and were, until the 1970s, the home grounds of Leeds United and Northampton Town respectively. Many of us that have played football and cricket at a decent amateur standard will have participated in both sports on the same ground on many occasions. For a short time I was chairman of a sports club that had three league cricket sides and six football teams all playing on Saturdays. With the extension of the football season over the past few years, one of the most complex tasks for the committee was to manage how both football and cricket could be played on the same ground when the two games overlapped in May, August and September. The matter was further complicated by the ground only having one set of changing rooms for both sports. We generally overcame this issue by having the cricketers change in the bar until the footballers had finished and had their showers. The whole scene often descended into 'Carry On'-like farce as the footballers insisted on larking around behind the bowlers arm and devouring the teas prepared for hungry cricketers. But somehow we survived until sympathetic fixtures secretaries took pity and factored our clashes into their computer programme.

There has been a long tradition of professional cricketers turning into footballers in September, the most famous of whom were Denis Compton and Willy Watson. More recently, Jim Standen kept goal for West Ham in the 1964 European Cup-Winners' Cup final, and the late Chris Balderstone played over 400 games for Carlisle United while simultaneously playing out a distinguished cricket career for Leicestershire that included County Championship and Benson & Hedges winners' medals and two England caps. Also Phil Neale, Jimmy Cumbes, Steve Ogrizovic, Ian Botham and Andy Goram all combined both sports with varying degrees of success. Perhaps the most interesting and least known cricketer/footballers were Brian Close and Viv Richards. Close represented England Youth against Scotland at football in 1948 and signed as an amateur for Leeds United before giving up football for a long and distinguished career in cricket. Close was also unusual for playing golf to single figures, either right-handed or left-handed. Viv Richards is best known as one the finest batsman to have ever played the game, but what is less well known is that he also turned out for the Antiguan football team. Richards played football for his country in their qualifying campaign for the 1974 World Cup, but sadly Antigua lost 6-0 to Surinam and 11-0 to Trinidad & Tobago and Richards' short international football career was over.

Doug Insole and Trevor Bailey knew just how to spend their winters. Both played football at senior amateur level, Insole with Corinthian Casuals, and Bailey, probably the more accomplished footballer, with great distinction for Walthamstow Avenue in the Isthmian League. In the 1960s Essex could boast a team that would have been better at football than they were at cricket. At a time when the club regularly finished in the wrong half of the County Championship they often fielded the following: Geoff Hurst (West Ham and England), Eddie Presland (West Ham), Gordon Barker (Southend United), Terry Kent (Millwall), Doug Insole (Pegasus and Corinthian Casuals), Trevor Bailey (Walthamstow Avenue), Brian Taylor (Brentford) and Paddy Phelan (local amateur). Second XI players included Cliff Holton (Arsenal), Dave Sexton (West Ham) and Alan Sealey (West Ham). The club offered terms to Bobby Moore, but the young footballer had other priorities and his Essex appearances were limited to testimonials. Geoff Hurst played one first-class match for Essex against Lancashire in the County Championship at Aigburth, Liverpool, in 1962. In his only appearance for the First XI, Hurst failed to trouble the scorers in either innings. Despite this setback to his cricket career, Hurst continued to turn out for the Essex Second XI. Both Keith Fletcher and Graham Gooch loved their amateur football and continued to play for fun before the demands of cricket completely took over (I am grateful to the website www.twohundredpercent.net for the information on footballer/cricketers).

Doug Insole, the old traditionalist, bemoans the fact that the excesses of professional football have robbed first-class cricket of some of its finest players. With the start of the soccer season now in mid-August and pre-season training beginning in early July, there is absolutely no chance of professional footballers playing county cricket even if they were inclined to do so.

Leading characters

By 1979 the days of football-playing cricketers and part-time jobs were well and truly over, enabling professional cricketers to concentrate fully on their day job. County cricketers, if they were to be successful, had to bring to their game a level of professionalism found in other sports. At Essex the players took to the new professionalism like ducks to water.

Keith Fletcher knew he had the right group of players to deliver the victory that Essex supporters craved. In Ken McEwan and Graham Gooch he had two world-class batsmen who scored their runs quickly and were happy playing long innings. Brian Hardie, Gooch's fellow opener, was a tough and obdurate Scot who acted as a perfect foil to his more belligerent partner. Fletcher averaged around 40 in 59 Tests for England and scored nearly 30,000 runs for his county, so as well as being an inspirational captain he was an accomplished international batsman. Established England opener Mike Denness had joined the club after winning the County Championship with his former county Kent. In the lower middle order, all-rounder Keith Pont, one of the team's great jokers, was a big-hitting batsman and useful seam bowler. Neil Smith was a competent wicketkeeper and his unorthodox stroke-making came to the rescue of his side on a number of occasions. As we shall see later, nobody contributed more to the club's change of fortune than all-rounder Norbert Phillip. Ray East was the side's left-arm slow bowler, night watchman and the principal joker in the pack. Former Cambridge University off-spinner David Acfield provided an alternative to East's left-arm spin and zany sense of humour. He was an interesting character who had represented England at fencing and became a close confidant of his captain. Acfield had come into the Essex side as replacement for the leg-spinner, Robin Hobbs, and while he never achieved the legendary status of the Chingford man the off-spinner provided a steady presence, even if his fielding and batting sometimes failed to reach the standards of his more athletic teammates.

The Essex pace attack of the side of 1979 was lethal. Norbert Phillip and Stuart Turner were both wicket takers, but they could also bowl long economic spells when the occasion demanded, while their batting could be relied on to turn games on a regular basis. Both were superb fielders. However, it was John Lever's incomparable bowling that contributed most to the successes of 1979 and to the glorious years that followed. Stepney-born, Lever was a left-arm, fast-medium opening bowler, which is a bit like saying Don Bradman was an orthodox right-hand batsman. It doesn't tell us very much. Lever reached his peak in the late seventies. In the 1977 season he took an impressive 108 wickets and his superb form continued in 1978 and 1979 when he took 102 and 104 wickets respectively. In

1979 he was named one of Wisden's Five Cricketers of the Year and carried off the coveted Players' Player of the Year award. More than any other player, Lever was responsible for Essex winning the Championship in 1979. His left-arm, rhythmical-swing bowling ran through sides in game after game, and he was simply unstoppable in that year as Essex went from victory to victory. The popular fast-bowler was in the form of his life. Lever prided himself on his physical fitness and later became the team's unofficial trainer. He could and did bowl long spells, and to his great credit, like his teammate Graham Gooch, his commitment to Essex never faltered when he became a regular member of the England team. Lever played 21 Tests for England at 26.72, including 7 for 46 on his debut against India in Delhi on the 1976/77 tour. He was later awarded the MBE for services to cricket and nobody deserved the honour more than the self-effacing but fiercely competitive J.K. Lever. Fletcher recognised his value to the team's success, as did thousands of grateful Essex supporters. In 1983 Fletcher wrote:

> *The ball swung for him almost throughout the whole of 1979, and he went from one set of astonishing figures to another as we simply walked off with the Championship.*
> *- Fletcher (1983), p.85*

On the fringe of the 1979 side were two young and aggressive batsmen. East Londoner Alan Lilley never quite fulfilled his exciting potential and went on to become a senior administrator at the club, while Mike McEvoy was another young player who found the going tough in the new pressurised atmosphere of Essex cricket. However, both players made a contribution to the Essex cause, and Lilley, in particular, was an outstanding fielder.

The Sobers effect

In the 1970s the introduction of overseas players into county cricket made a decisive contribution to raising playing standards and helped to increase public interest in the game in general. Overseas players became a regular feature of county cricket in the 1960s, and most counties, with one or two stubborn exceptions, employed overseas players for some or all of the season. Gary Sobers made the most immediate impact. Playing in a Sunday League match for Nottinghamshire against

Glamorgan at Swansea in 1968, the great West Indian all-rounder hit Malcolm Nash for six 6s in one over. The match was televised, only in black and white in those days, and must have been a sponsor's dream. Sobers' feat remains one of the most iconic moments in cricket history and is now immortalised on YouTube.

Essex did especially well with their overseas players. The exciting West Indian fast-bowler, hard-hitting batsman and superb fielder Keith Boyce played for the county from 1966 to 1977, cruelly missing out on the success that in 1977 was just around the corner. Boyce was brought to Essex from Barbados by Trevor Bailey and quickly made his mark. In his first game for the county, against Cambridge University, he took 9 for 61 in the University's first innings, unnerving the nervous students with some fierce fast-bowling. Keith Boyce had emphatically announced his arrival, and he became a hugely popular figure with the Essex supporters. He helped to transform the county's attitude to fielding, and his competitive instincts began to influence his teammates. Boyce played 211 matches for Essex, scoring 6,848 runs with an average of 22.75, and took 662 wickets at 23.72. One performance stands out and underlines his particular value to the county during the 1960s. Boyce was the first bowler to take 8 wickets in a one-day match when in 1971 he destroyed the Lancashire batting and achieved the rare figures of 8 for 26. To underline his genuine all-rounder status, he once hit a magnificent 98 off 54 balls in 50 minutes in a Sunday League match at The Oval. These two performances illustrate the type of player Boyce was much more adequately than any bare statistics. Tragically, Keith Boyce died of chronic cirrhosis of the liver in a pharmacist's chair in Barbados in 1996. Older Essex supporters will never forget the contribution he made to the improvement in the county's fortune during his time with the club.

South African batsman Lee Irvine signed for the 1968 and 1969 seasons and contributed 2,674 runs at 34.72. Bruce Francis succeeded Boyce in 1971 and the Australian scored 2,962 runs in two seasons with the club, at an average of 38.46 and with an impressive top score of 188. Although both Irvine and Francis made an impact at Chelmsford, after Keith Boyce the greatest contribution by an overseas player to Essex cricket came from another South African, Ken McEwan. McEwan, who played for the county between 1974 and 1985, became a vital member of the successful sides under Keith Fletcher in the 1970s and early 1980s. In all McEwan played 282 matches for Essex and scored 18,088 runs at an average of 43.37 and with a top score of 218. He contributed 52 centuries to the Essex cause and his runs were a major reason why the county became a dominant force in English county cricket. With South Africa ostracised from international cricket, McEwan was able to devote his best years to his adopted county. His 72 against Surrey in the 1979 Benson & Hedges final helped Essex towards a score that proved far beyond their South London rival's capabilities.

Ken McEwan left Essex at the peak of his career, claiming that he was tired of driving up and down the motorways of England without any prospect of playing Test cricket for his country. The great South African batsman spent many happy and successful years with Essex. Like Keith Boyce, McEwan was extremely popular with the Essex supporters. The official history of Essex cricket club describes him as

> *... a man without conceit, transparently honest and unflinchingly loyal, but because of his nationality, the ultimate honours were denied to him.*
> *- Lemmon and Marshall (1987), p.364*

McEwan retired to his farm in South Africa in 1985 following a season in which Essex won the NatWest Trophy and the JPL, were losing finalists in the B&H Cup, and finished fourth in the County Championship. Ken McEwan had been an integral part of the most glorious period in the county's history, and Essex, without his heavy run-scoring, struggled to maintain this success.

The Australian captain, Allan Border, was signed as a replacement for McEwan in 1986, and made an immediate impact during his brief stay at Chelmsford. He scored 1,385 runs, including 4 centuries, with a top score of 150. Border was signed to provide substance to a batting order suddenly deprived of the excellence of McEwan, while Graham Gooch was expected to be away from the club for long periods on Test Match duty. The Australian skipper had a very positive influence on the club with his winning habit, desire and sheer professionalism. The younger players were inspired by his attitude towards them and the brilliance of his batting. Once again the club had chosen the right man. Who would have thought, prior to 1979, that a successful Australian captain and near legend of cricket would sign for homely old Essex? How times had changed. Border ignited the club's season and helped to steer them to their third County Championship in four years and their fourth in eight. In addition, the club finished second in the JPL, just four points behind the winners Hampshire.

In the 1990s Essex continued to recruit high-quality, high-impact overseas players. Mark Waugh had a brief spell with the club and confirmed his reputation as one of the world's great natural stroke-makers. Nasser Hussain admits that he was in awe of Waugh and his effortless ability. Salim Malik, later involved in match-fixing allegations, never gave less than his best for Essex with his technical brilliance in playing spin bowling. In his two spells at Chelmsford he became a popular figure in the dressing room and he was a positive influence on Essex's two rising young stars, Nasser Hussain and Nadeem Shahid.

I have left arguably the best of Essex's parade of overseas stars, and a personal favourite, till last. Norbert 'Nobby' Phillip signed for Essex in 1978 and stayed for seven years, during which time the county had the most successful period in their history. The arrival of Phillip at Essex was fortuitous. The Test and County Cricket Board (TCCB) refused the club permission to sign the great New Zealander Richard Hadlee for part of the 1977 season, following Essex's reluctance to offer Hadlee a three-year contract. What a signing Hadlee would have been. But his replacement, the quiet and unassuming young Phillip, soon won over both his teammates and the Essex followers with his consistent, often match-winning bowling and his positive stroke-making.

In the 1970s Phillip played for the Windward Islands and regularly represented the Combined Islands. But, at a time when the West Indies had a wealth of quick bowlers, Phillip found it difficult to break into the West Indies side. Keen to further his career, he was anxious to pursue his dreams in England. Although he was an unknown quantity when he came to Essex, he appeared to be an almost an ideal replacement for the ailing Keith Boyce. He was a little quicker than Boyce, though not quite such a consistent batsman and not in the same class as a fielder. Phillip proved a more than adequate replacement for the popular Bajaan and proved the perfect foil for John Lever, as Essex again had the two-point pace attack necessary for winning trophies. Phillip's signing also allowed Stuart Turner to return to his favoured use of the older ball. In match after match during his time with the county Phillip proved his undoubted worth, including a match-winning maiden century. The bare statistics tell us that in his time with the club Phillip scored 3,784 runs at an average of 21.13, with a top score of 134. With his fast-medium bowling he took 423 wickets at 25.14. The numbers look fairly modest, those of a journeyman professional, but Nobby Phillip's contribution to the club's success in those incredible years cannot be measured solely in statistical terms. David Lemmon and Mike Marshall described one decisive contribution that Phillip made to the Essex cause:

> *As a batsman, he was never to hit the consistent power of his predecessor, but he produced one innings in his first season, 134, a maiden century of awesome brilliance, which brought a memorable victory at Gloucester.*
> *- Lemmon and Marshall (1987), P.306*

In the 1979 Benson & Hedges Cup final, Phillip took 3 for 42 from 10 over spell, a decisive contribution to the Essex victory. His bowling was crucial to the club's successes in the 1980s, when he achieved 5 wicket hauls 18 times and once took 10 wickets in a match. Building on his success with Essex, the Dominican-born Phillip played nine Tests for the West Indies between 1977 and 1980, with a best batting performance of 47, while taking 4 for 47 against India in Madras in his country's 1978/79 tour of the sub-continent. Norbert Phillip was one of Essex's unsung heroes and doesn't feature prominently in any of the accounts of Essex's glory years of the 1980s. Now in his mid-sixties, Phillip is thought to have retired to the USA, but little else is known about the West Indian all-rounder who was such a vital member of Keith Fletcher's all-conquering heroes of 1979.

The Essex success juggernaut rolled on into the 1990s with Championship wins in 1991 and 1992 under Graham Gooch, and the Benson & Hedges Cup again in 1998. They began the new century in style, winning Division 2 of the County Championship in 2002 and the Sunday Pro-40 in 2005 and 2006, and comfortably won the 2008 Friends Provident Cup against arch-rivals Kent. A succession of overseas players were drafted in at this time and usually made an impact, including Ryan ten Doeschate, Andy and Grant Flower, the popular and effective Andy Bichel and the immensely gifted Australian batsman Stuart Law, who joined Nasser Hussain's side in 1996. All contributed to Essex's continued success in their different ways. Law made a huge impact with his domination of county bowling, but he was selected only once to play for his country, when he would have walked into other international sides. The last of a line of outstanding international cricketers and perhaps the most interesting choice of overseas player in recent years has been the Pakistan leg-spinner Darnish Kaneria. He joined the club in 2005 for just seven matches and took 32 wickets. He rejoined in 2007 and enjoyed his most successful season with the county, taking an impressive 107 wickets. Kaneria broke a finger in 2008, and in the same season his wife gave birth to their second child, but despite the interruptions to his season he recovered to take his place in the Essex side that won the Friends Provident final at Lord's. Kaneria returned for the 2009 season and again made a telling contribution to the club's successful attempt at promotion to Division One of the County Championship. Kaneria is only the second Hindu to play Test Match cricket for Pakistan, and he has graced the game of cricket for both Essex and his country. Essex have not had a world-class leg-spinner in their side since the much-loved Robin Hobbs whirled away to such good effect in the 1960s and early 1970s. Such is his quality that Essex supporters have become used to the sight of Kaneria opening the bowling for Michael Pettini's team, and they will fervently hope that he is there in the 2010 season to support Essex's bid to win another County Championship trophy.

Graham Gooch has recognised the positive effect that overseas players have had on the performance of Essex teams over the past 30 years, but his views on the recent Kolpak 'invasion' of English cricket are quite different. For Gooch, counties that have come to rely on numbers of Kolpak players have been extremely short-sighted, hoping for a quick reward at the expense of developing local young talent. This is not the Essex way, he made clear, and the county would always place its future in the hands of a systematic scouting system, effective links with clubs and schools, and working with the Essex Cricket Board. The club are geared to developing young players through the Graham Gooch Cricket Academy at Chelmsford and Gooch's own Scholarship Scheme, from which Cook, Bopara and others have so clearly benefited. That said, the history of Essex cricket would have been the poorer without the brilliance of its overseas players.

Winning becomes a habit

The general improvement in the club's affairs was threatened by a financial crisis in 1960 that threatened the very future of the club. It is to the club's great credit that they not only survived the crisis but also prospered to the extent that a gleaming new ground is planned for 2012. Essex were not alone in having problems balancing their books at this time. Membership figures were declining at most counties as the County Championship's popularity began to recede in the public imagination. The English game was still reeling from the shock of being humiliated by Australia in the Ashes series of 1958. Keith Fletcher recalls the "harsher realities of life as a young county cricketer" of the time. In 1960 he received a letter from secretary Bailey, which, although accepting the progress that Fletcher had made in his short time at the club, left the promising youngster in no doubt as to the parlous state of the club's finances. Bailey wrote:

> *Unfortunately, the county's finances suffered a severe setback as a result of the weather and in consequence your winter retainer is very small. I shall be paying you a lump sum of £28 at the commencement of April.*
> *- Fletcher (1983), p.17-18*

Of course, the state of the English county game was due to a combination of factors, including naive management, an amateur approach to a professional game and a resistance to change. But all the counties received a wake-up call at this time and were forced to accept the harsh reality that county cricket had become a sporting lame duck and the preserve of only a few hardened enthusiasts. The saviour of the sleepy English professional game came in the form of one-day cricket: firstly, with the 60-over Gillette Cup in 1963; and secondly, the kick-up-the-backside cricket desperately needed, with the radical 40-over John Player League introduced in 1969. Keith Fletcher confirms the contribution that the JPL made to Essex's improvement:

The most fundamental reason was the introduction of the John Player League.
- Fletcher (1983), p.75

For Essex, a permanent move to Chelmsford could not be delayed for much longer. The improvements to the Chelmsford headquarters in the 1970s were achieved with an interest-free loan from Warwickshire Supporters' Club, negotiated by our schoolboy hero, Trevor Bailey. Fortunately for Essex, Warwickshire enjoyed considerable financial success at the time with their Pools syndicate and they were keen to use their money for the wider benefit of the English game.

Up until this time, on leaving their original home at Leyton (The history of the County Ground at Leyton is covered in more detail in the following chapter), deep in East London, Essex had wandered around the county to Brentwood, Colchester, Ilford, Southend, Westcliff, Clacton and Romford, much to the delight of local supporters. Essex began their first match at Leyton on the 14th May 1894, losing to Leicestershire by 66 runs. The club stayed at the old County Ground in Leyton High Road for much of the twentieth century, enduring the privation and damage of two world wars, before leaving in 1977 following a match against Glamorgan, which Essex won by 194 runs. Left-arm slow-bowler Ray East would have enjoyed the county's final match in East London with figures of 8 for 90 and 4 for 23. Only the festivals at Colchester and Southend have survived the cull, and the financial argument for playing all matches at Chelmsford is a very persuasive one. The last to go was the Ilford Festival and its demise was a big disappointment to the East London followers of the county. But the home club of two England captains, Graham Gooch and Nasser Hussain, could no longer cope with the demands of hosting first-class cricket. It did not help that Redbridge, the cheapskate local authority owners of Valentines Park, withdrew their small subsidy of the Ilford Festival. In addition, the county actually needed to play more matches at Chelmsford to justify the financial investment in the ground, now of a standard to compare with any in the country. In the end leaving Ilford was timely, as the Sunday crowd had become more and more objectionable. The effects of the sun combined with cheap lager brought out the worst in some elements of the home 'supporters', until one side of this beautiful parkland ground began to resemble the Western Terrace at Headingley at its drunken worst.

The end of festival cricket at club grounds such as Brentwood, Ilford, Leyton and Romford, if inevitable and in some cases welcome, did somewhat diminish the experience of being an Essex supporter. At the Festival grounds something odd or eccentric was always likely to occur. I can remember one Sunday at Ilford, just after lunch during a JPL match, when we witnessed the sight of the revered commentator John Arlott somewhat unsteadily climbing the ladder to the BBC commentary box. His ascent was hampered by the great man's inability to scale the ladder and carry a bottle of claret and two wine glasses at the same time. From the ground it was quite a spectacle and it seemed to take him a good ten minutes to reach the safety of the commentary box.

For many years during the 1950s and 1960s Essex used an old bus as a mobile scoreboard. The bus, painted black for the purpose, could often be seen trundling along the A13 on its quiet way to Southend, carrying on its side the news that Essex were 134-7, with Robin Hobbs unbeaten overnight on 22. The old bus retired to Chelmsford, where it continued to act as the official Essex scoreboard until it was replaced by its digital successor in the early 1990s. The bus, stripped of its workings, now enjoys a quiet retirement at Castle Park, home of Colchester CC. In August 1980 the old bus performed under the floodlights of Stamford Bridge when Essex played the West Indies in a night game experiment. On its side that evening, at the unlikely setting of the Chelsea ground, the bus carried on its side the news, not for the first time, that Graham Gooch scored 111 not out in the Essex innings.

With the loss of the festivals, the visions of an elderly match commentator precariously ascending ladders and scoreboard buses meandering across the Essex countryside are now only fond memories. Essex, along with the rest of cricket, has joined the technological revolution. It is not difficult to guess what Arlott might have thought of the likes of 'hawkeye', referrals and the 20/20 Indian Premier League.

The glorious Essex summer of 1979, and after ...

Under the business brain of Peter Edwards and the cricketing intelligence of Keith Fletcher, Essex were becoming increasingly professional both on and off the field. As they became accustomed to their new headquarters in the 1970s, the players slowly began to believe in themselves and develop a winning mentality, although there was a way to go before Fletcher's teams arrived at the point when they believed they were simply unbeatable. Great credit must go to Brian Taylor, who began the process of modernisation that was carried forward off the field by general secretary Edwards. As Fletcher remarks, "'Tonker', to his great credit, had learned from our wasteful attitude to the Gillette Cup." In the sixties Essex had acquired a deserved reputation for playing an attacking style of cricket with a sense of fun that stood in stark contrast to the more pragmatic and dour approach of the other counties. Things were about to change.

When success finally came it was sudden and dramatic. The defining year was 1979. In soccer Liverpool retained the First Division Championship, while Arsenal defeated Manchester United 3-2 in the FA Cup final, and Kevin Keegan was voted European Footballer of the Year in his final season for Hamburg. The cricket World Cup was won by the West Indies, who, rather too easily, beat England in the final by 92 runs. In 1979 *Star Trek: The Motion Picture* had its premiere, Phillips piloted the compact disc and Michael Jackson released his *Off the Wall* album, which quickly sold more than 7 million copies in the USA alone. And, last but not least, Essex CCC won the County Championship and the Benson & Hedges Cup. Readers will decide which of these events was the most significant in a memorable year.

The authors of the club's official history set the scene for a very special day in the life of Essex players, officials and supporters:

Whatever the future holds for Essex cricket, nothing will ever detract

from the events of 21 July 1979. In effect the day separates the past from the present and the future. Lord's was lapped in sunshine, and the crowd was happy and expectant ... Roger Knight won the toss and asked Essex to bat.
- Lemmon and Marshall (1987), p.322

Having made the first mistake of the day, Knight watched Essex reach 48 by the eleventh over when Essex lost their first wicket with Mike Denness caught at cover. Denness had made a contribution but his dismissal meant that the mercurial Ken McEwan had more time at the wicket. After a quiet start to the partnership, first Gooch and then McEwan accelerated as Essex went into lunch on 166 for 1 off 37 overs, with McEwan's 50 coming off just 68 balls. The South African was quickly out after lunch after contributing 72 in a record second wicket stand of 124. You could almost hear the sound of collective purring from the Essex supporters, but they knew only too well that the blue and gold ribbons could not yet be tied around the impressive looking trophy. But expectancy soared further when Keith Fletcher came in to bat, and sensing the enormity of the occasion he played one of the best cameo innings of his life. Fletcher hit 34 runs in half an hour as he and Gooch flayed the Surrey bowlers at nearly seven an over. With his captain back in the Lord's pavilion, Gooch went on his relentless way towards his inevitable century, flicking one ball from Wilson effortlessly to the top of the Mound Stand. He was eventually out in the 53rd over, his job well and truly done. In his incomparable innings Gooch hit 3 sixes and 11 fours in his 120 and effectively won the game for Essex, as he was destined to do. Essex finished their innings on 290 for 6, the highest score achieved in a Benson & Hedges Trophy final.

Despite making a valiant effort to reach their distant target and a few heart-stopping moments, with good knocks from Howarth, skipper Knight and England's Graham Roope, Surrey fell away and Essex won the match by 35 runs, with Graham Gooch announced as the winner of the Individual Gold Award and £200 for his match-winning innings, the first ever century in a Benson & Hedges final. Essex supporters went wild and the celebrations carried on long into that Saturday night. The long spell had been broken at last.

The new Essex now had a taste for victory and later that

season carried off their first ever County Championship, winning by the impressive margin of 77 points to complete a well-earned double. John Lever was deservedly chosen as one of the Wisden Cricketers of the Year for his outstanding swing-bowling over the season as a whole. And what a season it was. Gooch and Alan Lilley, who was left out of the Lord's final in favour of Mike Denness, set a new Benson & Hedges first wicket record in the match against the Combined Universities at Chelmsford, with a partnership of 223 (Gooch 133, Lilley 119) in an Essex total of 350 for 3. The county and the club's supporters owe Keith Fletcher a huge debt for his determined and inspirational captaincy and for leading Essex CCC to the very top of English cricket.

With their first trophies displayed proudly in the Chelmsford pavilion, Essex proceeded to dominate county cricket under Fletcher's inspired captaincy until he handed over to Graham Gooch in 1986, although he was to return as captain for the 1988 season while Gooch took a year off. Fletcher's achievements between 1979 and 1985 were extraordinary - three County Championships, the NatWest Trophy, three Sunday League triumphs and the Benson & Hedges Cup. In 1985, his final season as captain, Fletcher's team won the NatWest Trophy and the JPL, and lost in the final of the Benson & Hedges Cup. The season was notable for a record Sunday League partnership by Gooch and Brian Hardie. In the match against Nottinghamshire at Trent Bridge the Essex opening pair scored 239 runs for the first wicket, a new record for the competition. Gooch's contribution to the partnership was 171, with Hardie scoring a rather more modest 60. In the NatWest Trophy in the same season the same opening pair put on 202 runs, which at the time was the highest partnership score in any one-day final. This time Hardie outscored his more illustrious partner.

Graham Gooch's record as Essex captain does not quite match that of his mentor and inspiration, but it is impressive nonetheless. Gooch's Essex won the County Championship in 1986, his first year as captain, and again in 1991 and 1992, although one-day trophies alluded the county's greatest ever batsman.

Romantic Essex supporters like to think that their club moved steadily forward after the Second World War in a line that runs from Doug Insole to Trevor Bailey, Brian Taylor, Keith Fletcher and, finally, Graham Gooch. In a sense the romantics are correct. I think we can say that a project did grow in the minds of these quintessentially Essex men, but it was never fully articulated as a precise plan. Essex cricket did move forward through a combination of huge determination, belief and a burning desire for the county to take its place at the head of English cricket. None of the leading characters was dogmatic in his views, but each cleverly exploited the available options and made the correct decisions. For example, successive captains believed strongly in developing young local cricketers, improving the physical condition and mental strength of the team, and using the best of overseas talent available without resorting to the short-term Kolpak method adopted, perhaps too enthusiastically, by some county sides. That Essex captains from Insole to Gooch succeeded in their aims and objectives for the club, without losing sight of the underlying philosophy and ideals for which the club are well known, is a tribute to each of them and to the club in general. It helped that, including Graham Gooch, Essex had only six captains after the war in Tom Pearce, Insole, Bailey, Taylor and Fletcher. At the end of the 1994 season our Essex cricket romantics could sit contentedly in their members' seats outside the pavilion contemplating a golden future shaped by the dreams of a dynasty stretching back from Insole to Gooch. But just when the future looks assured, sport has a nasty habit of shattering illusions and breaking hearts.

End of an era?

When Graham Gooch handed over the captaincy to Paul Pritchard at the end of the 1994 season it felt like the end of an era. In fact, it was the end of an era. Essex have not won the County Championship since 1992 and for much of that time they languished in Division 2. (Keith Fletcher is strongly against the two-division County Championship because, as he says, "there are nine teams every year which cannot win it"). The winning tradition, carefully nurtured since the mid-1970s, slowly began to disintegrate. Pritchard's team did win the NatWest Trophy in 1997 and the Benson & Hedges Cup in 1998, more than enough for most teams, but expectations at Essex were extremely high. Pritchard, a highly talented batsman and the most congenial of men, handed over the captaincy to Nasser Hussain in 1999, following talk of dressing room factions, with the captain particularly close to the hugely talented Australian batsman, Stuart Law. The Hussain captaincy illustrates with great clarity the issues that Essex and other clubs have faced in county cricket from the mid-1990s onwards. He was born in Madras and grew up on the Essex/East London border just a few miles east of Graham Gooch's Leytonstone. Again, like Gooch, Hussain was coached by Bill Morris at Ilford CC. He was selected for the England Schools XI at the age of 14 and his teammates included Michael Atherton, Mark Ramprakash and Graham Thorpe. Originally a leg-spin bowler, Hussain established himself as a top-order batsman when a sudden growth spurt in his teens disturbed his bowling action. He captained England schoolboys and the Under 19s and appeared the natural successor to Fletcher and Gooch as Essex captain. In his autobiography Hussain acknowledges his debt to his great mentors at Essex:

> *Fletch was like God … leading Essex to all those victories and he seemed just a nice, down to earth bloke ….*
> *Gooch was another huge figure at this time … he played a massive part in my being selected for England … he was an absolute legend to me … I can't thank him enough for what he did for me as a young player, and I can't exaggerate his influence on me.*
> *- N. Hussain (2004), Playing with Fire: The Autobiography, Michael Joseph, p.55*

Hussain explains in his autobiography that, despite his almost hero worship of Gooch, he regrets never becoming close friends with the former England captain. Perhaps their shared passion for the game, their single-minded intensity and ambition and sheer determination prevented the development of a close relationship. Gooch and Hussain, outwardly so different, with Hussain the ultra-modern cricketer and Gooch more of a traditionalist, were more alike than either of them would have accepted. Both enjoyed a close relationship with their father, who was the principal inspiration and motivating force in their lives, and both were driven by a burning desire not to let their fathers down. Hussain writes of how he felt about his father's role in his early development:

... my relationship with my dad is crucial to explaining what makes me tick both as a person and a cricketer ... as a child I placed such a priority on trying to win Dad's approval that ... friendships took a back seat.
- Hussain (2004), p.40

Gooch has spoken in much the same way about the role that his father played in his early days. This does go some way to explaining both players' single-minded dedication to cricket and in particular to their own performances. But despite both enjoying the close support of eager parents, being brought up in the same area and having the same boyhood coach in Bill Morris at Ilford, Gooch and Hussain did differ in one respect. While Gooch attended his local comprehensive with mixed results, Hussain attended a minor Essex public school and Durham University. In terms of their education Gooch was closer to Fletcher than he was to Hussain. Fletcher and Gooch were similar in temperament, undemonstrative and even-tempered, while the university and privately educated Hussain was more of an emotional time bomb with a very short fuse. His legendary fiery temperament was to be tested to the limit both in his career at Essex and during the 2003 World Cup in South Africa, when he captained England in the most difficult of circumstances. Both Gooch and Hussain, in their different ways, were to have South Africa etched deeply into their respective careers, but for very different reasons, as we shall see.

Essex's three England captains in the years between 1981 and 2003 shared the same level of desire and drive to succeed that had served the county so well in the glory years. However, whereas Fletcher and Gooch were clearly happiest when applying their undoubted leadership and motivational skills in the relatively tranquil cricketing waters of Chelmsford or Ilford, Hussain was more at home in the fiery atmosphere of international cricket. For Hussain 1999 was a magnificent year. He raised in the region of £200,000 for his Benefit, he was made captain of Essex, and then on 1st July he captained England for the first time in the match against New Zealand at Edgbaston. The only downside for Hussain that year was the disappointment of being left out of the World Cup squad. His captaincy was to have an enormous impact on the performance of the England side and, in partnership with coach Duncan

Fletcher, he transformed the whole attitude and mentality of the England team for the next four years. One of England's greatest captain's, Mike Brearley, argues:

> *Whatever happens in the future, there has been under his captaincy a real change in the morale of the team as a whole, and of several individuals within it ... Hussain's captaincy has made a real difference to the England team.*
> *- Brearley (2001), p.2*

Brearley uses as an example the transformation of Andrew Caddick from a promising, if temperamental, quick bowler devoid of self-belief and confidence into one of the most destructive opening bowlers in world cricket. For Brearley, the improvement was the result of Hussain dealing with Caddick's anxiety about his own performance. Hussain recognised the problem, took it on and dealt with it and, most crucially, got Caddick bowling to his full potential. But great England captain though he undoubtedly was, his short spell of leadership of his county was anything but successful. While the fortunes of Essex continued to prosper during the England captaincies of Fletcher and Gooch, the club floundered in 1999, Hussain's one year as club captain.

Hussain was twice disciplined by Essex for saying the wrong thing to the wrong person. In the latter stages of his career he was often in conflict with the club, largely as a result of his non-selection in limited-overs matches. This became one of the principal reasons for his disagreements with Graham Gooch, who favoured giving young players experience at the expense of players close to retirement. Despite these minor squabbles, like his predecessors he was Essex through and through and loved the club, although the intense nature of his personality meant he was more respected, and deeply so, than loved by the club's supporters. In historical terms Hussain remains one of the county's most distinguished players with 96 England caps and 88 one-day international appearances, together with four years as captain of his country. He certainly paid back every minute of support that his dedicated parents had given to their son in his younger days. The details of Hussain's career are well documented and it is not my intention here to examine the minutiae of his time with Essex and England. What I am keen to do is to look at the reasons why his captaincy of Essex was so short-lived and how he became the first in a line of players produced by the county who became "an England player who played for Essex, rather than an Essex player who represented England".

Nigel Hilliard, the current chairman, Doug Insole, Keith Fletcher and Graham Gooch have each said that one of the purposes of the club is to provide future England cricketers. Gooch's Academy and Scholarship Scheme at Chelmsford is now producing players of international quality. And Essex see no contradiction in their county academy, made up of local boys and girls, producing England cricketers, who if successful will only play for their county club in a handful of matches each season. Hilliard, a seasoned observer of county cricket, recently confirmed that the club are happy producing England players and are not overly concerned that this might hold back the performances of his own team.

Gooch was unique in scoring heavily for Essex in between his Test Match duties. Hussain was less successful, scoring a modest 11,054 runs for Essex between 1987 and 2004. England skipper Keith Fletcher claimed 29,434 runs for his county, while Gooch accumulated 30,701 for Essex in his long career. It is interesting to look at the number of matches that the three England captains played for their county. Hussain played 189 first-class matches for Essex, Fletcher an impressive 429 and Gooch 391. These figures illustrate the changes that have occurred in English cricket over the past 20 years. That Hussain has played comparatively few county games indicates the priority that the TCCB places on the best players being England players rather than county players. This development, of course, has been formalised by the introduction of central contracts. The county statistics of Ravi Bopara and Alistair Cook are unlikely even to reach those of Hussain if they continue to play for England at the current rate of matches, let alone the giddy heights of Gooch and Fletcher.

In the 2009 season Andrew Flintoff is likely to play eight first-class matches in the long version of the game, five Test matches in the Ashes series and just three for his county, Lancashire. In 2008 Graham Gooch freely admitted that Bopara would play very little cricket for Essex during his international career. The astonishing thing is that the counties see no problem at all in this diminution of their role in English cricket. The TCCB pays the counties compensation for the loss of their best home-grown players. Nigel Hilliard is an astute chairman, instinctively collaborative, and steeped in Essex cricket, following a long and distinguished amateur career with Colchester CC. Interestingly, Hilliard is the first Essex chairman not to have played first-class cricket, but his business skills are serving the county well. He explained recently that Essex have Cook for free when he plays for the county, because he has a central contract with the ECB. For players without central contracts, such as Ravi Bopara, Essex pay the player's wages when he is not with England. In addition, the ECB pays around £45,000 for home-grown players like Cook and Bopara, as an incentive to counties to develop their youth programmes. This is all well and good, but with the loss of Bopara and Cook the club have struggled along in Division 2 of the County Championship, with an occasional one-day trophy being the best the county can hope for as long as they are denied the services of their best players. The counties spend the ECB money on overseas stars, but these can be under the same restrictions as England players and their services are lost to the clubs for weeks at a time. Nasser Hussain was the first player sacrificed by Essex to the cause of the national team, although, of course, he would not have seen it this way. As Graham Gooch has said in relation to the Indian Premier League,

> *... of course the best players will want to play in the ILP. All top players want to be where the other top players are.*
> *- Recored interview with author at Fenner's, Cambridge on 12th June 2009*

This happens in most sports, so why not in cricket? It is a difficult dilemma for county managers.

County cricket is set to change yet again in 2010. There are proposals by the ECB to reduce the number of four-day matches from 16 to 12 in 2010, with a 50-over league and 20/20 competitions. This will align the English game with State cricket in Australia, clearly the preferred model given the success of their national team. The changes have been proposed for two main reasons:

1. To build a successful England team; and
2. To generate maximum revenue for the counties.

Are these developments, which rob the counties of their best players for years at a time and drastically reduce the traditional county programme, in the best interests of English cricket? The English game was built on 28 three-day county matches with a national side that hosted Test matches in the summer and toured in the winter. Of course, just because first-class cricket in England developed in this way doesn't make it right for the twenty-first century and change is clearly necessary. But the truth of the matter is that the changes are being driven by the desire to increase 20/20 cricket, recently described by sports journalist Henry Blofeld as 'counterfeit cricket', for the money it will generate for the ECB and world cricket in general. The future of cricket is being shaped by the financial model of the Indian Premier League (IPL). Despite central contracts and almost 'full-time' England players for some years, there has been little noticeable improvement in the fluctuating performances of the England team. The players appear to lack the qualities of discipline, mental strength, self-belief and desire of the best team in world cricket, Australia. These are just the qualities that Keith Fletcher and Graham Gooch brought to the successful Essex sides of the 1980s and 1990s, and that Nasser Hussain, out of the same stable, engendered in the England teams from 1999 to 2004.

While there has been little or no improvement in the English national team, the above developments have reduced county cricket to a mere sideshow, where even the most enthusiastic of cricket lovers find the county season confusing and incoherent, and county supporters are denied the opportunity of seeing their favourite England player in action on all but a few occasions each season. County clubs have developed their grounds, installed floodlights, established academies, put in scouting systems and increased the effectiveness of their sponsorship and marketing operations. The demands of the England team are beginning to threaten the future of county cricket. Nasser Hussain's short spell as Essex captain and the absence of Cook and Bopara for all but a handful of matches are indicative of the ECB's policy of giving priority to the England team over and above everything else in the game, and of course it is not just Essex that are affected.

Today's elite international cricketers are required to balance their financial security against selection for their national team. I don't think there is any question that Graham Gooch, great patriot that he is, could have resisted the temptations of the IPL. International 20/20 cricket is beginning to provide top cricketers with the kind of earnings normally reserved for footballers, tennis players and golfers. If they are to retain their best players, pressure will be on individual countries to match these earnings. The IPL and its derivatives will also provide some county cricketers with out-of-season lucrative contracts, as Essex's attacking all-rounder Graham Napier will testify. As Gooch argues, finding the right balance between the interests of the players, the counties and the national team is absolutely crucial for the long-term future of cricket.

There is little question that the revolution in cricket has benefited the players. The car park at Chelmsford is full of sponsored cars, and players have kit and clothing deals as well as unlimited opportunities to earn money outside of their Essex contract. The top internationals on the Essex staff - Cook, Foster and Kaneria - are in particular demand and attract significant sponsorship income, and why not? In this respect cricket is catching up quickly with other sports. The days of winter jobs for county cricketers have well and truly passed.

There is a rather worrying downside to the modern cricket world of sponsored cars, millionaire cricketers and central contracts. The culture of county cricket has traditionally been marked by a real familiarity and closeness between players, members and supporters. At Essex, Cook, Kaneria and Bopara are international stars who play most of their cricket away from Chelmsford. Nasser Hussain gave up the Essex captaincy in 1999 for just this reason. Alistair Cook, appointed England captain for the Bangladesh tour, Spring 2010, will not be available to captain his county. Graham Gooch is likely to have been the last Essex captain able to combine leadership of club and country, while scoring heavily for both. The distancing of international cricketers from their county team and the club's supporters, the increasing intrusion of international 20/20 into the county game and the reduction of county cricket to a mere sideshow are all examples of a threat to a local sporting culture that has been eroded already Premier League football.

A period of uncertainty

On succeeding Paul Pritchard, Hussain quickly passed the Essex captaincy to the Lancastrian Ronnie Irani, largely because of his England responsibilities. Irani was a highly combative and aggressive Lancastrian, who led the county to Sunday League victories in 2005 and 2006, but in his seven-year reign the club struggled to adjust to the absence of Fletcher and Gooch. Despite their presence as coaches, the county missed their runs and on-field leadership. Irani's captaincy, like that of Pritchard before him, was characterised by dressing room friction and unrest. Talented local players such as John Stephenson, Nick Knight and Shahid Nadeem, whom supporters viewed as the future of the club, left for Hampshire and Warwickshire. Alan Lilley never became the successor to Gooch that many thought he would as a promising youngster. Neither Fletcher nor Gooch would have allowed factions to develop in the dressing room, and this was unusual for an Essex side known for their togetherness and ebullient spirit. Pritchard was a popular but ineffectual figure, while Irani, an outstanding cricketer and captain-by-example, lacked the more nuanced leadership qualities of some of his predecessors. England bowlers Neil Foster and Mark Ilot, and the dependable all-rounder Derek Pringle, were at the end of their careers and the conveyor belt of outstanding young local players, long a feature of this most local of clubs, appeared to dwindle to nothing. However, despite patchy success during his captaincy, Irani remains a tremendously popular figure at Essex, and had it not been for a serious injury he would have continued to lead the club for a few more years.

Nasser Hussain has been very critical about this period in the club's history, blaming the state of the club on a 'jobs for the boys' mentality whereby ex-players were appointed to roles of responsibility. Hussain compares the professionalism of the England management in the appointment of coach Duncan Fletcher with the way in which David East and Alan Lilley landed their jobs at Essex, and writes, rather unkindly:

> *I can't help comparing it to Essex. Any sort of appointment is done on seniority. Just look at Alan Lilley. Here's a bloke who, over ten years in the game, was known to everyone in the Essex team as cement-head. Now he's virtually running the club. …*

I would love someone at Essex to sit him down one day and say, 'Right Alan. What do you bring to this job? What have you done to deserve running a major company like Essex CCC?
- Hussain (2004), p.195

Hussain is an intelligent cricketer who understands that professional sport in the modern era has to take account of business priorities. He understood that a dressing room that lacked real leadership and where factions existed could not succeed. As Hussain rather brutally pointed out, the club was poorly led at this time and performances inevitably deteriorated. Had he been able to captain both his county and his country in the way that Fletcher and Gooch did with such success, Essex might well have prolonged their period of dominating county cricket. Hussain was the natural successor to Gooch in the line of distinguished Essex captains, as was Alistair Cook to Irani in 2007, when Mark Pettini was appointed. The club knew that, like Hussain before him, Cook would be unavailable for his county for most of the season. Cook captained England at U19 level and we can safely assume that he is being groomed as a future England captain.

Mark Pettini, surprisingly appointed captain in 2007, proceeded to win the Friends' Provident Trophy in his second season in charge. Brighton-born and university-educated Pettini, a close friend of Alistair Cook with whom he shares a house, also represented England at U19 and is seen as a promising cricketer with international potential. Regarded as a limited-over specialist, Pettini's personal performances as captain have been patchy and many supporters have questioned his place in the side. It is fair to say that his form was affected by a painful eye injury, and it is to be hoped that his undoubted playing and captaincy potential is realised over the next few years. Of the 18 trophies won by Essex since the memorable year of 1979, 11 were won by either Fletcher or Gooch. Of the captains after 1994, Irani's side won three competitions, Pritchard's succeeded on two occasions, and the current team under Pettini has secured three trophies to date, if we can describe promotion to Division 1 of the Championship in 2009 as a trophy. If we look more closely at this record, only Fletcher and Gooch have won the County Championship. There can be no question now that, in the club's history, the period between the years 1979 and 1992 will be seen as a golden age. Perhaps Fletcher and Gooch arrived at the club at the right time. Both county and international cricket changed dramatically when they left and the club, like many others, failed to come to terms with these changes. Even captains as successful as Keith Fletcher and Graham Gooch would have found it difficult to win trophies for the county after 1994.

Chairman Nigel Hilliard has some interesting ideas on captaincy. He suggests that often county cricketers just don't want the job and the responsibilities it brings, rather than seeing it as an honour and a privilege. They would simply prefer to concentrate on their own game. If they do, rather reluctantly, accept the job, county captains are often keen to pass it on at the earliest opportunity. I think this is true of Graham Gooch in his first spell as captain, and clearly Nasser Hussain realised quite quickly that his appointment was a mistake. For supporters of the club Paul Pritchard's captaincy appeared to sit rather heavily on his slim shoulders. After Fletcher, only Gooch in his second spell and Ronnie Irani seemed to grasp the nettle with some enthusiasm and sense of purpose. It is to be hoped that current captain Michael Pettini cherishes the opportunity to follow in the distinguished footsteps of Douglas, Insole, Bailey, Taylor, Fletcher and Gooch. To date, the signs are good.

The county has produced three England captains since 1981 in Keith Fletcher, Graham Gooch and Nasser Hussain. (J.W.H.T. Douglas and F.L. Fane both captained England in the early part of the twentieth century, and their careers are covered in detail in the county's official history: Lemmon and Marshall (1987). Like all England captains they had varying degrees of success and failure. Trevor Bailey and Doug Insole never captained their country, but Insole in particular served England with great distinction as an administrator, manager and selector. The influence of Essex cricket on the England national team in the years between 1960 and 2000 has been considerable. When Alistair Cook succeeds his illustrious Essex predecessors as England captain it will mean that Essex have produced four England captains since Fletcher was appointed to the post in 1981 - a truly remarkable achievement.

When the captaincy baton was passed to Keith Fletcher in 1974, Essex had transformed their whole approach and philosophy. Fletcher succeeded in adding a fierce competitive streak to the crazier antics of Ray East and others. While it was successful on the field the club had the opportunity to develop a sharp business edge and became adept at marketing and securing sponsorship. The next step was the development of the County Ground at Chelmsford. Essex was one of the first counties to install floodlights and they have submitted plans for an ambitious new cricket stadium at an adjacent site, to meet the revised ECB standards. The new ground will increase the capacity from 6,800 to 7,500 and provide a public space that will put cricket at the heart of Chelmsford city life. Unfortunately, the Environment Agency has stalled the proposals, claiming that the plans are unsafe because the site is situated on Chelmsford's flood plain. The club rejected these claims at their 2009 Annual General Meeting, arguing that the proposals have been included in the overall Chelmsford Flood Plan and therefore the EA's objections are groundless. A Public Enquiry was held in 2009 and the results have yet to be made public. The Secretary of State is due to decide on the dispute early in 2010 and Essex supporters will hope that common sense prevails. Essex Chairman Nigel Hilliard posted the following note on the Essex CCC website on 7th August 2009,

> *I can only hope that the Secretary of State will recognise the huge sporting, community, social and economic benefits this development will create.*

The club's modern-day, necessary preoccupation with commercial considerations has not diminished the special feeling of being an Essex member or supporter. Strolling around the New Writtle Road ground in the early season sunshine, enjoying a pint in the pavilion, or simply watching the cricket from the members' seats alongside some of the players and their families, you can feel the special atmosphere of Essex cricket. However, the graffiti-covered concrete subway walls of the river gate entrance to the ground betray the need for modernisation. The Chelmsford county ground has retained much of its peaceful and friendly atmosphere, despite Essex being one of the most forward-thinking counties. All members and supporters will hope that the club have included a 'friendly' atmosphere as an element within the design brief of the exciting new Chelmsford ground due to open in the 2012 season.

The club have contributed much to English cricket over the past 40 years in providing the England team with captains in Fletcher, Gooch and Hussain and players of the quality of Trevor Bailey, Barry Knight, Doug Insole, Robin Hobbs, Derek Pringle, John Lever, Neil Foster, Mark Ilot, Peter Such, John Childs, Alistair Cook and Ravinder Bopara. Despite Nasser Hussain's harsh criticism of the way the club has been managed in recent years and the failure to build on the successes of the 1980s and 1990s, the future of the club seems assured. Board cricket at Essex is flourishing, under the banner of 'Essex Cricket', with sides at every age level from Under 9s to Under 19s and the Academy XI for the most talented young players. The Essex Cricket Board is a partnership between local clubs and schools and is designed to give promising boys and girls the opportunity to play regular cricket of a high standard on decent grass wickets. The club's senior coaches, Paul Grayson and John Childs, lead a team of club volunteers, parents and schoolteachers, who selflessly give their time, as they have always done, in the interests of junior cricket. Essex have a thorough scouting system in place ready to spot the new Ravi Bopara deep in the East End or out in breezy Colchester on the Essex coast.

Most youngsters who progress in the game, either at club or county level, were introduced to cricket by their parents, who were probably club players themselves. Fletcher, Gooch and Hussain are perfect examples of this. The real challenge for county clubs such as Essex is to discover those talented youngsters who do not have cricket-playing parents but who show real talent in PE lessons or in the rudimentary cricket still played in state schools in East London, and places like Basildon, Harlow, Southend and Thurrock. It is important that these youngsters are given every encouragement to play proper cricket or the game could be in danger of going the way of English tennis. But at least in the county of Essex, with a new stadium due in 2012, the future looks bright and the philosophy of cricket painstakingly put together by the dynasty of Taylor, Fletcher and Gooch looks secure for now.

CHAPTER 8
CRICKET CLUBS AND PUBS

I was born in Walthamstow in 1946, but I was brought up on the council estates of leafy Chingford, close to the eastern edges of Epping Forest. Dad had been away for most of the war; missing, feared dead. Then the Red Cross found a prisoner-of-war list and my dad's name was on it. He had been incarcerated in Auschwitz for the last three years of the war. When he returned home in 1945 my parents moved from their council prefab in Chingford Hatch, close to the Old Dung Cow pub, to a three-bedroom house near the King George reservoir in Valley Side, where in 1952 Chingford Cricket Club planted a double flowering cherry to commemorate the Festival of Britain. When my youngest sister was born we moved again to a larger house out by Epping Forest. Here we disappeared into the forest for hours on end and grew to know every glade, stream and bomb crater. Once a year we would walk through the forest and across the football pitches on Chingford Plains to the Easter fair and be back in time for tea.

Chingford railway station is located a few hundred yards from the Royal Forest Hotel at the end of Station Road. The Chingford to Liverpool Street line was built at the end of the nineteenth century to transport East Enders to Epping Forest for day out in the fresh air. There was so much for them to do and see: fishing on Connaught Waters, tea at the café next door to the Queen Elizabeth Hunting Lodge, and bridleway walks through the forest. One particular bridleway led to a tea hut, which on Sundays would be surrounded by menacing-looking bikers from all over the county. If our cockney visitors were a little more adventurous they could wander down Station Road and gaze at the lovely Edwardian houses on the edge of the golf course.

For over 50 years the Chingford/Liverpool Street line has carried generations of Chingford folk in the opposite direction to the pleasure-seeking East Enders. The 30-minute journey takes passengers through Walthamstow, Hackney, London

Fields and Bethnal Green to Liverpool Street, deep in the heart of the City of London. A particular feature of Chingford Station was the wonderful Victorian station buffet, which doubled as the local pub when rush hour was over. Sadly, it was demolished years ago in an act of architectural vandalism, only to be replaced by a cold and unwelcoming waiting room.

Chingford has become notorious for its controversial MPs: the belligerent Norman 'on yer bike' Tebbit, and the current incumbent, Ian Duncan-Smith. The 'quiet man' persona of the latter hardly reflects the strident and clamorous tones often heard in the supermarkets and pubs of the town; if only it did. Tebbit was much more up their street, but I prefer to think about what might have been if the saintly John Arlott had succeeded in winning the seat for the Liberal Party when he stood as their candidate back in the 1960s. The area can also lay claim to being the family home of none other than Denis Compton, who, although born in Hendon, spent much of his childhood with brother Leslie and sister Hilda at the Compton family headquarters in Woodford Green (T. Heald, (1994) Denis Compton: An Authorized Biography, Pavilion Books, p.24).

Back in the 1960s on summer Saturday afternoons my brother and I would stroll across the forest to watch Chingford play cricket at their Forest Side ground at the back of the Queen Elizabeth pub. If the first team were at home we could enjoy watching a young Robin Hobbs whirling away, sleeves buttoned to the wrist, mesmerising the opposing batsmen with his bouncy leg-spin. Hobbs was actually born in Chippenham, but his parents settled in East London after the war. We had no idea that he would go on to play professionally for Essex for 14 years, score a first-class century against Australia and be awarded seven England caps. His century against Australia took just 44 minutes and was the fastest hundred in 55 years. He hit seven 6s and twelve 4s and his second 50 took just 12 minutes. Hobbs came out of retirement in 1979 to captain Glamorgan, but Essex were in his blood and he later returned to help with coaching the county's colts teams.

Cricket has been played at the Forest Side ground since the mid-eighteenth century, (Lemmon and Marshall's (1987) official history claims that the first recorded game of cricket in Essex was played in Chingford in 1726, although it is not clear if Forest Side was the ground on that occasion. It is more likely that the game was played on the more expansive Chingford Plains) although you wouldn't know from the modern pavilion and the housing estate that encroaches on three sides of the ground. Back in the late 1960s and early 1970s Chingford CC held lively dances in their pavilion on summer Saturday nights and Robin Hobbs was often there relaxing with some of his Essex teammates. The evenings were great fun and a little less raucous then the 'discos' held during the winter across town at Chingford Rugby Club. Hobbs remains a hugely popular figure in Chingford for his commitment to the club while playing for the county. The club secretary's report in 1974 includes the following tribute to our very own leg-spin genius:

After Robin Hobbs hit the headlines in the National Press by scoring 100 runs in 44 minutes against the Australians, he demonstrated his typical adaptability by turning out for the (club) 1st XI only a few days later in a closely contested league game. It is amusing to ponder that after facing Ashley Mallett and Co. and entertaining hundreds of paying spectators, Robin was soon afterwards participating in this match and paying for the privilege to do so.

Good old 'Obbsy.

Club and pub cricket has been the heart and soul of English cricket for 300 years and has its roots in the local communities. Back in the 1960s Chingford was a closely knit place, before it became blighted by the usual fast-food joints, cavernous football pubs and endless second-hand car showrooms. As teenagers we had lots of friends, life seemed secure and everybody knew one another. Our parents worked hard, and, although we didn't have much and never went on holidays, life was generally good and sport was at the heart of it, whether it was cricket at home or at school, golf at the municipal Chingford Golf Club, tennis at Ridgeway Park during Wimbledon or football just about everywhere. Today most young people have other priorities.

When we couldn't get to watch Chingford, we played fiercely competitive games of cricket in the street outside our house, much to the annoyance of the neighbours and passing motorists. When we couldn't raise sufficient numbers for a full game, a few of us would play French cricket for hours in the garden, careful to keep the ball away from my dad's lovingly tended vegetable patch and my mum's roses. Masses of cars, angry residents and gang activity ensure that nobody plays street cricket in Chingford today. If they are not scrabbling down in the streets with their mates, many youngsters flee to the safer option of their bedroom and their gaming consoles, which is not good for either their personal health or the general well-being of the community.

In the summer holidays we could get a bus outside our house down to south Chingford and then catch the famous No. 38 straight to the County Ground at Leyton High Road. During Essex matches at Leyton we were allowed to play cricket around the ground and within the boundary ropes at lunch – what a joy. The 38 bus ran from Chingford Station, through Walthamstow, Leyton and Hackney to Oxford Street in the heart of the West End. Sadly, today the route is a much reduced service, and in any case there hasn't been any county cricket at Leyton for years.

In the sixties and early seventies cricket could hold its own with football and both were a central part of the culture of the place for young people. It helped that in Chingford we had our own two giants of cricket, Doug Insole and Robin Hobbs, both of whom lived in Chingford and were often seen out and about. In Robin's case he could often be spotted in the pub, whereas the inestimable Insole was more likely to be seen shopping in the Co-op in Station Road on Saturday mornings - I was sent there to pay in my dad's union subs, as he was the treasurer of the Painters and Decorators' Union Chingford branch.

Chingford has managed to ward off developers and retain its Forest Side ground, in one form another, since 1884. Perhaps the club were helped by the fact that in the 1920s a certain Winston Churchill was among their patrons. The ground has experienced many changes over the years, and before the club installed their own bar at Forest Side they enjoyed the convenience of being next door to the Queen Elizabeth pub, which held a traditional 'flannel dance' during the annual cricket week in the 1930s. Doug Insole was a young player for Chingford in the 1930s and would have been present at these splendid events, I feel sure.

Members have been asked to make some momentous decisions in the club's long history. An entry from the club's General Committee minutes of 14th April 1936 states:

It was agreed that an experiment should be tried for a few weeks of serving 6d teas in the tea pavilion to consist of three pieces of bread and butter, two cakes and one cup of tea.

I can assure readers that today the teas at the lovely old Forest Side ground are far more generous than in 1936, and probably are no longer included as business in the proceedings of the club's General Committee meetings.

Today Chingford has just one cricket club for a population of 50,000 people. Walthamstow, its neighbour to the west, where Insole went to school, also has just one club but a much larger population. The population of the whole of the London Borough of Waltham Forest has just three serious cricket clubs for a population of 250,000 people. Leyton and Leytonstone, birthplace of Moore and Gooch, do not have an Essex League club between them. The former County Ground in Leyton High Road, where W.G. Grace, Hobbs and Sutcliffe, Ian Botham and Viv Richards could once be seen, is now home to some local football and enthusiastic but recreational cricket. The lovely old pavilion, which has been graced by visiting Australians and generations of Essex teams, now accommodates the Leyton Youth Centre, a worthy and popular facility, although surely the youth of Leyton deserve a more fitting, secure and better-equipped place to meet with their friends.

The third Waltham Forest facility lies somewhat in the shadow of its more illustrious neighbours, but it ought not to be forgotten. Highams Park is an East London 'village' sandwiched between Chingford to the east and Walthamstow to the west, and is the second stop on the Chingford to Liverpool Street line. In many ways Highams Park is a well-kept secret with lovely old houses around the lake and some good schools, and it is well-protected from the busy North Circular Road. Just beyond the railway crossing, past the tennis courts on Larkshall Road, is the Rolls Sports Ground, home of West Essex Cricket Club. The ground is bordered by woods, back gardens and a benign housing estate. The smart new clubhouse with bar indicates that this is a serious, well-run cricket club with high ambitions. The square is bigger than it used to be when it was squeezed between the two football pitches used by the local plastics factory. The club were formed in 1921 and today field four Saturday sides in the Essex League and one on Sundays. On 11th July 2009 the club fielded five Saturday teams for the first time in their 88-year history. West Essex have a thriving youth section led by ECB-qualified coaches and pride themselves on their community ethos and multi-ethnic membership. Although not as strong as their more influential neighbours, Chingford and Walthamstow, the club have much to be proud of as a gem of local community-based cricket.

Fortunately, in this cricket-deprived East London borough, the senior clubs are thriving, but it is deeply disappointing that there is no serious cricket in Leyton and Leytonstone. The picture is even more disheartening in downtown Newham and Tower Hamlets. With a combined population of 550,000, rising between 15 and 18 per cent every year, neither borough boasts a senior League cricket club. This is partly the result of a shortage of grounds, a lack of tradition, a tough working-class environment and a shifting population. Interestingly, Doug Insole has remarked on the quality and number of Essex players that came out of East London, describing the area as

> *A hotbed of sporting talent ... which is surprising because there isn't much cricket played in that London inner city bit.*
> *- D. Pracy (2004), Memories of Cricket at the County Ground at Leyton from the 1920s to the 1990s, London Borough of Waltham Forest oral history project.*

If Waltham Forest is visibly multi-ethnic, then Tower Hamlets and Newham have neighbourhoods that are as mixed as anywhere in the Western world, as we saw in Chapter 1. Cricket as a sport is unfamiliar to many of the people now living in the East End, while many others have a deep passion and love for the game. But if you look beyond what appears to be a depressing picture for the future of cricket in this sports-mad place and scratch beneath the surface, you begin to see signs of hope. If we include most of Hackney as belonging to East London then we really do see a more promising state of affairs. This is largely a result of the priceless open spaces that continue to flourish in the borough. Hackney Marshes and Victoria Park are the jewels in the Hackney crown and the latter has become the centre for a new and emerging inner-city cricketing culture. To understand just what is happening here, we need to forget for a while the more traditional vision of cricket of John Major's 'long shadows on the county ground' or summer afternoons on village greens with egg and cress sandwiches for tea followed by convivial evenings in the village pub. What we have in East London is a new type of game, played on weekday evenings as well as weekends, that has its roots in the roadside pick-up games in Jamaica or the volatile street cricket played out in the towns and beaches of Mumbai.

Community cricket, plantain chips and peachy ice tea

Victoria Park is the London equivalent of New York's Central Park, only more interesting. Central Park lacks Vicky Park's rambling vastness, its wonderful old Georgian houses and the Regent Canal and its towpath that takes you all the way to the Docklands. Vicky Park has a wonderful café where early risers can get a decent breakfast and where mums and toddlers can spend an hour together under the shade of the café's huge umbrella of ancient oak trees. And the good news is that cricket has returned to the Park.

The new urban cricket in East London is well organised and is linked to the ECB's development strategy and the Play Cricket initiative. Some of the new leagues are spread across the inner-city and metropolitan Essex, while others are located in one central venue. Among the latter is the Victoria Park Cricket League, which runs three divisions and an annual Cup competition. All matches are eight-a-side and are played on the park on weekday evenings. The names of the participating clubs are interesting and range from the exotic-sounding Bengal Tigers to the more prosaic Wrong 'Uns. And there is Chat's Palace CC, which represents the arts centre of the same name that operates in the building of the old Homerton Library up the road. The playfully named Ducks won the Premier League and Cup in 2009, a year that saw seven new teams join the League, making up the five clubs lost from the previous season. Vicky Park remains a dangerous place in which to wander alone after dark, but evening cricket has brought the park alive again on summer evenings and imbued this gem of an urban green space with a purposeful calm. Hackney does not have its own Fairlop, with its spacious sports fields out past Ilford that for generations was the spiritual home of metropolitan Essex cricket, but it does have Victoria Park where cricket thrives again.

The Lords International Essex League is also affiliated to the ECB but it operates on Saturday afternoons, with four divisions across the East London and Essex border. Grays & Chadwell were the Premier League champions in 2009, winning their first trophy for 11 years in the last League match of the season against Leyton County at the old County Ground in Leyton. The clubs play on West Ham Park at Fairlop, the Arena at Low Hall farm and the Ford Sports ground out at Dagenham. The Cosmopolitan Athletic & Social Club are one of the League's most impressive participants, with a healthy 70 members, and they won the First Division and the Caribbean Cup in 2008. To underline the strength of Cosmopolitan, they were able to enter a second team in the League in 2009 and have a full list of Sunday friendlies as well as a vibrant youth programme. Cosmopolitan are an inspiration to other clubs in the League and a model for urban cricket clubs across the East London area. They have strong links with their community, and in many ways this is community cricket. They are a long way from the peace and quiet of more traditional cricket venues such as Chingford's Forest Side ground, and Cosmopolitan's cricket reflects the vibrancy of their multi-ethnic neighbourhoods.

A particularly interesting East London initiative is the North East London Club League (NELCL). Played on Saturday afternoons, the NELCL was established in 2004 as a Hackney pub cricket league and all matches are 36 overs a side. They claim to be only of pub standard, but each club pays League registration fees of £300 per season as well as £120 for public liability insurance, protecting the players from being sued by hedge fund managers when cricket balls shatter the windows of their renovated park-view Georgian terraces. The League has seven teams, including Hackney Village, Island CC and the Coach & Horses. Matches are played across the three grounds of Springfield Park, London Fields and Millfields, just down the Lea Bridge Road from Hackney Wick. However, the NELCL has chosen not to affiliate to the ECB, with all the additional work that entails. You will not see many players with Gunn & Moore bats or tailored cricket shirts with ECB or sponsor logos, but it is genuine urban cricket played properly and seriously but with a huge sense of fun.

Finally, there is the wonderfully named Gujarati Metropolitan Cricket League (GMCL), formed in 1993 and based in Ilford.

The League is affiliated to the ECB and, despite its name, claims that its three divisions and youth teams are open to all regardless of race or religion. The GMCL spreads it activities across Ilford, Hainault and Goodmayes, the stretch of Essex that runs out from Ilford to Romford that has provided fertile ground for generations of West Ham footballers as well as Essex cricketers like Nasser Hussain.

It is often difficult in some communities to organise cricket for women and girls, but in April 2009 one of the heroes of England's World Cup winning team, Isa Guha, the highest ranked bowler in women's international cricket, launched the Streetchances girls' cricket event in Southwark, along with local boy Ravi Bopara. More than 120 girls from across the capital took part, and included among the teams were the Hackney Hurricanes, the Newham Knights and North London Muslim CC. The six-a-side format, called Street20, is a conditioned game played at an extremely fast pace. The winners of the inaugural competition were Tower Hamlets Tigers. At the end of the event Isa said:

> *Initiatives like this are very exciting and give the youth an opportunity to get involved in cricket easily, especially in areas of London where there is a lack of green space to play in.*
> *- I. Guha, this quotation is taken from comments made in the project newsletter which can be found on www.streetchances.org.uk*

All this is very encouraging for the future of cricket in the area. A very rough calculation shows us that at least 1,500 people of all ages are involved playing weekly, organised League cricket in East London and metropolitan Essex. Almost all matches are played on artificial wickets and there are often no changing facilities, showers or scoreboards, let alone sumptuous teas between innings. Where there are teas, the delights are likely to include potato masala, plantain chips and peachy iced tea rather than the egg and cress washed down with Earl Grey on offer out in the Rodings or Pleshey. But some of these clubs are wonderfully resourceful and provide what is necessary to stage a real game of cricket, and it is surprising what you can pile into a few cars in order to stage a proper cricket match. Long may they prosper.

To the top layer of Essex League clubs in Waltham Forest,

Chingford, Walthamstow and West Essex we can now add a complex matrix of about 60 or 70 clubs playing organised League cricket of varying quality across East London, an area that spreads from Bethnal Green out to Ilford and Hainault, and from Hackney out to Barking and Dagenham. We can now see that the picture generally painted of the terminal decline of cricket in the inner city is false, even though the schools may have lost touch with the game. The traditional form of the game may have declined, but in its place has emerged something different and exciting, and we might soon be talking about East London as a hotbed of cricket rather than football. Now that would be progress.

It is encouraging to discover that club and pub cricket in Waltham Forest, Hackney, Newham and Tower Hamlets is making a visible recovery, thanks largely to the efforts of scores of passionate and hard-working volunteers, who have established a strong and coherent structure of League and Cup competitions. Cricket in the area is recovering from the sale of school sports grounds and the destruction of grass pitches and looks to have a promising future. The golden age of school cricket on grass wickets in East London of the 1950s and 1960s, which produced Graham Gooch, is over and is unlikely to return. The future of the new form of the game in East London, however, is sustainable because it represents the multi-ethnic nature of the area. Some of the Leagues and clubs might appear exclusive and, although this is denied by clubs such as the GMCL, which openly welcomes all-comers, there is a feeling in some quarters that a few clubs operate subtle exclusion policies. Essex League club Ilford CC, where Graham Gooch, J.K. Lever and Nasser Hussain were given their opportunity as young boys, are now almost exclusively Asian in membership. Rather than this being viewed as a problem, it is perhaps more helpful to see it as an historical development, with the character of the club evolving to meet the changing ethnic composition of the town. In the 2008/09 season the club's first team finished mid-table in Division 1 of the County League, and the club fields four senior Saturday sides and has youth teams at every age group from nine years old. The Ilford CC Code of Conduct, adopted in 2008, states that the club will not discriminate against anyone on grounds of gender or ethnicity. Ilford are well run and successful, providing us with a fascinating example of how the sporting culture of East London has changed over the past 25 years, and it is a little ironic that Ilford are criticised for being exclusively Asian when senior clubs in the Essex League fall over themselves to recruit Indian and Pakistani players from the sub-continent.

'Proper' cricket

The Metropolitan Essex District Cricket Board (MEDCB) runs a winter indoor league of four divisions and a youth section and operates mainly at the Peter May Centre in Walthamstow, for those living close to London. In addition, many Essex towns such as Southend and Romford also run their own indoor cricket leagues. The MEDCB operates under the guidance of the ECB and aims to provide cricket for men and women of all ages and abilities, both indoor and outdoor. It also organises courses for coaches, scorers and umpires and generally acts as the local branch of the ECB. This is a nationwide network with varying degrees of success throughout England. The key to the effectiveness of local ECBs lies in their relationship with their county club, and fortunately for cricket in this area the Essex ECB has an excellent relationship with Essex CCC, which is not the case in all counties. True to the ideals of cricket in the county, the Essex Board and Essex CCC operate under the generic umbrella of 'Essex Cricket', a kind of family group sharing the same philosophy and objectives. It is a tribute to all concerned that the whole structure pretty much works for the benefit of the game in the county and East London. The structure in Essex is formalised through joint committee work and officials meeting and working together. The Essex CCC chairman, Nigel Hilliard, sits at the top of this network and talks proudly of how a potentially bureaucratic and complex system operates with a degree of cooperation and goodwill not found outside the county.

If you were beginning to think that cricketers of all abilities and backgrounds in Essex are well provided for, think again, for there is more. The Mid-Essex League has an astonishing 11 lower divisions, in addition to its Premier League. If we allow for ten teams in each division that means over 850 players involved in the League on any one match day. The clubs stretch out across an area south from Brentwood right down to Canvey Island, where cricket remains alive and well but presents a bit of a trek for clubs in the Chelmsford area.

The Essex Sunday Cricket League was established in 1996 and is made up of three divisions and 36 clubs. The League is a 40-over competition and membership is by invitation only. It is a particularly interesting set-up because the criteria for admission are strict and exacting. A high quality square and outfield, two sight screens, score-box, pavilion and bar, qualified umpires and a successful youth policy are all minimum requirements for membership. But one particular League rule is that opposition teams must pay £40 for teas, which are required to be of the highest quality, but no mention is made of whether sandwiches should be prepared with or without crusts, or if chocolate or fruitcake should be served, nor is there any mention of potato masala or peachy iced tea. The League could not be more different from the cricket played down in Hackney's Vicky Park. This is very serious cricket indeed, and with 36 clubs we can expect there to be around 430 good cricketers involved in playing in the Sunday League. We are now beginning to get the true picture of club cricket in this sports-mad area.

The North Essex League (NEL) is based in the Colchester area on the border between Essex and Suffolk. The NEL is a Sunday League with a Premier and five lower divisions and around 50 affiliated clubs and 500 registered players. One of these clubs is Bures & District CC, which are actually just over the border in Suffolk and locals say it is possible to hit the ball from one end of the Bures square right across into Essex. However, this feat has not been achieved in living memory, the ball general falling short into the stream at the southern end of the ground. As we shall see, Bures are also noted for the quality of their teas. With a nice sense of symmetry in this coastal place, the NEL seems to be won every year by either Frinton or Clacton cricket clubs. Graham Gooch has fond boyhood memories of the annual day trip out to Clacton with his dad's team, East Ham Corinthians, for a day's cricket at the seaside.

In our picture of club cricket in Essex and East London we should not forget the Herts & Essex League. The League has a wonderful story to tell and is a clear indication of the strength of cricket in the county. The League was established in 1993 with one division and by 2009 had grown to an incredible seven divisions, with ten clubs in each division. With 70 teams the

League can boast around 850 players playing cricket every Saturday of the season. If we include the League's youth section the numbers are extremely impressive. The League is really a competitive structure for village cricket in the area, but at 45-overs-a-side matches this is serious cricket played on good grounds with properly prepared grass wickets, with one or two exceptions, of course.

At the apex of club cricket in the county is the Shepherd Neame Essex League, the hub of competitive club cricket, which complements the local leagues and the newly emerging cricket down in the East End. The new Essex League is made up of 40 clubs and was established in 1973 when 19 clubs formed a breakaway from the old Essex Senior Competition. The League has separate sections for First, Second, Third and Fourth XIs, with four divisions in each in each section. With ten teams in each division, that means 160 teams playing in the League each Saturday of the season and nearly 2,000 cricketers playing Essex League cricket every single week of the summer. Of course, in addition to the League there are the usual Cup competitions, including the obligatory and highly popular 20/20, won in 2009, I am proud to say, by Chingford CC. The League operates under the auspices of the Essex Board umbrella with its computerised fixtures, results and averages system, employed by most county Leagues and their affiliated clubs. As with all county and other leagues under the ECB auspices, the Essex League operates within the Safe Hands scheme and all affiliated clubs are required to have rigorous child protection policies in place.

We can see from this outline of club cricket in East London and Essex that the sport in the area is in robust health and is extremely well organised, with a coherent mix of Leagues, Cups and friendlies linked together by affiliation to the ECB. There are opportunities to play serious indoor winter cricket, League matches on good pitches at every level from first to fifth team. If you wish you can play 20/20 evening competitions in the splendid setting of Castle Park in Colchester or the more clamorous surroundings of Hackney's inner-city Victoria Park. There are playing opportunities for boys and girls at every age group, as well as ethnic minority-based competitions, disability cricket, Kwik Cricket and joyful impromptu games at lunchtime on the outfield of the county grounds at Southend and

Colchester in festival weeks (but sadly not at Chelmsford). There is very little state school cricket today in comparison with the 1950s and 1960s, but in the minor public and grammar schools across Essex cricket continues to flourish. The renaissance of club cricket in East London and around Dagenham, Barking and Ilford is due to the enthusiasm of hundreds of cricket-loving, hard-working volunteers. Some of the clubs have no grounds, kit, money or 150-year old history, but by their own efforts they have achieved a structure that is both vibrant and sustainable, and they are now in a position to seek help from the ECB. And it is thanks to them that cricket is flourishing again in East London.

The picture out in Essex is very different, where there is a network and history of cricket in public and grammar schools that have sustained the county club over the years. As in many areas of life, social class has influenced the game of cricket in East London and Essex. In the former Essex metropolitan boroughs, even down as far as West Ham and East Ham, cricket continues to be a working-class game, if it is played at all. Occasionally it produces a Graham Gooch, but mostly footballers and athletes. Out in Essex, in towns like Brentwood and Colchester, public schools such as Bancrofts, Forest, Brentwood and Felstead ensure that there is a regular supply to the local clubs of well-coached youngsters with plenty of experience of playing on decent grass wickets. The best of these youngsters find their way to Gooch's Academy at Chelmsford, and, if they are good enough, they can end up playing for the county.

There is a real sense in which promising young cricketers who attend Essex public schools have a distinct advantage over those who go to the local comprehensives. However, it would be wrong to conclude from this that clubs in the more affluent parts of the county are full of public school toffs. After all, this is Essex, and, despite the undoubted influence of social class on cricket in the county, most clubs will have players from a range of backgrounds in their sides, including solicitors, doctors, teachers, plumbers and carpenters. By looking more closely at two of the more senior clubs, one from urban Waltham Forest and the other out in rural Essex, we should gain a greater understanding of the social nature of cricket in the county.

Walthamstow CC – an oasis of calm

My father's family originate from Wood Street, Walthamstow, which is located about a mile from the borough's famous old high street market. At one end of Wood Street is the public library and a junior school, and at the other is a roundabout that takes you down into Leyton and on into the East End. Wood Street connects Leyton with Highams Park and Chingford, and it is a busy urban place but with a village feel about it. In the past local people travelled to the City for work, or to the nearby Hawker Sidley plant or the Rael Brook shirt factory down on Forest Road, both now closed down. Today locals have to find other ways to earn a living and unemployment around Wood Street is high.

You can buy most things in Wood Street, from military memorabilia to wonderful pastries at the old bakers near the library. The street's best pub is the Flower Pot, watering hole to generations of Walthamstow teachers, who generally preferred the more relaxed ambience of the saloon bar to the noisy coarseness of the public one. I remember clearly one occasion in the early 1980s when a local builder, who had been banned from the pub by the no-nonsense landlord, dumped a huge pile of pre-mixed concrete from his truck onto the floor of the public bar. Wood Street is that sort of place. The Flower Pot also hosted the annual Wood Street Walk, a wonderful festive occasion that brings out the whole of the borough on a Spring Sunday morning. Just across the road from the pub is the street's railway station, which is the third stop from Chingford on the Liverpool Street line. If you turn right at the station up Greenaway Road, you will eventually reach the oasis of calm that is Buck Walk, home to Walthamstow Cricket Club, the last truly East London League cricket club.

The history of Walthamstow CC is a rare story of how an exclusively working-class area has sustained an ambitious and successful county League club that fields sides at senior level on Saturdays and Sundays and boasts a thriving youth section. Walthamstow has no grammar or public schools, and hardly any cricket is played today in either of the borough's primary or secondary schools. There is very little cricket in the Walthamstow area outside Buck Walk, apart from some recreational stuff played on the one or two artificial wickets that have managed to remain undamaged. Walthamstow is multicultural and is proud of its diversity and community spirit, and one can only imagine the potential for cricket among the borough's young people that remains unrealised, or downright squandered. Against this background, the story of Walthamstow CC is nothing short of heroic.

All county League clubs are required to sign up to the Play-Cricket website network. One of the facilities on the site allows clubs to create a history page, where they can write a brief, or not so brief in some cases, story about how and when their club started, important developments, notable performances, etc. Some clubs, who should know better, have a blank page where their history should be, but Walthamstow Cricket Club are clearly proud of their history and to commemorate their centenary in 1962 they commissioned a Mr Couzens to write an official club history. (www.play-cricket.com) Mr R.H. Williams, the club chairman, wrote at the time:

> *When Mr Couzens accepted the job of writing the club's history, I knew that the resulting work would be informative, accurate and entertaining. My belief was fully justified as will be seen from the following, which has been reproduced from his manuscript with very little alteration or amendment.*

Mr Couzens certainly "spent long and arduous hours" on researching his subject. He studied local newspapers, local government documents and club minutes, and he also had the ear of the local newspapers' editors of the time. It is clear from reading the results of his meticulous research that the work was very much a labour of love. Sid Couzens, however, was not a detached and dry historian but a very good club cricketer in his own right, with a distinguished playing record for his beloved Walthamstow. As the chairman wrote of his prowess as a cricketer:

> *If someone else tackled this task the name of Sid Couzens must surely have earned a chapter to itself.*

Couzens, a hostile fast-bowler in his time, took a record 1,843 wickets in 18 seasons for the club, an outstanding achievement at this level. Doug Insole up at Chingford, who knows a thing or two about these things, thought that Couzens was one of the most difficult bowlers he ever faced in club cricket. Fast-bowlers are not usually given to writing impressive club histories – Couzens was clearly a remarkable character. However, despite his impressive playing record, he was never invited to play for his county. He was content to be a club man, who, apart from his excellence as a player, contributed so much to the club in other ways. His chairman said that Walthamstow were the club "he undoubtedly loved and served so well". What follows in this brief summary of the history of one of the most esteemed sports clubs in East London owes a great debt to the fast-bowler, committee man and club historian, Sid Couzens.

Couzens starts his 'petite histoire' of his beloved club with the phrase:

It is generally accepted that very little of any good comes from war.

But, he argues, Walthamstow Cricket Club owe their Centenary Celebrations of 1962 to the threat of war, created by the threat to the country of the Russian Empire following the Crimean War of 1853-56. As a result of this threat a number of volunteer corps were established across East London and Essex between 1859 and 1860. The first of these were at Romford and Ilford in 1859 and 1860 respectively, and Walthamstow quickly followed their example. Volunteers were sworn in as the 'B' Company of the Second Essex Volunteer Rifle Corps at the Infants National School in St Mary's Churchyard, in the heart of the borough's historic village area. William Houghton, a vice-president of Walthamstow Cricket Club, was a founder member of the Company. Of course, one of the first things that the volunteer soldiers did was to form football and cricket clubs. However, the first matches were modest affairs, as Couzens points out:

From the numerous reports of volunteer rifle matches, musters and functions during 1861, it is reasonable to assume that the little cricket played was confined to 'scratch' matches on the Church Common.

But by the following year 'scratch' matches were much more serious affairs. In the *Chelmsford Chronicle* of Friday 27th June 1862 there is a report of a match between Walthamstow and

Upminster played at Church Common on 17th June. Upminster scored 54 and 80, and Walthamstow an even more modest 36 and 18. (The Church Common ground was sold by the Walthamstow Parish Council to the Great Eastern Railway Co. in May 1869. The Railway Co. deposited £2,800 for the purchase of the Recreation Ground between High Street and Selborne Road). In the *Chelmsford Chronicle* of Friday 1st August 1862, the following report appears:

> *Walthamstow v. Upminster*
> *On the 22nd July the return match between the above Clubs was played at Upminster, and was concluded in favour of the Walthamstow team on the first innings by 29 runs. It will be recollected that in the first match played, some five weeks since, the Upminster won by 80 runs, consequently in the present the gentlemen from West Essex considerably strengthened their team by bringing Messrs. Green, Greenhill and Mallett, with whose aid they succeeded in placing upon the telegraph at the fall of the last wicket a total of 101 runs. After dinner Upminster appeared at the wicket, and having run up a score of 72 runs, half of which were made by Grover, Abraham and Brewster, the last wicket was lowered. In the second innings of Walthamstow, which closed for 76, Wright marked 24 including a fine leg hit for 6 and Green 18.*

The thought of going out either to bat or to field "after dinner" clearly did not deter nineteenth-century cricketers. The scorecard shows that one of the opening batsmen for Walthamstow was H. Read, who became president of the club in 1875. The author of the report tells us that in a home match against Walthamstow a young man whom the visitors brought with them created a lasting impression on his mind:

> *He sent the ball repeatedly into my flower garden at the Mill, and into the road.*

This splendid hitter was none other than a young C. E. Green, who later played a prominent part in the founding of Essex County Cricket Club (Mr Abraham's notes were included in the centenary booklet issued by Upminster Cricket Club in 1958) and remains one of the most distinguished players to play for Walthamstow. Sir Pelham Warner, in his book about Lord's, (P.

Warner, Sir (1946), Lord's: 1787-1945, George G. Harrap & Co.) described Green as the life and soul of Essex cricket. Warner also paid tribute to Green's batting. Perhaps Green's finest innings was his 51 for the MCC v. Yorkshire at Lord's in 1870 when both Green and W.G. Grace (66) suffered a torrid time on a poor wicket from the Yorkshire fast-bowlers, Freeman and Emmett. Charlie Green was the first captain of Essex County Cricket Club in the old Leyton days and was later made club president. In 1905 he was elected president of the MCC, a distinguished predecessor of later stalwarts such as T.N. Pearce, Johnny Douglas and Doug Insole.

The *Stratford Times* and *South Essex Gazette* of Saturday, 6th October 1866 gives details of the end of season athletic event held by Walthamstow Cricket Club. Green won the 100 yards, high jump, kick football, throwing the cricket ball (103 yards), long jump (18' 9") and hurdle race. These astonishing performances confirm Charlie Green's brilliance as an all-round sportsman. He was also a skilled administrator and had a decisive impact on the development of both Walthamstow and the county club.

Lemmon and Marshall's Official History (1987) would not have been available to Sid Couzens when he wrote his history, or he would have seen that the first record of cricket being played in Walthamstow was actually in the mid-eighteenth century. It says:

> *By the second half of the century, cricket was abounding in all parts of Essex. In 1752, notice was given to all gentlemen cricketers 'that the long depending match to be played at Lowlayton, between the gentlemen of Hackney, and the gentlemen of Layton and Walthamstow, on Coppy Down, near the Bowling Green, July 29, for £50. ...*
> *The Gazetteer and London Daily Advertiser in 1765 ... reported: On Monday, August 5, Walthamstow beat Low Layton and Leytonstone by 62 runs, to the great mortification of the losers who had beaten all the villages thereabouts.*
> *- Lemmon and Marshall (1987), p.13*

The early eighteenth-century appearance of cricket in the area may have been loosely associated with the beginnings of the present club, but, interesting as this is, it probably cannot be claimed to part of the story of Walthamstow CC, which may explain its absence from Couzen's history of the club. In this sense Couzens is probably right to start his history with the rough games of cricket played by the local Volunteer Corps in the 1850s, which boosted the club's playing strength and turned a local cricket team into the strongest cricket club north of the Thames.

In 1865 Walthamstow CC moved to a new ground in Green Leaf Lane, just off Hoe Street, which links the borough with Chingford and Leyton. The ground was developed for housing many years ago and there are very few 'green leaves' in evidence today. William Morris School was built in 1902 on land adjacent to the old ground and was recently demolished to make way for 'affordable' housing. I was a pupil at the school for a couple of years in the early sixties. These were the days before smokeless fuel and I remember being sent home from school regularly during the winter months when a dense pea-soup fog descended on the borough. With no buses running we had to walk back home to Chingford, around 6 miles away, holding on to garden walls and railings because we literally couldn't see our hands in front of our faces.

The club captain at the time of the move to Green Leaf Road was P.J.G. Rouquette, who was likely to have been more interested in the formidable Walthamstow Football Club (Rugby), which in *The Victorian History of the County of Essex* is described as "the most historic, as well as the best in the point of view of active strength". (H.A. Doubleday and W. Page (1903), The Victorian History of the County of Essex, Constable). Rouquette, an old Rugbeian, is described by Couzens as "a forward of the heavy type which prevailed in his era and as the moving spirit of the Club at the time". He had three younger brothers who in turn captained the cricket and football clubs. The strength of the football side of the club is evident from the fixture lists of the time, which show that matches were played against St Bart's Hospital, West Kent, St Thomas's Hospital, Clevedon, St George's Hospital, Guys Hospital, R.M.A. Woolwich, Wasps, Ravenscourt Park, Marlborough Nomads, Richmond, Harlequins, London Scottish and Cambridge University. Like many clubs today, Walthamstow CC continues to operate within an overall sports club.

In 1873 the amalgamated Walthamstow Cricket and Football

Clubs were forced to move again, this time to St James's Street, situated opposite the club's headquarters, the Coach & Horses Tavern. In the same year, the *Stratford Times* of Wednesday 1st October 1873 gives details of the club's 'sports days' usually held at the end of the cricket season, a practice that has now sadly ceased. The *Walthamstow & Leyton Guardian* of 13th May 1876 gives the following colourful account of the club's sports day, held on this occasion in the spring of that year:

> *The spring meeting of these Clubs was held under favourable circumstances in the Club's Cricket Field, St. James's Street, Walthamstow, on Saturday, 6th May. No expense was spared to make the day's amusement all that could be desired. The prizes consisted of handsome cups, goblets and tankards, with two football caps of superior make, which were presented to Messrs. Echalaz and Ashmore. The Band of the 1st City of London Engineers (by permission of Lieut.-Col. Stillwell) were in attendance. Judges were C. Webb and P. J. G. Rouquette.*

Sports days were extremely popular and well-attended events, with local people dressing up and enjoying family picnics and beer from the pub next door. In 1873 the day's activities were graced by the appearance of the band of the Honorable Artillery Company, which regally entertained the competitors and their supporters. Among the committee and competitors during this period were members of the influential Borwick family, famous for their Victorian baking powder, whose factory was down in the East End at London Wall.

Cricket continued to develop in and around East London at this time. In both 1876 and 1877 the cricket club had a full fixture list for the First and Second XIs, including matches against local clubs Leytonstone, Clapton, Woodford, Enfield and Brentwood School. The journey from Walthamstow out to Brentwood would have taken at least half a day, at the time quite a feat of commitment and organisation. Of the fixtures completed in 1877, Walthamstow won 14, drew 5 and lost 11. The laws of cricket at this time did not allow for declarations, and one can just imagine the feelings of the Clapton captain and batsmen when their home match with Walthamstow on Saturday 21st July 1877 ended with the following result: "Walthamstow 200-6. Clapton did not bat. Walthamstow retaining possession of the wickets till call of time." (Details of match results taken from The History of Walthamstow Cricket and Lawn Tennis Club by Mr SA Couzens (1962) published on the clubs website www.walthamstowcc.hitscricket.com). Not much fun in the pub after the game that night. If Doug Insole had been playing in that game he would have almost certainly been called for throwing.

Towards the end of the nineteenth century the club's standing in the game was very high indeed, as we can see from this extract from the *Stratford Express* of Saturday 21st June 1879:

The annual sports in connection with the Walthamstow Cricket & Football Clubs came off on Saturday, 14th June, on the Club's ground St. James's Street. As usual there was quite an aristocratic gathering, the elite of the neighbourhood being present.

The *Gazetteer & Directory of the County of Essex* (1863) is highly complimentary about Walthamstow as a borough:

Walthamstow, one of the largest and handsomest sub-villages near the metropolis, is delightfully situated on the eastern side of the vale of the River Lea, within the southern verge of Epping Forest. It contains many handsome villas, with tasteful pleasure grounds, mostly occupied by merchants and others, who have their places of business in London.

It is interesting to compare this nineteenth-century version of Walthamstow with the lively, multi-ethnic borough of today, with its bustling market, noise and traffic pollution, and poor quality housing estates cheek by jowl with renovated Victorian villas.

Back in the nineteenth century the club were on the move once again and it is small wonder that, although Walthamstow survived these itinerant wanderings in their early days, inevitably the cricket club did suffer as a result of this continual moving around. Developers were slowly moving into the borough, forcing the club to vacate their St James's Street Ground at the end of the 1882 season. The football club acquired the use of the Cassiobury House Ground off Coppermil Road, used in the summer by Auburne and Elms cricket clubs. However, although the ground did not provide a new home for the cricket club, the move did have some positive consequences, as it brought the club into closer contact with Auburne, founded in 1878 by Major Guppy. Sadly, the club's link with the Volunteer Rifle Corps fell away and at the end of the 1884 season efforts were made to reorganise the cricket section under the presidency of Mr J.C. Rose of Longfield Lodge. Mr Rose generously allowed the club to use his land just off Blackhorse Lane for the following two seasons. Astonishingly, despite their wanderings, the club continued to maintain their impressive fixture list at this time, with matches against Clapton, Tottenham, Stamford Hill and Rochford Hundred (now Southend-on-Sea). Mr John Holmes, MP, was also added to their list of patrons at this time.

By an odd chance it was also at the end of the 1884 season that the Major's Auburne club amalgamated with the fashionable Mayfield Cricket Club of Clapton. This might be one of the few times that 'fashionable' and 'Clapton' have appeared in the same sentence, as that part of the East End is particularly run-down and neglected. The amalgamated club was known as Mayfield Auburne and enjoyed the use of the Cassiobury House Ground for the 1885 and 1886 seasons, under the captaincy of Josiah Gunton, a City Alderman, who but for his premature death might have become Lord Mayor of London. Mayfield Auburne CC was to play a major role in the future of the Walthamstow CC.

Towards the end of the century Walthamstow CC were becoming well used to being shifted around the borough. At the end of the 1886 season the club had to vacate their Rose's Farm Ground, again for housing development - a sure sign of the growth in population at the end of the nineteenth century and the increasing urbanisation of the outer London boroughs. This latest crisis forced a merger with the new Mayfield Auburne Club. The *Walthamstow Guardian* of Saturday 22nd October 1887 reported on the proceedings of the AGM of the newly improved Walthamstow Cricket Club, at which the treasurer, Major John Guppy, made the following statement:

In December, 1886, the Club had secured the lease for seven years of a private field, belonging to Mr. Courtenay Warner, in Blackhorse Lane and during the winter they had spent over £100 in preparing the ground for cricket and lawn tennis. A handsome pavilion had also been erected on the field. There were 64 gentlemen and 22 ladies at present on the books and two cricket matches would be arranged for every Saturday next season.

The Warner family owned great chunks of Walthamstow between Lloyd's Park and High Street, on which they built streets of flats and maisonettes for rent. My grandmother rented a first-floor Warner flat in Mersey Road by the entrance to the park. When I was a boy I used to visit her every Sunday morning and bring up her coal from the shelter in the side alley, and then I would go down to the off-licence on the corner to get her cigarettes and a bottle of stout. She had a bath in the kitchen with a wooden cover over the top that acted as a draining board when she did her washing-up. One of the attractions of the weekly trip was the Camp Coffee sweetened with Libby's canned milk that she always made me - a rare treat in those days. The Warner flats have all been sold off now and provide homes for young couples making a start on the property ladder.

The new ground was situated opposite Longfield Avenue in Blackhorse Lane, down towards Walthamstow Marshes, and a good way from their present ground off Wood Street. Settled for a period, the club began to enjoy a time of much-needed stability and prosperity, as we can see from the reports of the club's annual dinner that year. The *Walthamstow Guardian* of Saturday 14th December 1889 reported that the club enjoyed a successful annual dinner at the Holborn Restaurant in central London. By 1894 the club was running cricket tours for its First and Second XIs, a sure sign that the club had benefited from their latest move.

However, some local cricketers were not happy about the club's new, exalted position on the local scene. The Walthamstow Guardian of Friday 28th April 1893 carried the following comment:

There is a general feeling amongst local cricketers that the team bearing the name of the parish should be composed of local players. Unfortunately, the Walthamstow Cricket Club consists almost entirely of Stoke Newington and Clapton men. The Elmsdale Cricket Club are (in every way) more deserving of this honour ...

The fact that Walthamstow had so many 'ringers', or players

from outside the borough, was a direct result of the merger with Mayfield Aurbune. On Friday 3rd August 1894 the paper further reported news of a rival to the newly merged club:

By the way, I hear that next season it is intended to change the name of the Walthamstow Tradesmen Cricket Club (Thursdays only) to that of "Walthamstow Town" and to play Saturday matches. This is certainly a step in the right direction, as we certainly need a representative club.

The new Walthamstow Town Cricket Club was formed when the old Elmsdale and Walthamstow Tradesmen clubs joined forces. The Walthamstow Town Club had their first season in 1895, running one Thursday and two Saturday XIs. C.J. Kortright, the legendary Essex fast-bowler was their vice-captain. For a time they enjoyed considerable playing success and from 1896 to 1899 had First and Second XI matches with Walthamstow Cricket Club but owing to an apparent lack of interest the Walthamstow Town Club was wound up at a meeting on 17th April 1902. Walthamstow CC were now indisputably the premier cricket club in the borough. The club's next move, again provoked by rapacious developers, was to the Church Hill ground known as Rectory Field or Vicarage Field, now the site of the Girls' County High School, known to generations of locals simply as the 'green school' because of the girls' dark green school uniforms. The Church Hill ground was situated just a short walk from the club's current home, Buck Walk.

The club continued to develop in a positive fashion. In 1896, in an astute move, the club added Mr E. Widdrington Byrne, QC, MP, to their list of vice-presidents. The fixtures list was strengthened and now included Cheshunt, Edmonton, Ilford, Finchley, South Woodford, Woking, Enfield, Brighton Brunswick and Newhaven, an impressive list by any standard. One can only wonder at the travel arrangements to get to and from away games. Doug Insole wrote about such journeys in the 1930s when playing for Chingford:

... in those days a car was a noteworthy asset ... my memory is a little vague. I think we sometimes had lifts, but we often travelled, quite cheerfully, on the buses and trains humping on the shoulder a heavy

leather bag loaded with two bats, boots, pads, etc. On trips to Westcliff, Leigh and Shoeburyness a few of us would go down in the morning by train from Walthamstow Midland Station.
- M. Blake, Chingford Cricket Club 1884-2009: 125 Not Out (Chingford CC) and from theHistory section of the Chingford CC website www.chingfordcc.hitscricket.com

Late arrival for away matches often resulted in a loss of prestigious fixtures, but these difficulties would have been nothing compared with those encountered by our intrepid nineteenth-century cricketers when there were few trains or buses and hardly any cars. But the club continued to prosper and in 1897 they were delighted to report a total of over 100 cricket and tennis members and a financially sound position. The club's annual dinner that year was held in great style at the Trocadero Restaurant in London's West End, a definite upgrade from Holborn and an indication that the club were in very good shape indeed, with First and Second XIs tours to Kent and Surry respectively and a very full fixtures list.

After surviving a succession of enforced moves and local political infighting, Walthamstow CC began to be a real force in East London and Essex cricket, and in Charlie Cattell they had one of the finest club batsmen in the south of England. In the 1905 season Cattell made five successive centuries during a club tour and he was the first man in the club's history to complete 1,000 runs in a First XI season. His final figures for that year were 19 innings, with a highest score of 138, and 1,054 runs at 58.5. Even Graham Gooch in his heyday would have been proud of Cattell's figures that season. It was during the club's tour in 1905 that Cattell put on 245 for the first wicket with Harold Wilson (no, not that one) against Hastings Rovers at their Central Ground, a club record that still stands today.

The successful run at Church Hill was terminated at the end of the 1909 season when the ground was acquired by the Essex Education Committee, and in 1910 the club moved to their present home at Buck Walk and, as they say, the rest is history. The new ground was opened on Saturday 14th May, but unfortunately the First XI were badly beaten by a strong East Finchley side. However, despite this slightly embarrassing start, in the first season at the new ground membership increased from 110 to 150. To cope with this increase in interest three new tennis courts were laid for the following season, bringing the total of courts to nine. The Old Monovians Football & Hockey Clubs were granted permission to use the ground during the winter months, although the school had an extensive range of pitches on its own site in Chingford Road. The Old Monovians comprised former pupils of the Sir George Monoux Grammar School on the Walthamstow/Chingford border. The club later acquired their own sports ground just down the road from the Charlie Brown roundabout at Woodford. One the school's most famous old boys was Doug Insole CBE of Essex and England, although today some might consider that jazzman Johnny Dankworth and Teddy Sheringham have a stronger claim to the title of the school's most distinguished old boys.

In 1913 the club fielded First, Second and Third XIs for the first time in their history. Then, of course, the First World War intervened. Some infrequent cricket was played on the Buck Walk ground before it was taken over for the war effort. Many local sports grounds were turned over to military use in the First World War, including West Ham FC's Upton Park. The Buck Walk ground was reserved for the newly resurrected local Volunteers Corps, who used it for training and storing vehicles.

Cricket resumed quickly after the war and the club's first match was played at Blackhorse Lane on 17th May 1919, against the Gnome & Le Rhone Engine Cricket Club, when again they suffered an embarrassing defeat. This was hardly surprising since nine members of the team had just returned from four hard years in France and were playing their first cricket match in a very long time. But Walthamstow, along with many other clubs in the area, were to be congratulated on playing so soon after the war and after such a long period of inactivity.

In 1924 the two dilapidated sheds that had served as dressing rooms at the Buck Walk ground were replaced by a new pavilion. This pavilion was financed by 10 shilling shares repayable at a premium of sixpence for each year the shares were held. Initially the response was discouraging, but eventually sufficient funds were raised to meet the cost of £642. The reason for the bargain price was that almost all labour was supplied free by club members, a tradition that continues today in many clubs whose members almost always include builders, electricians and plumbers. The club had to raise about £200 a year to meet their debts, which they achieved through fundraising events, dances, sweepstakes, etc., again a practice that keeps many of today's clubs financially afloat. Thanks mainly to the energetic efforts of one particular member, Charles Hurst, the debt was cleared within five years. Incorporated into the capital charges repaid was the original £100 lent to the club at the time of the move from Church Hill in 1910.

At the Second Annual Supper held in the new Buck Walk pavilion in 1925, Jimmy Johns, the general secretary, informed the 140 members present that every effort should be made to purchase the Buck Walk ground in order to ensure the future of the club. Such ambition said a great deal about the club and what the facility meant to the members. As the committee members knew full well, no local club can be secure about their future when there is continued speculation about whether their ground might be sold to property speculators.

In a purely cricketing sense 1924 was the golden year of Walthamstow CC. One of the principal reasons for this was one Len Snaith. Snaith was still at the Sir George Monoux Grammar School when he played his first game for the club, scoring 108 not out for the Third XI against South Woodford on 21st June. The following week he scored 103 not out for the Second XI against nearby Hale End and completed his first season by heading the Second XI, batting with an average of 41.57. During the home cricket week, a feature of many cricket club calendars in the area, the Derelicts club turned up one player short and Snaith made up their number. He proceeded to score a century against his own club, which included several first team bowlers. All in all, a fine first season for the youngster. Predictably, the following year Snaith was promoted to the First XI and again headed the batting, scoring 854 runs at an average of 42.70. Inevitably, the prowess of Walthamstow's youthful protégé came to the attention of the county club. On Monday 19th July 1926, an Essex Club and Ground side visited Buck Walk under the captaincy of the redoubtable J.W.H.T. Douglas. Snaith scored 103 runs out of the Walthamstow total of 286 and the Club and Ground side replied with 127 for 3 wickets before rain stopped play. Sid Couzens claims:

> *... after the game the young upstart Snaith pointed out to Johnny where he had gone wrong, but Douglas did not appreciate the words of wisdom, for Snaith was never asked to play for any County XI.*

But Snaith continued to impress, leading the First XI batting averages on no fewer than 11 occasions before leaving Walthamstow in 1946 to join Leigh-on-Sea out on the estuary. In the 1933 season he became only the second player in the club's history to score a 1,000 runs in a First XI season, but it took him 26 innings as against Cattell's 19 innings back in 1905.

Jimmy Johns' campaign for the club to purchase their own ground eventually succeeded when in 1929 Walthamstow CC became the proud owners of Buck Walk. The ground had been the property of the Mills Trust and Miss Mills, who decreed that the ground should be retained as a sports field and had invited negotiations with this outcome in mind. The purchase put a tremendous financial burden on the committee members, who had to find people to buy the shares issued to finance the deal. Despite some anxious moments, the club succeeded in meeting their obligations, thanks largely to the financial support provided by the late Mr H.W. Dongray (club president from 1934 to 1961) and to the principal negotiator Charles Hurst (club chairman from 1934 to 1947).

With their home ground now secure, Walthamstow CC continued to build on their position as one of the strongest clubs north of the Thames, and their already strong batting was reinforced in 1934 by the arrival of M.R.J. 'Monty' Wood, who proceeded to head the First XI batting averages in five out of his first six seasons with the club. Monty made a name for himself in London for his powerful hitting. In 1935 he scored 971 runs in 24 innings at 40.45. These figures appear modest in comparison with today's club batting averages secured on dead, covered wickets and emasculated spin bowling. In the 1930s clubs traditionally prepared uncovered marl-prepared wickets while others, ever resourceful, used a compressed layer of cow dung to dampen and flatten the surface, which rendered the pitches more bowler friendly than today. With players like Monty Wood in their side the club were able to maintain their position at the head of club cricket in East London and Essex. However, just as the club were enjoying a deserved period of stability, war intervened again, this time with the most appalling results. Walthamstow was not hit as badly by the German bombers as the East End, but parts of the borough suffered terrible damage during the war, including the streets around Buck Walk and Wood Street.

Wartime cricket

It is worth pausing at this point in the history of Walthamstow CC to look at the effects of the Second World War on cricket in the county more generally. Cricket was not abandoned totally either at county or club level during the war. Of course, East London and metropolitan Essex region was one of the most vulnerable areas of the country and was subjected to prolonged and heavy bombing. Club grounds were often prohibited areas, and many were again under military occupation and not available until hostilities ceased. Many pavilions and playing areas were damaged by bombs, including the pavilion at Chelmsford. Travel was difficult to arrange and in certain areas was restricted altogether. In the early years of the war playing sport was seen by many as unpatriotic, but feelings subsided as the conflict dragged on, and playing sport came to be seen as a healthy distraction from the privations of war.

The Essex CCC committee agreed to carry on playing cricket, although the County Championship was suspended until 1945. Matches were arranged against local school sides, including Bancrofts, Forest, Chigwell and Brentwood. The club agreed to play one-day matches against local clubs and to pay the professionals, when they were home on leave, a mere £1 per match. There was an Essex and Middlesex match against Kent and Surrey at Lord's, with more than 15,000 people watching the first day's play. The match raised about £250 for King George's War Fund for sailors' families. Essex's Ray Smith regularly captained the British Empire side, scoring 2,155 runs and taking 308 wickets. An Essex XI played the British Empire at Chelmsford and raised £150 for the same fund, but efforts to arrange matches against other counties were largely unsuccessful. However, local matches were arranged against Colchester, Halstead and Braintree in order to provide the players with as much cricket as possible during wartime.

The Essex committee continued its policy of developing young talent that has served the club so well down the years, with coaching classes arranged at Chelmsford and Woodford Wells. (Annual Report 1944, D/Z 82/1/29/92, Essex Record Office.) The club were keen to be ready for the resumption of the County Championship at the end of the war, and Ray Smith, Trevor Bailey and Ken Farnes all began their playing careers during the war years. Three wickets in his first over was an impressive debut performance by the young Westcliff all-rounder, Bailey. The Essex committee also agreed to make grants of around £50 available to Ilford, Brentwood and Chelmsford CCs to ensure that their grounds were fit for county cricket when cricket began again.

At club level there were tremendous efforts to keep clubs intact, although travel was almost impossible and loss of both membership and playing staff was severe. At Upminster CC there was never any question of abandoning playing cricket. A side was fielded each Saturday, made up of youngsters and older members, a bit like fourth teams today. The club reported that one match

> *... was played whilst flying bombs were passing overhead, and throughout the war the preparation of wickets was hampered by shell splinters damaging the cutters.*
> *- 'Upminster Cricket Club 1858-1958', History and Centenary Programme, T/P 221/16, Essex Record Office.*

Upminster retained their links with the county club and regularly played matches against the local garrison side, and during the war relations were established with new clubs, which served to strengthen their fixtures list in the post-war period.

Clubs enjoyed mixed fortunes in wartime. Clacton CC cancelled all fixtures in 1939, but those for the 1940 season were allowed to stand in the hope that war would be over quickly. In the event, only a few matches were staged, club subscriptions were cancelled and the club really only recovered after 1945. The club resumed playing after the war with just one team, which played 18 fixtures in the 1946 season. (A.G. Lindfield and B. Naismith (eds) (1999), Cricket on the Green: A Celebration of Woodford Green Cricket Club, Woodford Green Cricket Club). All clubs were affected, even those out in the more remote areas of the county. In May 1940 the *Clacton Graphic* reported in its unpunctuated style:

> *St Osyth CC is officially defunct this season, but the members who remain in the village are determined to do all they can to arrange some matches during the summer so that cricket should not be altogether unknown at St Osyth during 1940.*

Some clubs took longer to recover from the war. In 1942 St Osyth CC's Cowley Park pavilion became the headquarters of the local Home Guard, and at the end of the war the ground was in no fit state for serious cricket, or cricket of any kind. The club finally re-emerged to play a few matches in 1950, paving the way for a full-scale resumption the following year. It was the same at Woodford Green, whose 1945 victory celebrations attracted thousands of people to their delightful ground, with Winston Churchill addressing the crowd in person.

Ilford CC staged matches throughout the war, including one between the British Empire XI and the Women's Cricket Association. During the war collections were made on the ground for the Red Cross, which amounted to nearly £400, and in 1943 and 1944 the club headed the donations made by Conference clubs to the war effort. Ilford fielded two XIs throughout the war, but it was impossible to continue popular fixtures against the likes of Southend because of travelling restrictions. (Ilford Cricket Club (1979), Ilford CC: A History of the First 100 years and a Centenary Souvenir 1878-1978, Valentine Press).

Walthamstow CC were perhaps more vulnerable than most to the bombing due to their proximity to the River Lea and the small arms and gunpowder works along its banks. The club continued to provide activities to keep its members interested when they were on leave from the Forces, and they maintained the ground in anticipation of the end of hostilities and the resumption of peacetime cricket. During the war the ground suffered severe bomb damage and only extensive internal strengthening kept the pavilion standing. The start of the 1942 season saw the members alternating between net practice and filling in bomb craters. In 1940 the club recruited Sid Couzens, one of the most outstanding players in the history of Walthamstow CC. They were clearly determined to keep things going, despite the war. One of only two bowlers in the club's history to have taken 1,000 wickets, Couzens took 1,843 in his 18 seasons - extremely impressive at this level of cricket.

Walthamstow CC emerges from the war

Club cricket, as with all sports, began to return to some kind of normality after the war. Following the settlement of their War Damage claim in 1954 the club were able to renovate the pavilion and in 1955 they were able to redeem the mortgage taken out in 1929. That Walthamstow CC emerged from the war ready to resume their role as one of London's top cricket clubs was due entirely to the wartime efforts of hard-working officials and committee members. One of their most notable achievements was in 1951 when the committee successfully fought off the threat of compulsory acquisition of the Buck Walk ground, a victory that demonstrated to the local council just how much the cricket club meant to the people of the borough.

Among the notable post-war performances by Walthamstow players were Alan Penman's ten wickets in a match between the Second XI and Maurice CC in 1957. This was the first time in the club's history that such a feat had been performed, yet within two years Denis Sayers took all ten for the First XI in a match with Old Stationers. Club officials must have been relieved that standards had not only been maintained but had actually improved since the war. With the security of a permanent ground behind them, the Buck Walk club entered a period of steady progress and improvement, particularly under the captaincy of the redoubtable Johnny Welch.

Welch captained the club for 14 years and was revered as a generous and understanding skipper. He was one of a number of Walthamstow players in the post-war period that could have played first-class cricket on a regular basis, including Barry Gymer and Mike Boyers. Such was his love for the game, Welch also captained Essex Seconds for a number of years during the 1960s. In the sixties, Walthamstow had a very strong side, which included wicketkeeper Frank Rist, West Indian Keith Boyce and the South African Lee Irvine, until Boyce and Irvine were required full-time by Essex. The club also had a close relationship with West Ham United, with Geoff Hurst, Alan Sealey and Alan Stephenson all playing under the captaincy of Welch, and even the great Bobby Moore made the occasional Sunday appearance.

Like many cricketers at the time, Welch was a decent amateur footballer and he had spells at Leytonstone and Romford. Now 85 years old, he is of the same generation as Trevor Bailey and Doug Insole and is remembered at the club as a self-effacing character and not one to seek glory for himself. He never played for the Essex First XI, but he was a wonderful ambassador for club cricket in the area. With typical generosity Welch donated a clock for the new pavilion at Chingford CC after the old one was destroyed by fire in 1966.

Under the Presidency of Bob Williams, who did such great work along with Charles Hurst in raising funds during the club's most difficult times, the club continued to prosper. The club are also indebted to the legendary sports shop owner, Arthur Sedgwick, one of their former vice-presidents, who in later years was instrumental in attracting many star-studded XIs to the ground. Most club cricket in the area is now League-based rather than the old run-chase game of the pre-war years. Up until fairly recent years there were no cricket Leagues in the south of England and a club's prestige was reflected in their fixtures list rather than where they might finish in the League. Clubs were expected to play the game in the correct spirit and go for the win at all times, and if the team failed there was the compensation of an honourable defeat - not a concept with which today's captains would be familiar. These days you are simply told which side you will play when the fixtures are announced. This is now the case on Sundays as well as Saturdays.

Like most clubs, Walthamstow have embraced the League structure. The club is currently thriving and fully signed up to the Essex Board's policies for club cricket in the county. They presently field four Saturday and two Sundays sides and compete in the area's winter indoor League. There is a flourishing youth section, with teams at under 11, 13 and 15. The standard remains high and in 2009 a young lad, Ashley Leat, put his name in the club's records by hitting six 6s in an over in a match against St Albans. Like most top Essex League clubs, Walthamstow engage an overseas player, and in 2009 New Zealander Nathan McNally took on a role that combines scoring runs, taking wickets, coaching the colts and generally representing the club with sponsors, and so on. Sadly, the club's Second XI were relegated from Division 2 in 2009, but I am sure this is a tiny blip in the distinguished history of this lovely old cricket club, deep in the heart of working-class East London. Having reached their centenary the club can look forward to their 150th anniversary with confidence, building on traditions inspired by generations of dedicated people who contributed, both on and off the field, to the continuing success of Walthamstow Cricket Club.

Brentwood CC, a gem of a cricket club

Walthamstow CC are an example of what can be achieved in cricket in an urban environment by sheer persistence and hard work, but if we travel further out into the county we see a very different picture, but an equally successful one. We might go south down to the estuary to visit the Essex League clubs at Leigh-on-Sea, Southend or Trevor Bailey's Westcliff, or into the Essex 'badlands' to watch an afternoon's play at Dagenham, Thurrock or Basildon, home of ex-East Enders and the quintessential 'Essex Man' of Daily Mail caricature. Seeing people as masses or generalisations is always a mistake. People themselves are far more individual and independent that any tabloid stereotype might suggest. My uncle was a porter in Smithfield Market, and like many who moved out to south Essex from the East End he rose early every morning to make the journey up the Southend Road into town. They were a good, hard-working family, as most were, with Thatcherite leanings, like the Moores and Gooches, but they were decent people who lived modestly and troubled nobody. However, let us leave south Essex people to their oil refineries, cockle sheds and Lakeside Shopping Centre and drive out from Walthamstow through Theydon Bois, Abridge and Ongar up to Brentwood in the heart of the county. We could have stopped at the ECB focus club Loughton CC, established in 1879, with their 75-year-old thatched pavilion, square with 18 pitches and 30-strong coaching staff, who field five Saturday and three Sunday sides, but Loughton is only a few miles from London and I was keen to get out further into rural Essex.

As we journey into the heart of Essex we might linger for a while in suburban Chigwell, former home of Bobby Moore and spiritual home of dozens of aspirational East Londoners, and turn into the Paddock Ground of the intriguingly named Fives & Heronians CC. The club run four Saturday and two Sunday sides and have a full indoor winter programme, plus the usual colts section. In 1999 the then chairman of the club served for 12 months as president of the Club Cricket Conference, such is the high regard in which the club are held in club cricket circles. It is worth noting that Loughton, Chigwell and Fives & Heronians are no more than a few miles apart - what a crucible of cricket.

Moving on into deepest Essex we arrive at the town of

Brentwood and its delightful cricket ground, just off the Shenfield Road. The Old County Ground, home of Brentwood CC, is situated at the eastern end of Brentwood High Street, only ten minutes' drive away from Junction 28 of the M25. It is within one mile of both Shenfield and Brentwood railway stations and only a 23-minute rail ride from London's Liverpool Street Station. Brentwood High Street has an array of lively pubs and restaurants and enjoys a reputation for being especially animated on Friday and Saturday nights. The cricket ground is at the end of High Street and has a delightful approach through a tree-lined avenue. It is difficult to do justice to the attractiveness of the Old County Ground. It was featured in the 1969 *Wisden*:

> *... of all the Essex grounds, the tree surrounded acres of Brentwood are the most beautiful. ... to play at Brentwood is to feel that one is playing in the grounds of some vast country mansion - which is virtually true.*
> *- N. Preston (ed.) (1969), Wisden Cricketers' Almanack 1969, Sporting Handbooks Ltd.*

Stephen Chalke describes Brentwood as the prettiest of Essex's venues:

> *There are trees on three sides of the ground, and by late June there are splashes of red among the various greens of the oaks, elms and planes. The ground belongs to Merrymeade, the adjoining stately home, and in a semi-circular enclosure an the old lady sits under a parasol, watching the play ... the old wooden pavilion is painted white, and it is so tiny that it contains just one hand basin for washing down after the game.*
> *- S. Chalke (1997), Runs in the Memory: County Cricket in the 1950s, Fairfield Books, p.25*

Things have barely changed at the old ground since Chalke wrote in 1997 and he paints an accurate picture of the place. Doug Insole remembers the ground from his playing days. He wrote in his typical blunt and honest style, in the context of class distinctions in county cricket:

> *If you ever went to Brentwood, the pavilion's about ten by eight so*

everybody chucked everything into the same room, about three blokes could change at a time. There was no question of any distinction, you all mucked in and that was that.
- Insole has written a short history of Chingford CC, which can be found on the club's website, www.chingfordcc.hitscricket.com

Insole was writing about the gentlemen and players division prevalent in cricket in his time, pointing out that class distinctions were "much less prevalent in Essex than elsewhere". It was probably easier to maintain a separation between gentlemen and players at Lord's than it was at Southend or Brentwood, not that Essex players would have put up with such snobbery for very long.

Sport has been played at the Old County Ground for well over 100 years and the *Official History* provides evidence of cricket being played by a team from Brentwood as far back as the eighteenth century:

... there were encounters ... between men, proud of their parish. Kelvedon met Witham, and in 1772, Ingatestone and Stock played each other three times. Ingatestone also played elevens from Brentwood, Navestock, Herongate, and Mountnessing ...
- Lemmon and Marshall (1987), p.15

This is a real indication of the sheer amount of cricket played around this time. Lemmon and Marshall also establish that cricket was played at Brentwood as far back as the eighteenth century:

Epping followed their sensational win over Ware (1768) by playing Brentwood at the Green Man on Navestock Common.

It is likely that the Brentwood team in 1768 was actually Navestock CC, created in that same year. Navestock is just outside Brentwood on the Ongar Road, a couple of miles from the Old County Ground, and the Green Man pub still stands proudly by the roadside. Navestock CC continue to occupy the common they have played on for an astonishing 370 years. The area of Essex around Brentwood must be one of the most cricket-mad places in the country. Within a short distance of the town there are cricket clubs with their own grounds at South Weald, whose Sandpit Lane ground lies in an enormous country park, Stock, Herongate, Ingatestone and, of course, Navestock itself. This is genuine village cricket but is well organised, with the clubs all entering sides in the Mid-Essex League. Stock CC, for example, field four sides, including one in the Premier League, and they have a thriving colts section. Also nearby are the Essex League clubs Shenfield and Ongar.

Back at Brentwood, in 1881 the county agreed that their headquarters should be at the newly formed Brentwood Cricket Club. The ground began to be used for tennis and hockey at the end of the nineteenth century, when the Brentwood Tennis Club and the Brentwood Hockey Club were formed. Like many similar grounds that had multiple use, an umbrella group was established to represent all interested parties.

Just over 90 years ago a leading executive of the Canadian National railway, Mr Robert Montgomery Horne-Payne, brought his bride to Brentwood and purchased 80 acres of land that included the Old County Ground, alongside which he built Merrymeade, a magnificent country house and now an old people's home. Mr and Mrs Horne-Payne were enthusiastic supporters of the club and used to watch matches under the shade of a great oak tree, which was once part of the playing area, in the same way as their more famous counterpart at Kent's County Ground at Canterbury.

The Old County Ground Club were formed in 1955 when the hockey, rugby, cricket and tennis clubs agreed to amalgamate while still retaining their separate identities – a compromise guaranteed to cause friction and conflict between the constituent groups. Since the mid-1950s there has been substantial investment in the ground, which, incidentally, provided the occasion for Graham Gooch's maiden century as a boy and was where the great Ray Smith made an unpromising Essex debut in 1934, with figures of 1 for 115. The Old County Ground can be rightly regarded as one of the finest sporting arenas in Essex, offering a range of sporting, social and other facilities to the people of Brentwood. Doug Insole would be delighted that the clubs have managed to retain the aesthetic appeal of the ground while modernising its facilities and also improving the quality of the square, a feat that has proved beyond many clubs in a similar position. Brentwood claims to be a true community club with a long-standing and successful commitment to youth development.

The club has existed in their present form since 1962 when

the rugby club departed to find a ground of their own. The Old County Ground Club, the umbrella body, bear most of the cost of the care and maintenance of the complex, including rent, utility bills and other expenses associated with running a thriving sports club. Of course, costs have increased considerably over the years and the club has gone from being a net contributor to individual club finances to relying on the individual clubs for any financial shortfall. But, like Walthamstow, the purchase of the Old County Ground has been completed, thereby securing the future of sport on this most desirable piece of real estate. The purchase of the ground will mean that the club will not have to pay rent, but there are considerable loans to repay and there will need to be extensive revenue-raising if the club are to continue to meets their obligations. However, they firmly believe that this is a small price to pay to secure the future of one of the most beautiful cricket grounds in Essex, or anywhere else.

Brentwood CC have a rich history, involving some great cricketers, wonderful characters and truly historic matches.

Outstanding matches at the Old County Ground

1. Essex v. Lancashire, 21st-24th June 1952

Dickie Dodds, the aggressive Essex opening batsman, played for the county between 1946 and 1959. He was a singular man, the son of a country vicar, and he donated all the proceeds of his benefit match in 1957 to his adopted cause, Moral Re-Armament. Dodds remembers a tied match against Lancashire at Brentwood in June 1952. Dodds was another who described the Brentwood ground as the loveliest of Essex's many cricketing venues. The groundsman at this time was Bill Hansell, whose preparations for a day's play were a little different from the scientific planning of today's highly trained grounds technicians, as Stephen Chalke describes:

> *Gone are the days when he uses his horse to pull the roller, but he still sprinkles wet cow dung over the wickets and rolls it till it dries like concrete under the sun … it is a batting paradise. In 1934 … Kent scored 803 for four. "What do you remember of that day, Bill?" … "The smell", he says. It is not a ground for a bowler to lick his lips.*
> *- Chalke (1997), p.27*

Lancashire batted first in the match and were bowled out for 266, with five wickets each for Ken Preston and Ray Smith. Essex replied in their first innings with a modest but competitive 261 against the pace bowling of Brian Statham and Roy Tattersall. Lancashire then declared their second innings on 226 for 7, setting Essex a sporting 232 runs to win. On the final day, with three balls remaining and nine wickets down, Essex needed just one run to win. Trevor Bailey, completely out of character and for reasons best known to himself, attempted a six off Malcolm Hilton to win the game and was duly caught out in the deep by the opposition captain Nigel Howard for a bold but insufficient 52 and the match was tied. The cricket reporter on the Brentwood Gazette wrote in astonishment of the shot:

> *... over 200 sun-drenched cricket lovers let loose a yell that was thrown skywards and must have reverberated through the county. They were all of one opinion that Trevor Bailey had made the winning hit.*
> *- Quoted in Chalke (1997). P.35*

"I don't know why he did it," Dickie Dodds said. "I'd never seen him hit a straight six before ...." Stephen Chalke claims that for once in his life Trevor was speechless. Bailey claims he had lost count of the score, an unlikely story for this most organised of cricketers. How could Trevor Bailey lose his head and throw away certain victory against a strong Lancashire side? The old Barnacle certainly learned his lesson on the hot sunny day on 24th June 1952.

2. Essex v. Worcestershire, 12th-14th May 1965
In a quirk of the fixtures list that season, Essex and Worcestershire had just played each other up at New Road. For the return fixture the teams made their way slowly down to Brentwood, where they were greeted by lovely sunny weather that lasted for all three days of the match. Robin Hobbs, the Essex and England leg-spinner, loved playing at Brentwood, describing it as "a lovely place to play ... so peaceful". Essex batted first and made 302 all out, with major contributions from skipper Trevor Bailey (74) and another Westcliff man, John Wilcox (87). Worcestershire were bowled out for 135, with Hobbs taking 5 for 46 off 25 overs. As is normal practice in

trying to arrange a run chase, Essex declared their second innings on 170 for 6, with another England man, all-rounder Barry Knight, scoring 53 not out and a youthful Keith Fletcher, batting at No. 3, contributing a useful 40. Worcestershire were set an improbable 338, and when the 41-year-old Trevor Bailey led his team out for the Worcestershire second innings Hobbs must have been licking his lips at the prospect of a long bowl on a pitch taking an increasing amount of spin. But Basil 'Dolly' D'Oliveira had other ideas and proceeded to play one of his very best innings. However, even the great Dolly could not deny Essex their deserved victory over the County Champions. He was eventually out LBW to Barry Knight for 169 out of his side's total of 289. Paddy Phelan, with his accurate off-spin, had the excellent figures of 7 for 80 from 35 overs and Essex won by 48 runs in the last half-hour of the third day. Robin Hobbs recalls:

As a game of cricket it had the lot. Dare I say it ... reasonable leg break bowling, fine swing bowling by Len Coldwell ... a magnificent innings by D'Oliveira. The sun shone ... A very good county match. It's always stood in the memory.
- Quoted in Chalke (1999), p110

The match was three-day county cricket at its very best.

Brentwood CC have had a long association with Essex CCC, and in addition to hosting county cricket regularly over the past 100 years they have secured the services of several England players, including Nick Knight and Gavin Hamilton. But perhaps the most distinguished of Brentwood's international players was Charles Kortright (1871-1952), who played for the club, Essex and England at the end of the nineteenth century. He was the fastest bowler of his day and arguably the fastest bowler of all time, as this comment from Sir Stanley Jackson confirms,

Kortright was generally regarded as the fastest bowler of his timein this country.
- D. Lemon and M. Marshall (1987) Essex County Cricket Club: The Official History, Kingswood Press, p.105-06

There are a number of cricket myths associated with Kortright. For example, he is reported to have bowled a ball that pitched on the wicket and, such was its ferocity, soared over the wicketkeeper's head and over the boundary before bouncing a second time. Kortright boasted that it was the first ever six in byes. He was also a hard-hitting batsman who was never selected to play in a Test match but played regularly for the Gentlemen against the Players, often in the same side as W.G. Grace. Even the incomparable W.G. Grace struggled against him, as this extract from a conversation between the two great players during a match between Essex and Gloucester in 1905 suggests:

The best WG Grace sledge was on him, though, not from him. Charles Kortright had dismissed him four or five times in a county game - only for the umpires to keep turning down his appeals. Finally, he uprooted two of Grace's three stumps. Grace stalled, as though waiting for a no-ball call or something, before reluctantly walking off with Kortright's words in his ears: "Surely you're not going, doctor? There's still one stump standing".
- Lemon and Marshall (1987), p.104

Kortright played for Essex between 1889 and 1907, taking 489 wickets for the county. Although he played for England, John Arlott, a good friend of Essex, included Kortright in his best 'never to have played for England' team. The great fast bowler spent his retirement playing golf at Thorndon Park Golf Club and was made a vice president of the county club. He must have been some character and Brentwood must be proud to include him as one of their ex-players. He was born just up the road in Ingatestone and once said, "I am proud to say I have never done a day's work in my life."

In more modern times Nick Knight played for Brentwood from 1990 to 1994 until he signed as a full-time young professional for the county. But at Essex he found himself competing for a place in the side with Nasser Hussain, Darren Robinson and others, and the club reluctantly agreed to release him after they had received an approach from Warwickshire. It was a good decision for Knight, who was quickly selected to play for England, becoming something of an international one-day specialist.

At home in the umpires' hut

The Essex Cricket League has over 300 registered overseas players spread across its 40 member clubs. The practice of engaging overseas players in club cricket has a long tradition in England, and most clubs in county Leagues register at least one each season. Overseas players are attracted to English club cricket for the opportunity to spend time in the country and to play serious cricket every week for five months of the year. Overseas players arrive from Australia, New Zealand, India, Pakistan, South Africa and the Caribbean and are usually expected to contribute both runs and wickets in every game. If the player is keen enough he will be asked to take coaching sessions and work with the club's colts section. Often a member of the committee will host the player for the duration of their stay, although there is one amusing story I heard about one overseas player in Essex who, failing to find a place to stay, lived in the umpires' room in the club's pavilion for the whole season, with rather chaotic consequences on match days.

Brentwood has engaged an overseas player most seasons since 1984. Sri Lankan Kasun Bodhisha, the club's 2009 recruit, true to tradition, arrived late in the country owing to visa problems. When he finally arrived in Brentwood he made an excellent start, scoring 66 not out and 123 not out in his first two innings. Boosted by Bodhisha's performances, the First XI won six of their first seven games and soon found themselves at the top of the Premier League. In a wonderful season for the club they went on to become Essex Premier League Champions for the first time in their history. Clearly Brentwood chose their overseas player wisely in 2009.

But perhaps the most successful of the long line of Brentwood's overseas players was the Indian batsman, Hrishikesh Kanitkar. Rishi, as he quickly became known, played 34 one-day internationals for India and two Test matches in Australia, and his arrival was greatly anticipated. The club was not disappointed. Rishi scored 1,066 League runs at an average of 76, hitting six 100s and helping to secure the club's promotion to the Essex League in 2005.

A thoroughly modern cricket club

Due to the deterioration of the Old County pitch and the redevelopment of their Chelmsford ground, Essex abandoned the Brentwood Festival in 1969, allowing the local club to develop their considerable potential. The club currently have approximately 100 senior members and a further 100 juniors at every age group from Under-11s to Under-17s. They run six Saturday sides, all in the Essex League, and one Sunday side. The old ground has undergone some changes: the old pavilion, fondly remembered by Trevor Bailey, was replaced in the 1980s by a brick-built version with showers, a kitchen and bar; and, sadly, the stately old trees on one side of the ground were blown away in 1987. Third team matches are played on the Brentwood School ground adjacent to the Old County Ground, reached through a gap in the fence. The cricket club have enjoyed a good relationship with the school for many years, and the latter has produced generations of well-coached youngsters for the club, some progressing to play for the county. Brentwood School is one of a number of minor public schools in this part of the county. The school has a modern approach and works hard to integrate with the local community, recently opening a wonderfully equipped sports centre, fully open to people from the town. With the high-performing Brentwood County High School as the state secondary in the town, Brentwood schools are among the best in the county. There is no question that the cricket club will benefit from having such schools to provide their future players. This is not the case back in Walthamstow, where there are no public schools and the state schools struggle to cope with a multitude of social and cultural problems. It is a small miracle that the borough's cricket club not only survives but also prospers.

In recognition of their achievements, Brentwood CC have been selected by the ECB as one of its Focus Clubs for the county of Essex. The ECB invited the first-class counties to apply for Focus Club status by submitting details of clubs in their county that they believed were torch-bearers for the cricket of the future - especially in terms of youth development. The 38 County Boards underwent an intensive two-year planning process to identify 1,453 Focus Clubs nationwide. Essex, through the Essex Board, chose Brentwood as one of their Focus Clubs. To be selected as a Focus Club Brentwood were required to produce a clear strategic plan for their future that was committed to a long-term youth development policy. One has the feeling, speaking to members around the club, that the youth development plan is not just something the club have put together to generate funds, but something to which they are committed, Focus Club or not. On Friday evenings you will see over 100 youngsters being put through their paces by club coaches. Like all these awards, Focus Club status has brought with it a heavier administrative workload, but I am sure the members will rise to the challenge.

A local hero

Most clubs have their unsung heroes who soldier on year after year, working quietly to keep clubs functioning, either by doing committee work, working on the ground, coaching or looking after the fixtures. One such hero at Brentwood is Ken Hobbs, who joined the club in 1969 at the age of 15. In his 41 years at the club, in addition to captaining the sixth team, which comprises a healthy mix of veterans and promising young colts, Ken helps with the coaching of 200 or so youngsters who attend the Fridays night colts sessions and, like others, does anything else required at the club.

What makes Ken's contribution to sport in the town so heroic is that he is also the fixtures secretary, webmaster and general helper at Brentwood Town FC, where he has been involved since 1978. Sports clubs need characters like Ken Hobbs and the thousands of unsung volunteer heroes in cricket clubs up and down the country, who give their time and effort for no other reason than a love for their game – they simply wouldn't know how else to live. I have an abiding memory of a colleague at a football club I was involved with. He could be seen every Saturday at the ground from about 9.00 a.m. for the afternoon kick-off. An hour before the game, there he was carrying two goal nets over one shoulder and a huge bag of footballs over the other. The pitch had a steep slope on one side, and during play our ageing hero, when he wasn't running the line, would sprint up and down the bank, fetching the ball from a tangle of bracken and brambles. In the after-match gloom, he would take down the nets and collect the corner flags and practice balls and carry them back to the changing rooms, where he would take his turn serving behind the bar and entertain and pay the officials, before going home to write up the programme notes for the next match. Clubs would die a slow death without these clubmen who are the real heroes of local sport from the chairman down.

Brentwood Cricket Club are in good hands with people like Ken and his colleagues and they appear to have a very bright future with a wonderful ground and a plentiful supply of local cricketers. The 2009 Essex Premier League Champions have much to be proud of.

Cricket teas and tea ladies

In this look at the different levels of club cricket in East London and Essex, its heroes and villains, and its rich history, it would be rude not to include some reference to what some consider the glory of our 'summer game': cricket teas. Club cricket would be poorer without the mid-afternoon teas, usually provided by cheery female volunteers, or teenage girls who need a little weekend pocket money. The subject of cricket teas deserves a book of its own, and probably does have one. Stories about them abound. But one thing is for sure: cricket teas as we knew them are changing, or have already changed, literally beyond recognition - yet another example of the ever-changing nature of the game. In Peter Tinniswood's *Tales from a Long Room*, the lead character talks whimsically about "angels on horseback, gentleman's relish, and the tea-urn dipstick," and we laugh (P. Tinniswood (1981), Tales from a Long Room, Arrow Books). But the state of the English cricket tea is a matter deserving of serious consideration.

Or it should be, but seemingly not for Bures CC just over the Essex border into Suffolk, a club that we have already encountered in a different context. The club have introduced a tea ladies Roll of Honour, a light-hearted look at the ladies who have fed the hearty rural appetites of club members over the years. They appear at first sight a formidable bunch. There is Kate 'the Dark Lady' Mitchell, sometime director of the Colchester Arts Centre, who made her much-awaited tea debut the season before last. Her colleague Ros allegedly makes the most stupendous homemade cakes, which "defy imperial measurement" according to the club and are only served when the other side field after tea, presumably to slow them down. Susie's sublime culinary skills are a treat and her sandwiches are of cordon bleu standard, claim the club. Susie is aided by her husband, honest Bob, who runs an illegal bar from the back of his van during home matches. Bures even boast a tea lady in possession of a university degree, who inevitably has a low tolerance of the annoying habits of the more agricultural club members, including her dad, Jim. Despite this gentle ribbing, the club clearly hold their tea ladies in the greatest esteem.

One club in Essex, which must remain nameless, have produced a 'top tips' list for players who, in a dire emergency, may have to make their own teas. Helpful hints include these on how to make egg sandwiches:

> *Who but a tea lady would know that you should buy Scotch eggs at the local supermarket, scrape off the sausage meat and slice up the ready-cooked egg, before placing between two slices of bread. Genius!*

Other helpful suggestions include slicing tomatoes before inserting them into a sandwich, otherwise they will never fit, and remembering that cakes should always be eaten *after* sandwiches. Some items on the list are more obvious. Even men know that tuna sandwiches should be kept out in the sun for three hours before serving. This light-hearted look at the activities of tea ladies is mildly disrespectful, but I am sure that no offence was taken.

One of the worst teas I have been served was at a rugby club whose pavilion the cricketers used at teatime. Everything was clearly bought at the nearby Spa grocers and consisted of limp pizza slices, damp crisps, freezing cold chicken thighs and, to add insult to possible injury, jaffa cakes - and all at £3.00 a head. Fortunately, most of it was consumed by the rugby players before their match. Apparently they thought it was the best thing they had ever eaten. On the other hand, the best tea I have ever eaten was at Yelverton CC in Devon, where the smoked salmon sandwiches and banoffee pie were simply beyond words. It helped that it was a sit-down tea, served by the ladies themselves – bliss.

Among the oddest cricket teas I can remember was one served at a Sunday game at Wadham Lodge in Chingford. We were sensibly advised by the opposition to take all valuables and playing gear out to the pitch, a good five minutes' walk away from the changing rooms. We batted first in that game and some of the lads spotted some kids climbing out of the skylight in the pavilion roof and shinning down the drainpipe to make their escape. We weren't too concerned as we had our valuables with us, but the opposing captain decided to check just the same, only to discover that they had actually stolen all the food for the teas, meaning that both sets of players had to drive down to the local petrol station for frozen sandwiches and stale crisps.

Among Essex clubs, Hornchurch's teas are legendary. The club, one time spiritual home of Essex cricket, provide such huge teas that supporters and passers-by are invited in for the leftovers, with a queue often forming around 4.00 p.m. on Saturday afternoons. Hot lasagna, curry and chips are all on the extensive menu, but, best of all, there is usually roast beef and all the trimmings for the umpires and scorers. Upminster teas are up there with best, especially on all-day matches when a full roast is often served – all for £35 per team. An honourable mention should go to Buckhurst Hill and Wickford, but we should not be too critical of any club in Essex, since that may incur a visit from celebrity chef Jamie Oliver, whose parents own the Cricketers pub at Clavering.

A summing up

This has been a necessarily brief study of pub and club cricket in the area of East London and Essex. It is particularly encouraging to discover that cricket is alive and well in the inner city, and that cricket there has evolved successfully with the changing times. Clubs in Hackney and Newham have adapted to the loss of grass pitches and traditional cricket grounds by introducing a lively new version of the game played on artificial wickets and bumpy outfields. But make no mistake - this is serious cricket played to a respectable standard.

The social composition of the game in the East End and metropolitan Essex has changed to reflect the vibrant multi-ethnic life of the area. The new urban cricket is almost always League-based and operates under the guidance of the Essex Cricket Board. It should not be dismissed as a trivial form of the game, because it is very likely that clubs such as Cosmopolitan CC will one day produce a steady stream of players for the county side – and, who knows, perhaps another Graham Gooch.

Out in Essex the more traditional form of the game is flourishing. We have seen how clubs like Walthamstow and Brentwood have responded positively to the new Essex League structure. Most Essex clubs have thriving youth sections, women's and girls' cricket, and, particularly in more affluent parts of the county, effective links with local schools. Unfortunately, clubs in urban locations like Walthamstow do not have cricket-loving grammar and public schools in their area, and are therefore not provided with a regular supply of experienced young players brought up on good grass wickets, as happens, for example, in Brentwood. In this sense cricket still retains much of its old class patterns and allegiances.

There exists a network of local and county Leagues right across the area, providing playing opportunities at every level, including cricket for boys and girls, men and women, over-50s, and people with disabilities, a cause dear to Graham Gooch's heart. At all levels, from street cricket in Newham to the glory of the County Ground at Chelmsford, cricket in this sports-mad area appears in great shape, the only serious downside being that the schools in East London and metropolitan Essex seem to have given up on the game altogether, perhaps in the interests of more pressing priorities.

CHAPTER 9
GOOD OLD GOOCHIE!
A TRULY GREAT CRICKETER

It is very difficult to imagine Essex CCC without Graham Gooch's looming presence. I was fortunate to interview Gooch in June 2009 on a glorious day at Fenner's, where Essex were playing Cambridge University. He had spent the morning in the nets with the young Essex batsman Varun Chopra, and in his shorts and training top he seemed entirely relaxed and comfortable in his surroundings. He was generous with his time and seemed pleased to have the opportunity to discuss his ideas on English cricket and some thoughts on his beloved Essex. He mused a little about his development as a young cricketer in East London and talked about the people who influenced him most in his early years. We discussed different ideas about coaching and the importance of the qualities of attitude and desire in today's young players. I was keen to ask Gooch about the way he had approached his retirement from international cricket, which seems to be in sharp contrast to his boyhood hero, Bobby Moore.

While we were talking a spectator interrupted the interview and asked Gooch to sign one of those tiny bats that youngsters use these days to collect their autographs. The man explained that he was raising money for a local charity and needed to fill his bat with famous names. As Gooch was signing the bat he asked the gentleman about his charity, where he was from and what he did for a living. He then returned to our conversation, ignoring repeated calls on his mobile phone. After an hour or so he ambled off towards the pavilion to rejoin the Essex players. Later that afternoon Gooch and a sprightly looking Keith Fletcher, now 65 years old, sat together on the boundary's edge watching the play, and I can only imagine the conversation that took place between these two lifelong friends and great Essex cricket legends.

Gooch only met Bobby Moore once, when the great footballer

turned out for Southend United in a game against Essex cricketers arranged for Gooch's benefit in 1985. There is something quite poetic in the two greatest sportsmen that East London has produced meeting, not in Rio, Sydney, Mumbai or New York, but down on the Thames Estuary at dear old Southend, home of that other great Essex legend, Trevor Bailey. Gooch said that he watched in awe on that evening as Moore strolled around at the back during the game, before giving way gracefully at half-time. Of course, Moore and Gooch shared much more than a benefit game at Southend. They were born and brought up within a few miles of each other, and both sets of parents lived through the war in Blitz-torn East London. Gooch's father, Alf, was the son of a merchant sailor from Plaistow, down the road from Upton Park. His wife, Rose, was from Leyton and a family of East End publicans. An old football injury kept Alf Gooch away from the action, but the couple experienced at first hand the horrors of the Nazi bombs on their neighbourhood. On 2nd Match 1945, close to the end of the war, a V2 rocket fell on Grove Road in Leyton, killing eight people and injuring scores of others. The Moore and Gooch families both struggled through the same hard times, but always with a spirit that typified the East End resistance to the Nazi bombardment. Graham's mother, Rose, explains:

> *... it was no good staying in all the time, or living down the bomb shelters ... you had to get out, had to have a little fun ... Alf and I went dancing all the time, or the pictures ... plus diving under tables, or ducking into doorways when the siren went. It was no good staying at home and letting it get you down, was it?*
> *- G. Gooch and F. Keating (1995), Gooch: My Autobiography, HarperCollinsWillow, p.16*

It is interesting that dancing seemed to unite the Moore and Gooch families. Tina, Moore's first wife, wrote about how her mother's family were great dancers, while Gooch's parents met at a dance in the Leyton Town Hall. Even dear old Keith Fletcher took to ballroom dancing as a young man, difficult though that might be to imagine.

Although born a few miles apart in that very ordinary strip of London where the East End meets the Essex border, Moore and Gooch were from different generations. The more outgoing of the two, Moore was a Conservative with a small 'c', while Gooch was a more vocal Tory supporter and very much a child of the 1980s. Both were astoundingly successful and eventually moved out to affluent Essex towns away from their roots in the booming and rapidly changing East End, with its huge mass of social and economic contradictions and cultural differences. Both scaled the heights of their different sports and became the best in the world. But neither of these two household names in world sport neglected their roots or lost affection for their 'manor', as East Enders ironically describe their neighbourhood. Moore and Gooch were extraordinarily similar in that respect. They were clearly proud of their upbringing and maintained a close bond with their families and friends from the area. They were both 'grafters', to use an old East End expression, and never forgot the values that their parents taught them.

Sadly, both Moore and Gooch's first marriages ended in separation, which must have been very difficult for these two family-oriented East Londoners. Moore stayed close to his two children and Gooch clearly adores his three daughters. The lives of great sporting figures are under intense media scrutiny these days, and long periods spent away from home can destabilise the steadiest relationships. In addition, both men married local girls at an early stage in their career, before they became household sporting names. Few marriages could survive the dramatic changes that overwhelmed both couples.

If Moore's mother was the dominant figure in his youth, Gooch's father Alf, a local carpenter, provided the support, encouragement and advice that were to prove so crucial to the young batsman's development. The Gooch family became the cricket family par excellence. He described how summer weekends were nothing but cricket, for the whole family - mum, dad and sister, Brenda. They simply knew no other life than sport.

Like many families in the area, the Gooches were keen to move up the housing ladder. They left James Lane for Mills Court, one of three low-rise council blocks near Harrow Green, and then to the house in Montague Road where Graham at last had his own room. It was in Montague Road, a 30-minute walk to Essex's original county ground, where the young Gooch began his education in cricket. In those days local people would not have seen Leyton as a deprived area but rather as a typical close-knit working-class East London community. Up until the early 1970s Leyton had some lovely old houses, leafy parks, friendly pubs and a few decent schools. Gooch's first school, Cann Hall Primary, not only had teachers willing to take cricket teams but also had a grass pitch - unimaginable today, on which they played matches against other local primary school teams. At his secondary school, Norlington High, which he attended in the mid-1960s, teachers would set up nets in the playground using an intricate system of poles and ropes, and the young Gooch and his mates would practise with composite balls on a tarmac surface. Further practice sessions would be held a short distance away at Ive Farm, and Mr Price, one of a growing group of Welsh teachers in London schools, would take them for matches on Draper's Field, where the local authority prepared grass wickets. He enjoyed batting practice in his schooldays, which held him in good stead for later in his career, and he had plenty of playing opportunities both for his school and the Waltham Forest District side. The playing fields that Gooch enjoyed as a young boy still exist, but the grass wickets have been replaced by a few sub-standard plastic strips, heavily scarred by tyre marks burned into their surface by local boy racers.

The greatest influence on Gooch's career was his dad, Alf. His father taught him 'the right way to play' and introduced him to East Ham Corinthians. The club played out at the Old Blues ground at Fairlop, a breeding ground for Essex cricketers. Gooch remembers as a youngster driving along the A12 every Sunday to play on Windy Ridge, the furthest of the Fairlop pitches and next to that of the East Saxons, who played to a higher standard and therefore got the better pitch. Gooch talks fondly about one of the great highlights of the Corinthians season: the annual away fixture against Clacton CC at their Recreational Ground, one of Essex's early Festival grounds. The players and their families would meet on a September Sunday morning at the corner of Catherine Street, close to Upton Park, for the long coach trip to the Essex coast. Gooch remembers the Clacton match as the biggest of the season and it was a very long way from home for a young 11-year-old. Of course, the cricket-mad youngster was not expecting to bat any higher than 10 or 11 in the order, but he loved the whole experience.

Apart from tips from his teachers and advice from his dad and the senior players at the Corinthians, Gooch did not have any formal coaching until he was 13 or 14 when he enrolled on a coaching course at the Ilford Cricket School around 1966/67. Gooch would have come to the attention of the senior clubs in the area with his performances for his school and district side, so it is likely that he was either invited to Ilford or taken there by his dad. His senior coach at the Cricket School was Bill Morris, who was assisted by young Essex players such as John Lever, who helped out at the School to supplement their Essex wages. The School was owned by Harold Faragher and Trevor Bailey and run day-to-day by Morris, a tough old West Indian who had played first-class cricket for Essex. Gooch received 20-minute lessons from Morris and slowly began to impress his coaches and people on the county circuit. At the age of 16 Graham was ready to play A grade club cricket and agreed to join Walthamstow, only to be 'poached' at the last minute by Ilford, who in those days were very influential at county level. The Essex players had winter nets at the Ilford Indoor School, and by now Graham had become part of the Essex system - Bill Morris could be very persuasive.

In the mid- to late sixties the Essex captain Brain Taylor was coming to the end of his career, and the county were keen to turn the young Gooch into a wicketkeeper batsman with a view to his replacing Taylor in the Essex First XI. By this time he was playing regularly for the Ilford Thirds, and at the age of 16 he made his debut for Essex Seconds at Northampton. The following year he played the whole season for the Essex Seconds, often with Bill Morris batting at the other end. He describes this time as "educationally the best experience I have had". It was in this crucible of club cricket that Gooch acquired the technique, skills and work ethic that would serve him so well later in his career.

Although cricket appeared to dominate Gooch's boyhood, he loved his football and the family were devout Hammers supporters. Winter Saturdays were spent on the South Bank at Upton Park with his dad and his Uncle George. By his own admission he was "a decent player, who probably wasn't quick enough to play at a high level". His dad played for Oxford City, but young Graham did play school district football, had a season with Redbridge College, and played a while for Mayfield Youth

Centre at Fairlop, a ground with which he was becoming very familiar.

In conversation with Gooch that day in Cambridge, what hit me most strongly was how ordinary his achievements and his elevated position in English sport seemed to him. It was just what he did. The clue to this is probably to be found in the engineering apprenticeship he took at Redbridge College, at the suggestion of his father. Today Gooch accepts that persuading him to go to college rather than straight into professional sport was showing typical good sense. The experience made him realise later how fortunate he was to be a professional cricketer. He expressed it this way:

> *I had been involved in a proper routine job, and this made me realise what playing sport professionally is really about. It was a reality check which young players today, who come into the game straight from school, never have.*

A positive family environment provided the right kind of support to Moore and Gooch, but there is a real sense in which their own personal qualities drove them to success. They were proud, well-mannered and intelligent men. Both were blessed with a good sense of humour and were fond of a joke, although Moore probably was more 'one of the boys' than Gooch. If Bobby Moore enjoyed the company of the rich and famous, one gets the feeling that Gooch was happiest with his own kind, having a quiet pint down the pub, or at home with his family. Both were hugely determined to reach the very top of their respective sports and trained extremely hard, listening carefully to their coaches and the older players. Moore had Noel Cantwell, Allison, Ron Greenwood and Alf Ramsey, whereas Gooch had his dad, Bill Morris and Keith Fletcher, who was there at the beginning and the end of his career. The combined qualities of dedication, desire and the ability to listen and learn set them apart from their contemporaries and enabled the pair to fulfil their enormous potential. They were taught well and understood that football and cricket were team games. Douglas Kemp, Gooch's teacher at Cann Hall Primary School in Leyton, has fond memories of his schoolboy prodigy:

He was a grand lad on the playing field, and never once forgot that cricket and football were team games, not unlike another, older, lad I took when I was involved earlier in district school's sides – Bobby Moore from the Tom Hood School nearby.
- Gooch and Keating (1995). p.18

Cann Hall Primary School stands on the edge of Wanstead Flats, where both Moore and Gooch spent their evenings and weekends kicking a ball about with their mates, learning the values of teamwork and honing their skills for hours on end. For a time his teachers thought the young Gooch was more likely to become a footballer than a cricketer, but fortunately, thanks to the likes of Mr Kemp, cricket was still being played in junior schools in the area, enabling Gooch's real talents to come to the fore.

As Gooch pointed out that day in Cambridge his life in cricket is well documented. There is his autobiography, a detailed biography by Ivo Tennant, and Gooch's own account of the 'rebel tour' of South Africa in 1982, written when he was just 28 years old. He has also produced coaching manuals and was the subject of the film, *The Wilderness Years*, an investigation into the South African episode and his subsequent three-year ban from Test cricket. Rather than repeating what has previously been written about Gooch's career with Essex and England, I am keen to explore his status as a sporting hero of East London and Essex and to examine his role as a coach with a growing reputation for producing outstanding young cricketers. This study of Graham Gooch's contribution to English cricket will consider the way in which he has decided to use his retirement, which in many ways stands in stark contrast to the non-playing years of his boyhood sporting hero, Bobby Moore.

Having said that I am not intending to replicate what has already been written about Gooch, it is worth summarising his 25 years in first-class cricket just to remind ourselves of his outstanding achievements. The burly six-foot, right-hand batsman and occasionally seam bowler was known as Goochie or 'Zap' to his teammates and most Essex supporters, the latter because of his distinctive moustache, which seemed to grow darker and more menacing as he got older. Peter Tinniswood's characterisation of Gooch as the village blacksmith in his fictional cricketing village of Whitney Scrotum in *Tales from a*

Long Room seems to me pretty accurate: strong, working-class, obstinate and a bit of a rebel.

And the crowd at Lord's rose to their feet

Gooch's career with Essex and England spanned the years between 1973 and 1997, a long 'innings' by any standards. But, unlike Bobby Moore, Gooch's international career was dogged by controversy and incident. He made his England debut against Australia in 1975 and famously 'bagged' a pair. He played in England's next match and contributed 6 and 31, before being dropped from the side for the next three years. Resuming his England career in 1978, Gooch was subsequently banned from playing for England for three years, as a result of his participation in the 'rebel tour' of apartheid South Africa in 1982. Following the ban he resumed playing for his country. The second phase of his England career was nothing short of extraordinary. It appeared that he was determined to show the world just how good a cricketer he really was. For example, at Lord's in July 1990 he scored a record-breaking 456 runs against India with his famous 333 in the first innings. It is easy to forget that in that match Gooch scored 123 in the England second innings, which in itself would have satisfied many lesser batsmen. To this day no other batsman in the world has scored 300 and 100 in the two innings of the same match, and his combined match total of 456 remains a world record for runs scored in one match. His first innings of 333 was the highest scored at Lord's and the highest ever by an England captain. In addition to these astonishing achievements, in the 1990 season Gooch averaged over 100 runs for the first time in his career. Such an insatiable appetite for run-scoring reveals much about Gooch's attitude to playing cricket, his mental strength, and his sheer desire to be as good as he possibly could be. On looking at his England record one can only guess what it might have been had he not succumbed to the approaches of the shady South African apologists for apartheid.

The list of impressive statistics continues. Gooch played what has been described as the greatest innings of all time, when he scored 154 not out in an England total of 252 against an outstanding West Indies attack at Headingley in the summer of 1991, joining the elite group of Pelham Warner, Len Hutton and Geoffrey Boycott as the only openers to have carried their bats for England. The Headingley pitch was green and lively and the day damp and overcast. For Gooch to carry his bat on such an occasion, and against such an attack, led the IOC to confirm the extraordinary performance as the highest-ranked Test innings of all time. His Essex teammate, Derek Pringle, scored 74 during Gooch's innings, sharing in a stand of 98 for the seventh wicket with the England captain. When Gooch finally ran out of partners he had been batting for over seven hours, scoring 61.60 per cent of England's total of 252, an unlikely score when they were 38 for 3 earlier in the innings. Of Gooch's innings, John Woodcock of *The Times* wrote:

> *Since World War II no innings by an England captain has surpassed this ... it stands out not for artistic merit but for skill and courage against a very formidable attack in awkward conditions at a crucial time.*
> *- Quoted in Gooch and Keating (1995) p.279*

As a result of this astonishing innings, his runs against India at Lord's in 1990 and his record as England captain, Gooch was awarded the OBE later that year. In the years between 1990 and 1995 Gooch was rated one of the very best batsmen in world cricket. He scored runs against all types of bowling and on good and bad wickets. Following his three-year ban he seemed to make a conscious decision to change his approach to batting from the attacking style of his younger days. In the early 1990s Gooch became a more careful player and, as a result, a prodigious accumulator of runs. He remains England's leading scorer with a total of 8,900 runs, including 20 centuries. He did have one or two technical problems playing across his front pads against medium-paced in-swingers, memorably against the Australian Terry Alderman. Despite this one aberration his career blossomed, as if he was determined to ensure that his record did justice to his unquestionable talent. Before he retired from international cricket in 1995, at the age of 41, and as England's all-time record run-scorer, Gooch had played 118 Test matches, 34 as captain. No England captain has scored more centuries than Gooch, a true example of the 'leading by example' leadership style that characterised the England football captaincy of Bobby Moore. Gooch's biographer, Frank Keating, summed up his renaissance in his late 30s when all his supreme skills and total commitment seemed to come together, particularly against the West Indies' fierce pace attack:

To carry his bat was historic feat enough. To do so in fashioning , almost single-handedly, a victory was unique for an Englishman.
- Gooch and Keating (1995), p. 280

Gooch even earned the grudging respect of the chairman of the England selectors, Ted Dexter, who said at the time, in his typical understated style:

...a very special guy.
Tennant (1992), p.202

Dexter had actually doubted the possibility of Gooch joining the shortlist of the greatest players because of his tendency to play the ball too far forward and away from his body. However, Gooch had worked out his technical difficulties and, to his great credit, overcame them. So join them he did, in 1991 following the Headingley Test victory, when according to the Coopers-Deloitte ratings Graham Gooch became officially the best batsman in the world. In 15 Tests as England captain he had scored 2,004 runs at 74.22. The dark cloud that had hung over Gooch during his three-year ban from Test cricket had well and truly lifted and the Essex 'blacksmith', through his own determination and desire, acquired a self-confidence and assurance that was noticeable to all those close to him. An Essex and England colleague said at the time:

... he became happier. He smiles more now. It is acknowledged what a good player he is, and human nature is such that he responds, just as he became melancholy over his ban and press criticism for going to South Africa.
- Tennant (1992), p.194

For England, also read Essex, for whom he saved some of his greatest performances. Gooch was asked on BBC Test Match Special, following his retirement, for his thoughts on a young batsman who had scored a century in one of his first matches for his country. Gooch recognised the potential of the youngster and praised the performance, and then said something that revealed his own desire and ambition as a player: "It was a good knock and the boy shows promise, but needs to move to the next level and make big scores, not just baby hundreds." Baby hundreds are fine for some, but not for Graham Gooch and the very best batsmen in the world.

To complete this summary of Gooch's career it is worth noting that his record in international one-day cricket is equally outstanding. He captained England in the 1992 World Cup final and played in the finals of 1979 and 1987. Of course, many Essex supporters would claim that Gooch's best ever year was 1979, when he scored the first century in a one-day final for Essex against Surrey in the Benson & Hedges Cup final at Lord's. His 120 prepared the way for Essex to win their first trophy in 103 years. This was a very special innings and signalled the emergence of a great batsman, as the *Wisden Cricketers' Almanack* of 1980 recognised:

> *With a mixture of frightening power and controlled fury, he not so much dictated to the bowlers but destroyed them. Those who witnessed it will treasure the innings for a long time to come.*

The Essex supporters certainly treasured the innings. Gooch's one-day performances for Essex in his early career are still discussed by the members at Chelmsford and he rarely failed to deliver on the big occasion. Unlike today, Gooch could slip easily from county cricket, Test matches and one-day internationals, never allowing his performances to drop.

Oh yes, he bowled a bit as well. His seam-up swing bowling gained him 246 first-class wickets with career best figures of 7-14. In his early England days, at the end of a dead match, he would deliver hilarious bowling impersonations of the likes of Bob Willis and Geoff Thompson – just imagine that happening in today's pressure-cooker atmosphere of Test cricket.

We can see that Gooch's record compares with the very best players who have played Test cricket. He seemed to make big scores when lesser players were obsessed with the state of the pitch, and when his country needed it most. In the days before central contracts deprived the counties of their best players for weeks on end, he continued to score heavily for Essex in all forms of the game. For this, more than anything else, the Essex supporters took him into their hearts. Following his retirement in 1997, the statistician Robert Brooke calculated that Gooch had scored 21,087 runs in one-day cricket. If we add this to his total of 44,841 first-class runs, he passes Jack Hobbs to become the leading English run-scorer of all time, an argument confirmed by Christopher Martin-Jenkins in *Wisden* in 1997. C.L.R. James's description of W.G. Grace seems to apply equally to the batting of Graham Gooch, when he writes:

He used all the strokes ... aggressively or defensively. As he approached forty he confessed to preferring a good slow wicket to a good fast one. In his prime it did not matter to him.
- James (1963), p.176

Not bad for our 'working-class sporting hero' from Leytonstone.

Time for a change

Like W.G. Grace, Graham Gooch thought deeply about cricket and his own game. When he returned from his South African ban, Gooch convinced himself that his performances for England had not matched his huge talent and that in his early career he had underachieved. Between the years of his ban, 1982-85, he had missed a possible 31 Test matches, and he began to be concerned about his Test record. In 1979 he had already made some technical changes to his batting, having adopted the now famous raised-bat stance. His new side-on position was widely copied, but he only made the change because he accepted Doug Insole's comment that he had acquired a tendency to play round his front pad, leaving him vulnerable to LBW decisions. He made further technical changes as he sought to improve his game, and greatness was not to be denied him as he set about improving his career statistics with a vengeance. As Keith Fletcher commented at the time, it was as if Gooch had suddenly become aware that he had the potential to become a great batsman. His sense of pride drove him to become the great batsman he knew he could be. He explained:

I want to be proud of my performances when I retire, and an important part of that concerns an improvement in my Test record ... at the moment my Test record is no more than OK.
- Tennant (1992), p.119

What Essex supporters will never forget is that not only did the great man improve his Test record he also continued to score heavily for his county, leading them to success after success in his time as captain. As he set about achieving his goals, the cricket public gradually took to 'good old Goochie', and cricket writers and fellow professionals have been unstinting in their praise for the tremendous contribution he has made, and continues to make, to English cricket. Gooch's new place in the affections of the British public rests largely on his leadership style. He led from the front, scoring century after century in his successful years as captain of England. The much missed John Arlott, that masterly communicator of all that is best in cricket, included Gooch in his list of great batsmen, writing:

He comes from East London, plays for Essex and in accent, outlook, and humour, reflects his birthplace. He did not find Test life easy at first. Twice again he fought his way in, and fell back, but his determination took him through.
- J. Arlott (1986), John Arlott's 100 Greatest Batsmen, MacDonald.

It is not entirely clear what Arlott meant by the East London 'outlook', but I think we can assume that it was intended as a compliment. Later Arlott pays further tribute to Gooch's courage in facing up to his problems following the South African rebel tour. Gooch also features prominently in Christopher Martin-Jenkins's list of top 100 cricketers. The distinguished Test Match Special commentator writes perceptively of our hero:

Opening the batting suited him. Tall, broad and developing a stance that told quick bowlers he is ready for them, with his bat crocked at shoulder height as they approached and his head turned over his left shoulder to keep his eyes level, he became the best player of blinding speed in the world ...
- C. Martin-Jenkins (2009), The Top 100 Cricketers of All Time, Corinthian.

But. betraying his own class prejudices, Martin-Jenkins continues:

By unusual diligence, an intelligence not always evident from his 'estuary' English, and unyielding determination to make the most of himself by keeping himself fit with long early morning runs that remained his virtuous habit into middle-age, he became England's most professional batsman in a long career devoted to the game.
- Martin-Jenkins (2009), p.164-67

Equating intelligence with a cut-glass accent has long been a conceit of the English upper-middle class. But, in fairness to Martin-Jenkins, he is generous with his praise of the Essex man and continues:

... Gooch could apply himself to run-scoring in any match of any duration. He was the pillar round which Essex built years of unprecedented success ... his mountain of runs, in Test and one-day cricket, was eventually higher than any man before him had built.
- Martin-Jenkins (2009), p.164-67

Warming to his task, Martin-Jenkins describes what has come to be regarded as Gooch's finest hour, including his 456 at Lord's against India in 1990:

... his greatest Test innings – as assessed by a computer which took into account all circumstances – was his 154 not out in gloomy weather conditions on a tricky pitch at Headingley against Ambrose, Patrick Patterson, Walsh and Marshall in 1991.... By all criteria, whatever a computer may say, it was one of the most noblest innings ever played.
- Martin-Jenkins (2009) p.164-67

I guess that settles it. This is high praise indeed from Martin-Jenkins and final confirmation of the official acceptance of Gooch as a batsman of the highest rank in Test cricket. His batting in the late flowering of his career, from the late 1980s to his retirement in 1997, ensured his rightful place in the history of the game. It is worth noting that Gooch was 36 years old in the summer of 1989, an age when many professional cricketers are contemplating an easier life running a pub out on the Essex coast, but not Graham Gooch. His determined effort to improve made him a more watchful player and less aggressive than in the early part of his career when he appeared to treat bowlers with complete disdain. In what Ivo Tennant has described as his 'Second Coming', Gooch decided that he wanted to bat and bat, play the percentages and make his way into the record books. That he succeeded in the task he set himself says much about the character of this surprisingly complicated man, as we will discover in looking more closely at his South African connections.

In the great man's footsteps

Before discussing the undoubted shadow on Gooch's career, it is worth looking at the thoughts about our hero from one of his successors in the roles of both Essex and England captain. Nasser Hussain was born in Madras but is effectively an Essex lad. His cricketing credentials are much the same as his mentor: coached by Bill Morris at Ilford CC and captain of England Schools, England U19s and the England B team, before being made captain of the England senior team. However, although the antecedents are similar, there are differences. Hussain attended private school and Gooch went to his local comprehensive. Hussain graduated from Durham University, while Gooch took an apprenticeship at Redbridge Technical College. Gooch was at the centre of Essex's successful years, while Hussain largely missed out, captaining his county for just one season. Gooch scored heavily for his county and his country, while Hussain, with the introduction of central contracts, became an England player rather than an Essex one. Both men were passionate about their cricket and both achieved their highest ambitions. Hussain and Gooch had hugely supportive parents and inspirational fathers who were also passionate about cricket and keen to see their sons achieve their dreams.

If the two former England captains came out of the same Essex cricketing stable, emotionally they could hardly have been more different. Early in Gooch's career he was the quiet, brooding introvert whom Keith Fletcher swore never spoke a word in his first season at the club, and who travelled to Ilford for coaching sessions on his moped with his bat strapped to his back. The parka-wearing young 'mod' seemed in awe of his older teammates. Hussain never had those kinds of inhibitions. Supremely confident, the younger man was an emotional firebrand, given to shouting, screaming and throwing his bat across the dressing room. However, despite Hussain's highly volatile nature as opposed to his senior's calm and brooding one, they shared a strong work ethic and a hunger to be the very best.

As England captains both had to deal with strong-willed characters: Gooch with David Gower, Allan Lamb and Ian Botham; and Hussain with Darren Gough, Andrew Flintoff and Michael Vaughan. Both men were highly successful England captains and possessed good man-management skills and powers of motivation. If Gooch led by example, Hussain became the more intuitive skipper and a much more strategic thinker, benefiting from an effective working relationship with the England coach, Duncan Fletcher. Gooch pioneered the idea that mental strength was allied to physical fitness, and a major part of Gooch's legacy is that this is now taken for granted in international cricket. Hussain dragged the England cricket team kicking and screaming into the modern sporting age before handing over, exhausted, to Michael Vaughan, who proceeded to win the Ashes in 2005 with a side imbued with the work ethic and professionalism instilled by Hussain and Fletcher.

In his lively and controversial autobiography (Hussain (2004), p. 55) Hussain writes respectfully and with great affection about his Essex colleague Gooch:

Gooch was an absolute legend to me. We travelled together to games, so I would soak up every word he uttered, and he had a profound influence on me. I can't thank him enough for what he did for me as a young player, and I can't exaggerate his influence on me.

Hussain has other reasons to be grateful to Gooch, as he admits:

Gooch was ... a huge figure at this time, and (even though he has never told me as such) he played a massive part in my being selected for England when he was captain and, I suspect, being made captain when he was a selector.

The young pretender acknowledges Gooch's contribution to the improved professionalism of the England team:

In many ways he was years ahead of his time when he brought a work ethic to the England side.

Sadly, the two former Essex and England captains, never

particularly close in the manner of Gooch and Keith Fletcher, became a little estranged. The estrangement was caused more by their respective ideas on captaincy and the handling of different players than as a result of any personal issues the pair had between them. Hussain saw Gooch's leadership style as inflexible and crude, based purely, as he has written, on 'work, work, work'. Hussain preferred a more subtle leadership style designed to get the best out of every player, rather than Gooch's 'one size fits all, follow my lead' method. Given what we know about Hussain's fierce temperament and reputation for flying off the handle, the estrangement between the two was probably more to do with Gooch leaving Hussain, the England captain at the time, out of Essex's one-day sides in favour of a promising youngster, as is the Essex way, than it was about any fundamental differences between these two strong-willed and passionate cricketers. To be fair to Hussain, he acknowledges Gooch and Keith Fletcher as "two of my greatest mentors".

The lure of the rand

Gooch and Hussain both went through torrid times in their careers when they were called on to make tough decisions based on either moral principle or financial gain. The pair became caught up in political turmoil way outside the comfort zone of a professional cricketer, and they were to witness at first hand the inadequacies and weak leadership of the people responsible for running first-class cricket in England. If Gooch and Hussain thought that sport should be kept out of politics, as Gooch certainly did, then their respective South Africa experiences tested this view to the limit. Gooch's decision to accept an invitation to play in apartheid South Africa with the rebel South African Breweries XI in 1982, when he was at the peak of his career, tells us a great deal about the motivations and character of this often quite, complex character.

Gooch became disillusioned with Test cricket following England's tedious series in India in 1981/82. His state of mind was not helped by his performances in the home series against Australia in 1981. After a run of low scores against the Aussies he was dropped down the order for the fourth Test and left out altogether for the final Test, although he was given assurances by the selectors that his name would be included on the list for the winter tour of India.

The Indian tour of 1981/82 was bad-tempered and marked by dubious umpiring decisions and appallingly dull cricket. This was too much for that exciting, guaranteed-to-get-your-pulse-racing opening batsman, Geoff Boycott. He left India early to return to the more familiar, if no less fractious, surroundings of Yorkshire. Keith Fletcher was the England captain for the 1981/82 series, and despite having his Essex colleague leading the side Gooch grew bored with the cricket and depressed by India's negative tactics following their victory in the first Test. But, despite his mood, he accumulated a total of 487 runs in six matches, including a century in the fifth Test, and completed the tour with a very respectable tour average of 54. However, the Indian experience, combined with having been dropped by the selectors in the previous series against Australia, made Gooch vulnerable, perhaps even open, to approaches from the South African money men, who were desperate to attract international cricketers to their country. Following the Indian tour and after a great deal of complex negotiations, Gooch agreed to sign the South African contract. The consequences of his controversial decision rocked his personal world and cricket in general.

The bare facts are that Gooch's decision cost him a three-year ban from Test cricket and consequent damage to his career statistics through missing a potential 32 Test matches. The South African tour party became known as 'Gooch's rebels', following his appointment as captain of this odd collection of ageing cricketers (with the exception of Gooch himself), who included Gooch's best mate, John Embury, Geoff Boycott and his Essex colleague, John Lever. Gooch became very fond of South Africa, and Cape Town in particular, and later supplemented his already substantial 'rebel' income by playing for Western Province for the duration of his ban. The results and statistics of Gooch's Eleven, or The Dirty Dozen as they came to be known, are an irrelevance given the political and ethical issues raised by the tour. Suffice to say that Gooch scored heavily, confirming Keith Fletcher's view that no cricketer absorbed pressure better than Gooch once he has a bat in his hands.

Gooch was shocked by the severity of the ban but remained adamant that his decision was the right one. When his ban expired in 1985 he refused to rule out the possibility of returning to South Africa, which created further trouble for the world's cricket authorities when he was selected by England to tour the West Indies in 1985/86. Gooch's stubbornness, independent spirit and anti-establishment instincts were proving both his greatest strengths and greatest weaknesses. The virtues that saw him recover from a disastrous first England appearance and enabled him to become a truly great international batsman were responsible for the working-class boy from a council flat in East London turning his back on the English cricket establishment by accepting the South African offer. Gooch's decision to go to South Africa shocked even his close family. His wife Brenda never supported her husband's decision, while his parents, Alf and Rose, could not understand why their son had put his England career on the line by signing up for a tour to a pariah state like South Africa. Gooch was, of course, upset by the reaction of his father to the rebel tour. He wrote:

He believed everything he read in the papers about me, believed that I was breaking up Test cricket for the sake of a good pay day, and he could not understand why I had done it.
- G. Gooch (1985), Out of the Wilderness, Willow Books, p.22

Did Gooch not think that his close family would be deeply affected by his decision, or what kind of media intrusion and public disapproval would descend on him personally, and on the lives of those closest to him? There is little evidence that he consulted widely before making his fateful decision. Admittedly, given the intrigue, deception and secrecy surrounding the whole affair, it would have been difficult for Gooch to talk at any length to those in the game that he trusted most. His great friend and mentor, Keith Fletcher, was not consulted, which seems incredible given the difficulty of the decision. Who could have offered more reliable and sensible advice than his Essex captain? Doug Insole was another whom Gooch might have approached for advice. In his biography of Gooch, Ivo Tennant writes:

Insole was the one person who might have been able to persuade Gooch to stay at home, yet he discovered what was going on too late.
- Tennant (1992), p.64

Tennant reveals that Insole was approached by the TCCB to try to persuade Gooch "not to be such a fool". But it was too late. Insole himself said later:

> *I wrote later in his benefit brochure that he was a bit naïve. Graham was either talked into or convinced into believing that the tour would loosen shackles on apartheid.*
> *- Tennant (1992), p.64*

So why did he risk disapproval from family, friends and colleagues and put his England career in jeopardy? The money would have been Gooch's main motivation, as it would have gone some way to providing the financial security that he craved for himself and his family. In this respect Gooch's instincts were no different to generations of young men and women from the East End of London, whether they were plumbers, nurses, shopkeepers or international cricketers. We know that Gooch had been in and out of the England team and that those selected to play for their country were not offered the security of central contracts in the 1980s as they are today. Had this financial security been available to Gooch, there is no question in my mind that he would have turned down the South African bribes. His income from county cricket was modest and there would have been very little money on offer through sponsorship or advertising contracts, although this was beginning to change in the mid-1980s. What was a young family man from Leytonstone to do? Turn down the South African money and the opportunity for financial security for his family? Gooch never had the luxury of the holier-than-thou position beloved of the liberal intelligentsia, most of whom enjoyed the privileged comforts of the salaried middle class. Nor did he support the hypocrisies of the English cricket establishment, who remained tainted by their behaviour during the D'Oliveira case. As British companies were actively trading with South Africa, Gooch's father Alf took the view: what could be wrong with a young professional cricketer taking part in a private tour, while visiting some townships during his stay? It was unfair that cricket should be the vehicle for anti-apartheid sentiments.

Of course, Gooch was naïve in the extreme. He failed to consult people who were in a position to offer him sound advice, and he never fully realised that the South Africans were attempting to host a fake Test series, with Gooch and others simply pawns in their nasty game. He never considered the wider implications of going; for example, the possibility that his actions, and those of the rest of the party, might threaten future series against cricketing Third World nations. These consequences were bad enough, but his harshest critics accused Gooch and his team of supporting apartheid and the odious South African regime. I have no doubt that Gooch felt that the presence of his team in the country would help to break down apartheid, but there is also little doubt that his main motive was financial gain, and for the reasons I have tried to explain.

Gooch had also experienced the insensitivities of the English cricket establishment, and the South African tour may have been partly an act of rebellion against the public school mafia that ran cricket in England at the time. The moral high ground is a good place from which to snipe at people and Graham Gooch was an easy target in 1982. Gooch may have unwittingly sold his soul to the South African devil in 1982, but his actions seems less vulgar and crass than the establishment figures who, in 2009, greedily accepted the convicted crook and embezzler David Sandford's millions, and who are preparing to sell the game to the highest bidder. Those who live in glass houses ....

He may have enjoyed his time in South Africa and the financial return, but there is no question that Gooch was deeply depressed by the reaction to the rebel tour in England. He had not only disappointed his family and close colleagues but had also become easy prey for the media, although he did manage to win a case against the *Sun* newspaper, which claimed that Gooch "didn't care about playing for England". Essex colleagues like John Lever and Keith Pont watched Gooch become introverted and withdrawn, and Pont said:

> *As the pressures on him increased he became more of a recluse and the derogatory letters he was sent hurt him more than he showed outwardly.*
> *- Tennant (1992), p.67*

Perhaps we should argue that in 1982 Gooch was an international sportsman and would have been fully aware of the implications of going to South Africa and how this would be received by people inside and outside the country who often risked their lives fighting apartheid. After all, it was a well-known fact that the unjust regime was brutal in its treatment of the black majority. But Gooch could see nothing wrong in what he was doing; he was providing financial security for his family by going on a short, private trip, which would not threaten his Test career. I don't suppose he thought much about the atrocities perpetrated against the people of South Africa by the regime. In some ways he was a child of his time. Mrs Thatcher was elected Prime Minister in 1979 and Gooch was an enthusiastic supporter – a classic working-class Tory. By 1982 the Iron Lady and her friends had destroyed the last vestiges of Britain's renowned reputation for fair play, and in its place had firmly established a new greedy and crude money-making ethic at the heart of British society. For our friend Mrs Thatcher and her apologists, there was no such thing as society; there was just 'me'. Gooch going to South Africa, although wrong, was in tune with much of the rhetoric of the time.

When Gooch's Essex colleague, Nasser Hussain, took his England team to South Africa for the 2003 World Cup he discovered what Gooch had learned in 1982: that sport and politics in this country are inextricably mixed. The England team were due to play a scheduled match in Zimbabwe, a country ruled by vicious despots who were maiming and murdering anybody who expressed dissent of any kind. A Channel 4 documentary, shown in the UK that year, highlighted the shocking events that were unfolding in that troubled country. The British Government had advised the England team not to go to Zimbabwe without officially instructing them to stay away, thereby abnegating responsibility and handing over the decision to the players. Hussain said, with refreshing honesty, that he was not interested in politics, to the extent that he had never voted in his life.

Abandoned by the British Government and the cricket establishment, political novice Hussain was called on to make the decision of his life. With help from senior players like Michael Atherton and Ashley Giles, the coach Duncan Fletcher, and Richard Bevan from the Professional Cricketers' Association, Hussain led his team away from the abyss and refused to go to Zimbabwe. He had the full support of his team, who were clear that they had made the decision as a show of support for the people of Zimbabwe. The team had also received death threats, which they took seriously, but Hussain makes clear in his autobiography that ultimately the decision was made on moral grounds:

> *I was sitting in front of my TV at home ... when a special News at Ten report came on highlighting the plight of four lads who had demonstrated against Australia's World Cup in Zimbabwe. They had been arrested outside, then tortured and raped, and had only just been released. ...*
> *It shocked me to the core ... Thank God we didn't go. If that had been England it would have been ten times worse. How could I have sat here and lived with myself?*
> *- Hussain (2004), p.21-22*

Thus two young Essex cricketers were thrust into the centre of world politics: Gooch, the working-class East Ender determined to secure his family's financial future and, against all advice, going to South Africa purely for the money; and Hussain, the university-educated but politically illiterate introvert, happier in his own company than in the political spotlight – the very last place he would want to be, and showing an enormous courage and leadership that characterised his England captaincy by making the decision not to go to Zimbabwe in 2003 on moral grounds. Perhaps Hussain's moral compass was a little more finely attuned than that of his Essex colleague.

However, drawing a conclusion of 'Gooch bad guy, Hussain good guy' is far too simplistic. The world changed dramatically between 1982 and 2003. Apartheid was defeated in South Africa and Nelson Mandela was freed from captivity to lead his country towards the change that its people and the world demanded. South Africa returned to the fold of international sport and again became a leading nation in international cricket. In England the Tories were out of power for years, to be replaced in 1989 by a softer-edged New Labour administration. Change was in the air at this time, and cricket was no exception. Nasser Hussain and his team benefited from central contracts, sponsorship and advertising income, a situation that Graham Gooch could only have dreamed about. The financially secure Hussain, an established international and England captain, never had to make the kind of decision that got Gooch into so much trouble and cost him three years of his international career.

It is easy to condemn Gooch out of hand for going to South Africa in 1982, but much more difficult to try to understand the circumstances surrounding his decision. There is no question that reactions to the rebel tour affected him deeply and probably changed him as a person. He served his three-year Test ban, continued to play for Essex, and made a careful reassessment of his life, particularly in terms of the future of his cricket. He would have been on an emotional roller-coaster as he sought to escape the complex ethical web in which he had become entangled. But redemption was not too far away. Although regarded as a mercenary in South Africa, Gooch received little criticism during his time in the country and was left alone to settle into his new routine. Back in the UK, during his enforced absence from Test cricket he continued to perform for Essex as though nothing had happened. His form was unaffected. In 1983 he scored three centuries in the final month of the season, securing another County Championship for his beloved county. Essex set new records in a John Player League match against Glamorgan at Southend, with Gooch making 176 in a total of 310 for 5.

George Orwell may have set his dystopian novel in 1984, but for Gooch in the summer of that year, the final year of his ban, he raised his batting to a new level. He scored 2,281 runs at an average of 69, a new Essex record. By any standards this was batting of the highest order and the Essex opener was now reaching a level that put him within reach of the greatness he now craved. Needless to say, largely as a result of Gooch's peerless batting, Essex won the Championship for the third time in five years in a close finish with Nottinghamshire and, just for good measure, won the John Player Special League Trophy by a clear eight points. Gooch's absence from the England side was highlighted when at Chelmsford he scored the only century of the summer against the touring West Indies team, who had just thrashed England 5-0 in the Test series of that year. Now 31 years of age, Gooch was reaching his peak. His white helmet, upright stance and bat aloft to face the bowler are etched in the memory. He had become disdainful of most bowling and appeared invincible, with his confidence at a new high. In a match against Middlesex, always a difficult game, Essex were set 210 to win in 33 overs, which seemed an impossible task even to Keith Fletcher, that most adventurous of captains. Gooch had other ideas, bludgeoning 120 runs against the Middlesex attack, which included John Embury. Essex won by four wickets and the Essex Blacksmith was now close to becoming the No. 1 batsman in the world.

Back in the fold

Gooch was now more than ready for the 1985 season and the end of his ban from international cricket, and what a year it proved to be. Essex won the NatWest Bank Trophy and the John Player League, and reached the final of the Benson & Hedges Trophy, losing to Leicestershire by five wickets. Gooch scored 91 in the NatWest final, sharing a record-breaking opening stand of 202 with Brian Hardie (110). In a John Player League game against Nottinghamshire at Trent Bridge the same pair scored a record 239 for the first wicket, with Gooch contributing 171 against Hardie's 66. His personal quest to become one of cricket's greats was well and truly on course. He had managed to combine great skill, mental toughness and physical fitness, in a huge effort of will, in a way that is rare in sport, let alone cricket. Outside Essex the press were clamouring for Gooch's return to the England side, and his comeback could no longer be delayed.

In the meantime Essex granted Gooch a benefit, and throughout 1985 he diligently attended pubs and clubs across the county, working tremendously hard and with his usual enthusiasm. Rather unexpectedly Gooch received great support from the City of London. The standard beneficiary City dinner attracted 1,224 guests, who had to be accommodated on two separate evenings. Gooch's benefit raised a phenomenal £153,906, almost double the amount that Keith Fletcher received in 1984. With his South African earnings and his benefit cheque, Gooch had finally achieved the financial security he had worked tirelessly to achieve. He was fortunate that his support from the City coincided with the excess of the Thatcher years. The East End City boys saw Gooch as one of their own; a West Ham supporter and self-made Essex man, who 'did his time' over South Africa quietly and without complaint. They gave generously to the greatest East London and Essex sporting hero since Bobby Moore.

In the same way that Christopher Martin-Jenkins sneered at

Gooch's 'estuary accent' (how else was he supposed to speak?), the journalist Simon Heffer revealed his own class prejudices when he wrote about his own daily commute to work from Chelmsford to Liverpool Street, a journey undertaken by generations of Essex people:

> *The people I shared carriages with were hard working, highly motivated by money, self-reliant and enjoy their leisure and lifestyle. Many of them could have been Graham Gooch if it was not for the fact that their behaviour was gross.*
> *- Quoted in Tennant (1992), p.75*

Heffer's patronising comments are not just unfair, they are simply a lie. Anyone who has travelled regularly on the Liverpool Street Chelmsford or Chingford lines will know that the journeys are generally peaceful, with commuters quietly reading or just recovering from their day. Mobile phones are a curse in public places and are as offensive on the posh Surrey commuter runs as they are anywhere else. But Heffer is right to say that Gooch has the Essex qualities of hard work and self-reliance, and thank goodness for Essex and England that he did.

In 1985 Gooch repeated his feat of scoring over 1,000 runs for Essex, this time at an average of 71, and passed 20,000 career runs late in the season. His return to the England side was now a formality, and he was duly recalled for the Test and one-day series against Australia, scoring two centuries in the one-day internationals and a magnificent 196 in the Oval Test. The challenge he had set himself of becoming one of the all-time batting greats was beginning to succeed. Gooch was back with a vengeance, his South African experience, it seemed, now firmly behind him.

Go jump in a lake, Goochie

It is tempting to conclude, given his South African experience, the issues around the Essex captaincy and his picking and choosing of overseas England tours, that Graham Gooch had courted controversy in his career. Although this would be harsh on Gooch, there is little question that in the 1980s he found himself at the heart of some of the major issues in sport, mostly related to his decision to go on the rebel tour. Following Gooch's part in Essex's triumphant season of 1985 and his successful return to the Test side against Australia that summer, it was inevitable that he would be selected for the winter tour of the West Indies. With his selection, however, his hope for a calm return to Test cricket was immediately shattered and his name, once again, was plastered all over the nation's front pages.

Before the party left for the Caribbean, Gooch was asked by a reporter if he would ever contemplate returning to South Africa. Gooch's answer was equivocal. Despite condemning apartheid, he replied that cricketers should have the right to tour South Africa as any other country. Oh dear! Gooch's dream of a seamless and successful return to international cricket was in pieces. He thought he had done his time. From the moment his comments reached the columns of the world's newspapers Gooch wanted to pull out of the tour, but he was persuaded to travel to the West Indies by the England selectors, probably against his own judgement. He was a reluctant tourist and was clearly depressed by the reception he received in the islands, and his form suffered as a consequence. On arrival the England opener was greeted by a burning effigy and newspaper headlines like 'Judas' and 'Go jump in a lake, Gooch', while Michael Manley, former Prime Minister of Jamaica and a well-respected figure in the islands, wrote of "lingering indignation about Gooch". Mid-tour he appeared to have made the decision to abandon the trip, but he was talked into staying by, among others, the England captain David Gower. Downcast, as only Gooch can be, he decided to support Gower and stay. In any case the protests had eased by the time the tour party reached Trinidad, where, in an innings that did much to repair Gooch's damaged reputation in the Caribbean, he scored a glorious and unbeaten 129 in just 37 overs. This was a commanding knock achieved in difficult personal circumstances. When Gooch responds to adversity in the way he has done repeatedly over his career, it is tempting to compare him with his hero and fellow East Ender, Bobby Moore. Moore's impeccable behaviour and glorious form on his return to the England team from his troubles in Bogota were an indication of the character of the man. Throughout his career Gooch also raised his game in the most difficult circumstances, whether scoring chanceless centuries against an almost unplayable West Indies attack or flaying the Australian bowling as he did in the one-day series in

1985. It is worth remembering at this point that Gooch's record-breaking career was founded on his embarrassing pair on his England debut in 1975. Strength in adversity is a laudable personal quality and one that Moore and Gooch shared and, perhaps, inherited from their parents' wartime generation.

Home sweet home, and a dip in form

Following his return from the highly politicised tour of the West Indies in 1986 Gooch was appointed Essex captain and the county duly won the Championship for the fourth time in eight years, helped by the 1,385 runs scored by the Australian captain Allan Border. In his first season as Essex skipper Gooch leaned heavily on his much-respected mentor Keith Fletcher, but they had different ideas about how to win cricket matches. For example, Gooch did not trust slow bowlers to win matches whereas Fletcher had used left-armer Ray East and off-spinner David Acfield to such good effect in his time as captain. Gooch's antipathy to slow bowlers might have something to do with the way in which he played them so dismissively in his own career, particularly his treatment of the highly regarded leg-spinner Abdul Qadir and the West Indian off-break bowler Roger Harper, both of whom he enjoyed sweeping out of their respective attacks. Gooch's lack of trust in slow bowlers did seem to confirm Nasser Hussain's charges of his inflexibility as a leader. However, despite their minor differences Fletcher and Gooch continued their close working relationship, which ensured Essex's run of success.

In the years between 1979 and 1986 Essex supporters had become used to their team winning trophies. Keith Fletcher has said that he was surprised how quickly supporters came to expect, even demand, success. They would certainly have been looking forward with anticipation to the beginning of the 1987 season, expecting their team to be competing for all the major trophies once again. The seamless dynastic progression from Gooch to Fletcher gave great comfort to supporters and a successful season appeared to be assured, a bit like the transition at West Ham from Greenwood to Lyall. But, sport being sport, and cricket being cricket, in 1987 Essex supporters could be forgiven for thinking that the wheels of the Essex juggernaut were beginning to wobble a little. The season started happily for the new captain and club talisman. Gooch scored 171 in the

Championship in the match against Gloucester, but when Essex returned to Chelmsford for their first home matches of the season Gooch failed to score a run in his four innings in the matches against Warwickshire and Pakistan. John Lever said at the time that he had never seen a batsman of Gooch's quality go through such a run of bad form. What was happening? Was the problem technical? Gooch, like Alistair Cook after him, did have a tendency to fall over to the off from time to time, leading him to play across his pads. Interestingly, Gooch thought that the umpire rumour mill exaggerated his vulnerability to the wicket-to-wicket ball delivered by medium-pace swing bowlers. "Oh yeah, old Goochie's doing it all the time, we don't have any choice, do we?" Gooch's answer to this was: "So what if I play a long way forward and occasionally fall to the offside? It's not a major problem."

Anyone who has played sport at a reasonable level will know the moment when, for no apparent reason, performance takes a downturn. For example, in golf the drive starts to curve an arc 50 yards to the right of the fairway and easy pitch shots hit bunker after bunker rather than settling down close to the pin. My tennis-playing friends tell me that they have experienced weeks when serve after serve thuds into the net, and they just cannot see how they will ever serve well again. At one stage in his career poor old Eric Bristow, former World Darts champion, simply could not let go of his darts when it was his time to throw. Graham Gooch's four consecutive ducks in 1987, although not of the order of the golfing 'yips', worried him enough to rethink his whole approach to batting. When the coach of Wimbledon champion Martina Navratilova was asked what he did to improve her game so dramatically at one point in her career, he told the gullible press that he cut down the handle of Navratilova's racket to give her more control. Of course it was a joke, implying that there is no one thing that can deliver us from bad form. Gooch, his form affected by a combination of factors, decided on the most sensible course of action. He told himself that he was going to play well and make runs. Clearing his mind of the rubble was the first step to scoring heavily again, along with a positive attitude. Gooch put it this way: "There was no more waiting for the worst to happen ... None of that stuff about 'Oh God, it's Malcolm Marshall today – is he going to knock my off-stump out of the ground for the tenth time on the trot?'"

The captaincy may have been a problem. Fletcher was still in the side and his presence may have inhibited the new captain or, as Allan Border suggested, the events of that winter's Caribbean tour and the earlier problems over his South African trip had at last caught up with the hitherto unflappable Gooch. Also, he had a very young family and had recently moved house. The collapse in his form was probably due to a combination of these things, as Gooch inevitably succumbed to the pressures of having been such a high-profile public figure over the past few years. His love of good red wine and the music of Van Morrison, usually guaranteed to smooth away the pressures, were clearly failing to do their job.

Thankfully, his succession of ducks proved short-lived and he began to regain his form over the course of the season, managing to top the Essex batting averages, this time mainly from a position in the middle order. But there was to be one casualty. He had discussed the Essex captaincy that season with chairman Doug Insole and Keith Fletcher. Reassured by the two men that he respected above all others, Gooch made some minor technical modifications to his technique. His form returned, as it was always bound to do, to the extent that he promptly scored 117 for MCC against the Rest of the World. Despite his return to form, Gooch handed back the Essex captaincy to Fletcher. Essex supporters might have held it against their hero for dropping the captaincy. But they would have been well aware of the mental juggling that Gooch was having to undergo.

Nigel Hilliard, the current Essex chairman, recently revealed that many county captains, initially enthusiastic about the job, quickly tire of it when they realise the responsibilities involved. They would rather be left to concentrate on their own performances. Fletcher was born to captaincy and again took over the reins, although the reluctant Gooch did captain the side from time to time that season when Fletcher left himself out to accommodate the promising young right-hand batsman Nasser Hussain.

Gooch's good late-season form continued and he played well in the 1988 World Cup in India and Pakistan, where England lost to Australia in the final. Gooch scored a match-winning 115 off 136 balls against the home side India, being particularly harsh on the Indian spinners Ravi Shastri and Maninder Singh. But he continued to cherry pick his tours, always preferring his beloved Essex to playing for England, which rather contradicted his desire to improve his Test record and ensure his place among the greats in world cricket. He went to Pakistan, but not to New Zealand. He may have regretted his decision when the Mike Gatting/Shakoor Rana incident threatened to blow up into yet another major international incident. But again he displayed his now familiar dogged determination in difficult circumstances, scoring 91 in 375 minutes to save the Karachi Test.

Back to his best

The power of positive thinking and a more relaxed mental approach certainly paid off for Gooch at the start of the 1988 season when he scored a majestic career best of 275 in the County Championship against Kent at Canterbury. In typical Gooch fashion, his insatiable appetite for runs was not satisfied until he scored a further 75 in the Essex second innings. He said of this innings, "When you are in the right frame of mind you just go out there and do it naturally." No playing across the line this season. In the season of experimental four-day matches, he scored 1,631 Championship runs for Essex, averaging 70. In the home Test series against the West Indies he averaged 45, with a top score of 146 in the first Test at Trent Bridge, accumulated in over six hours in England's second innings. Needless to say, he also scored a good 73 in the first innings. In this second stage of his career the relentless accumulation of runs and long match-saving innings were beginning to become habitual.

1988 was to be a keynote season for Gooch. Keith Fletcher announced his retirement from the game - a very sad day for Essex supporters, and Gooch was his obvious replacement as captain. He was ready this time and in the right frame of mind, his confidence sky high. In the series against the West Indies, England had three different captains. Mike Gatting began the series as skipper, but he lasted only one Test, resigning when stories about late-night drinks with a local barmaid made the press. John Embury replaced Gatting as captain for the next two matches before being unceremoniously dropped for the fourth Test. It felt a bit like the last man standing, but Gooch was made captain for the fifth and final Test. He must have been heartened to have Essex colleagues Derek Pringle and Neil Foster in his side. The pair duly came to the aid of their county captain and bowled out the West Indies for 183 in their first innings. In the hot Oval dust bowl England lost the match, but not before Gooch played a quintessential second phase of his career innings, being last out after batting for more than seven hours.

Gooch retained the captaincy for the single match 'series' against Sri Lanka that summer, which England won comfortably, their first win in a Lord's Test in five years. Now captain of Essex and England, and scoring runs for both, Gooch seemed to have got his career on an even keel at last and his destiny was within his grasp - and, at last, he had returned to the back pages, or at least for a time. If only Gooch's England career had progressed as smoothly as that of his boyhood hero, Bobby Moore. Moore may have had his troubles with West Ham, and there was the Bogota incident, but his England career was generally unblemished, culminating in captaining his country to World Cup triumph and achieving a record 108 caps. But Moore never had to play football in India, the West Indies or South Africa. Britain's imperial past returned to haunt the England cricket authorities and their successive captains. Following the spirited performance of his side in the final Test against the West Indies, and the victory against Sri Lanka at Lord's, Gooch was eventually made captain of the tour to India in 1988/89. But, just as he appeared to be established in the role, it was to be snatched away.

The curse of Alderman

Eight of the England party scheduled to tour India, including the captain, had sporting contacts with South Africa. Gooch himself had signed a contract to join Western Province for the winter of 1988/89, for which he would have to be released to allow him to lead the tour party. However, the Indian authorities announced in September that they would refuse to grant visas to any player that had sporting contacts with apartheid South Africa, so the tour was cancelled. Gooch did not go to South Africa that winter, but spent his time catching up with his children, running half-marathons and training with The Hammers. England's chairman of selectors, Ted Dexter, decided that Gooch had not done enough as captain in the games against the West Indies and Sri Lanka to deserve an automatic appointment for the home series against Australia in 1989. Instead he was given the job for the one-day matches preceding the Ashes series, in which he was named England's Man of the Series. But David Gower was made captain for the Test series, with disastrous results, amid rumours that a further rebel tour of South Africa was being put together. Gooch denied his involvement, and when the rebel captain Mike Gatting announced his touring party Gooch's name was not on the list, costing the *Daily Mirror* £20,000 in damages after the paper had alleged that Gooch had agreed to go on the rebel trip.

Gooch was, of course, selected for his batting against Australia, but in five Tests he scored just 183 runs. 'Gooch LWB bowled Alderman 0' is the abiding memory of the season. His form for Essex also dipped as the inevitable crisis of confidence followed. There is no question that Gooch liked hard wickets, with the ball coming onto the bat. The Australian medium pacers found him again playing around his front pad to the ball that nipped back and, as a result, generally posted two fielders close in on the leg side to restrict his scoring. Gooch sought advice from those he trusted, particularly Geoff Boycott, who suggested that he stopped going back and across as his initial movement, but keep his back leg outside leg stump, stopping him from playing across the line. This may have had some long-term benefit, but his low scores continued and he was dropped for the fifth Test and replaced by Yorkshire's Martyn Moxon. He was brought back for the sixth Test, but was out in the first over of England's innings, again LBW bowled Alderman for 0. It was enough to drive even the strongest, most level-headed batsman, as Gooch was, to distraction. He had lost the England captaincy and his form, and Essex had a frustrating season, winning nothing after being in contention in all competitions for most of the season. The final frustration was being docked 25 points for producing a pitch for the match at Southend against Yorkshire that was judged to have been unfit for first-class cricket. Essex won the match but were 'fined' 25 points by the TCCB, which virtually handed the Championship to Worcestershire by a margin of six points.

Gooch's career up to 1989, both for Essex and England, was an emotional roller-coaster, during which time he had been at the centre of political turmoil over his decision to lead the rebel tour of South Africa, putting him in contravention of the Gleneagles Agreement. The repercussions of his decision reverberated across the world of cricket. He was vilified in the West Indies and taunted by the British media with accusations of treachery. His stubborn refusal to admit his mistake and rule out the possibility of returning to South Africa put him in direct conflict with the English cricket establishment and ultimately cost him the England captaincy. Throughout this period he firmly believed that he had nothing wrong and that the position of the cricket authorities and the British press was based on blind hypocrisy. Gooch was instinctively anti-establishment and despised the class-ridden prejudices of cricket's elite, which he, more than most, had experienced at first hand.

His form fluctuated during these years from complete mastery over the best bowling attacks to wondering where his next run would come from. He was the pivotal figure in Essex's wonderful run of success from 1979, but he hadn't fully succeeded Keith Fletcher as club captain, which everyone at the club had expected. He was a magnificent but flawed batsman, and a complex, often contradictory character whom only a few people at Essex really knew well. His concern for the financial security of his family was a major motivating factor in his career, and by the end of this period he had become a relatively wealthy 36-year-old, with a large house in rural Essex, close to Chelmsford, but a long way from the streets of East London where he grew up. Like thousands of working-class East Londoners who had achieved the Essex dream in the 1980s, Gooch was a Conservative supporter. Rather than any ideological commitment, this was more to do with his beliefs in self-help and independence and wishing to adjust to his new economic and social standing. However, his Tory allegiance failed to protect him from the class prejudice and snobbery of the cricket authorities to which he was regularly subjected during his time as England captain. Dexter's 'wet fish' comments about Gooch must have hurt when he was first made England captain. Dexter was responding to Gooch's assertion that nobody could turn a bad team into a good one. Dexter interpreted this as Gooch virtually saying, "No David could ever kill a Goliath," criticising the new England captain's 'follow my example' leadership style. Establishment journalists like E.W.

Swanton and John Woodcock lined up behind Dexter with further criticisms of Gooch's captaincy that bordered on the personal. These comments were not so much to do with Gooch's South African trip in 1982, but rather Gooch being a working-class East Londoner who had offended the establishment's delicate sensibilities. It is clear that they always preferred the more clubbable, minor aristocratic David Gower and his semi-serious lightness of touch. Gooch had attended a comprehensive school where half the pupils failed their 'O' levels, and if he had not been blessed with sublime batting skills he would have become a humble toolmaker, although probably one of the very best in Essex. But his more privileged critics were to eat their words, particularly in the case of Dexter. Graeme Wright, shrewd and thoughtful judge, was one of the few who came to Gooch's defence at the time, writing:

> *He has an ability to distance himself sufficiently from his team-mates to gain their respect as leader. He will not need to be one of the lads. I do not share the concern that his batting will suffer from his being captain. Essex consider he is capable of doing the job and they are a county who plan carefully and have a commitment to success.*
> *- G. Wright (1988), Wisden Cricketers' Almanack.*

Gooch was not to be denied. He was handed the captaincy by Dexter for the England tour to the West Indies in 1989/90. He had seen off Gower, Gatting, Cowdrey and, briefly, John Embury, and would have been forgiven for thinking that he had regained what was rightfully his. In his biography of Gooch, Ivo Tennant claims the man reappointed as England captain was largely underestimated by the general cricket public, and media pundits.

Tennant's view was supported by the people in cricket who knew him best. Doug Insole remarked about how he thought Gooch had improved as a captain, becoming more thoughtful and acquiring good man-management skills. John Lever described how he would talk individually to members of the team and was particularly good at supporting young players. Notwithstanding Nasser Hussain's comments about the inflexibility of Gooch's leadership style, there is no doubt that Gooch began to think more deeply about captaincy as he moved into his late thirties.

Hero of the Caribbean

When the 1989/90 tour party to the West Indies was announced the names of Gower and Botham were missing from the list. Gooch now had a clear run at the captaincy and had the unopposed authority to apply his own ideas to the job. He was helped by the appointment of Mickey Stewart as tour manager, who, unlike many at this time, had a high opinion of Gooch and respected his work ethic and strength of character. Gooch and Stewart set about restoring some degree of professionalism and pride to English cricket. Players were expected to prepare properly and improve their fitness levels, and indoor practice and coaching facilities were set up at Lilleshall to this end. Gooch, with his marathon running, training with West Ham and understanding that consistent levels of performance required the correct balance of clear thinking, mental strength and physical fitness, was the perfect leader for a new time. Gooch had begun to be convinced that those running the England side were becoming more professional in their outlook. He saw that they were becoming increasingly interested in their players' fitness and in the way they practised and prepared for matches. This new and welcome attention to detail by the TCCB and the selectors was welcomed by Gooch, who always approached his cricket in the most meticulous fashion. Not for nothing did Keith Fletcher describe Gooch as the "hardest working cricketer" he had ever worked with.

Despite Essex failing to win a trophy, 1989 was proving a good year for Graham Gooch. It must have been a huge relief for him when his name was finally removed from the United Nations blacklist, following the International Cricket Council's commitment to ban players or coaches who agreed to ply their trade in South Africa. Gooch had decided that he would not return to the country, because he saw his Test match career as a priority. Having stated, "I do not agree with apartheid ... it is a terrible system," this episode of his life was now at last behind him. The prospect of facing Malcolm Marshall at Sabina Park must have seemed like a walk in the park after the media intrusion and political storm over his South African episode.

The England team had prepared properly for the challenge of facing the best team in the world in the hostile cricketing atmosphere of the Caribbean. The tour started well for Gooch when he made 239 in Jamaica, that beautiful but troubled island. He made the runs in 286 minutes and it was his highest score on an England overseas tour. It was an encouraging sign of the state of mind of the England captain. Perhaps the West Indies were complacent or perhaps they had underestimated Gooch's team, but England won the first Test by nine wickets thanks to the bowling of Gladstone Small, Gus Fraser, and particularly Devon Malcolm, who bowled with a ferocity that equalled the quickest of the West Indies pace attack. The bowlers were well supported by the resolute batting of Allan Lamb and Robin Smith. The victory at Sabina Park in Kingston marked the rebirth of Gooch's uncertain career and a radical revision of the public perception of their new hero. The moment for which he had worked so hard had finally arrived.

The second Test in rainy Guyana was completely lost to the weather and England approached the third Test in buoyant mood. Gooch won the toss and inserted the opposition. The England bowlers were again on top form, dismissing the West Indies for just 199 runs. England made a modest 288 in their first innings, with Gooch contributing a stubborn 84 runs. Devon Malcolm, bowling with pace and aggression, took 6 for 77 in the West Indies' second innings, leaving England to make a mere 151 runs to win and go two up in the series. Cruelly for Gooch and his team, pace bowler Ezra Moseley succeeded in breaking one of the England skipper's fingers and, with a combination of rain, bad light and a painfully slow over rate, the West Indies escaped with a draw they hardly deserved. But England's morale remained high despite victory slipping from their grasp in the cruellest manner. Gooch's broken finger, the first serious injury in his career, meant that his tour was over, but he remained with his players as tour leader, with the on-the-field duties handed over to Allan Lamb. Staying on the tour despite being injured was a clear message to the selectors as to how much the captaincy meant to Gooch. Understandably the loss of their captain, just when England were getting on top of a very good side, affected the England batting, as did a later injury to England's most reliable bowler, Gus Fraser. They lost the fourth Test in Barbados by 164 runs and the fifth Test in Antigua in four days, thanks to a record-breaking opening partnership of 298 by Gordon Greenidge and Desmond Haynes. The Wisden Trophy stayed in the Caribbean, despite a valiant attempt by a revitalised England team to take it from them.

The loss of their new captain undoubtedly affected the England players in the last two Tests of the tour. Their self-belief was dented and they lacked confidence on the field without Gooch's leadership. But if the tour fell away for England, Gooch emerged with a new reputation as a strong and popular leader, unopposed as the England captain. Almost single-handedly he had put the pride and self-respect back into English cricket. In a sense he had purged the England team of the factions and backbiting of previous tours and had introduced a new professionalism based on careful preparation, attention to detail, fitness and regular practice. He had rebuilt the England team in his own image, believing, as he always did, that unless the 'hard yards' were put in England would continue to fail. It was an approach that had served Essex well, and was to be spectacularly successful for Steve Waugh's Australian sides of the 1990s.

Gooch's past critics, some of them most vociferous, were now queuing up to praise England's new saviour. Ted Dexter revised his estimation of his new captain, admitting that the selectors were surprised at the way in which Gooch had settled quickly into the job. Previous England captains David Gower and Mike Gatting were both generous in their praise for their former colleague. The media, once his fiercest critics, began to take him up as the saviour of English cricket. Gooch would have taken all this in his stride. He was enough of a realist to know that success in sport can be very short-lived, but he had made a real attempt to change his approach to batting and captaincy. The career reassessment he made in 1986 included a look at his image and the way he engaged with colleagues and the media. By 1990 the adjustments he had made were becoming visible and he appeared more outgoing and self-assured. Gooch was now secure in the captaincy of Essex and England, the best English batsman by a mile, and one of the top three in world cricket. No wonder he was confident, and there was so much more to come.

Taking it to a new level

The summer of 1990 saw Gooch fully recovered from his broken finger and back in form for Essex. He scored 215 in a record 403 partnership with Paul Pritchard in the early season game against Middlesex at Chelmsford. His appetite for runs appeared to be insatiable as century followed century in batting of remarkable consistency and application. His technical problems had been resolved and runs came in all forms of the game, whether limited overs, County Championship matches or in the Test series against New Zealand. A particular feature of Gooch's 'second coming' was again the way in which he continued to make runs for Essex despite the pressures of the England captaincy. The responsibility and recognition that came with it appeared to spur him on. In between Test matches he scored a century in Essex's game against a New Zealand side at Chelmsford, and just to show he had lost none of his old attacking instincts he hammered 177 runs from 152 balls in a match against Lancashire.

In Michael Atherton Gooch found his most reliable opening partner since Geoff Boycott. Atherton scored 151 in the drawn first Test against New Zealand and the pair developed as an effective, often prolific opening partnership. Both were strong and determined batsmen as well as supremely talented. The first and second Tests were drawn but England won the third Test, with Gooch and Atherton contributing a first innings opening stand of 170. Eddie Hemmings and Devon Malcolm did the rest. England's performances against New Zealand maintained the improvement they had shown in the West Indies the previous winter, and they could look forward to India's with great confidence and anticipation.

Gooch continued to gain admirers and enjoyed the respect of his players and most people in the game. He had developed as a tactician and had improved his communication skills. His England team were an effective unit who had regained a real sense of purpose, a testament to the captain's motivational powers. His fitness and practice mantra was now accepted by the players and the authorities, as it was in most sports, and Gooch led by example. Not since Mike Brearley had England's captain enjoyed a position of such unassailable authority. It was in this spirit that Gooch's team anticipated the visit of the Indian team to Lord's for the first Test.

Gooch had warmed up for the Test series by hitting 177 from 152 balls against Lancashire, in soaring temperatures, in a run chase at Colchester. At Lord's Gooch lost the toss and England were put in by the Indian captain Mohammad Azharuddin, much to the surprise of his opposing skipper. England began their first innings in humid and overcast conditions, and with the score at 36 Gooch nicked a ball from Sharma to wicketkeeper More, who promptly dropped a regulation catch. How he and his captain were to regret his mistake. By the end of the day Gooch was on 194 not out. On the Thursday evening, somewhat poignantly, Gooch dined with his old Essex guide and mentor, Doug Insole, high above Lord's on Primrose Hill. The topic of conversation was as likely to have been about Essex and fine red wines as about Gooch's first day innings.

If the skipper was exhausted by his efforts on a sultry day, he showed no signs of this on the Friday when he moved quickly to 200, enthralling the Friday crowd in the ground and the English public at large. When tea arrived Gooch was 299 not out. He tickled the first ball from Ravi Shastri after tea down to fine leg and crossed with Robin Smith to reach 300, becoming only the third Englishman to score a triple hundred on home soil. The players had been on and off all day in the drizzle, so perhaps it was this, and thoughts about declaring, that caused Gooch momentarily to lose concentration. After a further short break he played lazily to a ball from Manoj Prabhakar that cannoned into his stumps and ended his epic and momentous effort. Gooch bowled Prabhakar 333. He strolled back to the old pavilion with the Lord's crowd on its feet in rapturous acclaim. What an innings! It is a characteristic of truly great players that they have several shots for any one ball. A shift in the wrist position or a subtle foot movement and the ball can be hit either through midwicket or straight down the ground. Gooch showed us he had all the shots in his mammoth innings. As C.L.R. James wrote about W.G. Grace's batting:

> *He turned the old one-stringed lyre into a many-chorded lyre … he turned batting from its many straight channels into one great winding river.*
> *- James (1963), p.177*

When it was at last over he gave his heavy 3lb record-breaking bat to wicketkeeper/artist Jack Russell, who used it in the composition of his commemorative painting of this historic innings. Russell's painting hangs proudly today in the Long Room at Lord's.

Not satisfied with his first innings effort, Gooch proceeded to score a century in England's second innings, taking his combined match total to 456 runs. At Lord's that Friday he became the first English player to score a triple century and a century in the same match. His 333 was the highest individual score at Lord's and the highest by an England captain. Among the milestones that Gooch passed that July day were those held by Jack Hobbs, Len Hutton and Don Bradman. The press went into raptures, leading to headlines such as:

- *Gooch attains greatness at last (The Times)*
- *Beyond the boundaries of belief (The Guardian)*

The tributes paid to the England captain for his remarkable achievement at Lord's came from all sections of the fickle British cricketing public. Forgotten were the cheerless South African episode and the subsequent ban. The resulting political problems in the West Indies had been put behind him. The pair he bagged in his debut Test appearance and the loss of form culminating in four 0s in succession for Essex were a distant memory. Even the phrase "Gooch LBW by Alderman" lost its potency as the enormity of his achievement against India began to sink in. Former critics and friends alike queued up to heap their praises on England cricket's new messiah.

Graeme Wright wrote of the experience of being at Lord's on the Friday of the first Test:

> *There, before us, the captain of England was approaching 300 and everyone took on board the awesomeness of his achievement.*
> *- G. Wright (1990), Wisden Cricketers' Almanack.*

Matthew Engel, a master of cricket writing, wrote in *The Guardian*:

> *Gooch batted sensationally … his on-driving was of a quality I have rarely seen surpassed … When he was finally out, even Gooch … may have been able to savour the romance of the moment. The crowd rose; it would have bowed to him. In his career he took one dreadful turn-off to South Africa, but history will concentrate on his path to glory. This year he has saved the honour of English cricket.*
> *- M. Engel, The Guardian, 28th July 1990.*

It is a pity that his recognition of Gooch's achievements had to include the phrase "even Gooch", indicating that the master had some way to go before he could completely throw off the rude and inaccurate stereotype. However, Engel neatly encapsulates the sense of the occasion. In a thoughtful piece in The Independent, Tim de Lisle put Gooch's two innings against India in the context of his whole career when he wrote:

His Test career has been a saga, a fifteen-year switchback ride ... an unlikely mixture of success, failure, joy and heartbreak, acceptance, rejection, leadership, self-doubt and political intrigue on four continents. Nobody has made more runs in a single Test match than Gooch, and nobody had made fewer.
- T. de Lisle, The Independent on Sunday, 29th July 1990.

From the sublime to the ridiculous
Gooch was to need all the qualities of courage, strength of purpose and resolve that he had demonstrated at Lord's for the winter tour of Australia. But for now he could bask in the glory of becoming the truly great cricketer that he and others thought might be his destiny. Never one to let his feet leave the ground for long, Gooch had Essex to occupy his thoughts for the remainder of the season. Unfortunately, his county were less successful than England, despite their captain continuing his purple patch of form in the Championship and one-day competitions. Essex drew their last two County Championship matches and had to settle for runners-up spot for the second year in succession. Without a one-day trophy either, Essex's crown looked to be slipping a little - something that would have worried Gooch and the county hierarchy. The captain suffered a further injury late in the season when he broke a thumb in two places while attempting a catch against Kent. As injuries go it was not thought to be serious and he began looking forward to the series in Australia, against whom he had a few old scores to settle. I am sure he realised that he was unlikely to repeat his feats of the summer of 1990 against a very strong Aussie team. He knew that the balance between bat and ball would be tilted much more in the direction of Australia, particularly the Aussie bowlers, and the Ashes would prove a far greater test than India at Lord's on a dead wicket. However, now he could relax in his new hard-won status as a great batsman and hugely influential

England captain. Referring to how the lives of great sports stars can change dramatically in a single season, Ivo Tennant writes:

> *Six years after Gooch had been outlawed from international cricket and two years after he had been on the brink of signing with Western Province, he was perceived in England not only as a sporting hero but also a true patriot.*
> *- Tennant (1992), p.165*

Tennant was quick to add that, of course, Essex were "still his first love".

Gooch had got as far as Heathrow Airport on his way to Australia when he was whisked away by Michael Aspel to appear on *This is Your Life*. Having said goodbye to Brenda and the kids back in Essex he now had to do the same thing again, which must have been difficult for the whole family. Uplifted by his TV appearance, he would have looked forward to his journey to Australia in hope and expectation. But his glorious summer was now a memory as they ran into the Australian steamroller. They lost the series 3-0 and in the most abject fashion, losing the first Test by 10 wickets, the second by 8 wickets and the fifth by 9 wickets. The Aussie bowlers Reid, Alderman and McDermott ripped through the England batting in match after match, with the only resistance coming from two Gower centuries and one from the young Michael Atherton. Injury kept Gooch out of the first Test and he returned for the second Test only for the inevitable to happen – Gooch LWB b Alderman 20. He did score 50 in the second innings in Melbourne, and he made 59 and 54 in the third Test in Sydney, before returning fully to form in Adelaide with 87 in the first innings and a match-saving 117 in the second, his first ever century against Australia.

The Aussie bowlers were devastating. Bruce Reid took 7 for 51 in the second Test in Adelaide with his left-arm seam bowling, only for Craig McDermott to better this effort with 8 for 97 in the fifth Test in Perth. Gus Fraser performed with his usual consistency in difficult circumstances with best figures of 6 for 82 in Adelaide, a match in which Mark Waugh made a magnificent 138. They are the bare facts of the tour and, once again, English cricket seemed to have repeated the habit of taking two steps forward and three back. Where have we heard that before?

Gooch and his team had left for the west coast of Australia the day after his TV appearance, where they spent some time in Perth practising, playing a few warm-up matches and generally acclimatising to their new conditions. Spirits would have been high following their success against India, and there was no reason to expect the carnage that was about to follow. But disaster struck within a few days when Robin Smith drove a ball back to Gooch in the nets, ripping open the ring finger on his right hand deep enough to expose the bone. Fortunately, there was no break and the injury was quite straightforward until it became infected, causing real alarm to Gooch and the England doctors. The injury led Gooch to miss the first Test in Brisbane, and one can only sense his frustration, having only recently recovered from another hand injury at the end of the summer of 1990.

As in the West Indies, Allan Lamb was to substitute as captain, while Gooch could only watch and wait for his hand to mend. Gooch's mood could easily be affected by events and as captain he would have felt responsible for the heavy defeats, which had started under Lamb's poor leadership in Brisbane. One senses with Gooch that if losing to Australia was the only thing to worry about, he could have coped, but it was the manner of the defeats and off-field behaviour that would have most disappointed him. There were individual transgressions, including the appearance of Lamb and David Gower at a Gold Coast casino on the second night of the first Test. Perhaps the most notorious incident on the tour was the 'fly past' over the ground by David Gower and John Morris in two Tiger Moth aircraft during a match in Melbourne in which they were actually playing. If that wasn't enough, Gower returned to the airport in full Biggles garb, to the delight of the waiting press. Captain Gooch had no idea that two of his team had left the ground without the permission of their captain. You really couldn't make it up. Gooch was understandably furious and as a member of the tour disciplinary committee fined both players £1,000. But the damage had been done. Gooch felt betrayed by his most senior player and the player that he was most likely to turn to in the field. He was also highly embarrassed because the party was becoming a laughing stock, having lost all their warm-up games and fielded abysmally. If England had been 2-0 up in the series, Gower might have got away with his silliness. In the event, the improvement that England had achieved the previous winter in the West Indies and during the Indian series in the summer was squandered through lazy and unprofessional conduct both on and off the field. And just to make matters worse, there were the tantrums of Phil Tufnell, who continued to exasperate his captain and teammates with his attitude, sloppy fielding and playing to the worst elements of the Australian crowd. Gooch was at crisis point and it seemed as though his captaincy and whole approach to the game were being questioned. How could this happen after the events of the previous summer?

David Gower was a most elegant and stylish batsman, to whom batting seemed effortless. His fluid and languid style was the kind that sparked the wish of the great West Indian commentator, C.L.R. James, to see cricket accepted as art. Watching Gower lean into a perfect off-drive, head right over the ball and right elbow pointing to the sky, or his delicious late cut that kissed the ball on its way to the third man boundary, provided ample evidence for the truth of James's ambitious claim for cricket. But, perhaps because the game came so easily to him, Gower never recognised the need to practise and prepare in the way that Gooch believed was necessary for a professional sportsman in the late twentieth century. Gower's laid-back manner must have infuriated the arch-professional Gooch, who was convinced that his method was the right one. He believed that success in the West Indies and against India the previous year vindicated his approach. Gower was perhaps the last of the supremely gifted but dilettante cricketers, in Gooch's era, before the professionalism that all other sports accepted as business as usual finally found its way into cricket. Interestingly, Gower had great respect for Gooch and their pubic spat has probably been over-hyped by the media. He once wrote of his erstwhile teammate:

> *Sometimes he seems to feel that no bowler can bowl at him ... you may have noticed the outward signs of determination to do well talking to himself as the bowler makes his approach ... Graham will maintain an excessive good humour – observant one-liners and more impressions.*
> *- Wisden Cricket Monthly, Vol. 2, No. 9, February 1981.*

So Gooch kept resolutely to his own beliefs about captaincy, leading to his successors, Hussain, Vaughan and Strauss accepting without question that this was the way to run an international cricket team. It is a tribute to Gooch that he got England started on this path.

In Australia Gooch felt betrayed by teammates and disheartened with their attitude. He was shocked by abject fielding, dropped catches and a general lack of commitment, intensity and desire. Was the captain to blame for the players' lack of commitment and indiscipline? Did his regime of hard word and endless practice backfire on a long tour, where a more flexible approach may have worked better? Truthfully, Gooch knew no other way. It had worked in the West Indies and in the home series against India. As he has said, at Essex he was brought up to win cricket matches. This was what motivated Keith Fletcher and later Nasser Hussain. Gooch could be forgiven for thinking that exceptional talents like David Gower were less interested in winning matches than in demonstrating their own sublime skills. I am sure that Gower liked to win, but for Gooch winning was everything. Late in his 333 innings against India at Lord's Gooch became preoccupied about the timing of his declaration in order to give his team the best chance of victory. He was far more interested in the result than in breaking individual batting records. One thing that did come out of the losing Ashes series of 1990/91 was that several senior players, Gower included, had put their international careers at risk.

Home again and new challenges

Despite the humiliating thrashing by the Australians, Gooch had no credible rival for the England captaincy, nor were the selectors questioning his leadership or his methods. Rather, they lined up behind him, a rare privilege for an England captain given the manner of the Ashes defeat. He was duly appointed as captain for the entire coming series against the West Indies, during which Gooch would be 38 years of age. Ted Dexter had come to trust his captain's leadership style and to admire his sheer professionalism. Despite his Australian nightmare, Gooch had retained his enthusiasm for the job, but this time he wanted to surround himself with tough-minded cricketers who understood what it took to win Test matches, even if they fell short of being the most talented available. It became clear that

Gower, Lamb and John Morris had been put on notice, and Tufnell must have wondered if he had played his last game for his country.

After a short trip to New Zealand the party returned to the UK, and Gooch to Essex. The club had failed to win a trophy since they won the County Championship in 1986. The glory of 1985 and the preceding years was looking a bit like a long-gone golden age. But before the season got under way again, there were some pleasant diversions: visiting Buckingham Palace to collect his OBE from the Queen; carrying out some after-dinner speaking engagements; and overseeing book publications and newspaper articles. The great man had reached a stage in his life when he was at ease with himself and content that, at least partially, the goals he had set himself in the mid-1980s had been achieved. He was financially secure and his general confidence had risen to the point where he could hold his own at any social gathering, including public speaking. But there was unfinished business to attend to at Essex, as a distraction from the soon to be faced Curtly Ambrose and Malcolm Marshall.

One senses that Gooch would not have been completely at ease until Essex were winning trophies again as they did back in the 1980s. The Essex team of the 1991 season were in a state of transition. Keith Fletcher had retired and there was no Hardie, McKewan, Phillip, Turner or Lever of the previous all-conquering generation. Pringle remained, as did David East and Neil Foster. Of the younger players the most promising included future captains Paul Pritchard and Nasser Hussain, and home-grown players Nick Knight, John Stephenson, Mark Ilot and Nadeem Shahid. The county had acquired the services of slow bowlers Peter Such and John Childs, an indication that Fletcher's influence at the club remained strong. Perhaps the best signing of 1991 was the Pakistan captain, Salim Malik. Essex had a good track record with overseas players, and Malik was to be no exception. An attacking right-hand batsman, a useful bowler and an excellent fielder, he played 39 matches and scored 2,889 runs at 55.55, with a highest score of 215 against Leicestershire at Ilford. Malik scored eight centuries for the county and took 39 wickets, with best figures of 5 for 67. 1991 was his finest season, when he accumulated an impressive 1,972 runs at 73.03. The county knew that, with their captain and best batsman away on Test duty for most of the summer, they would need someone to score the runs. Malik turned out to be just that player. The club approached the 1991 season in an optimistic mood, believing that they had a good blend of youth and experience. They had batsmen like Malik, Hussain and Knight, who could score quickly and play long innings; match-winning bowlers in Foster, Pringle, Such and Childs; and, of course, Gooch when he returned from England duty.

The 1991 season turned out to be a successful one for Essex, as they at last got back to their winning ways. Gooch also had good reason to be happy when he was voted England's best player in the 2-2 drawn series against the West Indies. Gooch's award was largely due to the 154 not out that he scored in England's second innings in the first Test at Headingley, setting up an unlikely fifth-day victory for his team. In many ways this innings, in terms of sheer quality and courage, surpassed his 333 at Lord's the previous summer. With a West Indies bowling attack of Ambrose, Marshall, Walsh and Patterson, and in overcast conditions, Gooch's innings is regarded one of the greatest in the history of the game. Praise for his innings was unstinting. The distinguished cricket writer, John Woodcock wrote:

> *... no innings by an England batsman has surpassed Gooch's. It stands out, not for artistic merit, but for skills and courage against a formidable attack in awkward conditions at a crucial time.*
> *- Quoted in Gooch and Keating (1995), p. 279*

Others had said it was the greatest Test innings ever played. *Wisden* insisted that it was "as fine a captain's innings as there has ever been". Robin Marlar wrote:

> *Carrying his bat for 154 in a total of 252 puts Gooch on a pedestal above anything he or any of his contemporaries have done ... It is a feature of cricket that when something happens like this, the nation gets a share of the glory too.*
> *- Wisden Cricketers' Almanack (1992)*

Gooch was now emphatically one of the greats. But, up against the man-of-the-series bowling of Curtly Ambrose, the England captain's figures in the next four Tests were fairly modest by his own lofty standards. However, he would be happy to have won two matches against the best side in the world, to some extent putting the horrors of the winter in Australia behind him. Once again, he had restored some pride and purpose to English cricket. Having rescued England again, the knight in the white helmet turned his attentions to his first love, Essex CCC. They did not let him down.

Essex were back. They reached the semi-final of the Benson & Hedges Cup, but lost ignominiously to Worcester at Chelmsford in a match they were expected to win at a canter. They could only muster 104 runs in their innings, and Worcester galloped home by nine wickets, silencing the usually boisterous Essex crowd. But success that season was not far away. They won their fifth Championship and their tenth major trophy in 13 years, finishing 11 points ahead of nearest rivals Warwickshire - not bad after 103 years of failure up to 1979. The two best performers of the season for Essex were Salim Malik, who scored nearly 2,000 runs at 73.03 and finished fourth in the national batting averages, and fast bowler Neil Foster, who took 97 wickets and gained third place in the bowling averages. Gooch, consistent as ever, finished the season fifth in the batting averages with 72.30. Very generously, Gooch agreed to the newly wed Malik's request to return home to Lahore in June of that season, where his young wife was sitting her university finals. As there was a short break in the Championship fixtures Malik's absence would not have damaged their campaign. He had agreed to return for the Sussex game at Horsham the following week, when Gooch and Pringle were playing in the second Test against the West Indies at Lord's. When the team assembled in their Horsham hotel the night before the match, there was no Malik, nor was his name on the flight list. But when the team arrived at the ground the following day there was the Pakistan captain, fit and ready for action. Gooch warmed to 'Sali' and Essex's judgement in their overseas players was sound once again.

The drawn series with the West Indies and Essex's victory in the County Championship led Gooch to declare that 1991 was the "best season of my career". Essex won six of their last seven matches, edging the title away from Warwickshire, who had led for most of the season. Gooch was determined that Essex would finish second for the third year running. Of course, they would have won the title in 1989 but for the 25 points deduction for an inferior Southend pitch. There were some notable individual performances in 1991: a June double hundred by Malik at Ilford, and a partnership of 287 for the fourth wicket between Gooch and Nasser Hussain against Northamptonshire at Colchester, to which Gooch contributed 177. In the final match of the season against 1990 winners Middlesex, he scored a belligerent 259 to help Essex win the game by an innings, in the process earning the gratitude of the Essex faithful who bestowed upon their captain something approaching god-like status. He returned their adulation in his victory speech with the words, "Essex cricket meant the world to me." Not Churchillian rhetoric to be honest, but every Essex supporter at Chelmsford that day understood the sentiments of their East London hero.

With the towering achievements of the 1991 season behind him – the enormity of his Headingley innings against the West Indies, his contribution to Essex's County Championship victory and the small matter of a century against the Sri Lankans in an end-of-season, one-off Test at Lord's, not to mention his inspirational captaincy - Gooch was looking forward to the World Cup in Australia and New Zealand in January and February 1992. As preparation for the World Cup England played three Test matches in New Zealand, beating the home side 2-0, with a century for Gooch in the second match. But the party's spirits were considerably damped following a horrific injury to the ever-popular David Lawrence. He had been brought into the side in the final two Tests against the West Indies and the one-off Test against Sri Lanka. Gooch was looking forward to working with the young fast bowler, who had impressed his captain as a team player with a strong work ethic. As he approached the wicket for the first ball of his third over, Lawrence collapsed as his knee buckled under him with a loud crack. Lawrence, a big man, was in the most awful pain as his knee cracked in two pieces, Gooch describing it as, "the worst sports injury I have ever witnessed". Lawrence was just 27 years old with his career ahead of him, but as a result he was never to play serious cricket again. He responded well to treatment in Wellington Hospital and was soon fit enough to undertake the long flight back to England, while his teammates turned to the preparations for the World Cup.

Gooch had received a ringing endorsement on his captaincy

from Chairman of Selectors, Ted Dexter, not always his greatest fan:

Appointing Graham as captain was one of the best decisions I've ever made. He's become an expert at winning cricket matches … He is very determined, very single-minded and demands high standards from his team.
- Tennant (1992), p.215

Dexter hinted that he was willing to give Gooch a break from touring to spend more time at home, so confident was he in his captain and England's leading batsman. Buoyed by this unqualified support for their captain, England had a good tournament, reaching the final at Melbourne where they faced a rampant Pakistan. There were some particular dilemmas for the England selectors prior to the 1992 World Cup. David Gower had failed to score a century in the 1991 season and, sadly, was never in contention for a place. Mike Gatting was serving his ban, even though Nelson Mandela had been released early in the summer of that year. The totemic Ian Botham was eventually selected after a decent series against the West Indies, and Gooch valued his presence in the squad for his experience and his inspirational influence on younger players. The 'podgy pantomime prince' had at least one match-winning performance left in the tank. Graeme Hick was in the party and England's batting line-up had a solid look about it.

Ups and downs at home and abroad

Sadly, not everything Gooch touched turned to gold. His team were well beaten in the World Cup final, struggling to a disappointing 227 all out in reply to Pakistan's modest total, at least by today's standards, of 249. Gooch's county teammate Derek Pringle returned the impressive figures of 3 for 22, while his captain scored just 29 of the England runs – most unlike Gooch. England's other main batsmen, Stewart and Botham, were also out cheaply, and only Neil Fairbrother and Allan Lamb offered real resistance. The bowling of Wasim Akram (3-49) and Mushtaq Ahmed (3-41) was a little too good for the English batsmen on the day. Gooch was bitterly disappointed to fall short by 22 runs, but he may have reflected on the fact that no side batting second had ever won the World Cup, and that any side in the world would have struggled against the Pakistan bowlers. The soon to retire Imran Khan's team were the better on the day, but Gooch could take heart from his side's performances on the tour and look forward to the visit of Pakistan for the five Test home series in the summer and perhaps taking some revenge on the fearsome duo of Wasim Akram and Waqar Younis.

Alas, it was not to be. Pakistan won the series 2-1, thanks largely to the 43 wickets of reverse swing by Wasim and Waqar, which completely bewildered the English batsmen. The Pakistan series was not a happy one and had its share of controversy. Captain Javed Miandad was a far more combustible character than his calmer and conciliatory predecessor Imran Khan, and the series was marred by on-field altercations, particularly with the umpires. Both captains were reminded of their responsibilities to the game by the match referee, Conrad Hunte. This infuriated Gooch, who argued that it was the Pakistan captain who had intimidated the umpires. The series was also played out against the backdrop of the tedious Gooch/Gower controversy or, as the media liked to refer to it, the Roundhead v. the Cavalier. Ex-players like Brearley and Botham usually backed Gower, who was left out for the first two Tests. Admittedly, Brearley's views were more nuanced than the ex-England all-rounder:

> *... the presence of a left-hander, curly-headed minor genius inclined to the ill-timed facetious remark, not very keen on physical training, would have hardly undermined the steadfast discipline of the team.*
> *- Gooch and Keating (1995), p.310*

Brearley qualified his plea for the recall of the erstwhile England "genius" with this assessment of the more prosaic Gooch:

> *Gooch's influence has been crucial. Not tactically ingenious, he inspires his players through his determination, personal skill and straightforwardness. As Atherton said, you feel you would like to do anything for him.*
> *- Gooch and Keating (1995). p.310*

In the event, Gower returned to the team for the last three

Tests, in which he averaged over 50, much to the delight of the beying critics of the England captain. As for the captain himself, he continued to defy the passing of time with 69 in the second Test at Lord's, 78 in the third in Manchester and 135 and 37 in the fourth Test at Headingley, a good ground for Gooch, which England won by six wickets. Just for good measure he scored 141 in Essex's match against the touring Pakistanis at Chelmsford in between Tests. In truth, the Gooch/Gower debate was a distraction, and Mike Gatting, whose ban had been rescinded, was chosen for the winter tour of India ahead of Gower, largely because the Middlesex man was thought to be a more accomplished player of spin. Although England lost the series against Pakistan, they were by no means disgraced. However, losing the fifth Test at The Oval by ten wickets would have been a huge disappointment, the reverse swing of Wasim and Wakar proving virtually unplayable for the English batsmen. The series had a fascinating Essex sub-plot in that Salim Malik appeared to be trying to outscore his county captain. Malik notched up 165 in Edgbaston and 153 and 50 in the county match at Chelmsford.

Gooch still had no serious rival for the captaincy as the 1992/93 tour of India approached, although he said later that he should have resigned after the defeat by Pakistan at The Oval that summer. Two things persuaded Gooch to stay on. Firstly, Keith Fletcher had replaced Mickey Stewart as England manager for the Indian tour and it would have been difficult to resist his great friend, who knew only too well the value of Gooch's runs. Secondly, the Australians were due to tour England in 1993 and an Ashes victory would have been the very best way, at the age of 40, to bow out. There was also a good reason not to go to India. Gooch shocked many people at the end of the Pakistan series, including his friends, when he announced that he and his wife Brenda were to separate after 16 years of marriage. Brought up on family values and a family man at heart, Gooch must have been deeply troubled by the separation and the effect it would have on Brenda, the girls and his wider family. But he decided to go and probably took his troubles and a heavy heart with him.

At this difficult time of his life Gooch's spirits would have been raised by the performance of his county side. The 1992 season started well for the Champions with a century for Derek Pringle and 75 from Gooch in the season opener against England A at Lord's. Gooch took his good form into the Championship with 160, his highest of the season, in the early match at Grace Road. Early exit from the Benson & Hedges Cup proved a temporary disappointment, as they maintained their Championship challenge and reached the semi-final of the NatWest Trophy. They proceeded to win the Championship for the second successive year, 41 points ahead of their closest rivals, Kent, winning 16 matches compared with a mere 11 the previous season. Essex supporters could be forgiven for believing that there might be no end to the achievements of their 'Captain Marvel'. He came second in the national averages that year behind Nick Folland of Somerset with 1,246 runs at 83.06, including six centuries. Apart from the personal heroics of the captain, the best performances for Essex that season came from the Australian Mark Waugh, the replacement for Salim Malik. Much admired by the Essex fans and hugely respected by the players, Waugh finished the season third in the national averages with 1,252 runs at 78.31. In a record partnership of 347 runs with Nasser Hussain at Ilford in June, Waugh contributed 219. The talented Australian clearly had a positive influence on the young Essex players. Nasser Hussain began to establish himself in the side, batting down the order, and, in Don Topley, Mark Ilot, Peter Such, Neil Foster Derek Pringle and John Childs, Gooch had the variety and penetration in attack required to win Championships. That Essex failed to win the County Championship again after 1992 is testimony to the quality of the team of the early nineties.

In retrospect, the end of the 1992 season would have been a perfect time for Gooch to retire. Essex were County Champions, and he was a successful and popular captain of his country, and in good form. However, because of his rigorous and demanding training regime over the years, as he neared 40 he remained fit for the job and he was keen to help Keith Fletcher on the winter tour of India.

Well established as England captain, Gooch would have travelled to India in the hope of further enhancing his growing reputation as a world-class skipper and one of the best England captains of all time. The tour started well with a Gooch century in a warm-up match. However, in general his impressive career took a backward step on the Indian trip. It did not help that he was beset by ill health and missed important matches, with Alec Stewart deputising. The New Year began in the worst possible way with India thrashing England in all three matches. The India skipper, Azharuddin, scored an impressive 182 in the first Test held in the heavily polluted city of Calcutta, to set up an eight wicket win and the tone for whole the series. The India captain was under tremendous pressure at home following the team's disastrous tour of South Africa, and in this context his innings was particularly impressive. As a mark of appreciation, 50,000 passionate supporters at Eden Gardens lit rolled-up newspapers for their beleaguered captain. Unusually for Gooch, he was out-stumped to a rare leg-spinner from Anil Kumble.

Things got worse in Madras, where England managed to lose by an innings and 22 runs, with centuries for Tendulkar and Sidhu, although Chris Lewis did make a creditable 117 to notch up a debut Test hundred. At the Wankhede in Bombay, England were beaten by an innings and 15 runs, despite scoring 347 in their first innings, which included a valiant knock of 178 by Graeme Hick. But the Indian batsman Kambli played the innings of the game with a magnificent 224 runs off a disheartened England attack. To rub salt into the wound England also lost the one-day series, which finally got under way after the first match at Ahmedabad was cancelled due to crowd disturbances.

The tour of India was a troubled one for the England party. A nasty virus ran through the squad, while Calcutta in particular was an unpleasant place to be with the searing heat and choking smog. The England team might have been intimidated by the massive crowds, with over 85,000 people in Eden Park for the final day's play. Prior to the tour there had been political and social unrest in the country, regularly spilling over into ugly violence. It was not a good time to be playing cricket in India. One or two members of the tour party expressed their dissatisfaction, including the insensitive and often boorish Phil Tufnell, who was reported to have said in frustration, "Done the elephants, done the poverty, now might as well go home." In fairness to Tufnell, the England captain's refusal to play a second spinner and his reluctance to bowl Ian Salisbury betrayed the inflexibility of his captaincy, previously highlighted by Nasser Hussain. India's bowling statistics for the first Test make interesting reading. Their spinners bowled 87 per cent of the total number of their overs in the match and took 17 of the 20 wickets. In stark contrast, only 27 per cent of England's overs were bowled by their single spinner, and of the 12 wickets they took in the match six were taken by slow bowlers.

The tour party moved to the idyllic cricket setting of Sri Lanka to gather their strength, recover from illness and regain some self-respect. In the end they did none of these things, losing all three ODIs and the one-off Test match by five wickets. By this time the England captain had returned home to recover from illness and to start a new life. At least the captain could claim legitimately that he had things on his mind other than cricket.

England continued to trundle out the usual excuses, and a few new ones, for their party's dismal showing in both India and Sri Lanka. The itinerary was too demanding and ill timed, and umpire decisions were poor at best and unfair at worst. Pitches were either under-prepared or over-prepared and, worst of all, the food was inedible and occasionally poisonous. In fairness to the party, the Calcutta smog was particularly noxious and a nasty virus ran through most members of the tour party. The media blamed Gooch's leadership and his inflexible work ethic and 'gloomy' training regime. The party descended into chaos, with complaints about their dress code and the new highly fashionable wearing of designer stubble. Ted Dexter felt so moved by this particular display of decadence that he was moved to condemn the outrageous use of designer stubble among international cricketers – such decadence!

As Gooch himself pointed out, the great West Indian captain Viv Richards possessed a neat goatee, while the Australian captain Steven Waugh regularly sported his own facial adornment. You would have expected a more in-depth analysis of England's performance on the tour from those responsible for running English cricket. But perhaps Dexter was right and wearing more traditional dress might have raised the level of the team's professionalism a little. Tracksuits, flip-flops and other casual gear just might give the appearance of a casual attitude to the business at hand. In the 2007 basketball season in America the NBA introduced a 'suits only' policy for all its players at press interviews and other formal occasions. The result was a rise in the self-esteem of the players, who, as a result of the more professional approach, were held in much higher regard by the fans. Fabio Capello, appointed England football manager in 2008, quickly introduced a strict dress code, a 'no mobile phones' policy and a much more focused and disciplined attitude among his players. The England football team's fortunes immediately improved, winning nine of their ten World Cup qualifying matches. Perhaps Gooch had lost his focus, and you would certainly have expected more from his partnership with Keith Fletcher.

The only players who enhanced their reputation on the tour were Graeme Hick and ,to a lesser extent, Robin Smith. Among those who disappointed were Gatting, Tufnell again, and Gooch himself, who averaged a paltry 11.75 in the Test series against India. Were tour manager Fletcher's limitations exposed as he failed to inspire and motivate the players? This is the Fletcher, of course, who had turned a hapless Essex into the dominant force in English cricket for over a decade. The tour gave both Gooch and Fletcher much to consider. The England party returned home despondent and in disarray. The Australians must have been licking their lips in anticipation of the Ashes series that summer.

Fletcher survived the chastening Indian and Sri Lankan winter tour and began to prepare for the Aussie challenge. For the time being Gooch remained unassailable as captain, despite his personal difficulties and the criticism of his leadership in India and Sri Lanka. He would have been anticipating the Ashes series with some apprehension and had begun to harbour doubts about his ability to motivate his players and score enough runs to lead them by his own example. The next couple of seasons were to settle the ultimate destiny of this undeniably great sportsman and establish his position in the history of the game. Gooch was aware that Michael Atherton was being groomed as his successor, as he prepared for what he expected to be his final series as captain of his country. Conscious of the increased demands on his time, the need to maintain his batting form and his advancing age, Gooch decided to give up the Essex captaincy at the end of the club's County Championship-winning season of 1992. He would need all of his considerable skill, determination and legendary fitness to face the Australians with any confidence. Gooch must have been keeping a watchful eye on his legacy, and in that sense it is worth looking at the 1993 Ashes series in some detail. The series was to be played over six Test matches, accompanied by the obligatory, money-driven, ODI series, which England inevitably lost, this time by an emphatic 3-0. They fared little better in the Test series, losing by a crushing four matches to one. At the end of the fourth match Gooch resigned and duly handed over the captaincy to his successor, Mike Atherton. The Lancashire man lost his first Test in charge, before rallying his team for an impressive win by 161 runs in the dead final rubber at The Oval.

The Australians began the series at Old Trafford with a victory by a hefty 179 runs. Graham Gooch had come a long way from his modest beginnings in Leytonstone and was a renowned fighter, but after his difficult time in the winter, his marriage break-up weighing heavily on his mind, the fight seemed to drain out of him. With thoughts of retirement ahead, he could be forgiven for weakening in the face of the merciless Australian onslaught. But he must have dug very deep that summer when again his fighting spirit, courage and sheer bloody-mindedness came through. He scored 65 and 133 in Manchester, but that wasn't enough to save England from the emergent Shane Warne, who was to prove a decisive influence in the series, as Mike Gatting quickly learned when he was out first ball to one of the most extraordinary deliveries that even the extravagantly gifted Warne had ever bowled. The Old Trafford Test has become known for Gooch's ball-handling incident, when the England captain instinctively brushed a ball from Merv Hughes away from his stumps in a desperate attempt to save his wicket. He was, of course, given out, 'handled the ball', the first Englishman to be dismissed in this way in the history of Test cricket. Perhaps his mind was elsewhere, but he was still the only English batsman to pass 50 in the match. The Old Trafford Test gave Essex fans some cheer, with Peter Such taking 6 for 67 in the Australian first innings.

The Aussies achieved their second victory of the series at Lord's, this time in the most emphatic manner. They amassed a huge 632-4 in their first innings, with centuries from skipper Allan Border, Mark Slater and David Boon, and 99 from the extremely promising Steve Waugh. England were never in the game, despite 80 and 99 from their captain-in-waiting, Mike Atherton. Shane Warne was again their main tormentor with his second eight-wicket haul in the series.

Gooch dropped down the order for the third Test, with some success when he scored 38 and 120 in a hard-fought draw at

Trent Bridge. It was Gooch's eleventh century as captain, during which he passed 8,000 runs in Test cricket. There was further good news for Essex supporters as the young Nasser Hussain scored 71 in the first innings and 47 not out in the second in a match-saving partnership with Graham Thorpe, who put together a courageous 114 on his debut. The England team for this match again included four Essex players, with Mark Ilot joining Gooch, Hussain and Such in the side.

England would have gained some confidence and encouragement from the drawn second Test at Lord's, but they were quickly brought down to earth with a bump at Headingley, where the Australians accumulated a match-winning 653 for 4 declared in their first innings, with a double century for Border and 100s for Waugh and Boon. They did not need to bat a second time, as England were dismissed for 200 and 305, Gooch contributing 59 and 26, again batting down the order.

Before the fifth Test at Edgbaston Gooch gracefully stepped down, clearing the way for Atherton to begin his time as England captain. Gooch, aware of his failing powers, had accepted the captaincy for the whole series reluctantly and this time could not be persuaded to stay, even by Keith Fletcher. This time he'd had enough. Gooch said later:

It was with some relief that Gooch passed the England captaincy over to Michael Atherton, much in the way that Nasser Hussain gave way to Michael Vaughan in 2003. To his credit Gooch gave Atherton his unstinting support, and his mood appeared to lighten as the responsibility was lifted from his shoulders. For the fifth Test he returned to his familiar opening position, but he lasted just 20 balls in the England first innings, in which they were limited to 276 runs largely due to the bowling of Paul Reiffel, who returned the impressive figures of 6 for 71. Shane Warne destroyed England in their second innings, with his magical leg-spin bowling earning him figures of 5-82.

Having won the Ashes, Australia could be forgiven for taking the foot off the gas a little for the sixth and final Test. To Atherton's great relief, England won the Oval Test by 161 runs, largely thanks to 56 and 79 from Gooch and fine quick bowling from Gus Fraser, who took 5-87 in the Australian first innings. Gooch was amused to find himself fielding under the helmet at short-leg in this match, the position usually reserved for junior members of the side, but he would have enjoyed taking two catches. When he returned home at the end of the day's play he found a telegram from David Gower that congratulated on his batting and catching, and how proud he must be of his new position under the helmet at short leg.

Gooch was now 39 and had relinquished both the Essex and England captaincies over the past two years, but he remained a valuable member of England's batting line-up and had a decent Ashes series with the bat. However, the young lions - Thorpe, Hick and Hussain - were impatient to make their mark on the England set-up.

England had lost the series by a thumping 4-1 margin, and Shane Warne and Graham Gooch were named men of the series. Over the summer manager Keith Fletcher had been publicly critical of some of his players, particularly the batsmen, whom he believed gave their wickets away far too easily, In contrast, the Australians, while wearing the baggy green cap, would die rather than give their wicket away cheaply.

Life begins at 40?

Gooch asked not to be considered for Atherton's tour to the West Indies in 1993/94, preferring to stay at home and try to settle into a new lifestyle. He had been separated from Brenda for over a year and, although living alone in Ingatestone, he was desperate to spend more time with daughters Hannah, Megan and Sally and to be as involved as much as possible in their daily lives. Apart from time with his family, Gooch spent the winter on a tour of speaking engagements with David Lloyd and Fred Trueman, in addition, of course, to watching The Hammers enjoy their first season in the Premier League after their recent promotion.

There were two home series of three Tests each in the 1994 season, the visitors being New Zealand and South Africa. New Zealand were first up and Gooch, despite approaching a venerable 41, was still keen to regain his batting place in the England side. Under Atherton, England had got off to an appalling start in the Caribbean, being bowled out for a wretched 46 runs in Trinidad, but later rallied and won in Barbados, where Alec Stewart scored a century in each innings. On the tourists' return, Gooch would not have expected the selectors to disturb the successful opening pair of Atherton and

Stewart. In the event the veteran opener was selected against New Zealand, but at No. 3. What happened next was typical Gooch. He made a terrific double hundred in England's first innings in an excellent partnership of 261 with Atherton. England's total of 567 meant that they did not have to bat for a second time, and New Zealand were beaten by an innings and 90 runs. Gooch achieved an unusual record in the match when he became only the fifth 40-year-old in the history of Test cricket to score a century, and this in his 108th Test. The remaining two matches in the series were drawn, with Atherton scoring a second century at Old Trafford, where Martin Crowe's batting in both innings saved his country from defeat. There were no records for Graham Gooch in this match. He was out for consecutive ducks for the first time since his debut for England in Birmingham back in July 1975. If he was concerned by this unexpected dip in form, he would have been reassured by scoring 101 and 205 in a Championship match at Worcester, becoming only the fifth man in history to achieve this feat five times. Chasing 405 to win, Gooch put on 245 for the fourth wicket with Ronnie Irani before Essex cruised to victory with four wickets in hand. This was the third successive time that Essex had successfully chased a target of over 400 runs in the Championship. Sadly, Essex could not maintain their early momentum and finished the season in sixth place, in what was a trophy-less season.

Even with his current good form, his three low scores in a row in Test matches led Gooch to be concerned about his England place against South Africa and the opportunity to test his, perhaps fading, skills against Allan Donald. The South Africans were welcome visitors to England after returning to the Test match fold following the release of Nelson Mandela and the holding of free elections across the country.

The England squad for the first Test against South Africa included Gooch's name but there was to be no revival in Gooch's form, as he could only manage 20 and 28 in a match in which the England side were thrashed by 356 runs. The only crumb of comfort for Gooch in this match was that he passed 2000 runs in Tests at Lord's. But the match, of course, was scarred by the Atherton 'dirt in the pocket' controversy, which rather spoiled what should have been a splendid sporting occasion. The second Test at Headingley saw England have the better of a drawn match, but, despite being restored to his preferred position as opener, Gooch's scores of 23 and 27 continued to give him and the selectors cause for concern. England won the third and final Test at The Oval by a handsome eight wickets to level a hard-fought series, mainly thanks to Devon Malcolm's match-winning 9 for 57 in South Africa's second innings. Gooch's own celebrations would have been rather muted with his return of 8 and 33 in the match. The great man was beginning to struggle, dropping a regulation catch in the outfield, which would have darkened an already gloomy mood, and no one could look gloomier than Gooch. He must have felt all of his 41 years as he heard the crowd's collective groan echo around Lord's when he spilled the catch. At the end of the series with South Africa, Gooch had won his 113th England cap, while at familiar Fenner's he completed one hundred 100s and passed 40,000 runs in first-class cricket. But his own memory of the season would have been his hugely disappointing run of low scores in Test matches. Was it time, at last, for the great man to leave the stage he had graced for so long?

Perhaps it was time, but the 1994/95 Ashes tour proved to be too tempting. Captain Michael Atherton wanted him in Australia for his potential runs and his massive experience, and Gooch himself was desperate to leave the international scene with a good series behind him. He must have wished he had stayed home in Ingatestone, as the tour was a near disaster. England were beset by injuries to key players from the start and went from match to match barely able to raise a team. The Australian team were cock-a-hoop, as only Australian teams can be, and were in no mood to 'remove the foot from the throat', as they say. The Aussies won the first Test at the Brisbane Cricket Ground by 184 runs, Shane Warne adding to his growing reputation with 8 for 71 in the England second innings, giving him 11 wickets in the match. Gooch, batting at No. 5, scored 20 and 56, a reasonable return but not for someone of his calibre. What would have annoyed and frustrated him more than anything was that he had made a start in both innings but had failed to go on to make a big score. At Brisbane he was undone by Shane Warne, England having decided to attack the young leg-spinner rather than let him totally dominate the batting.

England fared no better at the Melbourne Cricket Ground,

losing by a worrying 295 runs and with man-of-the-series Craig McDermott returning figures of 5 for 42 as England were bowled out for 92 in their second innings. The series seemed irrevocably lost at this stage as one England player after another either returned home for treatment or limped along more in hope than expectation. First Alec Stewart broke his thumb in practice and then Shaun Udal did the same in a provincial game. Devon Malcolm, Graeme Hick, Craig White and finally Darren Gough, who was beginning to make his mark on the tour, all suffered serious injuries or illness at some point in the tour. To add to Gooch's mounting frustration, he scored only 15 in the first innings before moving back to his customary opening slot due to Stewart's hand injury, but fared no better, being caught behind off Damien Fleming for just two.

The tour had begun with such promise for Gooch, with scores of 129, 38, 68, 50 and 101 in the warm-up games. On the morning of the first Test it seemed as if Gooch might have his wish and leave the international scene in a blaze of runs and an Ashes victory. But first Shane Warne and then Craig McDermott were to shatter the illusions of Gooch and his teammates as they demolished England's batting in the first two Tests. He just may have been comforted by the Australian cricketing public, who had a great respect for Gooch and welcomed him everywhere he went, according him almost royal status.

The third Test at Sydney gave some encouragement to the England supporters, as Australia collapsed to 116 in their first innings, thanks to 6 for 73 by Angus Fraser and Darren Gough's 6 for 29. This followed the young Yorkshireman's 51 runs in England's first innings total of 309. Australia held on for the draw, but England took great heart from their performance as the tour switched to Adelaide. The only England player unlikely to have his spirits lifted by the team's improvement was Graham Gooch, whose batting woes continued with 1 and 29 from his favoured opening position.

Ravaged by injuries to key players and facing a rampant Australian side, England travelled to Adelaide buoyed by their improved show in Sydney. Atherton set Australia 263 to win in their second innings, but they failed to withstand the pace of Devon Malcolm and Chris Lewis and England won a famous and unexpected victory by 106 runs. Thanks to a fine century by that other veteran, Mike Gatting, England had stemmed the

Aussie tide and could look forward to Perth in high spirits and with a reasonable chance of squaring the series.

Sadly, one England player, while welcoming the win, continued to be frustrated with his form. Gooch scored 47 and 34 in the match, and for some international batsmen this would have been acceptable, but not for Graham Gooch. Again, he had got in twice and failed to convert this into the hundred that he thought should have been there for the taking. He concluded from this that his reactions had slowed fatally and that at 41 years of age he would never again be the totally dominating batsman the cricket world had come to know. He clearly couldn't live with this, and following the Adelaide match Gooch announced his retirement from international cricket. The fifth Test in Perth would be his curtain call.

England's cricket could never be described as consistent. A terrific team performance similar to that in Adelaide is often followed by an embarrassing defeat, in which the batting is woeful, the bowling is all over the place and the fielding is a succession of dropped catches. For Gooch there would be no Michael Jordan-type, last-second, match-winning heroics in his final match; no glorious finale that he might have dreamed about. Australia won the toss and batted first on a hard, white, fast and true pitch. The unfortunate Mark Ramprakash was hit on the helmet by an express beamer from the young Glenn McGrath, his badly dented grill saving the England batsman from serious facial injury. Gooch himself began a rash of dropped catches. At the age of 41, he may have been the oldest England player to field at slip, which he did for much of the Australian batting.

In front of 70,000 people England lost the fifth Test by a depressing 329 runs. Craig McDermott, with 6 for 38, was again the Aussie hero, skittling out England in their second innings for 123 runs, and he was duly awarded the man-of-the-series. As Atherton and Gooch knew only too well, the Adelaide victory had temporarily papered over some very deep cracks indeed. Gooch scored 37 in the first innings and just 4 in the second . His final innings for England ended Gooch c&b McDermott 4. Overcome by the emotion of the occasion, Gooch was dropped twice before he was eventually out attempting to drive McDermott down the ground. Gooch has said, "Good players may lose their confidence, but they never lose their skill," but by the fifth Test in Australia, by his own admission, he had lost both. At the age of 41 it was time to go, as it was for his long-time England colleague Mike Gatting, who also retired from the international scene at the end of the tour.

As he strolled out to bat for the final time for his country, Gooch was greeted by a standing ovation from the huge Perth crowd. The Australian skipper, Mark Taylor, called his players together in a circle and gave the Essex man a resounding three cheers, and even Gooch admits that he was overcome by the respect paid to him by the Australian team. As he walked back to the pavilion, after only a short time at the crease, he was treated to another standing ovation. It was over. He would have dug deep in Australia, because it is the only thing he knows, but he could not give us a happy ending. But perhaps he knew that Australia, the greatest cricketing nation, was the best place for him to bow out. A couple of centuries would have been perfect, but the end did not diminish one of the two finest East London and Essex sporting heroes, as his last few England games failed to diminish the other, Bobby Moore.

An ordinary county pro

However, Gooch was not quite finished with cricket and set himself the goal of becoming an 'ordinary county working pro' for a couple of years with Essex, to try to get them back into winning ways. Gooch wrote in his autobiography, "I came in with Essex and Keith Fletcher and went out with England and Keith Fletcher." The newly appointed chairman of selectors, Ray Illingworth, never really saw eye to eye with the England manager and Fletcher was sacked at the end of the Ashes tour - the price for the manner of the defeat rather than the defeat itself. Both Gooch and Fletcher were now free to concentrate on their first love, county cricket. There cannot have been a closer relationship in cricket than that between Fletcher and Gooch and, thankfully for Essex supporters, it still had a few years to run. I am reminded of that day in June 2009 when I caught sight of them together, sitting quietly watching Essex playing the University in the Cambridge sunshine, and wondered just what it was they were talking about. My guess is that they were not looking back misty-eyed to past glories, but were eagerly discussing the techniques of Chopra, Bopara and the other young Essex players, checking with each other how they might help them improve. Both love the opportunity of working with young cricketers, and Essex are fortunate to have two such loyal and distinguished servants.

Gooch returned to his new home in Essex, complete with swimming pool, keen to see his daughters and pick up the pieces of his private life, which at least was showing signs of improvement. The praise that was heaped on Gooch on his retirement from the England scene must have more than compensated for the disappointment of his lack of runs in Australia. Even the modest Gooch would have been overwhelmed by the comments made about his career and his place in the affections of the cricketing public. He had become a truly great cricketer with a secure place in the history of the game and, to the surprise of many of us, a courageous and successful captain of England. But he wasn't finished. His new status in the game meant that he was always in demand. In the late winter and early spring of 1995 he had no time to nip down the M11 to watch The Hammers, let alone train with them, although at his age maybe that would not have been such a good idea anyway. But in the spring of 1995, as he prepared for his new life as a full-time county professional, tragedy and sorrow threw a dark shadow over the Gooch family.

Gooch's sister Brenda died of cancer in Romford Hospital that summer. She had been ill for some time, but nevertheless the family were terribly shocked at her death. Her brother was with her at the end, as was her husband Keith. The couple had two teenage boys and the whole extended family was devastated by the tragedy. Brenda had been, in Gooch's own words, "the smiling optimist of the family, always looking to the future". The funeral must have been a particularly distressing experience for all concerned. Gooch found some consolation back at Chelmsford with his Essex teammates, where Keith Fletcher had returned as a 'cricket consultant'. As Gooch remarked at the time, "It was a bit like the old, warm, comforting times of my boyhood."

Gooch threw himself into his work. This was to be his testimonial year, and he was desperate to make a real contribution to the Essex season. It was time to get some trophies back to New Writtle Road. He was 42 years old in the July of 1995, but he retained the thirst for runs that he'd had at the beginning of his career. He scored 1,600 runs in the season, including seven centuries, with an average of 50. He began the season modestly, but then hit his stride. In the summer's first two Championship matches, both at Chelmsford, he scored 139 and 92 against Leicestershire, and 86 and 165 against Worcestershire. He continued his outstanding form into June, when a century against Lancashire and Wasim Akram at Old Trafford confirmed his good form. Later in August he scored a wonderful century at Chelmsford against the touring West Indies side, which included his old tormentor, Curtly Ambrose. As he said later, "These were like old times, precious opportunities to re-live one's prime for a day." He followed this up with a century against Kent at Canterbury, which gave the 42-year-old four consecutive hundreds and his twentieth first-class century, leaving him just two behind Tom Graveney and three behind Denis Compton. Some 'ordinary county pro'. But all thoughts of a Gooch return to a struggling England team were quickly forgotten when his form dipped later in the season - just in time, many Essex's supporters were heard to whisper.

One century that Gooch scored late in the 1995 season is worth a special mention. He had recently undergone his now famous hair transplant operation, much to the hilarity of his Essex teammates, who gave him the obligatory stick he must have been expecting. Essex's next match was against Glamorgan at Swansea, where the crowd, in full voice, sang 'Hair of Graham' to the tune of their anthem 'Bread of Heaven'. Gooch's answer to the St Helen's choir was to score a 'hair-raising' century from 170 balls.

At the end of the 1995 season Essex finished a disappointing fifth in the County Championship, despite winning their last five matches, and again finished the season empty-handed. As Gooch has often said, he was brought up on winning cricket matches, and Essex had acquired the winning habit, particularly under Keith Fletcher. Gooch knew that expectations were high at the club and with the supporters, so he must have anticipated the 1996 season with some apprehension. He would have shown his customary enthusiasm and prepared as diligently as ever for the summer ahead, despite the fact that his international career was well behind him. But at the age of 43 he was fully aware that there was not much left in the tank. He need not have worried, however, because in 17 matches he scored 1,944 runs at 67.03 with a highest score of 201. This led his club captain, Paul

Pritchard, to remark:

> *He scored more runs than anybody else in the country and is a credit to himself and the club. What a man!*
> *- Essex CCC Yearbook 1997.*

One particular innings stands out that season, but for the wrong reasons. In a Championship match against Glamorgan at Chelmsford Gooch scored 170 in bad light before retiring (with the agreement of the opposing captain Matthew Maynard) to take his father Alf to hospital. He raced back to Chelmsford to resume his innings, as his dad would have wanted, but unfortunately Essex had been bowled out and he was unable to build on his score.

Despite Gooch's batting heroics and the runs of Stuart Law, the 1996 season was both disappointing and sad for the county. The distinguished ex-chairman and treasurer Tiny Waterman and the West Indian all-rounder Keith Boyce both passed away that year. Boyce was at the heart of the county's resurgence in the Fletcher era, while Walthamstow-born Waterman was a wonderful servant of the club and represented the East London branch of the Essex family. The season was disappointing for another fifth place finish in the County Championship and a woeful seventeenth place in the Sunday League with just four wins in the whole season.

The side had the opportunity to redeem their poor League performances when they reached the final of the NatWest Trophy – their first appearance at Lord's since 1989. Essex were well accustomed to the pressures of a one-day final and were confident of success. Their supporters, as ever, had high expectations of their team and could be relied upon to give Lord's the atmosphere of a Chelmsford Cup tie, despite their measly allocation of 4,500 tickets priced at £42 or higher. The day began encouragingly with Pritchard winning the toss for the lucky visitors' dressing room. The Essex captain invited Lancashire to bat first and the Essex bowlers performed superbly, restricting the opposition to a modest 186 all out. When the Essex side took the field after tea, victory seemed assured. However, sport being sport, and Essex being Essex, they quickly found themselves 34 for 8 with a humiliating defeat a certainty. They were eventually bowled out for 57 runs by the accurate seam bowling of Peter Martin and Glen Chapple, handing Lancashire a victory that they must have thought beyond them at tea.

All out for 57, chasing a meagre 186 - how could this happen? Graham Gooch had his own explanation for the catastrophic batting collapse. Opening the innings, he faced 55 balls and scored only 10 runs and he admitted he only middled the ball twice. Nine Essex players were out playing defensive shots and without giving excuses. The pitch was not up to scratch for a major final and Essex had the worst of it. In a Sunday League match a couple of months earlier the same teams scored a total of 481 runs in 80 overs - what a final that would have made. The Lord's pitch had deprived the cricketing public of what should have been a feast of runs, culminating in an exciting finish. Gooch was inconsolable. His final chance to make a big score in a prestigious final at Lord's ended in failure and abject defeat. He failed to join his teammates for the post-match 'celebrations' at the Sports Café, preferring the comfort of his home and family. Gooch was highly critical of the team's performance, but in contrast Nasser Hussain believed that Essex had equipped themselves well in the match, particularly with their bowling and fielding. It was simply the pitch that let the players down. It was neither the first nor the last time that Gooch and Hussain had differences of opinion.

Although the 1996 season ended in bitter disappointment for the club, for Gooch there were personal triumphs. He received the Bernard Stimson Award for the highest standards of general conduct in the sport, and the White & Mackay Award, worth £10,000, for scoring the most runs in the season, just ahead of the emerging Surrey left-hander, Graham Thorpe. If the season left Gooch with mixed emotions about his game and the performances of his club, the end of the year brought the personal heartbreak he must have been dreading for some time. Alf Gooch died at Oldchurch Hospital on 12th December, following a long illness, and just days before what would have been his 53rd wedding anniversary. He was devoted to his father and was grateful for the encouragement, support and advice that he had provided since Graham was a young boy running around on Wanstead Flats. He knew full well the debt he owed to his parents. The Gooches were a wonderful Essex sporting family, and after losing his sister in the summer of 1995 he had now lost his father. He would need all of his formidable personal resources to motivate himself to face yet another season. But if any player could find the motivation to play on into his 44th year it would be Graham Gooch. In the *Essex CCC Yearbook 1997*, club President Doug Insole, with a slightly heavy heart, listed the qualities that he believed all professional cricketers must possess to be successful:

> *Pride in personal performance and ambition for the success of the team must be major motivating forces. They are not present in all players.*

Gooch had all these qualities in abundance. But whether he still had sufficient desire and could maintain the levels of intensity that had marked his career to date, only time would tell. During the 1996 season he had overtaken Grace, Compton and Hutton in the all-time list of run-scorers with a career total of 44,000 runs. His benefit in the 1995 season had raised the handsome sum of £269,371, and there seemed little to be gained in going on for yet another season. What was there left to prove? Despite Essex failing again, 1996 had been a good season for Gooch personally and there was no real reason why he could not carry on scoring runs. His legendary fitness regime meant that he was physically up to the task, even at the age of 43, and Essex still needed his runs. So Gooch prepared for the 1997 season with his customary diligence.

However, it was to be one season too far. Gooch surprised everybody at Essex by announcing his retirement in mid-season, the day before a Sunday League match at Northampton. At this point he had scored just 369 runs at 23.06 with a highest score of 56. He could no longer continue to play first-class cricket while merely surviving against bowlers he would have dominated only the season before. It was time to go. By this time Gooch was playing little limited-over cricket, so his final appearance for Essex was to be a County Championship match at Chelmsford against Worcestershire. In his very last innings for the club, on his 44th birthday, he was bowled leg stump after scoring just four runs. As he strolled back to the pavilion that he had graced for 25 years, he waved briefly to his mother sitting in the players' area, gave a short farewell speech to a thin, final-day crowd, and one of the most distinguished careers in the history of English cricket came to a sudden end. True to form, as a retirement present from the club Gooch requested a high-tech multi-gym to keep him in shape.

There were mixed feelings among the Essex supporters, some of whom thought he might at least have played on to the end of the season. But the overwhelming emotion was one of sadness at losing the greatest player ever to have played for the county. He retired having scored 44,830 runs in all matches and, in addition, took 200 wickets with career best figures of 7 for 14. When he walked off the field after being dismissed against Worcestershire, Gooch held all batting records in the Benson & Hedges Cup and the NatWest Trophy. He had scored a first innings triple century for England against India at Lord's in 1990, and followed this up with a second innings century for a total of 456 runs in the match. It is generally agreed that he played one of cricket's supreme innings against a ferocious West Indies attack on a damp and treacherous pitch (despite Doug Insole describing it as "a true cricket wicket") at Headingley in 1991. His courageous 154 not out stood in contrast to the performances of his colleagues, only two of whom made double figures that day. Cricket statisticians often find reasons to disagree, but Christopher Martin-Jenkins writing in *Wisden* made a case for Gooch as the highest run-scorer in the history of first-class cricket. Gooch could leave his cherished Chelmsford with a deep sense of satisfaction. He had achieved all the lofty goals he had set himself in the late 1980s when he reassessed his career following his return after the three-year ban.

As England captain Gooch won 9 of his 23 Tests, losing just 5 at a time when the West Indies were at their peak. He succeeded simply by example and by convincing his players that they were good enough to win. But, unlike many international cricketers, his county remained extremely dear to his heart and, unlike many centrally contracted players of today, Gooch understood his obligations to his county and his roots. He had played some of the best innings of his career for Essex, in partnership with either Ken McEwan, Mark Waugh or Nasser Hussain. Essex member and *Daily Mail* journalist Simon Heffer paid this tribute to the great cricketer:

It has always been one of Gooch's best traits that he speaks with such

pride of representing the county in which he was born, grew up and still lives. I am sure that attitude has not been entirely coincidental to his magnificence as a player.
- Essex CCC Yearbook 1996.

For Essex followers, as journalist Michael Henderson put it, Gooch simply "enlightened our lives". We were proud of him because he was one of us and had overcome his own insecurities and humble background to fulfil every ounce of his considerable potential during his long career. As a cricketer and sportsman he was cut from the finest cloth, despite his often unsmiling and grim appearance. It is interesting that nobody ever accused the great Australian captain, the remorseless Steve Waugh, as unsmiling and dour when his country was beating everybody. Gooch recovered from his unwise South African venture, when he seemed to be at odds with himself, to become a national treasure. When the tributes came they were many and varied, genuine and fulsome. A personal favourite is one from the ex-Hampshire captain, Mark Nicholas, who wrote,

Gooch has been a remarkable cricketer, playing innings of rare genius and unshakeable tenacity which for a time made him the best of all the batsmen in the world.
- Gooch and Keating (1995), p.385

John Arlott, the very best of cricket writers, described a characteristically defiant Gooch innings against the West Indies:

Gooch boldly upstanding and unperturbed by the pace of Roberts, Holding, Garner and Croft drove, glanced and hooked with the air of command.
- J. Arlott, 'A Tale of Three Centuries', Wisden Cricket Monthly, Vol. 2, No. 3, August 1980.

Perhaps the most honest and well-deserved compliments about sporting careers come from people who have been great players themselves. Gooch would have enjoyed the ultimate mark of respect from one of the greatest cricketers of the twentieth century, Shane Warne, who, when remarking recently of ways of defeating opponents declared Gooch as the hardest England batsman he had ever bowled at. Case closed, we might say, but of course Gooch, who could look after himself against any bowling, never thought that spinners could bowl much, although even he might have made an exception in the case of Shane Warne.

Perhaps he might make an exception for the incomparable Shane Warne, but I wouldn't bet on it. What we know is that by the end of his career Graham Gooch had, as Scyld Berry wrote, "... transcended into that super league of Richards, Chappell and one or two others" (S. Berry, The Cricketer, Vol. 61, No. 10, October 1980). Devon Malcolm, the hero of England's victory against South Africa at The Oval in August 1994 was asked who was the best captain he played under and the fast bowler replied:

> *In 1989-90, we had a trip to the Caribbean and Graham Gooch made a concerted effort. We had training camps before we went away to improve our fitness so that, for the first time, England really looked professional. From the point of view of leading from the front, he was the best.*
> *- D. Malcolm, The Sunday Times, 23rd August 2009.*

Intensely determined, meticulously prepared, defiant and all-conquering are all virtues that Gooch would have admired in others, and which he himself possessed in abundance. The accolades at the end of his playing days were generous and welcome, but Gooch is not one to dwell on the past and when he stopped playing cricket at the age of 44 he would have already been thinking about the next stage of his eventful and successful career. In many respects it is the most interesting phase of his absorbing journey, and where we get to know him best.

Life begins at 44

Gooch had been asked to coach the England A team in Australia in 1996, but he declined the invitation in order to tend to his ailing father. When invited to go with the A team to Kenya and Sri Lanka in 1997, this time he was in a position to accept. He tried one or two things before settling into something more permanent. He was an England selector from 1997 to 1999, a period that included the World Cup. Gooch also took up an offer to join Durham as batting coach, but it seemed an unlikely pairing at the time and he returned to Essex in 2001 as head coach, replacing Keith Fletcher, who was probably ready for a break from the game to spend more time in the country pursuits he so much enjoyed. Gooch held the coaching job until stepping down just prior to the start of the 2005 season. He remains at Essex as the team's specialist batting coach and undertakes some promotional work for the county, acting as general ambassador. At the end of the 2009 season Gooch is still very much the club's centre of gravity and beating heart. He is the link in a line that connects the past and the present, and Doug Insole, Keith Fletcher and Trevor Bailey with the young lions Alistair Cook, Ravi Bopara and Varun Chopra. He misses playing terribly and never really enjoyed committee work, but he is comfortable in his role at the club developing young players, who hold him in the greatest regard.

He did make a one-off return to first-class cricket in July 2000, just a few days before his 47th birthday, when he captained MCC against New Zealand A in The Parks at Oxford. Perhaps it never pays to come back, as Gooch made only 0 and 5 in the game, after which he appreciatively returned to his retirement. There have been a few commercial projects: he promoted the Advanced Hair Studios for a while and produced two licensed computer games, *Graham Gooch's Test Cricket* in 1985 and *Graham Gooch World Class Cricket* in 1993. He agreed to become the president of the Essex Disabled Cricketers' Association, undertakes after-dinner speaking engagements, which by all accounts are a great success, and has helped to raise considerable sums for charity, including the Bobby Moore Cancer Fund.

Alongside his exemplary playing record with Essex and England, his greatest legacy is likely to be the Graham Gooch Cricket Academy and Scholarship Scheme based at Chelmsford. Not content with a playing career as one of the best batsmen this country has ever produced, his passion for the game has extended to a commitment and determination to produce the next generation of Essex and England cricketers. Although from time to time Gooch provides expert analysis for BBC Radio, he has no appetite for dishing out jeroboams of champagne or sitting for day after day in a TV studio. In his retirement Gooch has found a definite purpose, and he is fortunate that in Essex he has a club who have enthusiastically embraced his ideas. This is in stark contrast to how his boyhood hero, Bobby Moore, spent his own retirement, before his illness caused his untimely death. It is nothing short of a scandal that neither West Ham United nor the English FA cared enough to find a positive role for the greatest and most popular ambassador for football that this country has seen, or is ever likely to see. In the end the differences between the way these two great sporting heroes of East London and Essex spent their retirement are more to do with cricket being a more inclusive sporting family, while the world of professional football has become a shabby, money-grabbing machine that doesn't have an ounce of compassion or grace in its flabby debt-ridden body.

Gooch's Academy

The Graham Gooch Cricket Academy sits quietly behind the members' pavilion at the Ford County Ground at Chelmsford, just alongside the club museum. The River Chelmer runs gently around the ground located on the edge of Chelmsford Park, just a hundred yards from the city centre. Even on non-match days the ground is alive with activity: people erecting marquees, admin staff hurrying back and forth, and the groundsmen attending to the innumerable jobs that need doing out on the square. The last time I was there it was a non-match day and I had gone to look up some references in the club's museum. I wandered into the pavilion, looking for a cup of coffee, only to disturb a lively meeting of the Chelmsford Women's Institute. But it is the Academy that catches the eye, with young people, boys and girls, dragging huge cricket 'coffins' on wheels backwards and forwards. Heaven only knows what cricketing paraphernalia they contain. The youngsters are there during the long summer holidays for tuition, practice and to have fun. They are clearly having a brilliant time.

This wonderful coaching facility was renamed the Graham Gooch Cricket Academy in 2007 for reasons that speak volumes about the man who, it is worth remembering at this point, made a pair in his Test against Australia. In 2007 Gooch offered to provide financial support to the Essex Academy through his scholarship scheme to the tune of £30,000 a year for a three-year period, and in appreciation of this generous gesture the Academy now carries his name. A particular feature of the scholarship scheme is to provide opportunities for local young prospects to develop their game by spending their winters in

Australia and South Africa. For example, from October to December 2008 young Adam Wheater and Jaik Mickleburgh attended the Paul Terry Cricket Academy in Perth, Australia, before joining the England U19 squad for their tour of South Africa. John Childs, the former Essex off-spinner, who followed Peter Such as the Academy Director, told Essex members:

The injection of money into the Academy gives us the opportunity to further improve the coaching and training of our young Academy players and potential Essex professionals. The other main benefit is having Graham's name associated with our Academy. We can be proud of his career achievements with England and Essex which were further rewarded in 2008 when he was named in the ICC Hall of Fame 50 Great Cricketers of all time.
- Quotation by John Childs appears on the Academy section of the Essex CCC website, www.essexcricket.co.uk

The Academy and the scholarship scheme, unlike their football equivalent, are not just interested in developing youngsters who know only cricket, to paraphrase C.L.R. James. Gooch talks interestingly about young players maturing and how this is a necessary condition to becoming an established player. The scholarship players, whether they spend the winter in India, South Africa or Australia, have to cook for themselves, take responsibility for their everyday lives and handle their own finances. Gooch is convinced that the maturing process will make them better cricketers.

Since 2003 the Academy has produced young professionals for Essex, the England U19s and the full England side. Alastair Cook, Ravinder Bopara, Varun Chopra, Tony Palladino, Jahid Ahmed, Maurice Chambers, Mervyn Westfield, Tom Westley, Zoheb Sharif, Jaik Mickleburgh and Adam Wheater have all progressed through the Academy route, and Cook and Bopara in particular have benefited from the scholarship scheme. It seems, thanks to Gooch's generosity, that the future of Essex cricket looks assured.

The youngsters come from all corners of the county and up from East London. It is worth mentioning just a few of these exciting young prospects, all of whom attended the Academy in 2009. Dominic Hurst is a 15-year-old fast bowler from Hainault & Clayhall CC, Ravi Bopara's old club. Rishabh Shah is a promising young batsman and leg-spin bowler. Sixteen-year-old Beth McGregor is a left-hand bat and useful bowler and the fourth girl to be selected for the Academy. Beth plays for Chingford CC and has represented the county's U15s and Essex Women. But perhaps the best of a very promising bunch of young talent is 16-year-old wicketkeeper/batsman Ben Foakes. Ben plays his cricket for Frinton CC, has represented London & East Region and was awarded Most Valuable Player out of all the age groups in the Academy. Ben is currently being spoken of among the members as a future England international wicketkeeper, especially after his spectacular Second XI debut when he took four catches and four stumpings. The county has high hopes for these youngsters, all of whom have progressed from the Emerging Players' Group, and will follow their progress with great interest.

Gooch believes that Essex are in a good position to pick up any promising youngster who comes to the club's attention through their network, which includes the Essex Cricket Board and the Schools Associations, although he is aware that schools "are under strain" when it comes to cricket. Gooch looks for two main qualities in young players: natural ability and the desire to improve. The skills he identifies, like those in art, are difficult to specify, but he mentions balance, poise and simply 'something special'. However, without a desire and personal drive to improve, even the best young players are unlikely to develop to the next level. Some players, he pointed out, 'flat-line' - their attitude is not right. Youngsters like Cook and Bopara are already in 'receive mode', whereas no amount of coaching will help those players who remain in 'tell mode'. Cook and Bopara have been criticised by commentators for one fault or another, as was Gooch in his own day, because, as he said, "There is no such thing as a perfect player." A coach can shape technique but cannot keep telling a player how they should play. If the player has the right attitude and the necessary ability, "the coach is halfway there before saying a word," and the player can develop their most effective way of playing.

Gooch's gesture in helping the Academy and establishing the scholarship scheme is generous in the extreme and shows the strength of his commitment to the future of Essex and England cricket. Gooch and Essex chairman Nigel Hilliard see no problem in producing young cricketers like Cook and Bopara, who due to their England commitments play for their county no more than half a dozen times a season. Not all the club's supporters agree and some would like to see more of their stars, especially if it resulted in Essex returning to the glory years of the 1980s and early 1990s. But Gooch's commitment to the future of Essex cricket is total. Sitting on the boundary's edge at Fenner's he talked passionately about the "Essex cricket family having different priorities" to other county clubs whose short-sighted enthusiasm for Kolpak players has resulted in a loss of identity and purpose. The Essex way is to put into place layers of youth development, linked to a thorough scouting system throughout the county and East London.

Graham Gooch has become an *éminence grise* of English cricket. He was extremely proud to be appointed as Deputy Lieutenant for Essex in recognition of his great service to the county he adores, and his work with young players has enhanced his already towering reputation as a batsman and captain. His natural modesty prevents him from claiming any credit for the success of his scholarship scheme and the Essex Academy, simply describing them as "just another layer to the Essex coaching and youth system". One of the most impressive features of Gooch's retirement is his clearly expressed, fluent and analytical comments on cricket matters for BBC Radio. After hearing his thoughts on England's 2009 Ashes series win, a friend of mine - not a great cricket fan, but Essex through and through - commented in some surprise: "Was that Goochie?" If his coaching at the Academy is equally as clear and coherent, like the very best teacher, then no wonder the youngsters respond to him. Gone forever are the monosyllabic, guarded utterances to the press of his days as England captain. He cuts an impressive figure. But you feel he is most at home these days in a pair of shorts on the outfield at Chelmsford giving slip catches to the fielders before the start of play, coolly catching the quickest efforts of the young Essex bowlers in his huge baseball glove, or working quietly with Bopara, Cook or Chopra on some point of technique in the nets behind the pavilion.

At this stage of his life, now 56 years old, Graham Gooch remains deeply involved in cricket. He has achieved all the goals he set himself, apart from a century in his last Test match, and he is quietly working towards underpinning the future of Essex cricket. He cares passionately about the future of the game both at county and international level, understands that the map of cricket is changing and is concerned that 20/20 might become the dominant form of the game. Gooch is a great fan of the short game, but he believes that the biggest challenge in cricket is to find a way for the exciting, commercially driven side of the sport to sit alongside its more traditional form.

However, 20/20 is unlikely to be denied, as Gooch explained: "All the top players in the world are there, that's where it is happening, and the best players will want to be where it's happening." The balance of commercialism and traditional values is a delicate one and will require exceptional judgement if the right balance is to be maintained. The omens are not good. But rest assured that Graham Gooch will have something forthright and intelligent to say about the latest developments in the game, but Essex supporters will always remember him best at Lord's in July 1979 when, in his white helmet and bat raised with that balanced, purposeful intensity, he wrote himself and Essex into the record books and into cricket immortality.

LAST WORD

The remarkable success stories of Bobby Moore and Graham Gooch were based on a strong sense of self-belief, towering ambition, boundless natural ability and dedication to physical fitness. Our two sporting stars also possessed a spirit that runs through the people of East London and Essex and it was this that drove our two England captains to ever greater heights of achievement. Both Moore and Gooch knew how to dig down deep when it was necessary. They shared a potent sense of place and stayed close to their sports-loving local public, who in turn demonstrated an immense pride in the way in which they graced the world of international sport.

To know when to stop is an art and the last word should go to the authors of the official history of Essex County Cricket Club:

A nation which has no respect for its past has no hope for its future ...

SELECT BIBLIOGRAPHY

J. Arlott (1986), *John Arlott's 100 World's Greatest Batsmen*, MacDonald.

S. Bacon (1998), *Hammers in Focus: A Photographic History Over Three Decades*, Hallamshire Publications.

P. Bailey (ed.) (1995), *The Oxford Book of London*, Oxford University Press.

T. Bailey (1954), *Playing to Win*, Hutchinson's Library of Sports and Pastimes Series, Hutchinson.

T. Bailey (1986), *Wickets, Catches and the Odd Run*, Willow Books.

B. Belton (2006), *West Ham United Miscellany*, Pennant Books.

J. Bird (2002), *The Newham Story: A Short History of Newham*, ed. S.E. Kirby, London Borough of Newham.

D. Birley (1999), *A Social History of English Cricket*, Aurum Press.

C. Bray (1950), *Essex County Cricket Club*, Convoy Publications.

M. Brearley (2001), *The Art of Captaincy*, Channel 4 Books.

S. Chalke (1997), *Runs in the Memory: County Cricket in the 1950s*, Fairfield Books.

S. Chalke (1999), *Caught in the Memory: County Cricket in the 1960s*, Fairfield Books.

Essex County Cricket Club Handbook, 1969-2008.

K.W.R. Fletcher (1983), *A Captain's Innings: An Autobiography*, Hutchinson.

G. Gooch (1985), *Out of the Wilderness*, Willow Books.

G. Gooch and F. Keating (1995), *Gooch: My Autobiography*, HarperCollinsWillow.

M. Gorman (2009), *Homes for Heroes or Space to Breathe? The Struggle for Wanstead Flats 1946-47*, Leyton & Leytonstone Historical Society.

S. Inwood (1998), *A History of London*, MacMillan.

N. Hussain (2004), *Playing with Fire: The Autobiography*, Michael Joseph.

G. Imlach (2005), *My Father and Other Working-Class Football Heroes*, Yellow Jersey Press.

C.L.R. James (1963), *Beyond a Boundary*, Stanley Paul.

C. Kerrigan (2008), *East London: A Hotbed of Football 1867-1918*, 3-2 Books.

D. Lemmon and M. Marshall (1987), *Essex County Cricket Club: The Official History*, Kingswood.

C. Martin-Jenkins (2009), *The Top 100 Cricketers of All Time*, Corinthian.

T. Moore (2005), *Bobby Moore: By The Person Who Knew Him Best*, Harper Sport.

I. Oxborrow and R. Pritchard (2009), *Fletcher's Aces and Jokers: Essex – County Cricket Champions 1979*, Desert Island Books.

J. Powell (1993; 2nd edn 1998), *Bobby Moore: The Life and Times of a Sporting Hero*, Robson Books.

W.A. Powell (2002), *Essex County Cricket Club*, The History Press.

H. Redknapp (1998), *Harry Redknapp: My Autobiography*, Collins Willow.

A. Rippon (2005), *Gas Masks for Goal Posts: Football in Britain During the Second World War*, The History Press.

J. Rose (2001), *The Intellectual Life of the British Working Classes*, Yale University Press.

A. Sampson (1981), *Grounds of Appeal: Homes of First-Class Cricket*, Robert Hale.

I. Tennant (1992), *Graham Gooch: The Biography*, H.F. and G. Witherby.

D. Tossell (2007), *Grovel!: The Story and Legacy of the Summer of 1976* , Know the Score Books.

P. Warner, Sir (1946), *Lord's: 1787-1945*, George G. Harrap & Co.

B. Webber (2004), *The Way U's Were: A Personal History of Colchester United*, Tempus Publishing.

J. Wilson (2008), *Inverting the Pyramid: A History of Football Tactics*, Orion Books.

Wisden Cricketers' Alamanack, 1960-2008.

INDEX

OTHER SPORTS BOOKS PUBLISHED BY APEX

www.apexpublishing.co.uk

THE CRICKET QUIZ BOOK
ISBN: 978-1-906358-00-6 HARDBACK - £8.99

Did you know that cricket is the second most popular sport in the world and has been an established team sport for centuries, with more than 100 cricket-playing nations now recognised by the International Cricket Council? No doubt those questions haven't left cricket aficionados remotely stumped, but be prepared to be caught out by the 1,000 leg-breaking quiz questions in this book.
Your innings will require you to recall facts and figures relating to every possible aspect of the game of cricket from players to umpires and national to international matches, together with all kinds of trivia, so you could very easily find yourself in a real spin and may need to enlist the help of friends to bail you out before a sneaky Chinaman bowls you over, slips you up or reduces you to a pile of ashes.
Whether you find yourself top of the batting order or limping with a square leg, this book, with a fitting foreword by Dickie Bird, contains a wealth of knowledge about the sport that is guaranteed to enthral all cricket fans, and questions that will stimulate fond memories and friendly debates for many an entertaining hour.

THE WEST HAM UNITED QUIZ BOOK
ISBN: 978-1-906358-23-5 HARDBACK - £9.99

Now is the time to find out how much you West Ham United fans really know, but be warned – your brains are sure to take a hammering as you struggle to answer the 1,000 challenging questions in this quiz book, covering every aspect of the team's history, such as players, managers, opponents, scores, transfers, nationalities and every competition you can think of.
You'll be arguing with the referee and pleading for extra time as the questions spark recollections and ardent discussions of the legendary greats and nail-biting matches that have shaped the club over the years.
With a fitting foreword by Hammers legend Julian Dicks, and bulging with important facts and figures, this book will entertain as well as educate, but be prepared for a few fouls and yellow cards along the way.